THE ECONOMICS OF ECSTASY

The Economics of Ecstasy

Tantra, Secrecy, and Power in Colonial Bengal

Hugh B. Urban

OXFORD
UNIVERSITY PRESS

2001

OXFORD
UNIVERSITY PRESS

Oxford New York
Athens Auckland Bangkok Bogotá Buenos Aires Cape Town
Chennai Dar es Salaam Delhi Florence Hong Kong Istanbul Karachi
Kolkata Kuala Lumpur Madrid Melbourne Mexico City Mumbai Nairobi
Paris São Paulo Shanghai Singapore Taipei Tokyo Toronto Warsaw

and associated companies in
Berlin Ibadan

Published by Oxford University Press, Inc.
198 Madison Avenue, New York, New York 10016

Library of Congress Cataloging-in-Publication Data
Urban, Hugh B.
The economics of ecstasy: Tantra, secrecy, and power in Colonial Bengal / Hugh B. Urban.
p. cm.
Includes bibliographical references and index.
ISBN 0-19-513902-X
1. Kartābhajā.
BL1276.84.U63 2001
294.5′514—dc21 00-058911

9 8 7 6 5 4 3 2 1

Printed in the United States of America
on acid-free paper

Foreword

Hugh Urban's book *The Economics of Ecstasy* is a rare piece of work on many counts—it is extraordinarily learned, readable, and important. The scholarship is flawless and intense; Urban has worked through thousands of pages of Bengali texts that have never before been studied, some of which he discovered in forgotten places. This book demonstrates beyond a doubt that our ignorance of these texts has been an unfortunate lapse, for the texts reward both the scholar and the general reader on many levels: they contain passages of great beauty, humor, eroticism, obscenity, philosophy, and political significance. The translations manage to be simultaneously accurate and readable, sound and spirited. This alone would make the book well worth reading as a kind of sourcebook. But it is far more.

The historical topic—the Kartābhajā sect in Bengal and its place in the broader movement of Tantrism, an Indian religious movement that employed purposely shocking sexual language and rituals—is significant in itself. The Kartābhajā sect is little known and, like all Tantric sects and Tantric sex, much misunderstood. (A character in David Lodge's novel *The British Museum Is Falling Down* suggests helpfully to a friend who is groaning under the yoke of Anglican repression, "But if you must have religion, why not Hinduism? Then you can have sex as well.") Yes, but you also get a lot more than sex, as Urban demonstrates. He has done a magnificent job of contextualizing the Kartābhajā sect historically in the world of British economic and political domination. He sees the political and economic implications of a number of religious and sexual metaphors and ideologies deployed by the British, on the one hand, and the Kartābhajās, on the other, and the religious overtones of a number of political and economic policies advocated by the British, on the one hand, and resisted by the Kartābhajās, on the other. Urban manages both to incorporate and to transcend the contemporary hegemonic methodological stances of post-colonialism and subaltern studies as well as Foucault's pathbreaking studies of the relationship between power and sexuality. He employs a nuanced hermeneutic of suspicion (ultimately derived from Freud's suggestion that gold is a symbol of shit) to excavate the sexual meanings in apparent economic metaphors, and, more originally, the economic overtones of obscene phrases. He shows us how sex is money, and money is sex, and religion is both at once.

Even more interesting, I think, is the way that Urban has tackled the issue of secrecy in the political background and development of dissident groups. He presents secrecy as both an academic, methodological problem, as viewed from the outside (How can we find out about religions that, by definition, do not want us to know about them?) and a social, religious problem, as viewed from the inside (What is gained, and what lost, by people who create and inhabit a secret religious world?). The outside and inside merge in his own uneasy participatory observation, which he records with humorous self-deprecation. Drawing on his own broader studies of secrecy in other societies, including our own, Urban brings an implied but seldom revealed comparative stance to this study, producing insights that will have relevance for the study of other secret societies, and cults in general, far beyond the bounds of South Asia.

Wendy Doniger
Mircea Eliade Professor of History of Religions,
University of Chicago

Preface

There can be no final secret. The ultimate secret of Hermetic initiation is that everything is secret. Hence the Hermetic secret must be an empty one, because anyone who pretends to reveal any sort of secret is not himself initiated and has stopped at a superficial level. (Umberto Eco, *Interpretation and Overinterpretation*)

Better watch out!—There is nothing we like so much to communicate to others as the seal of secrecy—along with what lies under it. (Friedrich Nietzsche, *die fröhliche Wissenschaft*)

This book was born in large part out of the intense frustration and often maddening confusion that I encountered in the course of my research into the Kartābhajā tradition of West Bengal and Bangladesh between 1994 and 1997. For I was, after all, attempting to understand a tradition that is, by its own self-definition, a *secret* one—that is, a tradition that practices *active dissimulation,* intentionally conceals itself from unwanted outsiders, and makes explicit use of the most ingenious tactics of obfuscation, misinformation, and mystification. Not only was I trying to read and translate extremely difficult, deeply encoded esoteric texts, but I was also working with a number of gurus in Calcutta who seemed to take a real delight in the play of secrecy and the dialectic of lure and withdrawal, as they teased me with tantalizing glimpses of profound mysteries while always keeping me at a distance, always holding the deepest secrets just out of reach. In short, what I encountered—or, rather, ran quite naively and unwittingly headlong up against—was perhaps among the most difficult hermeneutic problems a scholar of religions might face, one that involves both profound epistemological and ethical questions: namely, how can one study something that is supposed to be secret—and, indeed, *should one in good conscience even try* to penetrate something that another culture wishes to keep hidden from the outside world?

By my own free admission, then, the initial impetus for this book was that disease which has stricken so many scholars in recent years—what Umberto Eco has aptly dubbed the "syndrome of the secret," or the morbid preoccupation with the tantalizing regions of the unknown and the occult. However, I also believe that, in the course of my research, I was forced in many ways to go through and beyond this syndrome of the secret, as a simple infatuation with the mysterious and the arcane; indeed, once I began to engage in more critical textual research and fieldwork, I began to appreciate just how complex, messy, infuriating, and also truly *interesting* the problem of secrecy is when we place it within its real living and social contexts. Beyond the simple tantalizing allure of the Hidden, which seems to have captivated so many historians of religions, I have tried to probe much deeper into the power of secrecy as a particular *discursive strategy,* as it is played out in real historical and material circumstances, in more mundane but no less interesting fields of society, politics, and economic exchange.

In the course of my research among Kartābahajā gurus of Bengal, I encountered a wide range of attitudes toward secrecy and toward my attempts to probe into their most sacred hidden traditions. On one side, I met some who were quite suspicious and even hostile toward my scholarly queries—particularly when they touched on the more sensitive questions of Tantric sexual rituals and other socially objectionable practices. On the other side, however, I also encountered a number of gurus—including one of the two living claimants to the title of Kartā, or God Incarnate—who seemed not only willing and able to reveal their most guarded secrets to a curious Western scholar, but perhaps even *too* enthusiastic about it. Particularly when the scholar happens to be backed by a generous research grant, the problem is often *not* one of finding no access to secret knowledge but, on the contrary, of encountering *too many secrets,* of finding almost endless hidden meanings and concealed truths, proliferating within a tradition which seems to enjoy the back-and-forth movement of the advertisement, partial revelation, and general obfuscation of elusive hidden truths. Indeed, I even met one individual who claimed to be a learned Kartābahajā master but later turned out to be a "pseudo Kartābhajā"—a rather remarkable and intriguing impostor who had no real connection with the tradition but had only heard that a rich Western scholar was coming in search of "secret knowledge."

After several years of interaction with this tradition, I thus came to realize that there simply is no easy or ultimately satisfactory way out of the epistemological and ethical quandary of secrecy. Even the act of receiving initiation, even the experience of studying as a disciple at the hands of a guru for many years would not resolve my double bind. After all, how could one ever be sure that what a guru tells in initiate (particularly a naive, rich Westerner) is ever the "final truth" or ultimate secrets and not simply another dissimulation? And once initiated, one faces the still more troubling ethical problems of whether one can ever reveal these secrets to an uninitiated audience of outside readers.

Initially quite frustrated and depressed by this methodological impasse, I was eventually forced to devise a series of alternative strategies for working around it, which allowed me to remain respectful of this tradition and its privacy while saying something useful about the phenomenon of secrecy. Most important, I decided to *shift my scholarly gaze* away from the elusive content or substance of the secret and toward the more visible *strategies and forms* through which secrecy operates in concrete social and material circumstances. What I found, then, was that the tactics of secrecy and the claims to possess very rare, valuable hidden truths very often function as a potent source of symbolic power, status, and prestige—though a rather ambivalent and dangerous one, which is always a potential liability for its owner.

The Economics of Ecstasy thus presents my own alternative approach to the problem of secrecy in the specific case of the Kartābhajās, as well as my attempt to interpret their complex history, politics, and economics over the last 200 years. A companion volume, *Songs of Ecstasy* (SE), will provide an introduction to and translation of over 100 of the Kartābhajās' highly esoteric, deeply enigmatic songs, which I have collected from a variety of textual and manuscript sources in West Bengal.

Columbus, Ohio H. B. U.
February 2001

Acknowledgments

As Georg Simmel long ago pointed out, the problem of secrecy is always a *social problem*—that is, a relationship between those who know and those who do not—and therefore the study of secret traditions is also very much a social problem, which involves the help, participation, and good counsel of a wide variety of significant others. The many persons and institutions to whom I owe a debt of gratitude are surely too numerous to cite here; however, my first and greatest thanks go to the various masters and disciples of the Kartābhajā tradition itself—not only for their invaluable aid and assistance, but perhaps even more so for their restrictive secretiveness and their more ingenious tactics of dissimulation, as they negotiated the strange encounter with a curious, persistent Western scholar. For the most part, the Kartābhajās I met were remarkably friendly and cooperative in their willingness to speak to me—though at times rather maddening in their playful use of secrecy, tantalizing mysteries, and intimations of ever more, still deeper, but more elusive hidden truths.

Second, and no less important, I also owe a tremendous debt of gratitude to my readers at the University of Chicago for their seemingly infinite patience with the often long-winded, sloppy, and poorly proofread early drafts of this text. Above all, Wendy Doniger provided both profound intellectual, emotional, and psychological support during some of Hyde Park's most depressing winters and invaluable aid with the style, structure, and grammar of this book. Bruce Lincoln has long been my most important theoretical influence and mentor in thinking through the various methodological problems in my work. Finally, Clinton Seely deserves perhaps the most gratitude of all for his truly saintly assistance with the maddeningly difficult task of translating the Kartābhajās' esoteric songs—a task that involved long hours of staring at seemingly incomprehensible Bengali gibberish until, between the two of us, we could reconstruct some vague kind of meaning amidst their cryptic obscurity.

Equal thanks belong to those outside the University of Chicago community who helped with the research, reading and editing of the text. First and foremost, I am enormously indebted to Ms. Hena Basu—one of the finest, most conscientious research consultants any scholar is likely to find anywhere in the Indian subcontinent, who not only dragged me through the most obscure back alleys and red-light districts of old Calcutta but also labored in the least friendly of Calcutta's libraries to hand-copy crumbling Bengali manuscripts. Second, I owe enormous gratitude to the friends and senior scholars who have taken the time to read and comment upon my work: above all, Edward C. Dimock, the Ādi-Guru of Bengal Studies, the master of the Sahajiyā traditions, and an invaluable aid in my translation of the Kartābhajā songs; Jeffrey Kripal, a close friend and (strangely) kindred spirit in the study of mysticism and crazy Bengali *tāntrikas*; Tony Stewart, one of my most respected mentors and scholarly exemplars, who has had a formative impact on my thinking about the ethics and epistemics of secrecy; and Rachel McDermott, a source of profound intellectual and psychological support, who, together with Jeff Kripal, has helped to show me that it is possible to survive, transcend, and transform the debilitating neuroses that plague so many of us in the academic world.

I also owe a great debt to the various institutions that provided the financial support for this book: first and foremost, I am especially grateful to the Social Science Research Council, who supported me with both their generous predissertation and dissertation fellowships in Bangladesh in 1994 and 1995–97; second, I wish to thank the University of Chicago Committee on South Asia, which supported me off and on during my research in West Bengal and my write-up period in Chicago.

Finally, I want to thank my dad, Hugh B. Urban Sr., for his painstaking help with the otherwise thankless task of proofreading this unwieldy manuscript, and also for just plain being a good dad.

Contents

A Note (or Apology) on Transliteration

Unfortunately, there is no standard or satisfactory system for transliterating Bengali script into Roman characters; indeed, there seem to be as many different systems as there are scholars of Bengali. After asking numerous authorities, both Western and Indian, I have found nothing but a wild diversity of idiosyncratic systems, nor have I ever come across a work that was entirely consistent within itself. On one side, authors who wish to emphasize the Sanskritic origins of Bengali use the same transliteration system as for *devanāgarī*: they distinguish between *v*'s and *b*'s and between different sibilants (*ś, ṣ, s*) and render all final open vowels. This purely Sanskritic system is perhaps the only truly "consistent" one, though it results in some rather bizarre constructions that have no real place in either the Sanskrit or Bengali languages (e.g., rendering the final vowel of a Bengali genitive inflection, such as *bhāvera,* which does not exist in Sanskrit and is not pronounced in Bengali). On the other side, those who wish to capture the actual sound of the Bengali language adopt a basically phonetic system: hence, all *v*'s turn into Bengali *b*'s, all sibilants become the Bengali aspirated *sh*'s, all final vowels drop off, and so on. This, too, produces some weird constructions—for example, *boishnab* for the Sanskritic *vaiṣṇava*—which are unrecognizable to most non-Bengali specialists. In sum, a purely Sanskritic system ultimately does violence to the uniquely Bengali character of the language, while a purely Bengali system is basically unintelligible to scholars of most non-Bengali traditions.

For my part, I have chosen to adopt a compromise system similar to that used by Jeffrey Kripal. As Kripal points out, Bengali writers, in their own self-representations, typically use a mixed system of transliteration, slipping easily back and forth between a Sanskritic and a vernacular.

> Because the culture itself rocks back and forth between venacular and Sanskritic transliterations, I too will alternate between the two options, trying as best I can to approximate the self-representation of the culture. . . . Such a system will no doubt strike the linguistically sensitive reader as a confused melange of broken rules and inconsistencies. I can only admit my compromises, note that they are at least partly a function of the culture's own history. (Jeffrey J. Kripal, *Kālī's Child: The Mystical and the Erotic in the Life and Teachings of Ramakrishna* [Chicago: University of Chicago Press, 1995], xxxii)

No one, for example, ever writes the name "Ramakrishna" the way it is actually pronounced (i.e., "Ramkrishno"). Instead, the tradition frequently Sanskritizes itself, though usually only partially, and often quite incorrectly. Moreover, this eclectic compromise method is itself a reflection of the complex and syncretic history of the Bengali people—a people who wish to identify themselves with the rich traditions of Sanskrit literature while asserting the uniquely "Bengali" quality of their own very rich history and literary creations. This may strike most specialists as inconsistent and contradictory; but one could argue equally that a purely "consistent" and rigidly governed system would do an injustice to this tradition, which is itself highly diverse, pluralistic, and often (like every language) quite inconsistent. However, I adopt a few basic ground rules:

1. The basic system is fundamentally Sanskritic, though tailored to the peculiarities of the Bengali language. This is intended, first, to make this book reasonably accessible to scholars of Sanskrit and other Indian languages, and, second, to preserve as much of the feel of the Bengali language as possible.
2. Therefore I follow the Sanskrit distinction between *v*'s and *b*'s and between different sibilants, and I render vowels in their Sanskrit form (*a* and *ā* instead of the Bengali *o* and *uh*).
3. Final *a*'s on genitive or locative constructions are not rendered, because this produces a form that makes no sense in either Bengali or Sanskrit. Thus, I use *Bhāver,* not *Bhāvera.*
4. Words of clearly Perso-Arabic origin are not Sanskritized: thus Pīr does not become Pīra, and terms like *gorib* ("poor") are not rendered as *goriva.*
5. Proper names are left more or less as pronounced and not Sanskritized unless that person has rendered his own name Sanskritically in English publications. Thus I refer to "Āulcāṅd" and "Dulālcāṅd" rather than "Āulacāṅda" and "Dulālacāṅda." This will no doubt produce a number of unsatisfactory contradictions—but no more than most native Bengalis produce when they attempt to render their own names into English.

Abbreviations

Citations in *Songs of Ecstasy* and in this book refer, first, to the original text and page number (e.g., KG 1 or BG 66), and, second, to the section and song number in the *Songs*. Hence, BG 160; II.1 refers to *Bhāver Gīta*, 160, translated in part II, song number 1.

BG	*Bhāver Gīta,* ed. Śāntirañjan Cakravartī. Calcutta: Indralekha Press, 1399 B.S. (1992).
BG (1882)	*Bhāver Gīta,* ed. Romeścandra Ghoṣe. Calcutta: Aurora Press, 1289 B.S. (1882).
KDA	Manulāl Miśra. *Kartābhajā Dharmer Ādi Vṛttānta Vā Sahajatattva Prakāśa.* Calcutta: Author, 1925.
KG	*Kartābhajā Gīta.* Bengali manuscript no. 964, Bāṅgīya Sāhitya Pariṣat Library (Calcutta), 1228-33 B.S. (1821–26 CE).
SE	Hugh B. Urban. *Songs of Ecstasy: Tantric and Devotional Songs from Colonial Bengal.* New York: Oxford University Press, 2001.
SS	*Sahajiyā Sāhitya,* ed. Manidra Mohan Bose. Calcutta: University of Calcutta, 1932.
STP	Manulāl Miśra. *Sahaja Tattva Prakāśa.* Calcutta: Author, 1309 B.S. (1902).

THE ECONOMICS OF ECSTASY

Introduction

Secrecy and Symbolic Power

From secrecy, which shades all that is profound and significant, grows the error according to which everything mysterious is something important and essential. Before the unknown man's natural impulse is to idealize . . . to intensify the unknown through imagination. (Georg Simmel)

It is perhaps only fitting that the phenomena of "secrecy" and "esotericism" should remain among the most persistent and pervasive, and yet also poorly studied and misunderstood, aspects of the history of religions. Derived from the Greek term *esoteros*, esotericism refers to what is "inner" or hidden—what is known only to the initiated few and closed to the majority of mankind in the exoteric world.[1] Despite the increasing preoccupation with the topic throughout the media, television series (e.g., the "X-Files"), popular novels (e.g., *Foucault's Pendulum*), and even now on the Internet (where we can shop at "Esotericism.com" or attend the "Church of Tantra" on line), the subject of secrecy remains poorly understood and theoretically confused within the academic study of religions.[2] Among historians of religions, such as Mircea Eliade and Kees Bolle, the study of secrecy has remained disappointingly general, universalistic, and largely divorced from all social and historical context. Even Antoine Faivre's extensive work on Western esotericism takes virtually no account of the very real social and political contexts in which esoteric traditions emerge and with which they are inextricably intertwined.[3]

The field of South Asian studies is no exception to this broader trend, which has generated a growing interest in the role of secrecy in Indian traditions, specifically in the texts and rituals of Tantrism. As Douglas Brooks has argued, just as the study of mystics such as Meister Eckhart has completely revised our traditional view of Christianity, and just as the recognition of the Kabbalah has transformed our understanding of Judaism, so, too, the recognition of the Tantras as a central and pervasive aspect of Indian religions has the potential to transform our understanding of Hinduism itself.[4]

Even amidst the growing body of Tantric studies, however, a number of profound lacunae in contemporary scholarship remain. First, as we see in the recent proliferation of scholarship on Kashmir Śaivism, much of the work has been almost entirely philosophical, extremely cerebral, and purely textual; with the exception of the more recent work of David White and Jeffrey Kripal, few scholars have made any inquiry into the real historical and social contexts in which Tantra is practiced, generally ignoring its complexity and messiness as a lived tradition.[5] In short, most scholars have ignored the basic fact that, as Simmel long ago pointed out, secrecy is always by definition a social phenomenon. It is deeply enmeshed in historical and political contexts, defining relations of power between those who know and those who do not.[6] Second, most of the recent literature on Tantra has been extremely specialized in focus, with little interest in the broader comparative issues involved in the study of esoteric traditions. Thus far, there has been little effort to grapple with the wider methodological problems of esotericism, nor has there been any attempt to integrate the rich body of sociological and anthropological theories of secrecy.

And third, there has yet been little critical reflection on the historical construction of the category of "Tantrism" itself. It is true that India has long known the existence of a large, diverse, and heterogeneous body of texts called *tantras*; however, as André Padoux points out, the abstract category of "Tantrism," used to refer to a distinct and coherent tradition, is "certainly a modern Western creation"—that is, largely the product of Orientalist scholars and colonial authorities of the nineteenth century.[7] We need to ask, therefore, what was the specific cultural and historical milieu, what were the deeper social and political interests, that led European authors to classify a certain body of texts and traditions under the collective title of "Tantrism?" And why specifically those that were considered, by Victorian standards, not only bizarre but also repulsive, sexually licentious, and morally offensive?

In this volume, I suggest a new approach to the study of Tantra and to the topic of secrecy in general, by focusing on one specific esoteric tradition—the Kartābhajās or "Worshipers of the Master"—which spread throughout the Calcutta area during the late eighteenth and nineteenth centuries. Precisely because of the unique and rather volatile milieu in which they emerged, in the early decades of colonial rule, during the first stages of the penetration of European capitalism into Bengal, the Kartābhajās offer an especially poignant case for the study of a secret tradition within its concrete, living historical contexts. Indeed, they are a striking illustration of the *power and the liability* of secrecy—its role both as a source of status, honor, or prestige and as a source of danger, scandal, censorship, or suppression.

In the first half of this introduction, I provide a general background on the Kartābhajās and their importance for our scholarly imagining of "Tantrism" and for the study of esoteric traditions as a whole. Then, in the second half, I engage the larger theoretical snarls inevitably involved in the study of something that is supposed to be "secret."

The Economics of Ecstasy: A Historical and Contextual Approach to the Study of Tantric Traditions

The Kartābhajās are a degenerate [*bhaṅga*] form of the Tantric religion. . . . In the Kali age, people are deluded by ignorance; therefore the desire for the five M's is the religion of this era. That's why the Kartābhajā teaching has secretly become very powerful in this land. (Rāmacandra Datta, *Tattvasāra*)

Founded by a semilegendary wandering madman named Āulcāṅd (d. 1779)—who was said to be Śrī Caitanya reincarnated in the form of a poor, crazy Fakir—the Kartābhajās stand out as perhaps the most important later branch of the Vaiṣṇava-Sahajiyā tradition, and as one of the few to have survived in the changing context of colonial Bengal. Throughout the Bengali world, moreover, they have a long and controversial reputation because of their supposed engagement in secret, scandalous, and immoral activities. As the orthodox Muslim leader Muhammad Riāzuddin Āhmad wrote in 1903, "The class of Fakirs called the Kartābhajās . . . is a group of necrophagous goblins [*piśāca*] who have spread their terrible poison throughout our community. . . . They are the refuse of our society."[8] Even today the dangerous power and lurid attraction of the Kartābhajās survive in the Bengali imagination; as we see in widely read novels such as Kālakūṭa's *Kothāy Se Jan Āche*, the Kartābhajās are surrounded with a tantalizing aura of danger and allure—an allure made all the more intense because any commerce with this group was explicitly forbidden by his conservative Brahmin family:

> My first trip [to the Kartābhajā festival in Ghoshpara] was not at all pleasant. . . . Even going to the gathering was forbidden. The instructions of my guardians were clear: That is a forbidden place. . . . In our family, as among many Brahmin families, it was forbidden because of its infamous reputation. *But the very fact that something is "forbidden" also means there is always an urge to transgress that prohibition. For every veil, there is a desire to unveil. The more secrecy there is, the more one's curiosity grows.*[9]

What I shall argue for in my discussion of the Kartābhajās is a profoundly contextual or *embodied* approach to Tantra, one deeply embedded in the concrete social, historical, and political circumstances in which these traditions emerge and with which they interact. Here I wish to follow the lead of Jeffrey Kripal and his work on the Calcutta mystic, Śrī Rāmakṛṣṇa. As Kripal suggests, we need to acknowledge not only the "pure" form of Tantra as presented in Sanskrit texts or in highly cerebral philosophical speculation but also its deeper ambiguities in concrete human experience—"not its ideal state but in its lived compromises and contradictions."[10] In the case of the Kartābhajās, I hope to demonstrate the profound impact of the changing social, political—and, above all, the economic—context of colonial Bengal on a highly esoteric Tantric tradition. In other words, I wish to delve into its *economics of ecstasy,* or (to borrow a phrase of Lise McKean), its *divine enterprise*[11]—the very material circumstances and practical conditions of its secret mysteries and hidden truths.

The Kartābhajās, it would seem, present an ideal case for this kind of a project. First, as one of the few esoteric sects about which we have a large amount of concrete historical data, drawn from a wide range of sources, the Kartābhajās provide a rare opportunity to study a Tantric tradition within its concrete sociohistorical context. Using primary textual material, firsthand accounts by well-known Bengali figures (Rāmakṛṣṇa, Dāśarathī Rāy, and many others), contemporary newspaper reports, and missionary accounts, we can reconstruct the historical trajectory and social composition of this group with a rare degree of accuracy. We know when and where the sect emerged, who participated in it, from which classes they came, how they interacted with the exoteric society around them, and how they changed in response to the changing social and economic circumstances of modern Bengal. Finally, we also have living representatives of the sect still practicing today, still publishing texts and converging at annual festivals in Ghoshpara, the sect's village center, north of Calcutta.[12]

Second, the Kartābhajās represent an especially clear example of an esoteric tradition. Not only did they develop a sophisticated system of secret discourse or *sandhābhāṣā*, called the Language of the Mint (*ṭyāṅkśālī bol*), which saturates their large corpus of mystical songs, but they also developed a strategy for cultivating a dual identity, maintaining at once the facade of an exoteric public identity (the *vyāvahārik* self), in conformity with exoteric social law while creating a secret, divinized identity (the *paramārthik* self).[13] At the same time, however, the Kartābhajās also provide an especially poignant example of what I shall call the inherent ambivalence and *liability* of secrecy—that is, the ways in which the very claim to secrecy often turns into a source of criticism, slander, and censorship from the surrounding exoteric society. Within the Kartābhajā tradition itself, in fact, we find repeated (though never successful) efforts at self-censorship, in the attempt to purge the tradition of its more objectionable esoteric, particularly Tantric and sexual, elements.

Third, the Kartābhajās also open up some especially important insights into the problematic category of "Tantra" itself. Not only did they emerge in the same area—Bengal, specifically around Calcutta—in which many of the foremost Orientalist scholars and Christian missionaries were working,[14] and in the same historical period—from the late eighteenth to early twentieth centuries—during which they first began to identify a certain body of texts and traditions as "Tantrism," but, by the end of the nineteenth century, the Kartābhajās were often singled out as the quintessence and most extreme example of the degenerate Tantric cult. In the words of the famous Bengali poet and satirist Dāśarathī Rāy, they are "the foremost of the *Aghora-panthīs.*"[15] Śrī Rāmakṛṣṇa, for example, often simply says *Kartābhajādi* (the Kartābhajās, etc.), to refer to a wide range of disreputable Tantric cults in the Calcutta area.[16]

The Kartābhajās, however, also illustrate with striking clarity just how flawed and ambiguous a category Tantra is. For if it is true, as Padoux suggests, that Tantrism is largely a modern scholarly construction, can we still use this category in a productive way? And what do we do with cases like the Kartābhajās, whom most critics outside the tradition denounce as Tantric, while many apologists within the tradition ardently deny that they have anything to do with the scandal and smut of Tantra?

As Douglas Brooks has argued, Tantra is perhaps best understood not in terms of a singular, monothetic definition but, rather, as a product of the scholarly imagination, a heuristic device or useful tool, which we employ in order to organize and understand a given body of texts and traditions. As such, it demands a more flexible and messier "polythetic" definition, which does not reify some single unifying essence but instead simply identifies a set of common characteristics and family resemblances. A given tradition therefore need not call itself "Tantric" but simply must share a significant number of these characteristics in order to be usefully classified as Tantric.[17] If we accept this polythetic definition, then the Kartābhajās would clearly appear to share virtually all of the ten characteristics Brooks identifies. They do indeed claim an extra-Vedic authority, beyond the traditional canon of Hindu scriptures[18]; they engage in special forms of bodily discipline, such as Kuṇḍalinī yoga[19]; they are at once theists and philosophical nondualists[20]; they employ the mystical power of sound and sacred formulae (*mantras*)[21]; they place extraordinary emphasis on the authority of the Guru (who is in fact identified as God incarnate); their theology and ritual center around the bipolar sexual symbolism of the male Deity and his Consort (Kṛṣṇa and Rādhā); their practice is at once highly esoteric (*gupta, rahasya*), and considered the most expedient, most natural, or innate (*Sahaja*) path to liberation[22]; they engage in acts which explicitly transgress conventional social boundaries—such as communal meals which ignore social hierarchies and (in some cases) sexual intercourse in violation of caste[23]; and finally, they demand forms of initiation (*dīkṣā*), in which caste and gender are not the primary criteria for *sādhanā*.[24]

Alternatively, we might also employ the simpler, more general definition suggested by Madeleine Biardeau and André Padoux: Tantric traditions, they argue, are most fundamentally those which aim to "harness *kāma*—desire (in every sense of the word) . . . to the service of deliverance"; that is to say, they adapt and employ the powers of the human body, the physical senses, and even sexuality as the most expedient means to liberation.[25] This is in fact the very basis of the Kartābhajā path, the end and goal of which are precisely to distill the nectar of desire, to transmute base physical lust (*kāma*) into pure, spiritual Love (*prema*). As two living Kartābhajā gurus explain, "The essential thing is that lust does not have to be abandoned; it has to be purified."[26] "The supreme essence is Sahaja; it cannot be attained through the repression of desire, but rather, in an innate, spontaneous, natural way. . . . The path to attaining the supreme essence. . . . is the method of Tantric yoga."[27]

Therefore, I would agree with D. C. Sen that the Kartābhajās may be regarded as the largest, most powerful, and "primary community among Sahajiyās" which survived in the colonial period and thus as part of the more general class of "Tantric" traditions of Bengal.[28] And yet, rather strikingly, the Kartābhajās themselves have always been deeply ambivalent about their relation to Tantrism—indeed, many members today vehemently deny that they bear any relation to things smacking of the scandal of Tantrism (which has become a kind of dirty word to most Bengalis).[29] Hence, the Kartābhajās not only offer a poignant illustration of just how problematic a category this is but also help us to reimagine and redefine this category in a more fruitful way in contemporary discourse.

Finally—and perhaps most important for our attempt to reimagine the category of Tantra—the Kartābhajās also demonstrate how deeply rooted Tantric traditions are within their specific social, political, or economic contexts. This tradition, I argue, cannot be understood apart from the very unique social and economic world in which it was born: the situation of Bengal under colonial rule, during the initial penetration of European capitalism into India. The sect emerged at a critical historical moment and at a pivotal geographic locus—the area around Calcutta, the imperial city, at the end of the eighteenth century. Much of its following was drawn from precisely those classes that had been most negatively affected by the changing socioeconomic changes in Calcutta and the surrounding countryside; they came from the "underworld of the imperial city," from the poor urban laborers and the dislocated peasantry of Nadia district.[30] This in turn had a formative impact both on the structure of the sect and on the symbolic language of its texts, which are filled with a remarkable amount of mercantile terms, such as "commodities," "capital," "brokers," "traders," "account books,"and so on. Indeed, not only do they borrow the mercantile imagery of contemporary Calcutta, but they also skillfully appropriate much of the discourse of the British East India Company itself. Throughout their highly metaphor and esoteric songs, the Kartābhajās often call themselves nothing less than a new Company, a "Poor Company" (*gorib Kompānī*), "Mad Company" (*pāgal kompānī*), or "Platoon of the Poor" (*kāṅgāler palṭan*) which had been founded because the "Old Company" of the mainstream Vaiṣṇava tradition was no longer relevant to a changing historical context. The Kartābhajās had come to reveal a host of "spiritual commodities" and a new form of "capital" for the poor low-class people who comprised its following.[31]

But beyond the basic social context in which they emerge, the Kartābhajās also show us how dramatically Tantric traditions may change and transform themselves with the changing course of history. "The people of Bengal have always been Tantrics and Sahajiyās," as one recent scholar put it, "In the Kartābhajā sect, this Tantric and Sahajiyā current has undergone many transformations and has been conceived in a new form."[32] Emerging during the critical period of early colonial rule, amidst the social and religious reforms of the Bengal Renaissance, the Kartābhajās clearly reflect the changing attitudes and anxieties about the very category of "Tantra" itself. As we see in each of the three parts of this volume, the Kartābhajās represent (at least) three fundamental transformations within the older Sahajiyā traditions, which emerged in response to the changing social and economic context of colonial Bengal. They might thus be called the following: (1) a kind of "popularized Tantra"—a more inclusive, less elitist tradition or "Religion of Man" (*Mānuṣer Dharma*), which made an explicit appeal to the poorer lower classes; (2) a "deodorized Tantra"—one that felt intense embarassment about the more objectionable aspects of the Sahajiyā traditions (above all, the use of sexual practices) and made a deliberate effort to sanitize, censor, or at least better disguise anything smacking of "Tantra"; and (3) a "commercialized Tantra"—one that developed a complex economic hierarchy, which ironically allowed this originally poor, lower-class sect to become perhaps the wealthiest and most successful of all the "obscure religious cults" of Bengal.

Therefore, in addition to its broader comparative implications for the history of religions, a thorough study of the Kartābhajās would also offer a much-needed contribution to the area of Bengal studies. As one of the few lower-class religious sects about which we have a good deal of historical data, the Kartābhajās open a fascinating and revealing window onto the lives of the poor lower orders of nineteenth-century Calcutta and the surrounding countryside—classes that were, as Sumanta Banerjee points out, otherwise largely invisible to Calcutta's upper-class bhadralok society, and long neglected by modern historiography.[33] Appearing ubiquitously throughout nineteenth-century Bengali literature, newspapers, and the writings of contemporary figures such as the disciples of Rāmakṛṣṇa, the Kartābhajās are a sect that every Bengali scholar has heard of; yet, thus far, there is not a single comprehensive study of this group. In many respects, the Kartābhajās are a group much like the Bāuls (who were ignored until made famous by Rabindranath Tagore) or the Vaiṣṇava-Sahajiyās (who were unknown until brought to our attention by Edward C. Dimock); in fact, until this century, the Kartābhajās were far more numerous and powerful than the Bāuls, the Sahajiyās, or any other of the so-called obscure religious cults of Bengal.[34] But, rather strangely, the Kartābhajās appear largely to have slipped through the cracks of modern scholarship. Apart from a few scattered articles by Geoffrey A. Oddie and Sumanta Banerjee, and Ramakanta Chakrabarty's brief chapter in his *Vaiṣṇavism in Bengal*, there is virtually nothing on this sect in the English language. Even in Bengali scholarship, there are only a few critical studies of this group. Indeed, no less an authority that Sukumār Sen himself reportedly stated that a thorough study of the Kartābhajās is among the most needed projects in the history of Bengali literature.[35]

The Enigma of the Kartābhajās: A History of Secrecy, Censorship, Scandal, Slander and a Gradual Decline into Obscurity

> At the very utterance of this word "Kartābhajā" my family and neighbors would make mocking and disgusted remarks. . . . "Oh! such a disgraceful thing has never before occurred in this world!" (Kālakūṭa, *Kathāy se Jan Āche*)

This scholarly neglect of the Kartābhajās, it would seem, is due in large part to the highly controversial and often quite scandalous reputation they acquired during the nineteenth century, when they became increasingly suspected of sexual licentiousness, fraud, and criminal behavior. Although it began as one of many small esoteric cults stemming from the much older Sahajiyā traditions of medieval Bengal, the Kartābhajās had, by the mid-nineteenth century, grown into a wealthy, powerful, and quite infamous tradition, which was widely discussed among the educated society of Calcutta. Initially a highly secretive obscure minor sect, the Kartābhajās also developed an important "exoteric" public dimension, which attracted a mass following and allowed its leadership to accumulate large amounts of land and revenue.

Unfortunately, in large part because of their "esoteric" heritage, the Kartābhajās also came under increasing attack, slander, and ridicule from the more conservative upper-class factions of nineteenth-century Bengal—above all, for their alleged immorality and Tantric sexual practices. As Rāmakṛṣṇa described them, for example, they were thought to be comprised mainly of "bitches" or "whores" (*māgī*), who engaged in sexual rituals, perverse relations with small boys, and other unspeakable acts. "Everybody shuddered at the name Kartābhajā. The vices which they imbibed from the Tantriks became most prominent. . . . Kartābhajā became a term of ridicule."[36] Even today, the *Samsad Bengali Dictionary* defines "Kartābhajā" as a sarcastic term of slander and insult. But, at the same time, ironically, the Kartābhajās were also praised by some of the most progressive reformers of the nineteenth century, such as Nabīncandra Sen, who admired their seemingly modern humanistic ideals. The semimythical founder, Āulcāṅd, has even been hailed by some as a kind of "folk Rāmmohun Roy."[37] Amidst all these conflicting accounts and scandalous accusations, the Kartābhajās have been largely ignored in modern scholarship. As the respected historian, Rameścandra Majumdār, put it, "up to the nineteenth century, many Sahajiyā sects such as the Kartābhajās. . . . became widespread throughout Bengal, but it is impossible to describe them without offending the judgments of good taste."[38]

Correspondingly, we find two parallel currents within the later Kartābhajā tradition of the nineteenth and twentieth century: on one hand, among the more esoteric disciples, a move further "underground", into the realm of increasing secrecy and silence; on the other hand, among the more "exoteric" and "orthodox" devotees, an attempt to clean up, sanitize, or deodorize the tradition, to purge all immoral or sexual elements—above all anything smacking of "Tantrism"—and to give the tradition a more "legitimate" Vaiṣṇava appearance. This attempt to legitimate and deodorize the tradition was never, however, successful. Increasingly throughout the twentieth century the Kartābhajās became the victim of severe ridicule, slander, and a gradual fall into obscurity. "Since the nineteenth century, this has been the most debated and most numerous of the folk sects," Cakravartī comments, "Because of the ill-repute and slander surrounding their Sahajiyā practices, they have now lost much respect."[39] Although many pockets of Kartābhajās still survive throughout Calcutta, rural West Bengal, and Bangladesh, and although one can still find many Kartābhajā subsects such as the Sāhebdhanīs, Bhagabāniyās, Gurusatyas, and Āuls, the current status of the tradition is a rather sad reflection of its impressive power and wealth at its height in the nineteenth century. Today, the Kartābhajās are typically remembered only for their large annual festival held in Ghoshpara at the time of Holi, which now survives largely as a kind of carnival event or popular entertainment (as well as the primary source of income for the current family of the Kartā). Ironically, this once profoundly "esoteric" Sahajiyā cult now survives as a relatively innocuous and "exoteric" devotional movement. "Many suppose that the Kartābhajās' Tantric bodily practices are the result of later external influence," Ratan Kumār Nandī explains, "But this is not the case. Rather, under the impact of later history, these practices underwent a transformation, and, in place of secret rituals [*guhyācāra*], a more devotional faith . . . became predominant."[40]

Method and Argument:
Putting Some History Back into the "History of Religions"

To penetrate a tradition as controversial and esoteric as the Kartābhajās, I submit, we must proceed by placing them within a broader cross-cultural framework, employing the tools and strategies of a historian of religions. These strategies I understand to be, (1) comparison in the *strong* sense of the word, that is, not only comparison across cultures but also across historical and disciplinary boundaries[41]; (2) a dialectical strategy of tacking back and forth between broad cross-cultural theory and specific historical detail; and (3) an attention to the *historical transformations* of the phenomenon and, above all, to the ways in which human agents appropriate and manipulate religious resources for specific historical interests. Here, I understand the task of the historian of religions to go far beyond a simple Eliadean quest for universal patterns and symbolic archetypes, or a search for the *sui generis* essence of religion as the product of *homo religiosus*. Rather, the historian of religions must also examine myths and symbols as the work of real, concretely situated, interested human beings, as products of *homo faber*, which are deeply enmeshed in real social, political, and historical contexts.[42] As Bruce Lincoln points out, the discipline of the "history of religions" therefore bears a deep tension at its very heart. To practice the history of religions is to examine the temporal, human, and material aspects of phenomena which claim to be transcendent, suprahuman and eternal:

> Religion . . . is that discourse whose defining characteristic is its desire to speak of things eternal and transcendent with an authority equally transcendent and eternal. History, in the sharpest possible contrast, is that discourse which speaks of things temporal and terrestrial in a human and fallible voice, while staking its claim to authority on rigorous critical practice.
>
> History of religions is thus a discourse that resists and reverses the orientation of that discourse with which it concerns itself. To practice history of religions . . . is to insist on discussing the temporal, contextual, situated, interested, human and material dimensions of those discourses, practices and institutions that characteristically represent themselves as eternal, transcendent, spiritual and divine.[43]

In sum, as a *historian* of religions, I will try to root the Kartābhajā tradition concretely within its greater social, economic, and historical context, examining the ways in which it interacted with, and was in turn historically transformed by, the cultural world around it. Hence I see my work as a complement and corrective to earlier works on the Vaiṣṇava Sahajiyā tradition like that of Edward C. Dimock, who provides an excellent analysis of the texts, theology, and practices of this tradition while largely ignoring the social and historical context in which it emerged. But simultaneously, as a historian of *religions*, I will also place this tradition within the much broader comparative framework of secrecy and esotericism cross-culturally, bringing to bear a wide range of anthropological and sociological theory, as well as comparative insights drawn from other non-Indian religious traditions.

Using some insights from Pierre Bourdieu and Michel Foucault, I argue for a theoretical shift in our approach to the problem of secrecy as a comparative and cross-cultural category. Instead of defining secrecy in terms of its content or substance, as most past scholars have done, I would suggest that it is far more fruitful to examine secrecy in terms of its form, or the ways in which secret information is exchanged.[44] Secrecy, I suggest, is best understood as a strategy for concealing and revealing information. It is a tactic which functions to transform certain knowledge into a rare and valuable commodity, a scarce resource, which in turn enhances the status and prestige—in Bourdieu's terms the "symbolic capital"—of its possessor. Unlike most forms of symbolic capital, however, secret knowledge can be exchanged and accumulated only within a highly restricted, often "illegal" or unorthodox social field, such as esoteric ritual. Hence, it might be thought of as a kind of "black market symbolic capital." Not unlike drugs or prostitution, it is a valuable but also dangerous and transgressive form of power which can only be exchanged outside the bounds of mainstream society, and which increases one's status only in an alternative, esoteric hierarchy.

Because this study concerns a sect that flowered during a situation of colonial rule, and because the texts of this group incorporate a large amount of capitalist language, in the course of my analysis I employ, criticize, and modify some of the insights of recent colonial and postcolonial studies.[45] On one hand, I am deeply sympathetic to scholars such as Jean Comaroff, Marshall Sahlins, the members of the Subaltern Studies Collective, and others who have dealt with situations of colonial contact and native resistance. As the Comaroffs argue, colonized peoples are never just assimilated passively into colonial and capitalist structures; rather, as creative agents, they also subvert and deform them in manifold ways, often by appropriating the structures of colonialism themselves, giving them new or radically transformed meanings.[46]

On the other hand, I am more critical of the recent proliferation of literature on postcolonial theory that has followed in the wake of Fanon, Said, Bhabha, and their disciples. I am indeed sympathetic to their critique of Eurocentric notions of language and literature and their concern with the "strategies of subversion" in the writings of colonized peoples[47]; however, as critics such as Aijaz Ahmad, Anne McClintock, and Sara Suleri have pointed out, there are a number of troubling problems inherent in the discourse of postcolonialism.

First, it tends to oversimplify the colonial situation, portraying it as a simple binarism of colonizer and colonized, imperial oppressor and native victim. By overemphasizing the radical impact of Western power on the rest of the world, much postcolonial discourse tends to divide all global history into pre- and postimperial epochs. In so doing, it is in danger of lapsing into a more subtle form of imperialism, viewing all human history from the standpoint of European expansion and the progress of modern capitalism.[48] As we will see, this is especially problematic in the case of colonial India, which represents an extremely complex interaction between indigenous and European factions. As recent historians such as C. A. Bayly and David Washbrook have argued, India was by no means suddenly and radically transformed from a pre-capitalist feudal society into a modern capitalist one. Not only were there many varieties of pre-colonial Indian capitalism, but even after the arrival of the British East India Company, the British were but one of several players in a complex field of economic relations. Pre-colonial and colonial structures existed simultaneously, while many competing factions, both foreign and indigenous, struggled over material and symbolic resources.[49]

Second, in their celebration of resistance and struggle, postcolonial studies too often overlook the more subtle forms of collusion and cooperation between colonizer and colonized. By romanticizing the struggle of colonized peoples, portraying them as noble champions of freedom against the expansion of global capitalism, they overlook the many ways in which colonized peoples do not simply struggle against oppressive colonial structures, but also introduce new, in some cases equally oppressive, hierarchies of their own. As John Kelly suggests, we need a more complex understanding of the colonial situation, emphasizing the ambivalent mixture of both resistance and accommodation. What we find is often "not a story of victory for the colonized in resistance to colonial hegemony" but, rather, one in which "the heroes are flawed and their successes mixed with failures."[50]

The Kartābhajās, I suggest, are a wonderful reflection of this deeper complexity of Bengal at the turn of the nineteenth century. According to the central metaphor of the main Kartābhajā text, the *Bhāver Gīta*, this world is one vast "bazaar"—a teeming marketplace, in which a host of merchants, both foreign and native, exchange the merchandise of their various religious and political beliefs.[51] Within the Kartābhajā songs and rituals, we find a rich mixture of colonial and precolonial, indigenous, and foreign discourse. Mercantile terminology and the language of the "company" (*kompānī*) mingle with traditional economic hierarchies, such as the precolonial Zamindārī system of revenue. At the same time, this group is also a fascinating mixture of both resistance and accommodation to colonial structures. The Kartābhajās do indeed strategically appropriate many elements of colonial discourse, investing them with highly subversive meanings and turning them into a powerful source of liberation. Yet simultaneously, it would seem that its poor, lower-class members are reinscribed into a new economic hierarchy, which serves primarily to benefit a small group of powerful gurus.

Structure and Plan of the Book: A Dialectical Argument

This volume proceeds by means of a dialectical movement, tacking back and forth between broad cross-cultural comparative theory and narrow, concrete historical detail. In the second half of this introduction, I engage in a detailed theoretical and comparative discussion, focusing on the larger cross-cultural problems of secrecy and esoteric traditions. The body of the volume will then be divided into three parts, with a total of seven chapters. In part I, the "The Secret Marketplace," I summarize the broader social and historical background of late-eighteenth-century Bengal and the basic religious and social ideals of the early Kartābhajā tradition. Part II, "The Power of Secrecy," then engages the role of secrecy as a source of symbolic power, in both esoteric discourse and in physical practice. And in part III, "The Liability of Secrecy," I examine the more problematic and negative side of secrecy as a potential source of scandal, slander, elitism, and exploitation.

Thus, although the overall focus of this volume is the role of secrecy as a strategy for acquiring symbolic capital, each of the seven chapters engages a specific substrategy or supporting tactic of secrecy. In chapter 1, "The Underworld of the Imperial City," I examine the role of secrecy as a *hermeneutic strategy,* or a means of appropriating the legitimating authority of traditional scriptures and sacred metanarratives while submitting them to a deeper, esoteric interpretation that undercuts or subverts them. In chapter 2, "The Religion of Man," I analyze the role of secrecy as a tactic of *religious appropriation and bricolage*: this is a method of borrowing elements from a variety of different "exoteric" traditions, while weaving them into a new esoteric synthesis that transcends them. At the same time, secrecy also operates as a *social ideal,* or a way of life, allowing the disciple to live a socially acceptable public life while cultivating an inner, autonomous esoteric identity.

In chapter 3, "The Language of the Mint," I engage secrecy specifically as a *discursive strategy*, a means of creating scarce, highy valued resources of knowledge. In chapter 4, "The Poor Company," I then look more closely at the specific *metaphoric strategies* and symbols employed in this Mint language—above all, the enigmatic use of mercantile imagery and the language of the "company." Chapter 5, "Secret Bodies," then shifts to the role of secrecy as a *practical and ritual strategy*, as a means of transforming the physical body and creating in its place an alternative spiritualized body.

In chapter 6, "The Stinking Fruit in the Garden of Love," I engage the more problematic side of secrecy as a source of scandal and embarrassment—above all, with regard to Tantric sexual practices—and the corresponding "metastrategies" of *self-censorship, concealment, deodorization, and disguise* which esoteric traditions must often employ in order to protect themselves. Finally, chapter 7, "The Economics of Ecstasy," discusses the more problematic aspects of secrecy as a potential strategy of *elitism and economic exploitation*, with special attention to the infamous annual festival held in Ghoshpara. As we will see in chapter 8, "The Progressive Exotericization and Institutionalization of an Esoteric Tradition," the esoteric elements of the Kartābhajā tradition would eventually become an increasing source of embarrassment, to be progressively marginalized as the later tradition evolved from a secretive obscure cult into a largely innocuous devotional faith.

The conclusion then zooms back out once again, to address the broader comparative issues of secrecy, particularly the changing shape of esoteric traditions under colonial rule.

The Torment of Secrecy: Methodological Problems in the Study of Esoteric Traditions

If we cannot agree about the nature of the secret, we are nevertheless compelled to agree that secrecy exists, the source of the interpreter's pleasures, but also of his necessary disappointment. (Frank Kermode, *The Genesis of Secrecy*)

With their profoundly enigmatic language and deeply encoded ritual practices, the Kartābhajās lead us directly into one of the most tangled methodological snarls any historian of religions might have to face: the question of secrecy.[52] Specifically, they raise two interrelated and deeply entangled problems—one epistemological and the other ethical—which are inevitably involved in the study of those traditions claiming to be "secret." This "double bind" of secrecy—or what Tony Stewart has aptly dubbed the "Gordion Knot" of secrecy[53]—may be formulated as follows: First, how can one study and say anything intelligent at all about a religious tradition which practices *active dissimulation* (i.e., which deliberately obfuscates its teachings and intentionally conceals itself from outsiders). And, second, if one does learn something about an esoteric tradition—above all, if one goes so far as to become an "insider," receiving initiation into secret teachings—how can one then say anything about this tradition to an uninitiated audience of "outsiders." In short, if one "knows," one cannot speak; and if one speaks, one must not really "know." As various scholars have described their own frustrated attempts to penetrate the Kartābhajās:

> There is no way of determining the numbers of this sect. . . . Because their practices are followed in secrecy, it is very difficult to study them.[54]

> It is very difficult to discuss the Kartābhajās' religious philosophy and methods of practice; secrecy with regard to its practices is a special characteristic of this sect.[55]

In the course of my own fieldwork among Kartābhajā disciples in West Bengal and Bangladesh, I was forced to grapple with this sticky double bind head on. Between the years 1994 and 1997, I interviewed and worked closely with a variety of Kartābhajās—among them, a female miracle worker and charismatic leader of north Calcutta, a dancing folk singer of rural Nadiya, a variety of begging minstrels of Bangladesh, a self-proclaimed wandering "madman" (*pāgal*), and two separate individuals who both claimed to be the Kartā (the supreme Incarnation of God in human form).[56] I encountered several gurus who would tell me nothing at all—or else, would only speak to me using the most obscure metaphors and incomprehensible riddles. Still more problematically, I encountered some gurus who seemed willing to tell me virtually anything they thought I might want to hear—even when it was apparent that they did not really know what they were talking about. Indeed, it quickly became clear to me that some members of "esoteric traditions" have a *vested interest* in letting people know they have a secret—in *advertising* their secrets—particularly if the person happens to be a wealthy American scholar, funded by a generous research grant. And it became equally apparent that, even if I did have access to a living oral tradition, or even if I were to undergo initiation, this would by no means resolve the epistemological and ethical double bind. If anything, it would only *compound* it a hundredfold.

In this sense, secrecy would appear to represent a particularly extreme example of the epistemological and ethical problems inherent in *every* attempt to understand another culture. It embodies the dilemma of *all* ethnography, which has become especially acute in the current "crisis of representation in the human sciences," as George Marcus and Michael Fischer have called it.[57] It is not only the question of whether one can ever accurately understand another culture; rather, does not the very presence of the scholar profoundly influence his or her data, that is, shape the ways in which his or her informants will act and speak? More important, can one represent another culture without distorting, exploiting, or otherwise violating it, without turning it into yet another colonial artifact or commodity to be consumed in the modern supermarket of cultures? As James Clifford suggests, the problem of secrecy is thus the most acute form of the basic problems inherent in every cross-cultural encounter. Just as, for example, elders in an African secret society employ "complex techniques of revelation and secrecy" to transmit their sacred knowledge to their sons, so too, the scholar encounters a similar dialectic of dissimulation and partial revelation in the effort to understand the other: "The strategies of ellipsis, concealment and partial discourse determine ethnographers' relations as much as they do the transmission of stories between generations."[58]

Entangled in the Double Bind:
Approaches to the Double Bind of Secrecy in the History of Religions

He who publicizes these things, I know, is lost and will certainly go to hell.
(*Nāyikā Sādhanā ṭīkā* of Rūpānugā Dāsa)

Despite the recent proliferation of interest in the topics of secrecy and esotericism, in both the popular and the scholarly imaginations, these categories still remain poorly understood and theoretically confused within the academic community.[59] As Beryl Bellman has argued in his work on the African Poro secret societies, most past approaches to secrecy have been hampered by a persistent problem, namely, a tendency to neglect or confuse the key distinction between the *form* and the *content* of secrecy. Even as early as 1906, Georg Simmel's classic study had pointed out this crucial distinction: for secrecy is a "sociological form that stands in neutrality above the functions of its contents."[60] Nevertheless, Bellman argues, most studies of secrecy have ignored this distinction and instead defined secrecy primarily in terms of a "hidden content." Much of the past literature, as we see in the work Norman MacKenzie, E. J. Hobsbawm, and Mak Lou Fong, has been limited to the creation of various different, often conflicting typological schemes based on the content of secrecy or the resultant forms of secret organization (e.g., religious, political, revolutionary, and criminal).[61]

All these approaches to the "content" of the secret, however, run into a basic and troubling obstacle—namely, the double bind of epistemology and ethics, the question of how one can ever know with certainty the true substance of what is hidden, and then, supposing one *can*, should one reveal it publicly? As Tony Stewart asks, "is it professionally ethical to reveal that which was intentionally concealed? Is this not one more form of exploitation and the brutal wielding of power?"[62] There is a real danger, it would seem, of doing violence to another culture, looting the cultural artifacts of another people and replicating the destructive practices of imperialism in a more subtle form. Among the first and clearest cases of this ethico-epistemological dilemma, for example, can be found in the early work of Marcel Griaule among the Dogon. As Clifford has shown, Griaule consistently treated the secret knowledge of the Dogon as a kind of precious artifact which had to be wrested—often forcibly and underhandedly—from the hand of the native: "The ethnographer must keep up the pressure . . . in Sudanese societies, with their long process of initiation, one had to force the revelation of occult doctrines."[63] As Griaule himself comments in two rather astonishing passages:

> We would make asses of the old hesitators, confound the traitors, abominate the silent. We were going to see mysteries leap like reptiles from the mouths of the neatly caught liars. We would play with the victim; we would rub his nose in his words. We'd make him spit up the truth, and we'd turn out of his pockets the last secret polished by the centuries, a secret to make him . . . blanch with fear.[64]

> The role of the person sniffing out social facts is comparable to that of a detective or examining magistrate. The fact is the crime, the interlocutoer the guilty party, all of society's members are acomplices.[65]

But of course, native cultures do not always react passively to the attempts of Western scholars to penetrate their treasured knowledge and esoteric traditions. Lamont Lindstrom, for example, has shown the ways in which the peoples of the South Pacific have gone to even greater lengths than ever to conceal their secret knowledge, to resist the probing inquiries of the white man: "Our totalizing, textualizing mode of information with a discursive will to truth continues to penetrate and absorb resistant pockets of silence . . . islanders have blocked exotic knowledge and disengaged from external conversational conjunctions in order to protect local truths by burying Christian Bibles . . . and by silencing anthropologists."[66]

Rather remarkably, few scholars have tried seriously to grapple with these problems,[67] and even among those who have, the various approaches to the double bind have seldom proven satisfying. The first and most common approach, we might call the "textual" approach, the one that limits itself to historical texts and makes no effort to penetrate the esoteric tradition "from within."[68] In the field of Tantric studies, this is the method adopted by the majority of scholars, such as Giuseppe Tucci, André Padoux, Teun Goudriaan, and most recent authors. However, the more honest among them—for example Edward C. Dimock—will frankly admit that their knowledge is always partial, and severely limited by the fact that they had never received initiation or oral instruction.[69]

Second, there is the "initiate's" approach, that is, the approach taken by those who insist that a merely textual understanding of an esoteric tradition is simply inadequate, and that the only way to really understand such a tradition is through direct, firsthand personal experience with its living "oral" form.[70] In her work on women in Tantric Buddhism, for example, Miranda Shaw claims to have undergone extensive initiations among contemporary Tantric Buddhists and thereby to have gained access to an enormous body of hitherto unknown texts and commentarial traditions.[71] Similarly, in his work on South Indian Tantra, Douglas Brooks has argued that the only way the scholar can gain access to esoteric knowledge is by tapping into the living representatives of the oral, commentarial tradition, as it has been handed down from guru to disciple over centuries: "Since Tantrics maintain a vigilant guard over the secret meanings of texts, the scholar's access to tradition is limited to those living Tantrics willing to discuss openly Tantric concepts and practices. . . . Tantric traditions are most thorougly understood when both written and oral sources are taken into account."[72] Although I am sympathetic to Brooks's broader and more nuanced approach, I do not think he really solves the epistemological problem; if anything he has only rendered it even *more* complex. For how can one be sure that anything a contemporary practitioner says—particularly to a Western scholar—is any more accurate than what a text says? And how can one be sure that what a contemporary guru says about a tenth-century text is anything like what a tenth-century guru might have said? But perhaps most strikingly, even though Brooks himself spent much time living in close contact with Tantric pundits in South India, undergoing numerous initiations and instructions in esoteric doctrine, he never grapples with the more difficult epistemological problems, nor does he ever address the sticky moral issues involved in placing these teachings within the public domain.[73]

Third, there is what we might call (borrowing Eliade's phrase) the "Noah's ark" approach to esoteric traditions, namely, provided that he or she has the culture's permission, the scholar is in fact doing a service by preserving ancient traditions which are in many cases rapidly being lost in the face of the modern world. One of the few scholars who has attempted to grapple with the ethical questions raised by his research is Fredrik Barth, in his work on the Baktaman tribe of New Guinea. Barth himself received numerous esoteric initiations, going as far as the fifth of the seven degrees in the Baktaman system. However, Barth seems to have been far more aware than most scholars of the ethical issues involved, and he made a clear effort to be as open as possible about his intentions in learning the Baktaman secret traditions. "Publishing this monograph raises a vexing question, since much of its data are part of a cult secret . . . I was told these secrets in trust and never failed this trust while I was part of the Baktaman. I made it clear that in my distant home I would share their knowledge with others who had passed through all our initiations; and that was acceptable."[74] Moreover, Barth offers a persuasive rationale for his work: His intention is not to exploit and plunder the Baktaman esoteric lore but, rather, to preserve a rich religious tradition which is rapidly being lost in the face of modernization: "I hope this text will repay them by salvaging some of what they value from the oblivion of imposed change which looms ahead."[75] Now, Barth's position may indeed be the most ethically responsible; however, it does *not* resolve the epistemological problem (and in fact only compounds it, as the scholar is only "preserving" what the tradition *wants* him or her to preserve). Moreover, it also does not tell us what, if anything, the scholar can do if he or she is not so fortunate to receive the permission of the esoteric tradition.

In view of these deep and fundamental obstacles to the study of secrecy, some authors have concluded that it is simply an insoluble and futile task. As Edward Conze flatly asserts in his discussion of Buddhist Tantra, the problem of secrecy presents an impassible barrier, and we can in fact say nothing intelligent at all about esoteric traditions like Tantra:

> These doctrines are essentially esoteric, or secret (*guhya*), This means what it says. Esoteric knowledge can . . . under no circumstances be transmitted to an indiscriminate multitude. There are only two alternatives. Either the author has not been initiated . . . then what he says is not first hand knowledge. Or he has been initiated. Then if he were to divulge the secrets . . . he has broken the trust placed in him and is morally so depraved he is not worth listening to. . . . There is something both indecent and ridiculous about the public discussion of the esoteric in words that can be generally understood.[76]

Such is the impasse faced by the student of esoteric traditions, the one smitten by the syndrome of the secret: Either, it seems, we must leave these traditions alone altogether, letting them remain respectfully pure and untouched, or we must risk doing violence to ancient esoteric traditions to which we have no right. In what follows, I offer my own, admittedly tenuous and provisional alternative means of dealing with this impasse.

Secrecy and the "Black Market" of Symbolic Capital

> Among children, pride and bragging are often based on a child's being able to say to the other: I know something you don't know. . . . This jealousy of the knowledge about facts hidden to others is shown in all contexts from the smallest to the largest. . . . The secret gives one a position of exception . . . all superior persons . . . have something mysterious . . . From secrecy . . . grows the error according to which everything mysterious is something important and essential. (Georg Simmel)

For my own part, I do not believe there is any real "way out" of this double bind. But I do believe there are a few alternative strategies for dealing with it, which would still allow us to say something useful about the phenomenon of secrecy. Hence, I wish to suggest a new approach to the problem by employing some of the insights of Pierre Bourdieu and Michel Foucault. It is generally more fruitful, I would argue, to turn the focus of our analysis away from the *content* of secrecy and instead toward the *forms and the strategies* through which secret information is concealed, revealed and exchanged. Here I wish to undertake a "theoretical shift" similar to the series of shifts undertaken by Foucault in his study of power and sexuality. As Foucault suggests, it is necessary to turn from the study of power as an oppressive, centralized force, imposed from the "top down " in the political hierarchy, to a study of the *strategies* through which power is manifested.[77] So too, I would suggest that we make a shift from the "secret" as simply a hidden content and instead investigate the strategies or "games of truth" through which the complex "effect" (to use Bruce Lincoln's phrase) of secrecy is constructed.[78] That is, how is a given body of information endowed with the mystery, awe, and value of a "secret"? Under what circumstances, in what contexts, and through what relations of power is it exchanged? How does possession of that secret information affect the status of the "one who knows"? As Bellman suggests, "secrets cannot be characterized either by the contents of the concealed message or by the consequences . . . they are understood by the way concealed information is withheld, restricted . . . and exposed. Secrecy is . . . a sociological form . . . constituted by the very procedures whereby secrets are communicated."[79] This turn to the "strategies" or forms of secrecy does *not,* however, mean that the content is simply meaningless, worthless, or "semantically empty"—a kind of "McGuffin," to use Hitchcock's metaphor.[80] On the contrary, it is more often the case that secrets are *semantically overdetermined* (i.e., subject to an enormous variety of possible interpretations and meanings), depending on the specific social and historical context, which guru you ask, when you ask him, what stage of initiation you have attained, and so on. Nor does this mean that we can say *nothing at all* about the substance of secrecy; indeed, I have a great deal to say about the nature of Kartābhajā esoteric discourse and practice, as well as the many conflicting interpretations thereof. My point here is simply that, in most cases, the analysis of the strategies and forms of secrecy is both more *fruitful* (or at least less frustrating) and often more *interesting* than the search for the ever-elusive hidden content.

As I wish to define it, secrecy is best understood as a strategy for accumulating "capital," in Bourdieu's sense of the term. Extending Marx's definition of the term, Bourdieu defines capital as including not only economic wealth but also the nonmaterial resources of status, prestige, valued knowledge, and privileged relationships. It refers in short to "all goods, material and symbolic, that present themselves as rare and worthy of being sought after in a particular social formation."[81] Like economic capital, however, symbolic capital is not mere wealth which is hoarded and stockpiled; rather, it is a *self-reproducing* form of wealth—a kind of "accumulated labor," which gives its owner "credit," or the ability to appropriate the labor and products of other agents. Bourdieu then distinguishes between several varieties of capital. Most important, in addition to economic capital, there is social capital (valued relations with significant others), cultural capital (valued information or educational qualifications), and symbolic capital (the other forms of capital when recognized as "legitimate," in the form of prestige and honor).[82]

Symbolic capital is itself the product of a kind of "social alchemy," a process of misrecognition, through which material capital is transformed and "legitimated" in the form of status or distinction. This is the process at work, for example, in the purchase of an expensive work of art, which confers the mark of "taste" and "distinction" on its owner, or in the investment in a good education, which bestows "cultivation" and "cultural capital." As such, the dynamics of the social field are determined largely by the strategies and maneuvers of agents in their ongoing competition for these symbolic resources: "Symbolic capital is the product of a struggle in which each agent is both a ruthless competitor and supreme judge. . . . This capital can only be defended by a permanent struggle to keep up with the group above . . . and distinguish oneself from the group below."[83]

In the context of the esoteric organization, I believe, two processes are at work which serve to transform secret knowledge into a kind of capital. First, the strict guarding of information transforms knowledge into a scarce resource, a good that is "rare and worthy of being sought after." To use Bourdieu's terms, secrecy involves an extreme form of the "censorship" imposed on all statements within the "market of symbolic goods"; for every individual modifies and censors his or her expressions in anticipation of their reception by the other members of the social field.[84] Secrecy, however, is a *deliberate and self-imposed censorship*, whose function is to maximize the scarcity, value and desirability of a given piece of knowledge.

> Secrecy is about control. It is about the individual possession of knowledge that others do not have. . . . Secrecy elevates the value of the thing concealed. That which is hidden grows desirable and seems powerful.
>
> All knowledge is a form of property in that it can be possessed. Knowledge can be given, acquired, sold . . . Secret knowledge evokes the sense of possession most clearly.[85]

As Lindstrom suggests in his work on the Tanna peoples of the South Pacific, secrecy is thus a central part of the "conversational economy" which constitutes every social order. Secrecy converts information into something that can be owned, exchanged, accumulated—"a commodity, something that can be bought and sold." Thus, what is most important about secrets is not the hidden meanings they profess to contain but, rather, the "economy of exchanges" or resale value which secrets have as a commodity in a given information market: "Secrets turn knowledge into property that can be exchanged. People swap or sell their secrets for money and other goods. . . . By preserving patterns of ignorance in the information market, secrecy fuels talk between people who do not know and those who do."[86]

Second, once it has been converted into this kind of valuable commodity, secret knowledge can serve as a source of "symbolic capital" in Bourdieu's sense, as a form of status and power accumulated by social actors and recognized as "legitimate" in a given social field. As Simmel himself long ago pointed out: "The secret gives one a position of exception . . . all superior persons have something mysterious."[87] Secret knowledge thereby functions both as a form of "cultural capital"—special information or "legitimate knowledge"—and as a form of "social capital"—a sign of membership within a community and hierarchical relationships with significant others. Particularly when combined with a series of initiations or a hierarchy of grades, this is, like all capital, a self-reproducing form of wealth, which grows increasingly powerful as one advances in the ranks of knowledge and ritual degrees.

However, in distinction to most of the forms of "capital" which Bourdieu discusses, the symbolic goods of the secret society can only be exchanged behind closed doors, in the esoteric realm of ritual. Secret knowledge is not exchanged publicly in mainstream society or in the "field" of exoteric relations but solely within the field of the esoteric society. Hence, we might even call it a kind of *black market symbolic capital*, a form of capital which is valued only in special circumstances outside of ordinary social transactions. Indeed, in some cases, this knowledge may even be considered dangerous, threatening, or illegal in the eyes of mainstream society. This danger, however, only makes it all the more powerful, valued, and desirable.

A Nonreductionist Economics of Ecstasy: "Economism" Turned on Its Head

Now, in response to some anticipated objections from my readers, I should note that this use of Bourdieu's notion of "capital" and the "market metaphor" of social action is by no means a matter of simple reductionism or "economic determinism." On the contrary, Bourdieu proposed his own model largely as a reaction against rigid Marxism or "vulgar economism." For Bourdieu, the economic realm is itself but one of many "fields" in the social order, alongside the political, religious, artistic, and so on, each of which has its own laws of exchange and forms of capital.[88] Moreover, the use of the economic metaphor is not only justifiable but in fact quite appropriate in the case of eighteenth- and nineteenth-century Bengal. As Sudipta Sen has shown, the image of the market or bazaar (*bājār*) was among the most common metaphors used throughout pre- and post-colonial Bengali literature to describe the world as a whole—this mortal realm of constant exchange, buying and selling, haggling and swindling. This is nowhere more evident than in the Kartābhajā songs, which center around the image of the "bazaar of the world" and are saturated with mercantile terminology borrowed from the East India Company.[89]

Moreover, while making use of Bourdieu's economic model, I also hope to criticize and modify it in several important respects. Most significantly, as many critics have argued, Bourdieu consistently tends to belittle and deemphasize the role of agency, awareness, and intentionality in social practice. As Michel de Certeau, Jean Comaroff, Richard Jenkins, and others have argued, Bourdieu tends to reduce social actors to unconscious "dupes" within a rather static structural system, and hence to reduce social practice to a kind of "celebration of mindless conformity," which merely reproduces the existing social order: "the role of consciousness is almost totally eclipsed; his actors seem doomed to reproduce their world mindlessly without its contradictions leaving any mark on their awareness."[90] Hence, Bourdieu gives little attention to the possibilities for resistance, struggle, and subversion of the dominant social order. With his key emphasis on the importance of *strategy*—the agent's capacity for creative manipulation of the structures of the social order—Bourdieu's model *should*, at least implicitly, leave some room for the possibility of resistance.[91] Unfortunately, Bourdieu's own remarks on the potential for resistance are oddly brief and undeveloped.[92] Therefore, I suggest that we follow the lead of de Certeau, Comaroff, and others, by building on Bourdieu's notion of strategy and more fully developing the possibilities for struggle and subversion of the dominant social order. We need to ask, in short, How do lower-class, marginalized, and oppressed members of society struggle to achieve "capital," status, or prestige. How do the poor "make do" within a social field that is clearly dominated, within a market where all the prices are inflated and all the scales rigged? As de Certeau suggests (modifying Bourdieu's model), there are not only a variety of *strategies* at play in the social field (i.e., techniques by which elite and dominant classes struggle to accumulate power and capital) but also a wide array of *tactics* (i.e., the more "everyday" struggles and maneuvers on the part of the dominated classes, by which they appropriate, manipulate, and turn to their own advantage the structures of the dominant social order).[93] These are what de Certeau calls the more subtle *tactics of consumption* among dominated classes, "the ingenious ways in which the weak make use of the strong," or the manifold ways in which social consumers "*poach* on the property of others."[94]

In fact, far from a simple reductionist economic argument, which would explain religious ideas by reference to underlying material forces, what I am really arguing for here is a profoundly antireductionist approach to the Kartābhajās, and even a kind of economism turned on its head. That is, instead of reducing the Kartābhajās' mystical language to deeper economic causes, I show the many ingenious ways in which the Kartābhajās have appropriated and transformed economic, mercantile, and even European capitalist discourse, turning it to the advantage of a largely poor, lower-class esoteric religious movement.

The practice of secrecy, we will see, may be employed by a variety of different social factions. Like all discourse, as Bruce Lincoln has noted, it may be used to reinforce existing sociopolitical hierarchies and to maximize the power of a small elite. But, at the same time, it may also be manipulated by oppressed or deviant factions in order to subvert and contest those same hierarchies.[95] As Foucault keenly observes, "the very same strategy can be both repressive and liberating;" thus "silence and secrecy are a shelter for power, anchoring its prohibitions; but they also loosen its hold and provide for relatively obscure areas of tolerance."[96]

On the one hand, esotericism often goes hand in hand with *elitism*, the power and privilege of the few over the many. Its aim is often "not to disrupt order and conformity, but *reinforce* it."[97] As a key source of *distinction*—of privilege, exclusivity, and the mystery of power—secrecy is often among the most powerful tools of ruling elites and powerful aristocracies. Simmel himself long ago pointed out the following: "This significance of the secret society as the intensification of sociological exclusiveness is strikingly shown in political aristocracies. Secrecy has always been among the requirements of their regime. . . . By trying to conceal the numerical insignificance of the ruling class, aristocracies exploit the psychological fact that the unknown itself appears to be fearsome, mighty threatening."[98] As Ian Keen has argued in the case of the Yolngu people in the northeaster Arnhem land of Australia, secrecy, deliberate mystification, and systematic ambiguity are deployed in large part to reinforce the dominant social order. Through the "technologies of secrecy," such as the control of space and the encoding of information in ambiguous forms, the Yolngu define relations of power and status. The careful control of access to sacred knowledge is a key mechanism reinforcing the authority of men over women, and of elders over youths:

> Mystery was in the hands of the few, who deliberately used devices of obscurity and ambiguity in the control of religious ideology.
>
> Yolngu religious secrecy was as much about the authority of older men in relation to younger men as men's exclusion and domination of women.[99]

For example, even secret traditions such as freemasonry—which had so long been accused of subversive activities or revolutionary politics—have been shown by more recent scholars to have been predominantly a highly conservative, largely aristocratic and elitist tradition: "Far from being suspect as a cabal of . . . libertines and subversives . . . Masonry was a prestigious and important organization. Joining masonry was the accepted thing to do."[100]

Many of the more powerful schools of Hindu Tantrism, in fact, present clear examples of the "elitist" nature of esotericism. Whereas, in the popular imagination and in much past scholarship, Tantrism has been portrayed as a subversive and revolutionary countercultural phenomenon, more recent studies have shown that this is in many cases quite incorrect. As Brooks has argued in the case of the South Indian Śrīvidyā tradition, the most important Tantric authors such as Bhāskararāya were in fact conservative, highly orthodox Brahmans; their aim was not to undermine or subvert existing social hierarchies and the structures of brahminical religion but, on the contrary, to reinforce them precisely at a time when they were being threatened by the rise of various non-Brahminical movements, such as bhakti or Advaita Vedānta: "Tantric ritual and ideology continues to provide a means by which Brahman society perpetuate the perception of itself as religiously privileged in the midst of radical social and economic changes that do not always privilege Brahmans."[101]

By contrast, the tactic of secrecy is also among the most frequently used tactics of the disenfranchised, discontented, or simply disgruntled members of society. It is among the most important survival strategies deployed by marginal groups, such as homosexuals, who wish to conceal and protect their identity or behavior from the eyes of mainstream society, or by oppressed classes, slaves, or exploited peasantry, as we see, for example, among Haitian secret societies such as the Bizango and Sans

Poel. As Karen McCarthy Brown suggests, the need for secrecy in the case of Vodou not only persisted throughout the difficult history of slavery and colonialism but has even been carried over and continued with the immigration of Haitians to this country: "Secrecy has long been part of Vodou. A great deal of discretion was required during the days of slavery . . . Vodou was forced underground. In New York, where prejudice against Haitians and Vodou is rampant, these habits of secrecy are reinforced. Maintaining two discrete worlds side by side is a skill even children must learn."[102] In its most extreme forms, the tactic of secrecy may be deployed by subversive, dissident, and revolutionary groups—the Assassins, the Mau Mau, the Bavarian Illuminati, and, particularly in the case of Bengal, the revolutionary secret societies of the Nationalist Movement, such as the Jugantar society and the Dacca Anushilan.[103]

In this sense, I suggest, secrecy functions as an extreme form of what James C. Scott calls a "hidden transcript"—that is, a "discourse that takes place offstage, beyond direct observation," which "consists of offstage speeches, gestures, and practices that confirm, contradict, or inflect what appears in the public transcript."[104] Hidden transcripts may be deployed by both the subordinate and the elite members of society. On one hand, as the realm of "concealed" and backstage discourse, the hidden transcript is the "privileged site of subversion and resistance," the realm in which the subordinate deploy the various "weapons of the weak" such as backbiting, gossip, poaching, pilfering, and footdragging, in order to undermine dominant authority: "offstage, where subordinates may gather outside the intimidating gaze of power, a dissonant political culture is possible;" indeed, "the social location *par excellence* for the hidden transcript lies in the unauthorized and unmonitored secret assemblies of subordinates." But on the other hand, Scott points out, dominant groups and elite factions themselves "often have much to conceal and they have the wherewithal to conceal what they wish"; hence, they also develop their own offstage discourses and "hidden transcripts."[105]

In the Kartābhajā tradition, we find both of these strategies at work simultaneously—a process of both resistance to or subversion of the existing social structures and the construction of new, in some ways equally oppressive, hierarchies of power. If the secrecy of the Kartābhajās offered a new realm of freedom and apparent equality for women, peasants, and urban laborers of Calcutta, it also reinforced the wealth and status of a small group of powerful gurus in the upper echelons of the Kartābhajā hierarchy.

Secrecy and Censorship: The Ambivalence and the Liability of Secrecy

Where in social life can a similar misrepresentation be found? Only where two persons are concerned one of whom possesses a certain power while the other has to act with consideration on account of this power. The second person will then distort his psychic actions. . . . He will mask himself. . . . The political writer who has unpleasant truths to tell to those in power finds himself in a like position. If he tells everything without reserve the Government will suppress them. . . . The writer stands in fear of censorship; he therefore . . . must conceal his statements in an innocent disguise. . . . The stricter the domination of the censorship, the more thorough becomes the disguise and . . . the more ingenious the means employed to put the reader on the track of actual meaning. (Sigmund Freud, *The Interpretation of Dreams*)

As Bachelard so neatly put it, "there is no science but of the hidden." The sociologist is better or worse equipped to discover what is hidden depending on . . . the degree of interest he has in uncovering what is censored and repressed in the social world. (Pierre Bourdieu, *Sociology in Question*)

Now, if it is true that secrecy can serve as a profound source of status, power, prestige, and symbolic capital for its owner, it is also a deeply ambivalent kind of power. As a kind of "black market capital," secrecy is always highly dangerous and often a potential *liability* for its owner. For whatever is secret can always be accused of being immoral, scandalous, and politically or morally subversive. Hence, secrecy very often goes hand in hand with tactics of *censorship*—a censorship both on the part of critics, who want to eliminate or silence potentially threatening or subversive esoteric traditions, and on the part of initiates, who subject their own ideas and practices to a form of *self-censorship,* masking, encoding, or concealing those elements which might be objectionable to outsiders.[106]

On one side, censorship is always among the most important instruments employed by those in power in order to reinforce their status and to suppress deviant or threatening members of society. Whether in the form of legal regulations, deliberate editing, or destruction of threatening publications, or forceful silencing of outspoken individuals, censorship is a key part of virtually every form of domination: "censorship is a form of surveillance: a mechanism . . . the powerful use to tighten control over people or ideas that threaten to disrupt established systems of order."[107] In this sense, censorship functions as what Susan Jansen appropriately calls (using the terms of Michel Foucault) "the knot that binds power and knowledge." For, if knowledge is power—the power to define, categorize, and control society and our perception of the "way things are"—then those in power must also be able to supervise, control, and restrict access to that knowledge; they must be able to silence those who challenge the taken for granted interpretation of reality. As such, secret societies and esoteric organizations—particularly those believed to engage in immoral, transgressive, or illegal activities—are often quickly singled out as the most immediate targets of censorship: for they have the potential to threaten the very order of society itself: "Those who attract the attention of censors are a strategic category of outlaws. They are epistemological criminals, cosmological mess-makers who dirty the discrete (sacred) presuppositions in which the prevailing order is secured."[108]

On the other hand, however, the tactics of censorship and enforced silence are also just as frequently exercised by dominated groups themselves on their own texts and utterances, in the form of self-censorship. Marginal or deviant groups in all societies must censure themselves, not so much to make themselves appear more powerful or mysterious but simply to avoid persecution by the dominant order. As Scott suggests, this systematic editing of one's discourse is among the most common "arts of resistance" of the weapons of the weak. It can be a powerful tactical means of communicating potentially dangerous or subversive information, at the same time staying within the boundaries of official law: "Like prudent opposition newspaper editors under strict censorship, subordinate groups must find ways of getting their message across, while staying somehow within the law. This requires . . . a capacity to exploit all the loopholes, ambiguities and lapses. . . . It means carving out a tenuous life in a political order that . . . forbids such a life."[109]

Self-censorship is therefore not a simple matter of silencing; rather, it involves a complex and ingenious use of concealed, encrypted language, a veiled discourse designed to pass by the censors while still transmitting its message in covert form to its intended audience. As Leo Strauss has argued, heterodox individuals have always had to cultivate the subtle art of "writing between the lines," of distinguishing between exoteric and esoteric teachings: those intended for all citizens (and censors) and those intended to be deciphered only by a carefully screened audience of sympathizers. For, "where there is censorship, there is usually clandestine activity," and in fact, the tactics of "dissimulation, double-entendre, and satiric irreverence have their genesis in persecution."[110] As Freud himself has put in his classic work on the dream process: "the stricter the censorship the more far reaching the disguise."[111]

The problems of secrecy, censorship, and self-censorship, it would seem, only become all the more intense in cases of colonial contact, in which esoteric traditions are confronted by different, often threatening, political and moral forces. Throughout the European colonial imagination of the late nineteenth and early twentieth centuries, the fear of violent, subversive political activities often went hand in hand with the fear of perverse, transgressive, or immoral practices among the natives under their rule. As we see in the cases of the Mau Mau in Kenya or in various native uprisings in South and North America, political rebellion was, in the colonial imagination, often associated with immorality, sexual transgression, perverse secret rituals, and the violation of social taboos. The rebellious colonial subject threatened, not only to subvert the colonial government but also to unravel the moral fabric of society itself.[112] Nowhere was this more true than in the case of colonial India, as the British officials became increasingly nervous about, and increasingly severe in the repression of, subversive secret organizations—both real and imaginary (such as the Thuggee). As Sir George MacMunn put it in his widely read account *The Underworld of India*, "secrecy goes with savagery"; or as Valentine Chirol warned in *Indian Unrest*, there was believed to be a deep and intimate connection between the Tantric secret societies and revolutionary political organizations; sexual depravity and political subversion were believed to go hand in hand: "The unnatural depravity represented in the form of erotomania is certainly more common among Hindu political fanatics."[113]

Correspondingly, we also find that secret organizations under colonial rule often develop even more elaborate and sophisticated techniques of self-censorship and disguise in order to elude and deceive their imperial masters.[114] Nowhere is this more apparent than in the case of the Tantric traditions during the colonial period in Bengal: "Tantric traditions were being made more respectable through excisions, and at times suppressed altogether . . . as stricter ideas about gentility developed in the shadow of Victorian norms in the late nineteenth century."[115] On one hand, as we see in the case of texts such as the highly unusual and enigmatic *Mahānirvāṇa Tantra* (which was probably a product of the late eighteenth century) there was a clear effort to censor, sanitize and "deodorize" the Tantras, to make them less offensive and to purge them of their more objectionable elements. For Bengali mystics, such as Śrī Rāmakṛṣṇa, Tantra had become not only a thing of awesome power and erotic allure but also a source of intense ambivalence, of "shame, disgust and fear" and thus the object of extreme censorship among his disciples.[116] On the other hand, as we see in the Sahajiyā traditions, there was also a movement further "underground," ever deeper into the realms of secrecy, disguise and self-obfuscation. "[T]he movement does not appear to have gone 'underground' until the nineteenth century, when the British exert full control over the delta," as Stewart suggests, "with the growth of colonial power, the Sahajiyās began to feel pressure to become more invisible than ever."[117]

The Kartābhajā tradition, as we see in the remainder of this book, stands out as among the most acute examples of this dialectic of secrecy and censorship. Regularly singled out as the most threatening, most dangerous, and potentially most subversive of the so-called deviant sects of colonial Bengal, the Kartābhajās cultivated the skills of dissimulation in ever new and more ingenious ways. With the Kartābhajās, however, we find two different kinds of self-imposed censorship at work—tactics of both *deodorization* and *disguise*. On one hand, many of the more conservative Kartābhajās of the twentieth century made a concerted effort to clean up and sanitize the tradition, to purge it of its Tantric elements, and to re-form it as an essentially innocuous devotional movement, in line with the mainstream Gauḍīya Vaiṣṇava tradition. On the other hand, many Kartābhajās sought to employ the tactics of concealment in ever new and more creative ways, to continue their highly esoteric, in many cases transgressive, practices while presenting an outward show of social conformity. As we see throughout their highly cryptic songs, the Kartābhajās learned to become masters of the arts of coded discourse and disguise. According to one of the Kartābhajās' cryptic esoteric phrases or "Mint Sayings," "The one who is secret is liberated; but the one who is open (outside the veil), is an adulteress" (STP 80; III.159). Or, as the Kartābhajās' primary text, the collection of mystical songs called the *Bhāver Gīta* (The Songs of Ecstasy), puts it:

Brother, I'm afraid to speak of such things,
lest whoever hears it be scared shitless!![118] (BG 159; II.89)

Part I

THE SECRET MARKETPLACE

Historical Origins and Socioeconomic Contexts

1

The Underworld of the Imperial City

The Religious, Social, and Economic Context of Early Colonial Bengal and the Rise of the Kartābhajās

In the final chapter of the great sixteenth-century hagiography of Śrī Caitanya, the *Caitanya-caritāmṛta*, there is one particularly enigmatic little verse, which Advaita Ācārya sends as a coded message to his master, Caitanya. As the text itself informs us, this verse is intentionally esoteric, encoded in a highly elliptical expression—a "mysterious or puzzling" (*praheli*) verse, whose meaning "only the Lord could understand, and others could not."[1] As the most recent translator, Edward C. Dimock, has commented, this verse is "one of the biggest problems the whole unwieldy text presents."[2] Although a coherent English rendering of this odd verse is difficult, Dimock suggests the following (admittedly inadequate) literal translation: "Tell the madman that people have become mad; tell the madman that they do not sell rice in the market; tell the madman that there is [i.e., he should have] no anxiety [*āul*] about the matter; and tell the madman this is what the madman has said."[3]

According to the more "orthodox" or mainstream Vaiṣṇava interpretation, such as that of the Bengali commentator Rādhāgovinda Nāth, this verse is a message sent by Advaita Ācārya to his master, Caitanya, in order to reassure him that his divine work on this earth has been successfully completed. The first madman (*bāul*), Rādhāgovinda suggests, is Caitanya himself, who has become mad with *prema* or divine Love. "That the people have become mad" means that all the people of the world have likewise become maddened with the bliss of divine love. And the statement that "they do not sell rice in the marketplace" means there is sufficient Love (that is, spiritual goods or rice), and so there need be no anxiety (*āul*, which he thinks is derived from the Sanskrit *ākula*). The second madman (*bāul*) is Advaita himself, who has sent this message to Caitanya to assure him that his work is done.[4]

Rather significantly, at the turn of the nineteenth century, this verse would also be reappropriated and adapted as the justification for the birth of a new religious movement—the Kartābhajā tradition. However, the Kartābhajā interpretation of this verse differs quite radically and would seem to turn the mainstream Vaiṣṇava interpretation entirely on its head (STP 4–5). For the Kartābhajās, the statement that "the rice is not sold in the marketplace" does not mean that there is now sufficient Love in the world: On the contrary, it means that the market of spiritual practice in the old, mainstream Vaiṣṇava tradition has become corrupt and fraudulent: the Vaiṣṇava Gosvāmins are no longer distributing the "spiritual goods" to their poor lower class followers but are hoarding all the wealth and power for themselves.[5]

In the Kartābhajā reading, moreover, the *āul* here does not mean "anxiety" or "worry" in the mundane sense. Rather, it refers to the supreme madman, Āulcāṅd, who is none other than the new incarnation of Caitanya and the founder of the Kartābhajā religion (STP 5). Because the "bazaar of love" had been corrupted by greedy self-serving Brahmins, Caitanya decided it was necessary to become incarnate in a new form, in the secret disguise of a crazy, wandering Fakir named Āulcāṅd, in order to redistribute the goods of love and truth to his disciples. As one modern Kartābhajā devotee, Debendranāth De, explains this riddle: "The original religion of Love founded by Caitanya was no longer being followed. . . . 'The rice is unsold in the marketplace'—this means that there was no longer any respect for the Religion of Love. . . . It was necessary for Caitanya to become incarnate in a new form. . . . Thus, 150 years after his death he became incarnate as Āulcāṅd."[6] As one Kartābhajā guru, Advaita Dās, explained this verse to me, the Kartābhajā path was founded as the "*Gupta Hāṭ,*" the *Secret Marketplace,* where the genuine goods of Caitanya's teachings can still be obtained, though only behind the veils of mystery and concealment.[7]

In sum, what we have here is a classic strategy of *esoteric hermeneutics,* one employed by many esoteric traditions—a tactic of appropriating classic religious texts or legitimating metanarratives, at the same time reinterpreting them and giving them a new *secret meaning*, which subverts the official, exoteric interpretation. This is a strategy much like what Harold Bloom has called, in the case of Kabbalistic hermeneutics, a *strong misreading*, or, to borrow a phrase of Daniel O'Keefe, it is a tactic of "stealing the lightning" of the orthodox tradition and using it to legitimate a new esoteric tradition.[8]

At the same time, it is also rather appropriate that the Kartābhajās have seized on the specific metaphor of the *marketplace*—an image used in a variety of earlier Vaiṣṇava texts, which is itself the root metaphor used throughout the Kartābhajā songs. Still more important, the use of the "market" metaphor is especially fitting because of the unique economic context in which the Kartābhajās emerged. The marketplace (*bājār, hāṭ*), as Sudipta Sen has shown, was a critical center of eighteenth-century Bengali life—not only economically but culturally, politically, and religiously. Throughout eighteenth-century literature, the image of the "market appears" as a key metaphor for what Bourdieu calls the "social field" as a whole, for the complex webs of exchange in all arenas of social action.[9] However, amidst the rapidly changing field of colonial Bengal, as power shifted hands from indigenous rulers to foreign merchants, the shape of the market also began to change. While many wealthy merchants and bankers of Calcutta may have profited from the shifting balance of power, most of the poorer classes only faced a new series of hardships.[10] The marketplace—as the Kartābhajās so often remind us—had become increasingly a place of deception, thievery, suffering and debt:

Brother, you've come here in the hope of doing business—
But until now, nothing good has happened; the days merely go by.
. . . You've written your name in the Moneylender's account book
and all the capital he gave you, he has now tricked you out of!
Your affairs are all in his hands—
like an earthworm, singing and dancing, crawling upon the road!
And even now I can see [the moneylender's] face, laughing at the fun!
(BG 213; II.26)

So too, it would seem, the "religious marketplace" underwent a number of similar transformations, in reaction to the changes taking place within the economic market. Throughout Bengal, a host of new "rice merchants" began to emerge—wandering fakirs, folk poets, divine madmen, and founders of "obscure religious cults," of which the Kartābhajās were the most numerous and most notorious. And it was largely to this poor rural peasantry, and to the porters, petty merchants, and small traders of Calcutta, most negatively affected by the changing economic context, that the Kartābhajās appealed, offering a new kind of power, status, and identity. "Change was in the air . . . because of chronic rural indebtedness, landlord oppression and famine . . . thousands of poor low caste people were seeking something better. . . . It was in this atmosphere of economic hardship . . . that the Kartābhajā movement flourished."[11]

The rise of the Kartābhajās, I argue in this chapter, occurred at a pivotal historical moment and at a key geographic locus in early colonial Bengal: on the critical margins between the urban streets of Calcutta and the rural hinterland, amidst the economic transition from pre-capitalist to colonial capitalist forms, as power changed hands from indigenous Hindu and Muslim elites to the East India Company. After briefly describing the religious background and the social and economic context of early colonial Bengal, I then describe the early history of the Kartābhajās as they emerged within this critical period. Indeed, as we see in this chapter, another favorite Kartābhajā legend states that the wandering madman, Āulcāṅd, appeared *precisely at the time of the Battle of Plassey* (1757). As the troops of the Muslim Nawab were returning from their looting raids, the story goes, Āulcāṅd cryptically warned them that the Muslims would fall from power and the Foreign Men (*phiriṅgī*) would soon take possession of the land.[12] It was at this pivotal moment that the Kartābhajā sect emerged, hailing itself as a new "company"—a "Company of the Poor."

The Dark Side of the Tradition of Caitanya: The Religious Roots of the Kartābhajās

The vital, true religion of Caitanya had awakened the minds of all mankind . . . . But the Sahaja tradition also endured continuously and gave some solace to the very poor, uneducated people on the fringes of society. Known by the names of the Āuls, Bāuls, Dervishes and Saiṅs, this class of "Sahaja" disciples was the inherent underside of the worship of Caitanya. (Sukumār Sen"Kartābhajār Kathā o Gān)

Like the sacred place of the Triveṇī—the holy meeting place of the Ganges, Sarasvati, and Jamuna rivers, where the Kartābhajā founder, Āulcāṅd, is said to have miraculously appeared[13]—the Kartābhajā tradition emerged out of the rich confluence of a number of very old religious currents of Bengal. The Kartābhajā teachings are rooted in a long tradition of esoteric mystical sects, which have been labeled variously as "obscure religious cults," "deviant orders," "heterodox cults," or what Sen aptly dubs the "underside" or the dark side of the tradition of Caitanya—the side of the Bengal Vaiṣṇava tradition that rejects social and religious structures such as caste, Vedic authority, and Brahminical ritual, explicitly transgressing basic moral codes and social laws.[14]

The common substratum of most of these "obscure religious cults" is an old current of mystical eroticism and secret practice in Bengal known as the Sahajiyā tradition. Derived from *sahaja*, meaning "together-born" (*saha-ja*), and thus "innate," "simple," "natural," or "easy," the Sahajiyā path is meant to be the most rapid, most expedient, and also the most "natural" road to liberation. It is the path to realizing the supreme state of *Sahaja*—the ultimate experience of all things in their own original state, in blissful unity, beyond the dichotomies of the phenomenal world.[15] Deeply rooted in the Tantric traditions of Bengal, the heart of the Sahajiyā path is the belief that the human body, desire, and even sexuality do not need to be suppressed in order to achieve liberation; on the contrary, if properly sublimated and transformed, they become the most powerful means to enlightenment and ecstasy. If the "poisonous serpent" of lust (*kāma*) can be caught hold of and controlled, it can be transformed into the golden nectar of spiritual love (*prema*). In the words of Caṇḍīdās, "Using one's body as a medium of prayer and loving spontaneously is the *Sahaja* love."[16]

Most modern scholars have traced this tradition to the time of the Buddhist Caryāpadas (composed sometime between the eighth and twelfth centuries), a body of mystical songs which express the most profound and mystical teachings through the medium of secret discourse and coded language. Indeed, it is not insignificant that the oldest known form of Bengali literature is in fact this same deeply esoteric, heavily Tantric, and extremely cryptic body of songs, composed in the difficult "intentional language" or *sandhābhāṣā*.[17]

During the sixteenth century, with the revival of Vaiṣṇava bhakti inspired by Śrī Caitanya (1486–1533), the old traditions of esoteric ritual and coded discourse of the Sahajiyā Buddhists began to merge with the devotional love of the playful, erotic child-God, Kṛṣṇa, resulting in a new "Vaiṣṇava Sahajiyā synthesis."[18] For the Sahajiyā, classic Vaiṣṇava texts such as the *Caitanaya Caritāmṛta* are now given a deeper, often highly unorthodox interpretation, in line with the secret, transgressive, and explicitly sexual practices of the Sahajiyās. Indeed, in the Sahajiyā's rather radical revisioning and esoteric rereading (or "misreading") of the tradition, Caitanya himself becomes a secret practitioner of sexual rituals, who passed on his *true* teachings in a concealed form, preserved only by the Sahajiyās.[19] And the physical union of male and female disciples, joined in illicit love, becomes the supreme embodiment of the divine love of Kṛṣṇa and Rādhā in paradise: "The end of man is the perpetual experience of divine joy. . . . When one realizes himself as divine, one experiences in union not the insignificant joys of human love, but the perpetual joys of Rādhā and Kṛṣṇa."[20]

Although the "easiest" and most expedient means to liberation, the Sahaja path is also the most dangerous and—from an exoteric point of view—the most socially objectionable. The Sahajiyā locates his authority not in Brahminical orthodoxy, Vedic injunctions, or caste status but within the human body itself: "The laws of the Vedas will totally erupt," sings Caṇḍīdās, "I have thrown in the river the care of my caste. . . . I have demolished all religious rites."[21] Explicitly rejecting and willfully overturning many of the basic structures of caste and Brahminic authority, the Sahajiyā path must be concealed behind the layers of secrecy and silence, transmitted only through guarded initiations at the hands of authoritative Masters: "The Sahajiyā is an esoteric cult that needs esoterism to live; it is a flower that blooms in darkness and is destroyed by exposure to light of day. . . . To take on the protective coloring of orthodox Vaiṣṇavism is . . . to allow the Sahajiyā to remain unseen."[22]

From a very early date, it seems, the Sahajiyā and other Tantric traditions began to commingle with the rich traditions of Islamic mysticism embodied in the various Sufi orders of Bengal. Since at least the ninth century, Muslims had begun to penetrate into Bengal, finally conquering the region in 1203, and with them, they brought a long tradition of Indian Sufism, with its own sophisticated theology and mystical practice. Among the most powerful orders in Bengal were, first and foremost, the Chisthi, followed by lesser orders such as the Sohrawardi, Qadari, and Naqshbandi. The Bengali Sufis, moreover, continued the complex process of fusion with indigenous Hindu traditions which had already begun among earlier Indian Sufi orders.[23] Despite their wide diversity, the Sufi traditions of Bengal all share a number of basic characteristics, which would offer fertile soil for synthesis with Hindu Tantric traditions. Foremost among these are a rich tradition of devotional mysticism and the erotic relation between God and the soul, the central relation between the Master and disciple (Pīr and Murīd), and elaborate systems of bodily cosmography and meditative practice (such as the system of *laṭīfs* or spiritual energy centers and the practice of *ḍhikr* or invocation of the Divine Name). Most important, like the Tantric schools, the Sufis developed sophisticated tactics of secrecy, with elaborate systems of initiation and well-organized lineages for the transmission of esoteric knowledge. Like the Sahajiyās, they also cultivated the art of esoteric hermeneutics, with a twofold reading of the Koran: one exoteric (*zāhir*), based on Sharī'at or Islamic Law, meant for ordinary men, and one esoteic (*bātin*), based on Ma'riffat or mystic knowledge, "aimed at the select few able to grasp its meaning, passed down from heart to heart."[24]

At some unknown time in history, the frequent cross-fertilization between the Sahajiyās, Vaiṣṇavas, and Sufis gave birth to an eclectic class of wandering minstrels or holy "madmen," popularly known as the "Bāuls."[25] With the Sahajiyās, the Bāuls celebrate the divinity of the body and sexuality, engage in a variety of esoteric Tantric rituals, and explicitly violate moral and religious laws. Even more so than most Sahajiyās, however, the Bāuls are openly iconoclastic, rejecting the most basic social conventions, ignoring religious boundaries, and taking delight in overturning the laws of mainstream society: "A Bāul is one who, dressed in a tattered garment made of remnants of clothing . . . of both Hindus and Muslims, wanders incessantly living on whatever those who listen to his songs give him. . . . The Bāul is thought mad because he goes deliberately . . . againt the current of custom."[26] Willfully inhabiting the "Topsy-turvy land" (*ulṭa deś*), the Bāul may violate any social convention for the sake of spiritual love: "Reverse are the modes and manners of the man who . . . is a lover of true love; none is sure about the how and when of his behavior. . . . Awkwardly wild are his manners and customs. . . . He is as satisfied with mud as with sandal-paste. . . . He builds his house in the sky, even as the fourteen worlds are burnt to ashes."[27]

The question of the precise historical origins of the Bāul tradition is an extremely difficult and tangled one, which has given rise to an enormous variety of scholarly conjecture. Most authors today want to date the Bāuls to the early seventeenth century, if not before; however, although the term *Bāul* appears in Bengali texts as early as the sixteenth century (e.g., in the *Caitanya Caritāmṛta* where Caitanya is called "Bāul" or mad), there is in fact no clear reference to an actual "sect" or coherent religious group identified as "Bāuls" until the end of the nineteenth century. Akṣaykumār Datta's *Bhāratavarṣīya Upāsaka Sampradāya* (1870) is the first known text which actually refers to a sect called "Bāuls."[28] My own opinion is that there have probably been a variety of wandering minstrels, crazy holy men, and mad yogis traveling throughout the countryside of Bengal, known under a variety of different names—Dervish, Fakir, Bāul, Āul, Sāiṅ, and so on. Yet it was only in the later nineteenth century, as these groups came increasingly under the categorizing, classifying eye of Orientalist scholars—and above all, as they came under increasing persecution by the orthodox Muslim and Hindu communities—that the term "Bāul" began to be applied generally to these otherwise very diverse groups.[29] And it was not really until Rabindranath Tagore began to popularize the songs of Lālan Shāh and exalt the figure of the Bāul as a kind of embodiment of Bengali popular culture that we see the Bāul emerge as a kind of "icon of folk culture" in the Bengali imagination.[30]

Yet whatever the precise origins of the Bāuls and their beautifully simple yet profoundly haunting songs, there is no question that Bāuls and Kartābhajās have a long history of close interaction. Whether the Kartābhajās are basically a "subsect" of the Bāuls—as some believe—or whether the Kartābhajās in fact predated and profoundly influenced the Bāuls—as others like myself suspect—the two continue to this day to be closely intertwined.[31]

Although the Bengal area had long been a fertile breeding ground for various small heterodox sects, we appear to find an increasing proliferation of these "deviant orders" during the latter half of the eighteenth and the beginning of the nineteenth century. Combining elements of Sahajiyā, Tantric, Vaiṣṇava, and Sufi traditions, a huge number of small esoteric sects emerged throughout Bengal. Known under various names such as Sāhebdhanīs, Balarāmīs, Kiśorī-bhajanas,

Āuls, Rāmaballabhīs, and some fifty-six other "heterodox sects" identified by Ramakanta Chakrabarty, these groups typically rejected caste hierarchies and Brahminical authority, transgressing social norms and offering new roles to women and lower classes.[32]

A variety of scholars have speculated about the historical reasons for this proliferation of "minor sects" among the lower classes in the eighteenth and nineteenth centuries. Some have suggested that following Caitanya's death, the Gauḍīya Vaiṣṇava community underwent an increasing process of "Brahmanization"—a reintroduction of priestly authority, ritualism, and caste distinctions, which in turn alienated many of the poorer lower classes.[33] Others point to political causes, specifically the declining power of the Muslims in the eighteenth century, and the displacement of both Muslim and Hindu authority by the British Company; as Ajit Dās suggests, the collapse of both Hindu and Muslim rule opened a kind of spiritual vacuum, giving the opportunity for the rise of lower-class, "heterodox" groups, many of which rejected both orthodox Islamic and Hindu authority and opened their doors to men and women of all religions.[34] And still others point to various environmental factors—the Maratha raids of the 1740s, the famine of the 1770s, and so on. As Chakrabarty summarizes this complex situation:

> The reasons for the sprouting of numerous deviant orders . . . are not far to seek. The slow consolidation of British power in Bengal . . . and the quick downfall of the Moghuls after 1709 made life . . . in Bengal hazardous. . . . The Bengalis . . . were harassed by the Maratha raids. . . . The penetration of British mercantile capital into the traditional Bengali industries upset the economic order. . . . Brahminical exclusiveness led to the development of diverse sects among the lower orders.[35]

However, while certainly not the only reason for this proliferation of minor sects, perhaps among the most important factors—at least in the specific case of the Kartābhajās—was the rapidly changing economic context of early colonial Bengal. Both the religious and the economic marketplaces underwent a series of significant transformations, as old centers of trade began to crumble, as a host of foreign goods began to flood into Bengal, as the urban center of Calcutta began to emerge as the new center of exchange, and as the British Company introduced new forms of mercantile capital into the traditional economy.

Toil and Trade in the Marketplace of the World (*Bhava-Bājār*): The Social and Economic Context of the Kartābhajā Tradition

You had come to this land to work as a merchant,
but when that business failed, you found a lot of work in this market and bazaar.
But now the small and great Porters all control you!
. . . You've labored for the Company for so long a time—
And Śaśī Lāl laughs and says, "Oh, see how manly you are!" (BG 215; II.31)

Throughout the esoteric songs of the Kartābhajās, the key metaphor and dominant motif is an economic one: labor and trade, credit and debt, lending and brokerage amidst the "business of the world." This is particularly noteworthy given the rapidly changing, often tumultuous economic context in which they emerged: the Calcutta environs at the turn of the nineteenth century, a critical moment in the history of Bengal under the East India Company.

The question of the impact of British colonialism and the penetration of European capitalism into Bengal has long been one of the most contested issues in all of Indian studies.[36] Contrary to earlier nationalist and Marxist historians, a number of recent "revisionist" historians have rejected the idea that British Rule very suddenly and violently transformed the Indian economy. As C. A. Bayly, David Washbrook, and others have argued, it is a common misconception to suppose that India had been devoid of the capitalist spirit prior to the advent of the British; on the contrary, India had a long tradition of banking, trade, and large-scale exchange, which in many ways resembled what we call modern capitalism. The East India Company was, initially at least, only one player among many competing factions in the complex field of Indian economics.[37] Indians, moreover, were by no means passive victims of colonial and capitalist encroachment; rather, Bayly suggests, they showed remarkable resilience and resistance to the colonial powers, which "transformed and frustrated the feeble European impulse." Even long after the establishment of British Rule, precolonial economic forms would continue well into the nineteenth century, shaping and limiting the expansion of European capital within the structure of the *ancien regime.*[38]

The East India Company's primary aim, as Washbrook argues, was not to dismantle the precolonial economic structures but, rather, to *exploit* them, to use them even more efficiently. In the process, the colonial administration helped reinforce the indigenous capitalist elements, giving them a new governmental protection and enhancing the power of the privileged classes to accumulate wealth and property: "The Company was not bent on creating a free market economy. It did not . . . dismantle the ancien regime's institutions of economic management. Indeed, it worked them more intensively than they had ever been worked before."[39]

Nevertheless, while we need to take very seriously the revisionists' rereading of colonial history and their emphasis on its complexity and continuities, we must also be wary of another danger—that of belittling or ignoring the very real effects of colonial rule. As the members of the Subaltern Studies group (e.g., Ranajit Guha and Partha Chatterjee) warn, the revisionist historians are in danger of minimizing the very real, often destructive consequences of colonialism and the incursion of capitalist interests—that is, of suggesting that "*it never happened,*" or "erasing colonialism out of existence."[40] We must not forget, they remind us, the often devastating impact of colonial power—above all, upon the peasantry and lower classes, who remained often fiercely resistant to the increasing impositions of the colonial state. As a whole, Sugata Bose suggests, early colonial Bengal must be seen as an intricate and shifting "admixture of pre-capitalist and capitalist relations"—but one in which the peasantry and lower classes faced in most cases increasing exploitation and impoverishment: "Non-capitalist agrarian production and capitalist economic development were bound in a dialectical relationship. . . . The productive role of Bengal's peasantry did not free labor but merely enhanced colonial capital and magnified its dominating power over an increasingly impoverished rural population."[41]

The Bazaar of the World and the Marketplace of Religion: The Centrality of the Marketplace in Eighteenth- and Nineteenth-Century Bengal

This land has been secured with a Contract [*koṇṭrakṭ*]:
There's an Emperor in this land,
and beneath him is the Good-Mannered Company [*ādab Kompānī*].
In the twinkling of an eye, they produce and sell so much merchandise!
(BG 265; II.6)

If the songs of the Kartābhajās center around the imagery of business and trade, then the key metaphor in all their cryptic verses is that of the marketplace. Whether in the form of the *bājār* (the permanent market for general merchandise), the *hāṭ* (the local periodic market), the *gañj* (the wholesale market for bulk goods), or the *melā* (the annual fair, usually attached to religious sites), the world of the market held a central role in the cultural fabric as both a material locus and a key metaphor in the Bengali imagination.[42] An intricate hierarchized market network stretched from the urban centers, throughout the Ganga river system, to the *ghāṭs* and warehouses (*āṛat*) of the hinterland. At the top of this hierarchy stood the wealthy bankers (*bāniāns*), moneylenders (*mahājans*), and wholesale dealers (*āṛatdārs*), and they in turn employed a variety of middlemen or brokers (*dālāls, pāikārs*) to acquire the goods and distribute them to the petty traders and shopkeepers (*dokāndār*) in the bazaars.[43]

As Sudipta Sen has argued, the marketplace was the nexus amidst a complex web of relationships permeating all levels of culture, a meeting point of economic forces, political power, and religious patronage. Amidst the dispersed and shifting political realm of the eighteenth century, in a society without a single centralized locus of authority, it was the marketplace that bound together the many diverse fields of power—economic, religious, and political alike: "The marketplace . . . was not just a site of transaction, but a knot in the fabric of social mediation woven around manufacturing villages, quays on the river, checks and tolls, granaries and storages, and weekly or permanent markets."[44] Not only were there intimate connections between political power and control of the market, but there was an equally close relationship between religious patronage and the marketplace. Indeed, the marketplace shows us just how difficult it is to separate the economic and religious fields, how material, social and religious capital are all bound together in a complex fabric: "Marketplaces [were] inevitably attached to religious sites. . . . [M]arketplaces were set up to keep up a whole range of religious commitments—not only to direct resources to the prosperity of a sacred site, but to enjoin trade in commodities of ritual significance."[45]

Thus we find that throughout the literature of eighteenth-century Bengal, the image of the "marketplace" often serves as the most basic image for the world as a whole—a fitting symbol for the complex relations and exchanges within a highly mobile, fluid, transient society. Not only in travel literature and secular accounts but also in religious texts and devotional works—such as the *Caṇḍīmaṅgal* or the *Hāṭ Pattan* (the Foundation of the Marketplace) attributed to the Vaiṣṇava poet, Narottam Dās—the market represents the knot in a fabric of political, religious, and economic relations, and thus it is the key symbol for power as a whole: "*Bazaars, gañjs* and *hāṭs* . . . had come to signify political authority and material clout in an unprecedented way. . . . The marketplace stood as a powerful metaphor of world authority for the ruling elite."[46]

Not surprisingly, with the victory of the East India Company and the establishment of colonial rule, the British made it one of their central tasks to take control of and regulate the marketplaces of Bengal. Indeed, the bazaar was in a sense an *epicenter* of the battle for colonial conquest. The result is what Sen calls a "Conquest of Marketplaces" as the company progressively displaced indigenous sources of market patronage, imposing instead a singular, more closely supervised administration of the marketplace. In place of the precolonial marketplace—with its complex networks of royal and religious patronage, its shifting relations of power between Mughal rulers, Hindu Zamindārs, and various religious factions—the company sought to impose a new "terrain of regulation," marked by uniform laws of revenue controlled through the departments of customs and police. In fact, Sen suggests, the company set out to establish a kind of "settlement of marketplaces" which paralleled the new system of land revenue in rural Bengal under the Permanent Settlement of Lord Cornwallis. "In the decades following 1790, marketplaces were made directly accountable to the political economy of the colonizing state. The company administration attempted a thorough overhauling of every kind of duty, privilege or grant in the marketplaces."[47] However, as Kumkum Chatterjee points out, these efforts to "conquer the marketplaces" were never entirely successful, and local rulers and merchants would continue to resist, thwart and frustrate British incursions into the marketplace throughout the colonial period.[48]

The New Babylon: The Lower Orders of Calcutta at the Turn of the Nineteenth Century

Calcutta was like the sea: streams of money flowed into it, and rivers of money flowed away. (Bhabanicharan Banerji, Bengali newspaper editor, 1787–1848)

So freely, I know, you abandoned all your wealth,
wandering and searching throughout the entire Company [*kompānī*];
that's why you break your back working here!
Now your name is written in the account books of the Company warehouse!
(BG 215; II.31)

Perhaps nowhere were these rapid changes in the marketplace more apparent than in the colonial capital of Calcutta. From its very foundation in the seventeenth century under the inspiration of Job Charnock, Calcutta had been intended as a commercial center and primary locus of trade with the hinterland of agrarian Bengal. As it grew rapidly toward the beginning of the nineteenth century, the imperial city took shape as a vast and intricate series of marketplaces, a thriving network of small villages, hutments, and bazaars.[49]

As the population of the city expanded in the nineteenth century (from 179,000 in 1821 to half a million by 1850 to almost a million by the early twentieth century), and as a new influx of immigrants from Orissa, Assam, Bihar, and other regions began to flood into the slums, a variety of new social patterns began to evolve. Most fundamental was the cleavage of Calcutta into the "White Town" and "Black Town." Whereas the former was the wealthy, well-ordered European quarter, linking the imperial city to the global capitalist network, the latter was a vast teeming settlement, described as a kind of "New Babylon, a huge and mixed crowd of people."[50] As one observer, H. E. A. Cotton, put it, Calcutta was "a queen of two faces: a city of startling contrasts, of palaces and hovels . . . of royal grandeur and squalor that beggars description."[51]

As Sumanta Banerjee suggests, Calcutta of the early nineteenth century witnessed the rise of two new cultural groups, spawned by the changing social and economic context. On the one hand, there were the wealthy elite or the *bhadraloks*, largely comprised of intermediaries helping the East India Company conduct business and administration, absentee landlords, and a middle class of professionals. This was, in short, "a class of persons, Indian in blood and color, but English in taste, opinions, morals and intellect."[52] Deeply informed by British values, many of these urban elite hoped to reform society and religion along Western lines. As we see in the case of the Brāhmo Sabhā (later Brāhmo Samāj), led by Rāmmohun Roy (1772–1833), many of the more progressive bhadraloks hoped to reform caste, eliminate *satī*, child marriage, and other social ills while instituting a more universal, rational and nonidolatrous form of religion, based on the monotheism of the Upaniṣads and Vedānta.[53]

On the other hand, Calcutta also gave birth to a growing substratum of urban poor—the "lower orders" (*itar lok*), inhabiting the slums and bazaars of the Black Town. Many of these were laborers and artisans, drawn from the villages to the city in the hopes of new opportunities in a rapidly expanding city, but often quickly displaced amidst an increasingly exploitative environment. Comprising some three-quarters of the city's population, these *itar lok* included the artisans, potters, palanquin bearers, oil makers, the first generation of an industrial proletariat, jute and textile millworkers, barbers, washermen, fishermen, and boatmen: "The lower orders [were] migrants who came to Calcutta from the neighboring villages in search of jobs. A large number were traditional artisans who practiced rural cultural forms . . . and thus evolved a new urban folk culture, to be marginalized by the end of the 19th century."[54] As the new class of urban elite began to set up their little chiefdoms (*rājyas*) in various sections of the city, clusters of lower-class slums grew up around them, creating a contradictory landscape of opulent mansions surrounded by poor and crowded slum/bazaars: "Thus developed the bazaars and hutments where the artisans and laborers lived . . . Modeled on small villages, these became replicas of the landed estates owned by feudal chieftains, their contours changing in response to urban needs. Calcutta became a city of hutments, palatial buildings of opulent Bengalis surrounded by bazaars and slums."[55]

However, as the rapid influx of English imported commodities progressively came to dominate the Calcutta marketplace, flooding the city with "boots and shoes, carriages, looking glasses, liquors, and miscellaneous items described as 'treasure,'"[56] many of Bengal's traditional industries—particularly those of spinning and weaving—were deeply undermined. Even as the industrial revolution was rapidly getting under way in England, in Bengal, "domestic industry was almost completely destroyed within a quarter of a century."[57] As a result, many of the city's traditional craftsmen found themselves profoundly displaced, increasingly reduced to a "landless proletariat" manufacturing raw materials for export back to England. "Through their wretched living conditions and endemic poverty . . . the laboring men felt the brunt of colonial rule even more keenly than others. European foremen could kick them to death; policemen could beat them. . . . Slum dwellers could be evicted by landlords, beaten by musclemen, and thrown out by the municipal administration."[58]

However, as Banerjee has shown with such amusing detail, the lower orders would always find ways to give voice to their resentment against their oppressed condition, to parody the foppish babus and satirize the pretences of the upper classes, both native and foreign. Not only did they develop a variety of new popular arts—music, dance, poetry, and painting—combining traditional rural styles with those of the new urban context, but many would also turn to ecstatic devotion and mystical experience in the worship of the smaller, heterodox, non-Brahminical sects, such as the Bāuls, Āuls, Dervishes, or Fakirs:

> Uprooted from the social and economic base of the villages . . . and still to discover a new identity in . . . the alien metropolis, Calcutta's lower orders were groping for their own distinct forms of self-expression. Religion was one such form.
>
> The various groups of Āuls and Bāuls who used to roam around the streets of Calcutta . . . were some of the earliest followers of lower class religious radicalism. While Calcutta's *sambhranta* people were . . . debating subtle points of the caste system and how to protect their religion from contamination, the Bāuls made fun of such pedantry in songs.[59]

The Fringes of the Imperial City: The Changing Economics of Rural Bengal

Meanwhile, in the countryside surrounding the imperial city, the Kartābhajās and other small sects would also draw much of their following from the poorer peasantry of rural Nadiya, Jessore, Khulna, and twenty-four Parganas districts. Like the complex marketplace of Calcutta, rural Bengal of the nineteenth century reflects a dynamic interplay between precolonial and colonial, precapitalist systems and the increasing pressures of the global capitalist economy.[60]

Perhaps nowhere were complex changes and continuities in the Bengali economy more apparent than in the series of reforms in land revenue which took place under the company's administration in the late eighteenth century. This began in the 1760s when the company began to replace the feudal tax system of the Zamindārs with an administrative system run by European tax collectors, and it culminated in the permanent settlement by Lord Cornwallis in 1793. To govern the land in the most efficient manner, Cornwallis wished to create a new kind of propertied class, comparable to the British landed gentry, a class with "heritable, personal and transferable rights on their estates."[61] The rate of tax was thus permanently fixed, with a determined percentage to be collected for the district government. Ironically, as Ranajit Guha argues, even though the settlement had been intended to optimize the indigenous economy and promote antifeudal capitalist interests, its effect appears to have been quite the reverse.[62] As Bayly comments, though "they had wanted an 'English gentry' with deep control over deferential yeomanry," instead "they formed an 'Irish' class of non-productive rentiers lording it over an impoverished peasantry."[63]

On one hand, there was a sudden and rapid transfer of landholdings, as many hereditary Zamindār families found it increasingly difficult to meet the demands of rent and were in many cases stripped of their land. Meanwhile, much of the land passed into the hands of the rising class of urban nouveaux riches or "comprador landlords," mainly drawn from the bankers, merchants, and company servants of Calcutta. On the other hand, these changes had an equally profound impact on Bengal's peasantry. Although early historians had probably overexaggerated the profoundly disruptive impact of the settlement,[64] more recent scholars such as Sugata Bose agree that the overall impact of these changes was generally quite negative for the peasantry of Bengal. As the Zamindārs came under increasing pressure to meet the revenue demands, the burden of the rent was in turn passed on to the peasantry, and as a new class of landholders and moneylenders moved in under the protection of the company, an ever more efficient form of oppression was imposed, which only "intensified 'feudal' exploitation of the peasantry":

> Under the Raj the state assisted directly in the reproduction of landlordism. . . . The British infused new blood in the proprietary body by the Permanent Settlement. . . . The outcome was to revitalize a quasi-feudal structure by transferring resources from older less effective members of the landlord class to . . . financially more dependable ones. For the peasant this meant not less but more intensive ex-

ploitation: the crude medieval type of oppression . . . was replaced by the more regulated will of a foreign power which . . . was to leave the landlords free to collect . . . from their tenants and evict them.[65]

It is no accident that the late eighteenth and early nineteenth centuries witnessed an increasing outburst of rebellions and insurrections throughout the countryside of Bengal. From at least the 1760s, when peasants under the leadership of the Hindu Sannyasis and Muslim Fakirs burst into rebellion in different part of Bengal, and continuing with the Wahabi rebellion under Titu Meer in 1831, the Faraizi rebellion in 1838–48, the 1855–57 uprising of the Santal tribals, and the resistance by the indigo cultivators against the English planters in 1859–61, rural Bengal would be shaken by agrarian violence for more than a century. Often combining religious ideals with immediate economic interests, messianic and eschatological beliefs with political violence, these peasant uprisings reveal a profound hope for an entirely new world:

> Under colonial domination India's network of community relationships verged on complete breakdown . . . Even as the community was eroded, the masses became subject to the plunder of capital, pre-capitalist wealth and state power. It is in such circumstances that subaltern consciousness seeks . . . a paradise lost. The insurgencies . . . hang on eschatological prophecy and faith in the magical elimination of enemies. But in this fusion of the mystic and the earthly they signify a challenge to alien domination.[66]

In short, it would seem that the stage was very much set for the descent of a new *avatār*, a new God-made-Flesh to heal both the spiritual and economic miseries of the lower orders of early colonial Bengal.

The Secret Vṛndāvana: The Birth of the Kartābhajās

At the Ghoṣpāṛā festival, there's no consideration of caste—
In Ghoṣpāṛā, the secret Vṛndāvana [*gupta vṛndāvana*], I can find the Man of the Heart! (Bāul song attributed to Lālan Shāh)

Ghoṣpāṛā has become the secret Vṛndāvana!
Shining rays of red sun light upon all boys and girls! (Kubir Gosāiṅ, Sāhebdhanī poet)

The Kartābhajās stand out both as the most powerful of the various "minor sects" of late eighteenth-century Bengal, and as among the clearest reflections of the complex social and economic events of this rapidly changing period. Not only did they emerge during the first decades of colonial rule and the critical period in the transition to colonial capitalism, but the height of Kartābhajā power—during the decades of the 1830s to 1850s—also coincided with the height of peasant unrest throughout rural Bengal. Thus, within the Kartābhajā songs and rituals, we find a rich mixture of colonial and pre-colonial, indigenous, and foreign elements. The mercantile terminology of colonial Calcutta and the language of the "company" mingle with traditional economic hierarchies, woven together in a rich bricolage of pre-capitalist economic structures, precolonial social arrangements, and a wide variety of religious elements drawn from Hindu, Muslim, and even Christian traditions alike.

Literary Sources for an Illiterate Tradition: An Evaluation of the Historical Sources

They have a separate Tantra; abandoning the mantras of all other gods,
they are initiated by the Human mantra [*Mānuṣa-mantra*].
Religion is mixed up with all irreligion;
they turn every deed into the enjoyment of sensual pleasures!
The basis of all their trachings is deception and fraud. (Dāśarathī Rāy, "Kartābhajā,"
a satirical poem ridiculing the Kartābhajās)

Among the most valuable aspects of the Kartābhajā tradition, and the one that makes them so important for our knowledge of Bengali religious and cultural life, is the fact that we have such a large amount of historical evidence about this group. In addition to primary texts, there is a large and diverse body of data—missionary accounts, newspaper reports, and the commentaries of contemporary literary figures. As the Kartābhajās became increasingly notorious and controversial throughout the Calcutta area, they also came to be discussed, debated, attacked, and sometimes even praised, by the most learned minds of Bengal.

PRIMARY SOURCES In the eyes of their critics, the Kartābhajās have frequently been dismissed as an illiterate sect without written scriptures or a textual tradition. According to the Baptist journal, *Friend of India*, "the sect have not yet produced any account of their doctrines. Indeed they hold pens, ink and paper in contempt."[67] An essentially esoteric tradition, rooted in intimate master-disciple relationships and secret initiation, the Kartābhajās have always transmitted most of their teachings orally, primarly through the medium of highly cryptic esoteric songs. The oldest handwritten manuscript that I have found is a collection of 126 songs entitled the "Kartābhajā Gīta" (dated 1228 [1821 C.E.]); however, their large corpus of mystical and deeply encoded songs was never consigned to print until 1870, when it was collected under the title of *Bhāver Gīta* ("Songs of Ecstasy"[68]) or *Śrī Juter Pada*. Although traditionally attributed to the second, most famous Kartā, Dulālcāṅd (a.k.a. Lālśaśī, d. 1833), these songs are a rather chaotic and eclectic hodgepodge, which probably reflect a variety of conflicting authorial voices (see SE, part I; the content of the BG will be analyzed in chapters 3–5).[69]

After the *Bhāver Gīta*, the most important works are those of the early-twentieth-century devotee Manulāl Miśra, who made some efforts to systematize and organize the rather chaotic Kartābhajā tradition. In addition to his major commentary on the *Bhāver Gīta,* Miśra also published several other, very Tantric-influenced, treatises on Kartābhajā belief and practice.[70] Finally, we have a number of collections of songs gathered by various scholars and published under titles such as "Kartābhajāsaṅgīta" or "Saṅgītamālā," as well as several other more popular texts written by contemporary Kartābhajā gurus—including the recently deceased Kartā Satyaśiva Pāl and one of the two living Kartās, Rañjit Kumār Pāl—who continue to promote the tradition throughout the Calcutta area.[71]

Some of the most intriguing primary material on the movement, however, comes from the personal testimonies of early Kartābhajā devotees. The first of these is the *Brief Memoir of Krishna Pal*, recorded by the Baptist missionary, William Ward. After recounting his own life as a Kartābhajā convert and guru, Pal describes his later conversion to Christianity—and so became, according to Ward, the very first Hindu in Bengal to adopt the missionaries' faith.[72] Another firsthand account of the movement appears in J. H. E. Garrett's *Bengal District Gazetteers, Nadia* (1910). Here a Kartābhajā disciple named Babu Gopal Krishna Pal offers a strong defense of the Kartābhajā tradition against its critics, as well as a useful summary of its major doctrines. Refuting all charges of licentiousness and immorality, Gopal Krishna praises the Kartābhajā religion as the "Religion of Man," which is truly egalitarian, and in which "degraded humanity finds a cordial welcome and ready recognition."[73]

SECONDARY SOURCES: MISSIONARY AND ORIENTALIST SOURCES It is not insignificant that the first known secondary sources on the Kartābhajās come from the early Christian missionaries and British Orientalists. Perhaps the most energetic of the early British missionary groups, the Baptist Missionary Society (BMS), founded in 1792 by William Carey, set up its center in Serampore, not far from the Kartābhajā homeland in Ghoshpara. As Oddie points out, the missionaries were extremely interested in small sects like the Kartābhajās, which they saw as fertile ground for the spread of their own religion. In the Kartābahajas' rejection of caste, and their worship of a human being as "God incarnate," the fathers thought they had found some very promising parallels to Christian doctrine, which could be turned to their own advantage.[74] Most of the early missionaries were extremely critical of, and often quite shocked by, the seemingly licentious practices of the Kartā. Perhaps the most often cited of all the early accounts of this sect is that of Reverend William Ward (1817), who describes the Kartā as charlatan claiming to cure disease and exploiting his poor ignorant followers in order to build up his own wealth and power.[75] So, too, the widely read work of H. H. Wilson, the *Sketch of the Religious Sects of the Hindus* (1828–32) stands out as a classic of early Orientalist scholarship, and also as one of the most often cited sources on the smaller "deviant orders" such as the Kartābhajās. Even more so than Ward, Wilson is especially cynical in his comments on the economic motivations behind the sect: the worship of the Kartā as God incarnate is essentially "an artful encroachment upon the authority of the old hereditary teachers or Gossains, and an attempt to invest a new family with spiritual power."[76]

Finally, in addition to Ward and Wilson, we have a large body of other Missionary records, the most significant of which are the *Church Missionary Register, Christian Intelligencer, Friend of India,* and the Missionary histories of James Long and Eugene Stock. Most important, these sources recount the events of the late 1830s, when several hundred poor, disgruntled Kartābhajā devotees converted en masse to Christianity (see chapter 7).[77]

NEWSPAPER ACCOUNTS After the missionaries, our next major body of information comes from the contemporary newspaper accounts—the *Saṃvāda Prabhākara, Somprakāśa* and *Tattvabodhinī* foremost among them. The *Saṃvāda Prabhākara,* edited by the famous scholar of Bengali literature, Īśvara Gupta, published an anonymous report on the Kartābhajā festival of 1848. The account is a mixed and ambivalent one, to say the least. On the one hand, it gives vivid descriptions of the opulent lifestyle of the Kartā surrounded by fawning women, while the poor, afflicted devotees are beaten and extorted by the gurus. But, on the other hand, he also praises the egalitarianism and humanism of the Kartābhajā faith.[78] Even more important is the account of Akṣaykumār Datta (1820–1886), editor of the key Brāhmo paper, *Tattvabodhinī,* and one of the earliest sources for the various "deviant sects" of Bengal, the Bāuls, Sahajiyās, Balahāṛīs, Kartābhajās, and others.[79] On the whole, Datta's is an unusually balanced view of the Kartābhajā sect, both sympathetic to its religious content but also critical of what he regarded as its fall into immorality and corruption.

LITERARY FIGURES Some of our most colorful accounts are written by well-known literary and religious figures of Bengal, who viewed the sect from both very positive and very negative perspectives. Among the most important of the former is Rāja Jayanārāyaṇ Ghoṣāl (1752–1818) of Bhukailash, Calcutta, a wealthy and affluent man who is said according to legend to have been a disciple of Dulālcāṅd. Described by some as the "most progressive man of his era," Jayanārāyaṇ was a merchant and banian who had "enjoyed the confidence of Warren Hastings and helped the Government of the Company in their survey of Bengal," and so was honored with the title of Mahārāja.[80] Jayanārāyaṇ was also the author of an enormous poetic epic called the *Karuṇānidhānavilāsa* (1813), in which he depicts a series of divine *avatārs* for the modern era: Kabīr, Jesus Christ, and Rāmśaraṇ Pāl (the first Kartā).[81] These three great incarnations, he suggests, will unite their three countries and holy scriptures, creating a harmonious "religion of Man" for a new age (see chapter 2).

The Kartābhajās also had great admirers among the newly emerging Hindu reform movement, the Brāhmo Samāj, who were attracted by the Kartābhajās apparent egalitarianism, universalism, and humanism. Among these were the famous Brāhmo leaders, Vijaykṛṣṇa Gosvāmi, Śaśīpad Banerjee (who started the first Brāhmo Samāj among India's new class of industrial proletariat), and Nabīncandra Sen (1847–1909) (a well-known poet, who advocated humanitarian ideals, the reform of caste, and new roles for women). In the Kartābhajā religion, they supposed, they had found a kind of popular lower-class analogue to the progressive ideals of the *bhadraloks* of Calcutta. In Nabīncandra's biography, *Āmār Jīvana,* we have an invaluable account of his visit to the Ghoshpara festival, where he was sent as a government official. He even claims that on the train ride home from Ghoshpara, he met the great Rabindranath Tagore, who, although formerly skeptical of the scandalous Kartābhajās, heard Nabīncandra's account and was deeply moved by the sincerity and humanism of this religion.[82]

Side by side with these laudatory views, however, we also have a series of far less positive, often extremely cynical attacks on the Kartābhajās by contemporary literary figures, and particularly by the Western-educated elite bhadralok society of Calcutta.[83] Among the most severe attacks on the Kartābhajās came from the well-known Calcutta poet Dāśarathī Rāy (1806–57), in his satirical poem "Kartābhajā." The most degenerate and perverse of all the low-class sects of his day, the Kartābhajā is, in Dāśarathī's scathing verse, nothing but "a dog in the wretched hut where the paddy-grinder is kept . . . a ghost in a field strewn with rotten carcasses; an ugly old whore in a place full of rubbish and dung."[84]

RĀMAKṚṢṆA AND THE KARTĀBHAJĀ BITCHES Perhaps the most important of all our nineteenth-century sources is the great Calcutta saint, Śrī Rāmakṛṣṇa (1836–86). Because of his own experience in Tantric practice and his close contact with a number of Kartābhajās in Calcutta, Rāmakṛṣṇa provides an invaluable insight into the esoteric life of the sect. The saint was closely associated with one particularly mysterious pundit named Vaiṣṇavacaraṇ—an enigmatic Janus-faced figure, at once a respected Vaiṣṇava pundit and a secret Kartābhajā master—who introduced him to a variety of Tantric groups in the underworld of Calcutta. Rāmakṛṣṇa describes several encounters with Kartābhajā practitioners, whom he regarded with profound suspicion and fear: "their way of life is so repugnant that I am unable to reveal it to the public," as one of his biographers put it.[85] After he had had some further experience with the sect, however, Rāmakṛṣṇa seems to have softened his originally harsh judgment, admitting that this may be a dirty or "backdoor" kind of path—like entering a house through the latrine door instead of the front door—but a possible religious path nonetheless.[86]

On the whole, although it is a rather chaotic and mixed assortment, this large body of historical material does, I think, provide a reasonably solid basis for understanding the social context and early development of the Kartābhajās. Provided that we read these sources against one another, ever wary of the deeper political, religious, or personal biases that inform them, they provide some remarkable insights into this otherwise obscure and esoteric tradition.

The Secret Caitanya—A Poor Mad Fakir:
Āulcāṅd and the Legendary Origins of the Kartābhajā Tradition

[Caitanya] became incarnate in Nadiyā and engaged in the supreme Play—
Then He was revealed in Ghoṣpāṛā, and stayed a few days in Jaṅgīpur.
He remained in secrecy, immersed in His own delight, with His devotees
Man is Truth; the Guru is Truth; the Truth of [all] Truth is Hari, the friend of the Poor! (Kubir Gosāiṅ, from Cakravartī, *Sāhebdhanī Sampradāya*, song 61)

Now that we have outlined the social and religious context, as well as the primary sources for the Kartābhajās, let us place this tradition within this context and trace its early origins. The Kartābhajās trace their own origins to an extremely colorful, highly idiosyncratic, and at least partly legendary figure name "Āulcāṅd" or "Baba Āul." Described in the *Bhāver Gīta* as the "Wretched Mad Man" and the crazy rag-clad "Poor God" (*gorib bidhatā*), Āulcāṅd appears at once as a divine incarnation, a mischievous trickster, a criminal, and a wandering lunatic.[87] Although the origins of the name "Āul" are unclear, most scholars believe that it derives from the Persian *āulīya,* the plural of *walīya,* which designates a "friend of God" and thus "a man who has fully realized the nature of the Lord." To this day in scattered regions of Bengal, there is a highly esoteric sect, closely related to the Bāuls and Sufis, known as the Āuls or Āulīya, and many speculate that Āulcāṅd was in some way connected with this tradition.[88] More likely, however, is that the image of Āulcāṅd as a rag-clad, mad fakir has been borrowed from the cult of Satya Pīr or Satya Nārāyaṇa, which spread thrughout the Hindu and Muslim communities of Bengal since the sixteenth centruy. Like Āulcāṅd, Satya Pīr is typically represented as a poor crazy fakir—"a wandering mendicant Sufi in tattered rags, harsh to those who spurn him, but gracious to those who show him respect." In the late nineteenth century, moreover, Satya Nārāyaṇa was appropriated by the orthodox Vaiṣṇava community, now identified as Viṣṇu's avatār who had come specifically for the age of Muslim rule: "Lord Viṣṇu . . . in this final aeon, the Kali yuga, assumed the image of a holy man of India's conquerers prior to the British."[89]

The subject of a wide number of different legends and folk stories, Āulcāṅd is said to have been born around 1686 and died in 1779. According to some legends, he is said to have been somehow involved in the raids of the Marāṭhās (1744), when he was arrested by the officers of the Nawāb Ālivardi Khān, and then miraculously escaped from the dungeon.[90] Indeed, according to one particularly noteworthy account, mentioned briefly earlier, Āulcāṅd appeared precisely at the time of the Battle of Plassey—and, in fact, even uttered the cryptic prophesy of the downfall of the Muslim Nawāb and the triumph of the British in Bengal: "In 1757, when the Muslims had looted the land and were returning to Murshidabad, a soldier placed his trunk on the Fakir's shoulder, struck him with his gun, and told him to carry it. The fakir went a little distance, put the trunk down and said that the Muslims would be driven out and the Europeans [*phiriṅgī*] would seize the land."[91]

The most "historical," or perhaps the least mythological, of these various stories is that Āulcāṅd was an orphan who was discovered in a field in 1774 by a man of unknown descent named Mahādeva, a betel grower of Ula village (Nadiyā district). He lived with Mahādeva for twelve years, and afterward lived among different persons throughout Bengal until the age of 27. He then renounced the world and became a wandering Fakir, traveling widely and meeting with various holy men (many believe he may have been initiated into the Qadiri Sufi order). Eventually Āulcāṅd arrived at Beria village where he met Rāmśaraṇ Pāl; after miraculously curing him of his colic pain (or in some accounts, after curing his wife Sarasvatī), he made Rāmśaraṇ his chief disciple, followed by twenty-one other fakirs.[92]

According to Kartābhajā belief, however, Āulcāṅd was no mere human being; indeed, he was none other than Śrī Caitanya in secret disguise, now reappearing on earth in the form of a Muslim Fakir. This is extremely telling, for it points to the Kartābhajās' key strategy of *esoteric hermeneutics*—or "strong misreading"—which involves a simultaneous appropriation and criticism of the mainstream Gauḍīya Vaiṣṇava tradition, its founding scriptures and its legitimizing metanarratives. With their ingenious tactic of "stolen lightning," the Kartābhajās have at once pilfered and yet also undercut or subverted the sacred mythistory of the exoteric tradition, investing it with a deeper secret interpretation known only to initiates.[93] According to the Kartābhajās' esoteric rereading of the *Caitanya Caritāmṛta*, the Gauḍīya tradition had gradually become coopted by greedy self-serving gurus, and so Caitanya decided to incarnate himself in a new form. After remaining hidden for several centuries, he donned the garb of a poor, crazy fakir and appeared at the Triveṇī, the meeting point of the Jamuna, Sarasvati, and Ganges rivers, where he miraculously crossed over the waters (a legend which may also bear some esoteric reference to Tantric yogic techniques; STP 4–6).[94] He then established his "secret Vṛndāvana" (*gupta vṛndāvana)* in Ghoshpara village:

> This Madman [*khepā*] is the Lord, "the Destroyer of Doubt." . . . In every age, he assumes the human form, becomes incarnate on this earth and engages in play with mankind. . . . He appeared in the Satya, Tretā and Dvāpara yugas; so too . . . in the Kali yuga, he appeared as Caitanya. Then he remained hidden for long time. But he reappeared in Ghoshpara, and devotees can know him if they gaze upon him secretly [*rahasya kare*], with half-closed eyes.[95]

Now, it is really rather significant that Caitanya-Āulcāṅd should have chosen the specific locus of Ghoshpara—a small village some twenty miles north of Calcutta—as the site for his new incarnation. Within the geography of colonial Bengal, Ghoshpara occupies a key place, situated on the critical margins of the Imperial City, where rural Bengal and the urban center overlap, on a central commercial route by which people and goods come and go between city and country. Hence, it offered an ideal place for a new Vṛndāvana or a "*secret marketplace*"—*an alternative social space*, where the poor lower classes of Calcutta could temporarily escape the burdens of caste and labor in the city, to retreat to the sacred confines of the Kartābhajā path. The purpose of Caitanya's new incarnation in this Secret Vṛndāvana was precisely to reveal a simple, easy (*sahaja*) means of worship for the lower classes, who were neglected and downtrodden by the orthodox Vaiṣṇavas. "At present," Caitanya-Āulcāṅd thought, "'there is no easy method of worship for the lowly, powerless people; that's why I have revealed the easy [*sahaja*] path, so they can worship the truth within them, the worship of Man.' Thus he took another kind of body. He could not reveal his true nature as Caitanya deva to many people, but only to his close disciples."[96]

In addition to his divine status, Āulcāṅd is also the subject of a variety of miraculous tales and humorous anecdotes describing his eccentric, often shocking behavior. Indeed, it is said that when he first entered Ghosphara, the villagers took him to be a dangerous madman, and pelted him with filth.[97] Their reaction was perhaps not entirely unjustified. When he felt the need to express himself candidly, Āulcāṅd was not beyond displaying the most bizarre behavior. On one occasion, for example, he is said to have appeared unexpectedly at the wedding ceremony of Rāmśaraṇ's daughter, where he promptly stripped naked before the attending women and began to dance.[98] According to another rather bizarre story, Āulcāṅd used to engage in rambunctious horseplay with the local children—so rambunctious, in fact, that one day he accidentally slapped a little cowherd boy in the head so hard that he killed the child. Fortunately, his disciple Rāmśaraṇ was able to use his own magic powers to remedy the situation: in desperation, he kicked the dead boy in the head, whereupon the child sat up immediately and opened his eyes.[99]

It would seem there was more than a little tension between the eccentric Āulcāṅd and his disciple Rāmśaraṇ—particularly as the latter began to claim supernatural powers and spiritual authority of his own. Āulcāṅd eventually abandoned Ghoshpara and went off wandering in East Bengal. Having traveled through the regions of Bakarganj, Khulna, Jessore, and the Sundarbans, he is believed to have initiated a number of Bengali Muslims and to have spawned several offshoot sects. To this day, Kartābhajā splinter groups such as the Satya-Gurus and Bhagabānīyas may still be found in the districts of Jessore, Khulna, and Barisal.[100]

Finally, we should also note one very telling legend about Āulcāṅd which is current among some Bāul traditions of East Bengal. According to this narrative, Caitanya had reappeared in the secret form of Āulcāṅd precisely in order to reveal the Tantric practice of *parakīyā* love, or sexual intercourse with another man's wife. Indeed, as the chief exponent of *parakīyā* love, so the story goes, Āulcāṅd was himself the founder of the Bāul tradition. "Among some Bāuls, there is a popular belief that Caitanya himself knew a secret method of practice—the practice of sexual union between man and woman . . . out of the desire to spread this *parakīyā* teaching, Caitanya himself became reincarnated in the form of Āulcāṅd. . . . This is itself the Bāul practice and Bāul philosophy."[101] This legend is especially striking precisely because, as we will see later, there is intense debate and controversy within the Kartābhajā tradition itself over the question of *parakīyā* love; indeed, most of the more orthodox contemporary leadership would strongly deny that there is any trace of *parakīyā prema* in the Kartābhajā path (chapter 6).

Rāmśaraṇ and the Twenty-two Fakirs: The Historical Origins of the Kartābhajās

According to Kartābhajā tradition, Āulcāṅd gathered twenty-two primary disciples before his death. The precise names and birthplaces of these twenty-two are preserved in at least five different lists, which vary considerably.[102] Rather significantly, however, most of them are said to have come from the poorer lower classes of Bengal: "Most were milkmen [*sadgops*], some were fishermen, some were Rājputs, some were braziers; that is, they belonged to classes which had fallen to a low place in society."[103] According to most traditions, eight of these twenty-two were considered foremost: Rāmśaraṇ Pāl, the future Kartā, and, after him, Bhīma Rāy Rājput, Becu Ghoṣe, Hari Ghoṣe, Hāṭu Ghoṣe, Kānāi Ghoṣe, Nidhirām, and Śyāmadās. Yet apart from Rāmśaraṇ and the dissident disciple Kānāi Ghoṣe (who would later reject Rāmśaraṇ's authority and found his own sect) little is known about the original disciples.[104]

According to the later Kartābhajā tradition, as represented in Miśra's list, each of the disciples is said to have been a reincarnation of one of the original followers of Caitanya. Becu Ghoṣe, for example, is the incarnation of Rāmānanda Basu; Bhīma Rāy Rājput the incarnation of Jīva Gosvāmin; Kinu Govinda the incarnation of Raghunātha Bhaṭṭa, and so on. In short, just as the Kartābhajās appropriated the legitimating authority of Caitanya (in the new incarnation of Āulcāṅd), so too, they sought to appropriate the authority of the later Gauḍīya tradition as passed on to Caitanya's disciples. As Chakrabarty suggests, it is no accident that the Kartābhajās made these claims in the late nineteenth century—"a time when the orthodox Vaiṣṇavas mounted a massive assault on the Kartābhajās and other deviant orders."[105]

Rāmśaraṇ Pāl quickly emerged as the most important, or at least most ambitious, of the twenty-two fakirs. A *sadgop* (milkman) by caste and a cultivator by profession, Rāmśaraṇ is said to have been the son of one Nanda Ghoṣe of Jagadishpur village. Because of his intense religious devotion, he caused dissension within his family and so left them to wander, finally arriving at the village of Ghoshpara. After the unexpected death of his first wife and daughters, Rāmśaraṇ married Sarasvatī, daughter of Govinda Ghoṣe, the wealthy landlord of Govindapur village. This wedding, it seems, would later prove to be an extremely expedient and highly lucrative maneuver. As Māṇik Sarkār points out, the leaders of the Kartābhajā sect were thereby endowed with the inheritance of a wealthy Zamindār's estate, while, at the same time, the local Zamindāri was given a new kind of divine patronage and sacred legitimation: "The landholding of that region was then . . . in the hands of a Sadgop (milkman) . . . Rāmśaraṇ Pāl's wife was Sarasvatī Devī, the daughter of the Zamindār, Govinda Ghoṣe, and she later became known as Satī Mā. Thus the Kartā was the Zamindār's son-in-law; and the

Zamindār's daughter gained divine power as Kartā Mā."[106] As we will see in chapter 7, this link between the Kartā and the Zamindāri economic system is an important one, which would help to structure the organization of the sect as a whole.

Not long after his marriage, Rāmśaraṇ was visited by the strange mad fakir, Āulcāṅd. Amazed by Āulcāṅd's miraculous healing powers, he immediately fell down and became a disciple of the wandering madman. After Āulcāṅd's mysterious departure (perhaps incited by the spiritual rivalry between the two), Rāmśaraṇ proclaimed himself the Kartā, the Master or Lord, of this new religion and as the incarnation of God (Kṛṣṇa-Caitanya-Āulcāṅd) in human form. In the eyes of their devotees, Rāmśaraṇ Pāl and his wife Sarasvatī thus came to be regarded as far more than mere mortals but, rather, as the eternal male and female principles of the universe—the *Ādi-Puruṣa* and *Ādyā-Śakti* incarnate (see KDA 9, 57–69).

The Holy Mother: Satī Mā and Her Miraculous Grace

In its more popular "exoteric" dimension, particularly among the poorer lower classes, the most widely worshiped figure in the Kartābhajā tradition is Rāmśaraṇ's wife—Sarasvatī, better known as Satī Mā or Kartā Mā.[107] From a fairly early date, it would seem, Satī Mā began to be famed throughout Bengal as a source of profound spiritual power, the worker of miracles, the giver of blessings and supernatural deeds. With the professed power to heal sickness, cure blindness, and relieve poverty, she became especially beloved among the poor lower classes—above all among women, particularly widows, barren wives, and mothers of sick or dead children. By the early twentieth century, as we see in the work of Manulāl Miśra, we find a fully developed theology of Satī Mā as the Divine Mother. In works such as *Satīmār Mahātmyā* (the majesty of Satī-Mā), Satī Mā appears as far more than just a giver of divine grace but as a Divine being and metaphysical Reality: she is none other than the *Ādyā-Śakti* or *Prakṛti* itself, the divine feminine principle at the source of all creation. Indeed, she even assumes the role of divine Savior, who has—like Āulcāṅd himself—descended from her eternal heavenly state to become secretly incarnate in the form of a mortal human body: "Woman is the root of the primordial tree. Who would exist without woman? Consider semen and menstrual blood: the body of Woman is the vessel of the whole world. From woman, all creation occurs. She is this very earth. Without woman, there would be no creation, preservation of destruction. . . . Now Satī Mā has become the savior of this world. Secretly (*gopane*), she became incarnate in the form of a human being."[108]

For Miśra and for many later Kartābhajās, Satī Mā and her miraculous child Dulālcāṅd (who is said to have been Caitanya-Āulcāṅd himself, having secretly entered into the womb of Satī mā) almost become a kind of "Virgin Mother and Child," not entirely unlike the Christian Virgin and Christ. Indeed, it is tempting to hypothesize that, in his theological doctrine of Dulālcāṅd as the divine incarnation of Kṛṣṇa-Caitanya, with Satī Mā as his holy mother, Miśra was trying to construct a kind of Indian answer to the Christian virgin and holy child. (Jeffrey Kripal has suggested similar motivations at work behind the construction of the divine status of Rāmakṛṣṇa of the same period in Bengal.[109])

At the same time, however, Satī Mā's promises of supernatural grace, spiritual healing, and miraculous powers also became among the primary sources of ridicule and satire among the Kartābhajās' many critics. Since at least the late nineteenth century, the more cynical Bengali poets and humorists have delighted in poking fun at the superstition and magical quackery surrounding the image of Satī mā. One satirical play of early-twentieth-century Calcutta, the *Jelepāṛār Saṅg* (1914) humorously depicts Kartā Mā and her magical abilities:

A pure *Muci* [leather worker] by caste, I am Kartā Ma, O I am Kartā Mā;
The Barren woman to whom I show my Grace will hear the cry of a son!
If a child-widow, wearing a Sari, becomes pregnant, O if she becomes pregnant,
when she takes refuge at my feet, she will have no fear!
. . . And if a chaste wife remains at home, then, due to my boon, she will find a pure husband; she will get a pure husband!
And if the husband of a middle aged or old woman leaves her
and wastes his money uselessly,
then, by the virtues of my sacred earth, he'll fall and grovel at her feet![110]

We will see in chapter 2 that this ambivalent role of Satī Mā, as both a figure of both tremendous female power and an icon of superstition, hucksterism, and delusion of the poor, also reflects the ambivalent status of women in this tradition as a whole: their potential for new roles of leadership and empowerment as well as new forms of exploitation and manipulation.

Two Red Moons over the Ocean of Love: Dulālcāṅd (Lālśaśī), and the Full Flowering of the Kartābhajā Tradition

In a certain kingdom, a King sits upon a throne.
The people engage freely in business.
There are horripilations of joy at the beautiful sight!
Everyone engages in thousands of transactions,
and the business in that realm goes along easily [*sahaje*]
. . . Look—*Śaśī appears amidst the society of merchants.* [*byabsādārer samāje*]!
(BG 54, II.40; my italics)

The most famous and widely known figure in the early history of the Kartābhajā lineage is the son of Rāmśaraṇ and Satī-Mā, Dulālcāṅd ("Two Red Moons," also known as Śaśī-lāl or Lālśaṣī ["Red Moon"] or Rāmdulāl Pāl). According to Kartābhajā tradition, Dulālcāṅd was none other than the reincarnation of Āulcāṅd (thus also of Caitanya and Kṛṣṇa) who entered into Satī-Mā's womb at the time of his death. Said to have been educated in Bengali, Sanskrit, English, and Persian, and reputed to be a great pundit in all the *śāstras*, Dulālcāṅd first promulgated the Kartābhajā faith as a coherent religious system, now making it palatable not only to the poor lower classes but also to some of the mot respected elites of Calcutta.[111] In fact, so widespread was Dulālcāṅd's fame as a spiritual leader, that he was even invited to the World Parliament of Religions—some sixty years after his own death![112] According to Kartābhajā tradition, Dulālcāṅd was visited by the greatest figures of nineteenth-century Bengal, including a variety of Europeans and even Rammohun Roy himself, who is said to have sought his advice. One popular Kartābhajā song recounts:

Rājā Rāmmohun Roy used to go to his side
and satisfy his desire, drinking the nectar of immortality.
Many Europeans used to go to him
Reverend Duff, the Christian, went to his side
and received instructions at his home in Ghoshpara.[113]

Well known to the British missionaries of the time, Dulālcāṅd was visited by several of the most active preachers of the Calcutta area, including John Marshman and William Carey. According to the account of the *Calcutta Review*, the missionaries found Dulāl living in enormous elegance and wealth, dwelling in a rich estate with a splendid Rājbāṛī-style mansion: "Drs. Marshman and Carey visited Rāmdulāl . . . in 1802 . . . at his house, which was handsome, stately and exceeding that of many Rajas. He was no less plump than Bacchus. . . . He argued with them, defending the doctrine of pantheism."[114]

Born the son of simple *sadgop*-farmer, Dulālcāṅd appears to have been a remarkably shrewd businessman and to have achieved an unusually affluent lifestyle. There is much evidence, in fact, that he had firsthand experience in the world of commerce and mercantile trade. The songs of the *Bhāver Gīta* which are attributed to him, at least, suggest an author who had an intimate knowledge of the world of business and the marketplace, particularly that connected with the East India Company. "The language which most often appears in the text and which seems most intimate and personal," as Sukumār Sen comments, "is that of commerce."[115] Indeed, Chakrabarty has even suggested that Dulālcāṅd not only had experience in the marketplace but also used his earnings to build up the Kartā's estate in Ghoshpara; hence his mystical songs, with their unique blend of economics and ecstatic devotion, are at once spiritual dialogues and accounts of his own business dealings: "Dulālcāṅd had much experience as a businessman. Like many landlords he invested his earnings in building up a big estate. The income from his estate was reinvested in trade. . . . Dulālcāṅd talked both shop and mysticism."[116] The irony—and perhaps the flagrant hypocrisy—of this growing wealth and power among the leadership of an avowedly lower-class movement or "Poor Company" would become increasingly evident throughout the nineteenth century; it is, moreover, a paradox which we will encounter repeately throughout this volume (see especially chapter 7).

Dulālcāṅd, moreover, stands out as the single greatest systematizer and theologian of the Kartābhajā tradition. Indeed, he must be regarded as a kind of organizational genius, who fused a small, largely obscure secret cult with a mass popular movement, combining the rural folk traditions of village Bengal with the urban styles of Calcutta, and forging a new religious movement which would become remarkably powerful among lower-class Hindus and Muslims alike. Under Dulālcāṅd's skillful leadership, the originally highly esoteric practices of the Sahajiyā traditions were combined with a more popular exoteric dimension, centering around the miraculous deeds of Satī Mā. Indeed, not only was he the Kartābhajās' greatest financier, building up a large Rājbāṛī mansion in Ghoshpara, but Dulālcāṅd also made a certain attempt to appeal to some of the educated bhadraloks and Zamindārs. According to popular tradition, he was a close friend of the famous Zamindār, Jayanārāyaṇ Ghoṣāl, and in fact initiated the Rājā into the tradition. In sum, Dulālcāṅd constructed a remarkably effective and lucrative—even if rather weird and somewhat schizoid—religious synthesis:

> There is a very intelligent organization in the Kartābhajā religion, whose foundation lies in the lofty imagination and clever skill of Dulālcāṅd. On one hand, there is the philosophy of the Avatār, and on the other, tales of miraculous healing. . . . On one hand, there is accumulation of wealth at the guru's Office; on the other, the promise of sons to barren women. The learned were attracted by the harmony of religions; the ignorant were deluded by the magic power of Satī Mā.[117]

A Platoon of the Poor (kāṅgāler palṭan): The Social Composition of the Kartābhajās

If Dulālcāṅd and the Pāl lineage of Kartās seem to have enjoyed a fairly wealthy and comfortable lifestyle, rather strikingly, the majority of their following appear to have come quite predominantly from the poorer lower classes of colonial Calcutta and rural Bengal. Indeed, among the most valuable aspects of the Kartābhajā sect as a whole is the rare insight it gives us into the lives of the so-called *itar lok* or "lower orders" at the dawn of the nineteenth century. Obviously, because this is an esoteric tradition, one which actively conceals itself, it is extremely difficult to discern the social makeup of the Kartābhajās; however, if we scan the historical sources, from Ward's 1817 account down to the Bhattacharya report of 1897, we find almost unanimous agreement that by far the majority of its following was drawn from the poorest and most disadvantaged classes of Calcutta and rural Bengal. "All the contemporary records," Banerjee comments, repeatedly stress that most of the Kartābhajās have always come from the "lower orders mainly from the depressed castes, untouchables, Muslim peasants and artisans."[118] Now, it is indeed true that a few *bhadraloks* and upper classes, such as Jayanārāyaṇ, Nabīncandra or Vijaykṛṣṇa, had shown a passing interest in the Kartābhajās[119]; yet, as Datta pointed out in his account of 1870, by far the majority had always been poor, low caste, and uneducated: "Very secretly (*gopane gopane*) this movement has become powerful. Even if many educated Bhadraloks have also participated in it, the majority are lower class and female."[120] Likewise, as the Calcutta paper, *Somaprakāśa*, reported in 1864, "this is an especially influential religion among the lower classes. The bhadraloks respectfully stay far away. . . . The cause for the popularity of their religion is obvious: it offers a great opportunity for independence. In the law books of the Hindus, they have very little freedom . . . but in the Kartābhajā religion they find great freedom."[121] In rural Nadiya district, as Oddie has shown, the movement was extremely popular among the poorer cultivators and *śūdras*, particularly those who had suffered most from the new system of taxation.[122] In the colonial center of Calcutta, it attracted the poor laboring classes who had recently migrated to the city from the villages, especially "the *kaivartas* (farmers and fishermen), oilmen, dealers in spices, grocers, weavers, and other lower-caste Hindus."[123]

Specifically, however, the Kartābhajās of the early nineteenth century appear to have been drawn particularly from those men and women who were involved, in way one or another, in the world of the *marketplace*. As Cakravartī suggests, they were "largely persons involved in trade," in the the world of labor and commerce in Calcutta's teeming bazaars.[124] Throughout the *Bhāver Gīta*, there is constant reference to the buying and selling of the marketplace, particularly in the thriving bazaars of Calcutta and Dhaka. However, its characters are not for the most part the wealthy men of the marketplace—such as the bankers (*bāniāns*), moneylenders (*mahājans*), and intermediaries of the Company who profited most from trade with European capitalists. Rather, its heroes are the "poor" (*gorib*) on the bottom of the mercantile hierarchy, and specifically the small shopkeepers (*dokāndār*), porters (*muṭe*), and laborers involved in shipping and transfer of merchandise to the *ghāṭs* and *gañjs* (wholesale markets). These are the men who had in most cases, as Śaktināth Jhā points out, profited least and suffered most amidst the new economic changes: "The East India Company monopolised control of business in this era, and many small merchants had to take loans from Moneylenders, lost their wealth and fell into poverty."[125] As the *Bhāver Gīta* laments,

> I've quit this business, brother,
> There was no profit in it—I had to give up my earnings too easily!
> Is one more merchant any use in this land?
> I work in some city; I go to the marketplace and toil, breaking my back,
> And as the days pass, do I get even a piece of bread in this kingdom?
> I conducted business in this land eight million times—
> but see, brother, my troubles haven't left me!
> Seeing and hearing all this, I've gone mad! (BG 214; II.27)

The villains and objects of ridicule in these songs, on the other hand, are chiefly the "moneylender" (*mahājan*), the "middlemen" or "brokers" (*dālāl, pāikār*), and the rent collectors (*gomastās*), who went back and forth between the foreign companies and the poorer shopkeepers or labourers. The *dālāls* or brokers, for example, are frequently ridiculed as both "thieving charlatans," out to swindle the poor, and as pathetic fools, who are just as easily swindled themselves. "Overwhelmed with the madness of the brokers, everything became corrupt! . . . They tell you 'it's genuine,' but sell you the fakes!" (BG 267; II.38). The *gomasthā* or rent collector, likewise, is depicted as a "stupid snub-nosed" wretch tagging along at the heels of the company.[126] Take, for example, the following humorous songs, which playfully describe the plight of a poor merchant who had come to the city in the hope of doing business, but had instead only fallen into poverty; he has now been forced into the life of a lowly porter laboring under the company, bound by debt at the merciless hands of a moneylender (*mahājan*):

O, how wonderfully funny!
You've quit your business, and now, I see, you're working as a Porter in the marketplace and at the ghat!
. . . So freely, I know, you had abandoned all your wealth,
wandering and searching throughout the entire Company—
that's why you break your back working here!
Your name is written in the account books of the Company Warehouse!
. . . You had come to work as a merchant in this land,
but when that business failed, you found a lot of work in this market and bazaar.
And now the Porters, both petty and great, all control you!
. . . You've labored for the Company for so long a time—
And Śaśī Lāl laughs and says, "oh, see how manly you are!" (BG 215; II.31)

Will the Porters' Headman protect you,
when the Moneylender's men come to arrest you for your debts?
Then you'll suffer everything!
For what's overdue is recorded in the Money-lender's account book.
(BG 217; II.34)

Even today, most of the Kartābhajās whom I met in Calcutta were this sort of poor trader or petty shopkeeper. Among those I interviewed were a pair of brothers who run a small umbrella-making business in north Calcutta, the owner of a tiny printing shop in the middle of one of Calcutta's worst red-light districts, and one of the most respected living Kartābhajā gurus, who works as a clerk in a small Āyurvedic medicine shop. Even one of the two living Kartās works as a low-level accountant in a small office in downtown Calcutta.[127] As we see in one recent report on the Kartābhajā Melā (1976), some 340 of 381 disciples surveyed were found to be illiterate; 184 of the 301 women were widows; and 57 of the 103 families owned less a single *bigha* (.33 acre) of land, while 16 were homeless beggars.[128] Thus, the vast bulk of the following has always been and remains today largely poor, lower class and illiterate.

Conclusions: A "Marginal" Tradition

In the enigmatic, colorful, often humorous figures of Āulcāṅd, Dulālcāṅd, and their first disciples in Ghoshpara, we find a striking illustration of the early Kartābhajā synthesis and its unique role in colonial Bengal at the dawn of the nineteenth century. A poor wandering half-Muslim, half-Hindu madman, who emerged just after the Battle of Plassey at a critical transition in Bengali history, Āulcāṅd is a profoundly "liminal" character, seated on the borderline of religious and political boundaries. So, too, his greatest successor, Dulālcāṅd, appears as a fundamentally ambivalent, even schizoid figure: born the poor son of a milkman, he assumed leadership of a small lower-class sect, and somehow he constructed a powerful (and apparently very lucrative) new religious movement.

On the whole, the Kartābhajās may be said to represent, in several important senses, a "marginal tradition," a tradition that emerged at the critical interstices and cultural boundaries of late-eighteenth-century Bengal. If the Kartābhajās presented themselves as a "new marketplace" (an alternative spiritual path which would replace the corrupt "marketplace" of the mainstream Vaiṣṇava tradition), this was also very much a "secret marketplace"—a tradition that could only operate on the fringes and underworld of the dominant social order. Born in the key geographic space of Ghoshpara, on the border between the village of Bengal and the imperial city, they arose on the critical margin between the urban center of Calcutta and the rural hinterland. Coming to prominence at the key historical moment of the late eighteenth century, amidst the collapse of both traditional Hindu and Muslim power and the rise of the British East India Company, they also emerged at a very liminal and transitional time in the political history of Bengal, amidst the rapid transfer of power between indigenous and foreign rulers. And finally, founded by a wandering madman said to have been Caitanya in the disguise of a Sufi Fakir, they also emerged on the margins of religious boundaries, between Hindu and Muslim, and between the established "orthodox" tradition of the Gauḍīya Vaiṣṇavas and the various "heterodox" sects on the fringes of mainstream religion.

As we will see in the following chapter, this "marginality" is reflected in the Kartābhajās' religious teachings and in their social ideals. Not only did they draw the majority of their following from the marginal classes of colonial Bengal, but they also forged a remarkable synthesis of a number of religious currents, combining Hindu and Muslim, Tantric Sahajiyā, and mainstream Vaiṣṇava elements into an original and highly profitable new spiritual product amidst the competitive "marketplace of religions" of nineteenth-century Bengal.

2

The Religion of Man (Mānuṣer Dharma)

The Religious Ideals and Social Vision of the Kartābhajās

Sahaja is of the human caste;
It dwells in the *Sahaja* land.
Know, in a hint [*ābhāse*] what its nature is:
Revealing this publicly is impossible, but a taste of it is possible:
Its origin lies within the body itself!
It is unrestricted by good or evil;
So what use will known laws be?
It is without refuge in any religious views.
. . . Hear this law: "Man is supreme!" (BG 48; II.68)

I'm the pure-blooded son of a woman of good family,
but I've been deluded by the charms of an enchanting woman
I've taken up residence in Kartā Mā's house.
In this religion there is no differentiation of caste—Hāṛīs and Mucis all come together.
The religion in this terrible Kali Yuga is "the Supremacy of Man" [*Puruṣottama*].
("Jelepāṛer Saṅg," a satirical play ridiculing the Kartābhajās)

Like the economic field of the late eighteenth century, the religious world of early colonial Bengal was also (to use the *Bhāver Gīta's* favorite metaphor) a vast "bazaar," a marketplace of spiritual goods, both genuine and fake, in which traders from all lands haggled and bartered. Amidst this teeming market, with its host of Hindu, Muslim, Christian, and other competing factions, the Kartābhajās would emerge as perhaps the most successful of the various "minor sects" that spread among the lower classes. As I argue in this chapter, not only did the Kartābhajās emerge at a key locus and critical historical moment, but also they represent a profound transformation within the older Sahajiyā tradition, which was especially well suited to this changing social context, and which offered a highly marketable set of spiritual commodities.

The primary appeal of the Kartābhajās, and the main reason for their striking growth and success, lay in their remarkable capacity for synthesis. This tradition represents a rich bricolage of diverse elements, operating on at least three levels, which I examine in each of the three sections of this chapter. First, on the religious level, the Kartābhajās skillfully combine elements of esoteric Sahajiyā Tantric teachings, more orthodox Gauḍīya Vaiṣṇava theology, a strong element of Sufism, and even a degree of Christian influence. Second, on the social level, the Kartābhajās bring together members of all classes and social factions, rejecting caste distinctions and proclaiming the divinity of all human beings. And third, on the level of gender, the Kartābhajās also offered a new social space in which men and women could mix freely, even providing new opportunities for women in roles of spiritual authority. The result is a rather ingenious religious fusion—or "subversive bricolage," to borrow a phrase of Jean Comaroff[1]—which skillfully adapts and reconfigures elements from a wide range of sources. In de Certeau's terms, it is the result of a kind of "poaching" or pilfering by poor lower-class consumers in a dominated religious market.[2]

As a kind of poaching, however, this bricolage also demanded subtle use of the tactics of secrecy. In the previous chapter, we examined the Kartābhajās' key strategy of *esoteric hermeneutics*—their rereading of the scriptures and narratives of the mainstream Vaiṣṇava tradition, which at the same time gives them a new, secret interpretation. In this chapter, we explore two additional strategies. First, secrecy functions as a *tactic of appropriation*. If the Kartābhajās are able to draw on or "steal" elements from a variety of religious traditions, this is because all these religions only appear to be separate when seen from the "exoteric," outward, or orthodox point of view. On the inner or esoteric level (known only to the Kartābhajā initiate), they are in fact all one, all the same "Religion of Truth" or "Religion of Man."[3] Second, secrecy operates as a key *social strategy* or a way of life: The Kartābhajā social ideal involves a basic double norm, which allows the initiate to live a perfectly conventional, worldly life in conformity with the laws of exoteric society, while at the same time leading a secret inner life, explicitly violating the laws of caste, gender, and purity that govern mainstream society.

To understand the rich bricolage of the Kartābhajās, however, we must also place it in relation to the changing ideals taking place among the upper classes of nineteenth-century Calcutta. Even as the great reform movements of the "Bengal Renaissance," such as the Brāhmo Sabhā led by Rammohun Roy, were spreading among the wealthy educated classes of the city, the Kartābhajās and other lower-class sects were engaged in their own kinds of social and religious "reforms." Not unlike the Brāhmos, they too criticized polytheism and idolatry, offered new roles for women, fought the rigidities of caste, and proposed a universal, nonsectarian religion. Hence we find some authors praising Dulālcāṅd as a kind of "Folk Rammohun"—a lower-class reflection of the *bhadralok* reformer.[4] The impetus for the Kartābhajās and other sects, however, was really quite different than that of the Brāhmos. If the upper-class reforms were motivated by the confrontation with Western education, science, and capitalism, the lower-class sects were motivated primarily by the effects of social dislocation, poverty, and the search for meaning amidst the often alienating world of colonial Bengal.

Indeed, we might say that the Kartābhajās' Religion of Man represents a kind of "popularized Tantra"—a new transformation within the Sahajiyā tradition which invests many older Tantric ideals with broader social implications in the changing context of colonial Bengal. The concept of *Sahaja* itself—the inborn or innate path to liberation—becomes for the Kartābhajās the "simple" path for the poor, an easy religion for the downtrodden lower classes. So, too, the Tantric ideals of the divinity of man and the body, freedom from caste, and new roles for women, all took on larger social implications as the Kartābhajās grew from a small "obscure religious cult" to one of the most powerful movements of Bengal. The Kartābhajās offered, in short, a new kind of identity, status, and symbolic capital—though perhaps a kind of stolen or "counterfeit capital," based on a range of elements adapted from other sources.[5]

However, if it is true that the Kartābhajā path offered new sources of status and prestige for those on the margins of Bengali society, it seems no less true that it also opened up new possibilities for exploitation. Despite its ideals of egalitarianism, the Kartābhajā tradition was clearly internally divided by its own inequities and asymmetrical hierarchies. This ambivalence becomes even more acute in the controversial status of women. If the female Kartābhajā can be "empowered" or given divine authority as a guru or spiritual leader, she may also be manipulated as a source of easy income or as a sexual partner in esoteric ritual. Hence if the Kartābhajās proclaim themselves a new "Mānuṣer Dharma," it remains unclear whether this is best understood as a "Religion of Humanity," in the most universal sense, a "Religion of Man," in which it is primarily males who hold the power, or the "Religion of *a* Man," in which one particular individual, or small group of individuals, are revered as divine.

The Subversive Bricolage of the Kartābhajā Path: Shopping in the Spiritual Marketplace of Colonial Bengal

> Users make (*bricolent*) innumerable and infinitesimal transformations of and within the dominant cultural economy in order to adapt it to their own interests and their own rules. (Michel de Certeau, *The Practice of Everyday Life*)

Precisely because they are part of an esoteric tradition, the Kartābhajās are able to manipulate selected elements from a variety of mainstream or "exoteric" traditions, fusing them into new "secret tradition" which transcends and surpasses them. "The conflict between religions (Hindus, Muslim, Christian, etc.) is only the conventional or exoteric level of truth (*vyavahārik*)," Manulāl Miśra explains, "The *Sahaja Dharma* is the religion of liberation" (STP 76). Just as the center of a circle unites all the points of the periphery, so too, the innermost, hidden core of esoteric Truth—the *Sahaja Dharma*—unites and underlies all the exoteric religions of Hinduism, Christianity, or Islam (STP 79).

However, because of its confusing and seemingly chaotic mixture of elements, the Kartābhajā tradition has often been dubbed a kind of "syncretism," an accidental, unconscious mishmash of various ideas floating around nineteenth-century Bengal.[6] As I wish to argue, however, this is by no means a simple haphazard melange but, in fact, an ingenious appropriation of elements from many different traditions. Rather than "syncretism"—which I believe is a misleading, ambiguous, and in most cases entirely inaccurate term[7]—I prefer to speak of *strategic appropriation* and *conscious manipulation* in the construction of the Kartābhajā faith. Above all, I wish to emphasize the real creative ingenuity by which the Kartābhajās have "stolen" and reinterpreted various elements from each of these traditions. Rather than the product of unconscious assimilation, this is more like what de Certeau calls the "tactics of consumption," by which the dominated classes poach upon the dominant order. "The social order constrains and oppresses the people, but at the same time offers them resources to fight against those constraints. . . . Yet the everyday culture of the oppressed takes the signs of that which oppresses them and uses them for its own purposes. Popular creativity . . . is a creativity of practice as bricolage."[8] Let us now examine the elements of the Kartābhajās' rich bricolage in more detail.

The Sahaja Path: An "Easy" Religion for the Poor

One must understand lower class religion (*nicu dharma bujhiyā sujhiyā loite habe*).
(Mint Saying [*Ṭyāṅkśālī Bol*], no. 62—STP 62; III.62)

Although there is a wide range of opinion as to which of the many elements in this bricolage (Vaiṣṇava, Tantric, Sahajiyā, Sufi, Bāul, etc.) is the most important,[9] the majority of scholars seem to agree that the esoteric tradition of Vaiṣṇava-Sahajiyā Tantra is its underlying basis. In fact, the Kartābhajās may well be regarded as the most important later branch of the Sahajiyā tradition that survived in colonial Bengal: "Among the sects spawned by the Sahajiyās, the Kartābhajās are to be mentioned first and foremost. In terms of age, it is also the oldest."[10] Not only are the songs of the *Bhāver Gīta* saturated with Sahajiyā philosophical concepts (the divinity of Man, the mystery of the human body, the quest for the *Sahaja Mānuṣa*), but the Kartābhajās identify themselves as essentially *Sahajayāna*: a natural, innate, spontaneous religion (*sahaja-dharma*). The *Bhāver Gīta* sings:

There is no division between human beings.
So brother, why is there sorrow in this land?
Look and understand: In *Sahaja,* in their own Self nature,
the infinite forms in every land,
all the activities of human beings,
the expanse of all events—all things dwell [in this very *Sahaja*].
Good and bad desires
are equally erroneous, and go astray from the lawful path.
Every human heart is rich.
It is not possible in separate forms,
for it is eternally conceived within the every man and woman [*nityā nārī puruṣe*]
(BG 32; II.57)

Like the older Sahajiyā tradition, moreover, the Kartābhajās embody a certain "spirit of protest and criticism," rejecting the authority of the Vedas and all other sacred scriptures, and praising the human body itself as the supreme vehicle of truth (BG 32–3; II.58–9):

There are so many views in the Tantras and Vedānta,
and as may in the Āgamas and Nigamas—
they're all delusions, and whoever abandons them will find peace! (BG 35; II.60)

But at the same time, the Kartābhajās also represent a profound transformation of the Sahajiyā tradition within a changing historical context. For the most part, as Dimock points out, the Vaiṣṇava-Sahajiyās of the seventeenth and eighteenth centuries had not been particularly concerned with the affairs of the outer social world; Sahajiyā *sādhanā* may have been "subversive" within the realm of secret ritual, but it had little impact in the exoteric world; "the Sahajiyā was an esoteric school. Its deviation was not socially visible."[11] The Kartābhajās, on the other hand, appear to be far more socially conscious than most Sahajiyā traditions. Indeed, they have newly adapted and reinterpreted the Tantric concept of *Sahaja* itself, deliberately playing on its dual sense as both *innate* or *inborn*—the supreme reality dwelling within every human body—and as *simple* or *easy*—a "Simple Religion for the Poor" or an "easy" path for the downtrodden lower classes. Caitanya himself, we have seen, is said to have become reincarnate in the form of Āulcāṅd in order to reveal this "simple religion" (*sahaja dharma*) for the poorer lower orders who had been neglected by the orthodox Vaiṣṇava community. With the revelation of the Kartābhajā path, as Manulāl Miśra explains, the most secret practices of the Sahajiyā tradition have become accessible to the weak and the oppressed: "In His desire to give a taste of this teaching to men of little intelligence, he revealed the deepest secrets of practice very briefly and in simple language. . . . The fact that such a difficult task can be achieved by poor men like us is remarkable indeed!"[12]

So, too, the Kartābhajās have transformed a variety of other Tantric concepts—the divinity of the human body, the rejection of caste, the criticism of the Vedas and Brahminical authority, the offer of new roles to women and lower classes—giving them markedly more socially conscious implications. As Debendranāth De suggests, the older Sahajiyā ideals have now "appeared in a new and more accessible form."[13] The *Bhāver Gīta* sings:

Straightway, that [*Sahaja*] Man who is compassionate to the Poor
dispels all dangers with the gift of fearlessness.
The pleasures and sufferings of *karma* are destroyed
The difficult path has become easily accessible to the lowly folk.
. . . Brother, abandon all your wealth and stand waiting upon the path;
For at the Festival of the Poor, all troubles are dispelled!
. . . At the sight of these Poor Men, raise your two hands,
immersed in bliss, crying "Alas, Poor Men!" (BG 97; II.73)

Yet rather ironically, as we will see later, this "democratic" or universalist ideal was not always played out in actual practice within the Kartābhajās' own, often quite asymmetrical and unegalitarian, spiritual hierarchy.

Concealed in the Secret Vṛndāvana: Vaiṣṇava Orthodoxy and Sahajiyā Heterodoxy

While deeply rooted in the esoteric traditions of Sahajiyā Tantra, the Kartābhajās also skillfully appropriated many elements of the more "orthodox" Vaiṣṇava tradition. To legitimate their new, often highly unorthodox, tradition, and to establish their own kind of sacred "metanarrative" or mythistory, they made a number of bold claims on the authority of the Gauḍīya Vaiṣṇavas. As Dimock suggests, this kind of duplicity or "schizoid identity" had long be an integral part of the Vaiṣṇava-Sahajiyā school. The Sahajiyā disciple had to cultivate the outward appearance of an orthodox Vaiṣṇava, in conformity with the traditional laws of mainstream society and religion: "The Vaiṣṇava self. . . . is the official self. . . . The unofficial self is the Sahajiyā self, which . . . goes beyond all normal standards."[14]

However, born as they were within a particularly sensitive social climate, the Kartābhajās appear to have gone to even greater lengths (though never very successfully) to don the outer garb of the more respectable Vaiṣṇava tradition. Not only was Āulcāṅd identified as the "secret" Caitanya (BG 410–11; II.42–43) and his initial disciples with the six Gosvāmis and other Vaiṣṇava leaders, but, particularly in the later Kartābhajā tradition, we find an increasing number of Vaiṣṇava elements which have a suspiciously artificial and "tacked on" appearance. The last portion of the *Bhāver Gīta* itself is a rather uncharacteristically (for this text) readable and largely innocuous section titled "Kṛṣṇa Līlā" (BG 442ff.; II.90ff.). Unlike the majority of the Kartābhajā songs, as Debendranāth De has argued, those of the *Kṛṣṇa Līlā* are not only unusually intelligible and far less cryptic but also markedly more conservative in their theology and symbolism, employing standard language borrowed from the long tradition of Gauḍīya Vaiṣṇava poetry.[15] But as Bhaṭṭācārya argues, even though the Kartābhajās made various efforts to give themselves a kind of mainstream Vaiṣṇava veneer, the deeper presence of Tantric and Bāul elements continually pokes through to the surface:

> Since its first inception, there was an attempt to give this movement an outward cover of Hindu orthodoxy. In the songs of the *Bhāver Gīta* . . . there is an effort to create the outer appearance of the Vaiṣṇava and Hindu traditions by mentioning Brahmā, Kālī, Rāma, Caitanya, Nityānanda, etc. But still within these verses one can easily see many Bāul and Tantric ideas such as . . . the worship of Man . . . yogic practices, the concept of "the woman becoming a Hijṛā, the man a eunuch," etc.[16]

Even as early as 1828, H. H. Wilson had observed the rather effective political strategy behind the Kartābhajās' theological maneuvers. This strategy allowed them to appropriate much of the power and following of the orthodox Vaiṣṇava tradition while subverting and undermining this tradition with their own rather unorthodox teachings: "The innovation is . . . an artful encroachment upon the authority of the old hereditary teachers or Gosains and an attempt to invest a new family with spiritual power. The attempt has been so far successful that it gave affluence and celebrity to the founder."[17]

The Religion of "Truth:" Kartābhajā as a "Meta-Religion" or "Infra-Religion," at Once Transcending and Infiltrating Both Hinduism and Islam

Emerging as they did at a critical moment of historical change, when both traditional Hindu and Muslim ruling powers were being displaced by the British Company, the Kartābhajās also represents an explicit attempt to unite both Hindus and Muslims under a single more generic title: the "Religion of Truth" (*Satya Dharma*) or Religion of Man. Because virtually all past research on the Kartābhajās has been conducted by West Bengali, largely Hindu scholars, the Islamic element, largely drawn from the Muslim regions of East Bengal, has long been the most neglected and misunderstood side of the Kartābhajā tradition. It is, however, obvious and undeniable from the very beginning. Not only was Āulcāṅd himself a kind of weird fusion of Hindu and Muslim—none other than Śrī Caitanya in the disguise of a Sufi Fakir—but also the Kartābhajās have from the very start promoted themselves as a religion open to both Hindus and Muslims: "Hindus and Muslims have all come from one God; his essence is equal within every body; if everyone has been born in one and the same place, how can we call anyone 'true' or 'false'?"[18] In fact, many have suggested that the central emphasis on "Truth" (Satya) and the idea of the Kartābhajā path as the "Religion of Truth" may well be borrowed from the Muslim concept of *al' Haq*, God as Supreme Truth.

> Truth is Truth, and lying and swindling is untruth [*hakke hak nā hakke ṭhakaṭhaki*]
> If one doesn't undertand this, he'll be drowned in troubles again and again!
> (BG 71)

It is equally likely, however, that this emphasis on "Truth" was influenced by the cult of Satya Pīr or Satya Nārāyaṇa, a nonsectarian tradition that had spread throughout both the Hindu and Muslim communities of Bengal since at least the sixteenth century and which became especially popular during the eighteenth century.[19]

Particularly in their practice and spiritual life, moreover, the Kartābhajās adopted a number of Sufi and Muslim elements. Their weekly gatherings, for example, are on Friday, the traditional Muslim holy day, and also closely resemble more esoteric weekly gathering or *majlis* of the Sufi orders. Their central emphasis on the recitation of the Name of God reflects not only earlier Vaiṣṇava influence but also the practice of *ḍhikṛ* or invocation of the Name of Allah in the Sufi tradition. The songs of the *Bhāver Gīta* are peppered throughout with Sufi mystical and metaphysical terms—dervishes and fakirs (BG 276), the metaphysics of the divine Light (*nur*) of God, the description of Āulcāṅd as "*Ādam Bāorā*" or the "Mad Adam" (BG 229), and so on. In fact, the highest stage of ecstasy and liberating bliss at the peak of the Kartābhajā path, the stage of "extinction" or cessation (*nivṛtti*), is commonly described using classic Sufi language and imagery—the imagery of annihilation (*fanā*) of the self in God. According to two of the Kartābhajās' Mint Sayings, which are both classic Sufi phrases: "I am not; you are not; He [i.e., God] is." And "If one dies before he dies, he never dies."[20]

Hence, on the more exoteric level, the Kartābhajā path might be called a kind of "*metareligion*"—an avowedly universal path that appealed to both Hindu and Muslim devotees, while claiming to transcend all sectarian differences. On the esoteric level, however, it also served as a kind of "*infrareligion:*" it allowed these disciples to lead an outward, public life as orthodox Hindus or Muslims, while secretly following the path of the Kartābhajās in the closed realm of privacy. With their key distinction between the exoteric and esoteric identities—the *vyavahārik* or conventional self and the *paramārthik* or supremely liberated self—the Kartābhajās could live a dual life, outwardly pious Muslims or Hindus while inwardly disciples of the Kartā: "Outwardly they present themselves as Hindu or Muslim. . . . But the inner practices of this sect are followed in secrecy."[21]

In sum, just as the mad fakir Āulcāṅd had appeared precisely at the time of the Battle of Plassey to predict the downfall of the Muslims and the triumph of the Foreigners (STP 3–6), and just as the foreign Company had arrived to take the place of indigenous Hindu and Muslim rule, so, too, the "new Company" of the Kartābhajās had arrived to offer a new alternative to traditional, exoteric Hinduism and Islam.

The Man of the Heart: The Divinity of Man and the Human Body

This Kali yuga has been blessed
In the Kali yuga Man is the Avatār
Having attained the human body,
can't you recognize this Man?
Look and consider—without Man, there is no other path. (song of Bāṅkācāṅd;
SE IV.18)

Like most earlier Sahajiyā and other Tantric traditions, the Kartābhajās believe that the supreme reality, the ultimate bliss of Sahaja, dwells within all things and forms of the universe—including every human being and every human body. Indeed, among all the creatures of the universe, the human being (*Mānuṣa*) is the most perfect image and realization of the divine: "Hear this law," sings the *Bhāver Gīta*, "Man is supreme" (BG 48; II.68). As one outspoken devotee, Babu Gopal Krishna Pal explained to the *Bengal District Gazetteer* in 1910, "The Kartābhajā sect . . . is a man-worshipping sect, and its object is to call forth the latent divinity in man.

This it seeks to accomplish, not by renouncing the world . . . as transitory and illusive, but by going through life's struggles manfully and heroically."[22] If the human being is the noblest creature in the universe, the image of God on earth, so too, the human body is its the supreme receptacle of Sahaja and the epitome of the universe, a microcosm reflecting all the myriad forms of the macrocosm. Like most other Tantric schools of Bengal, the Kartābhajās imagine the body to be a vast and elaborate "interior landscape," with its own mountains and rivers, oceans and islands:

All things and all events
lie within the microcosm of the human body;
Whatever is or will be lies within the Self-Nature (BG 33; II.59).

Sahaja is of the human caste;
It dwells in the *Sahaja* land.
Know, in a hint [*ābhāse*] what its nature is:
Revealing this publicly is impossible, but a taste of it is possible:
Its origin lies within the body itself! (BG 48; II.68)

As such, the path to liberation does not lie in external rituals, Vedic injunctions, or philosophical speculation; rather, it lies within the body and through physical *sādhana*, which is the most expedient means to salvation. "The natural faculties are not destroyed; rather one must seek the supreme reality in a natural, easy way (*sahaje*), within one's own nature. The path to the supreme truth is the physical method of Tantric Yoga."[23]

Dwelling within the innermost secret core of every human body, the Supreme Reality of Sahaja takes the mysterious form of the "Man of the Heart" or *Maner Mānuṣa*. Of course, ever since Rabindranath Tagore first popularized the songs of the great Bāul Lālan Shāh in the early twentieth century, the concept of the "Man of the Heart" has become well known throughout both Bengali and Western scholarship.[24] Moreover, most authors have assumed, that this is a very ancient concept, dating back to the earliest Sahajiyā authors of medieval Bengal. Historically, however, there is no evidence that the precise term *Maner Mānuṣa* was ever used prior to the nineteenth century. Although many Sahajiyā texts had employed terms such as the *Sahaja Mānuṣa,* or the innate, spontaneous Self,[25] the concept of the *Maner Mānuṣa* which would later become so famous in the songs of Lālan seems to have made its first known literary appearance in the Kartābhajā songs (BG 240–3 II.77–8; BG[1882] 135ff.).

At least one author, Tushar Chatterjee, has even argued that Lālan's well-known image of the *Maner Mānuṣa* is itself pilfered from the songs of Lālśaśī.[26] There are, moreover, popular legends that Lālan used to go to the Kartābhajā festival in Ghoshpara, as well as a number of songs attributed (probably falsely) to Lālan which praise Āulcāṅd and the wonders of Ghoshpara. For example, "At the Ghoshpara Melā there's no consideration of caste; I can find the Man of the

Heart in Ghoshpara, the secret Vṛndāvana!"[27] Although Chatterjee's claims are clearly exaggerated, and although there is no way of proving that Lālan actually stole the idea from the Kartābhajās, it does appear that the 1870 edition of the *Kartābhajār Gitāvalī* is the oldest known text in which the phrase *Maner Mānuṣa* first occurs. [28]

But in any case, both the BG and Lālan share the same frustration in their quest for the Man of the Heart, complaining how difficult it is to find or even speak of this mysterious Person who is at once the most intimate companion and the most estranged "other" to oneself;

What use is there in trying to bring that Man of the Heart outside?
Always eternally happy, united with the Self, he remains seated within the heart.
So why now would he come out?
. . . O my mind, who knows what of sort are the habits of the Man of the
  Heart?
And if one could know them, could he express their form?
The mind cannot know Him; for [only] the beauty of His outward form is
  known.
As long as life remains in my body, I fear to speak of Him—
I saw Him in a dream, and my heart was rent! (BG 243; II.80)[29]

Yet rather strikingly, unlike the songs of either the earlier Sahajiyās or the later Bāuls, the Kartābhajā songs regularly describe this man of the heart, or Sahaja Man, using language borrowed from the world of business, commerce, and economics. And they do so in a rather paradoxical, seemingly contradictory way. The *Maner Mānuṣa* is sometimes depicted as a wealthy merchant or king, and sometimes as a wretched beggar or a poor man. In some songs, for example, he is described as the "Kartā" or owner of a merchant ship,[30] or as the "rich man" (*dhanī lok*) who has set up his office and now engages in merchant trade:

The Sahaja Man has gone and built his Office [*kuṭhi*] in this Land,
. . . You heard the news of this Rich Man [*dhanī lok*] from someone or other,
That's why now, at every moment, your heart longs to see him.
That Sahaja Man easily comes to this Sahaja land and engages in business.
. . . Supplied with *Rasa*, that Man has come to this land and engages in debt and
  profit.
Lālśaśī says "that Man has come and engages in debt and profit!" (BG 309;
  II.72)

In other songs, however, this *Maner Mānuṣa* or *Sahaja Mānuṣa* appears (like Āulcāṅd) as a pathetic beggar, wearing rags, as the "lowliest of the low," or as the "great poor God" (*Gorib Bidhātā*); he has come to show his compassion to the poor, wretched, lowly men, revealing himself openly amidst the Festival of the Poor (*kāṅgāler melā*) (BG 112; II.10):

Just look—when that Sahaja Mānuṣa comes here,
if anyone reviles him, He embraces them!
If anyone offends Him, He simply speaks and laughs!
Come on brother, let's go bring Him here, who wears the garb of a Poor Man,
as if He had no wealth or self interest or power in hand!
Who can forbid Him from begging for alms?
. . . He dwells within the lotus of the Heart, the fountain of nectar!
(BG 272; II.69)

However, this apparent contradiction between the Maner Mānuṣa as both a great "rich man" and a "poor beggar" it is probably not accidental: it is the same paradox at the heart of the Poor Company itself—a "platoon of the Poor" who would, at the same time, hail themselves as the proprietors of the Forty worlds and the true "Rulers of the Land." And it is the same ironic paradox of a collective of poverty stricken lower classes, whose Kartā would eventually became one of the wealthiest and most powerful sectarian leaders of the nineteenth century.

The Worship of the Master (or "Big-Boss"): God Made Flesh

If the Kartābhajās share the more general Tantric belief in the divinity of the human being and the physical body, they are unique in their belief that one human being in particular—the Kartā or Master—is the supreme incarnation of the divinity in human form. The Kartā is Āulcāṅd reborn; thus he is also Śrī Caitanya, Lord Kṛṣṇa, and the supreme Godhead in the flesh. Moreover, the use of the term "Kartā" to refer to the supreme Divinity is extremely noteworthy here and has very few precedents in earlier in Bengali religious literature. Derived from the Sanskrit root *kṛ*, to make or do, and thus denoting an "agent," creator, or doer, the term "Kartā" is generally rather secular. It typically refers to the head of a business or family—a "master or boss." And particularly in the case of early nineteenth-century Calcutta, the term "Kartā" had clear economic implications, referring specifically to the "Owner" or "Boss" of a business or mercantile office.[31] This is all the more plausible because, as we see in detail in chapter 7, the Kartābhajā sect was organized much like a "business," with its own *gadis* (mercantile office or throne), complex economic hierarchy, and regular systems of taxation. In fact, this image of the Kartā as a Boss or proprietor, complete with a business office and an account book for recording sins, recurs throughout the Kartābhajā songs and prayers. Consider, for example, the following "Friday Song," which is one of the most common songs used at every weekly gathering:

Pardon my sins, Lord—
Oh such delusion from birth to death!
. . . How many millions are my sins!

when one starts recording my delusions in the account book,
there's no limit to them!
Now, having become a poor man, I run after you without fear!
. . . I am the Bailiff [*bellik*], and You are the Proprietor [*Mālik*] of everything;
I say, "Yes," and You make it so.
Take and control all my wealth, my self-will, my strength.
Save me, in your record office [*sereste,* typically a business office],
from the guns of the slanderers! (BG 3; II.95)

Drawing much of the membership from the poor working classes and petty shopkeepers in the marketplace of Calcutta, the Kartābhajās quite naturally borrowed the image of the Kartā as Boss or Proprietor to describe the leader of their own poor company. Seated in the alternative "office" (*gadi*) of Ghoshpara, outside the tumult of Calcutta, the Kartā offered an alternative kind of authority, beyond the Māliks and bosses of the city (though one which demanded its own kinds of obedience and financial burdens; see chapter 7).

The Kartā and the Christ:
Probable Christian Elements in the Kartābhajā Bricolage

Like the Christian missionaries, [the Kartābhajās] have tried to spread their religion with various devices and strategies. (Akṣaykumār Datta, *Tattvabodhinī,* no. 81, 12 Baisakh, 1772 Śaka [1850])

More than a few authors have noticed that the doctrine of the Kartā as "God incarnate" bears some rather suspicious resemblance to Christian theology. As Sukumār Sen points out, the ideal of the Kartā may well reflect the influence of Christian missionary teachings, which were rapidly circulating throughout colonial Bengal.[32] Since the late eighteenth century, the Baptist Missionary Society had begun to work industriously in the Bengal area, spreading the message of the Savior, the Son of God, at about the same time that Rāmśaraṇ Pāl began to declare himself God incarnate. The famous Scottish missionary, Alexander Duff, even established a Christian school at the very entrance to Ghoshpara village, which must have had more than a little impact upon the evolution of the Kartābhajā tradition. One of the primary reasons for the mass conversions of Kartābhajā devotees to Christianity in the early nineteenth century, as Geoffrey Oddie argues, was precisely because of the many obvious similarities between the two religions.[33] We know, moreover, that Dulālcāṅd had conversations and even debates with the Baptist Missionaries, whom he regarded as their competitors in the "marketplace of souls." According to the *Calcutta Review*, Marshman and Carey visited Dulāl in 1802 and debated various theological issues with him, arguing the finer points of pantheism.[34]

It seems equally likely, moreover, that the Kartābhajās quickly absorbed and adapted certain other Christian ideas. Most notably, they adopted a system of "ten commandments" which they likely at least in part pilfered from their Christian neighbors. These commandments consist of three forbidden acts pertaining to the body (sleeping with another man's wife, stealing, or coveting another's things), three mental prohibitions (those things which were forbidden for the body, now on the mental level of even thinking such things), and four forbidden things relating to speech (lying, harsh words, talking too much, and improper words). Although these commandments do not correspond precisely to the Christian commandments, the fact that there are ten is, as many scholars have noted, rather suspicious.[35] Still more strikingly, Manulāl Miśra's collection of the "Mint Sayings" (*ṭyāṅkśālī bol*), compiled in the early twentieth century, contains an alternative list of commandments, which reflect even more Christian influence: Now the Kartābhajā is further enjoined to "honor his father and mother" and to "love his neighbor": "The laws of the Religion of Truth: speak the truth; do not speak falsehood. One must not kill. One must not steal. Honor your father and mother. Love your neighbor. Do not commit adultery. Do not eat remnants of food. Do not become intoxicated. Do not eat meat" (STP 68; III.151–59). Even most Kartābhajā devotees freely acknowledge the resemblance between their ten laws and the Bible's Ten Commandments. "He established ten laws, extending his power over the hearts and bodies of his devotees," Advaita Candra Dās explains, "These laws are written in close similarity to the Bible's Ten Commandments. Thus, the Christian preachers could view the newly founded Kartābhajā religion with the eyes of faith."[36]

In addition to their ten commandments, the Kartābhajās also developed a curious practice of repentance and confession of sin—known as the Dāyika Majlis (from *dāy*, debt or mortgage)—which also bears a suspicious resemblance to the Christian practice. Rather significantly, however, a key part of the atonement for one's sins is the payment of a "fine" or "mortgage fee" in order to attain full forgiveness: "The Kartābhajās have a practice called the Dāyika Majlis, which is like the Christians' 'Confession' . . . Many devotees meet together and sing Satī Mā's or Dulālcāṅd's name. . . . At the end of the service everyone looks in the direction of the confessor. The confessor has to a pay a fine of 5 1/2 annas for his sins. . . . Then his heart is made clean."[37]

At least some of Dulālcāṅd's own disciples, moreover, quickly made the connection between the Kartābhajā and Christian religions. Already by the early nineteenth century, a sect called the Guru-Satyas or Satya-Gurus had splintered off from the main body of the Kartābhajās, settling in East Bengal in the regions of Bakarganj, Khulna, and the Sundarbans and preaching an explicit synthesis of Kartābhajā and Christian faiths. For the Guru Satyas, Dulālcāṅd is identified with Christ himself, while the divine Mother, Satī Mā, becomes the Virgin Mary, Mother of God. As Henry Beveridge described them in 1876: "The Sayta Guru . . . originated about 1804 with a native who read the Gospel narrative and had some personal intercourse with Serampore Missionaries. Giving himself out to be a modern incarnation of Jesus Christ, and able to work miracles, he succeeded in obtaining a number of followers."[38] Indeed, the recently deceased Kartā, Satyaśiva Pāl himself, suggests that

Dulālcāṅd had been so moved by his conversations with the Baptist Missionaries that he decided to establish a new branch of the tradition, as a deliberate fusion of Christian and Kartābhajā belief: "Dulālcāṅd was closely associated with the missionaries of Serampore. After his debates with Marshman and Carey in 1802, he was inspired by Christianity and established the Gurusatya sect."[39]

A similar fusion of Kartā and Christ appears in the writings of one of the most famous of all Kartābhajā devotees—Jayanārāyaṇ Ghoṣāl, the affluent Zamindār of Bhukailas, who is widely believed to have been a friend of Dulālcāṅd himself.[40] In the history of Bengali literature, he is best known as the author of the longest Kṛṣṇalīlā poem of Bengal, the *Karuṇānidhānavilās* (1815). Herein, Jayanārāyaṇ offers a prophecy for a new age, in which a series of Avatārs will arise and join together to promote a new, universal religion. Together with the names of Jesus Christ, Kabīr, and Nanak, we find the first Kartā, Rāmśaraṇ Pāl, described as one of these great *avatārs*. Representing the "East," Rāmśaraṇ will unite with Christ, the divine Son from the West, in a global wedding which gives birth to a new universal faith:

From the West, Icchamoni [Jesus]; from the north Kabīr, the virtuous one;
From the East Śrī Rāmśaraṇ.
. . . One named Rāmśaraṇ will come from the Eastern lands.
In the form of a Son, the Avatār will come from the West.
Let His Name be known as Jesus Christ.
From three countries, three paths will join.
They will all revere Jesus as the foremost;
Without Jesus there is no other means.[41]

Among many of the educated classes and progressive reformers in Calcutta, there had of course been similar attempts to achieve a synthesis or at least a reconciliation between Hindu and Christian ideals. As Kopf suggests, the presence of Christianity and the person of Christ posed a real dilemma for progressive, liberal-minded men such as Rāmmohun Roy. If the West was to be emulated for its scientific and economic superiority, should the Hindu simply convert to Christianity? "Rāmmohun was confronted by the central question as to whether India should follow Christ. . . or whether India should follow some Christ-like figure in her own tradition who represented the same principles."[42] Among the lower-class sects, however, this question was probably formulated quite differently. For the Kartābhajās, the missionaries were rivals and competitors in the spiritual marketplace—but so many "market brokers" (*dālāl*) holding some packets made in England.[43] Hence the best solution for the Kartābhajās was perhaps that of bricolage in de Certeau's sense—a pilfering or poaching from those in power, turning the tools of the dominant to the advantage of the weak.

But whatever its origins—whether economic or Christian—the ideal of the Kartā as God incarnate was to become a powerful and influential one in nineteenth-century Bengal. Rather strikingly, there is a good deal of evidence that the

Kartābhajā doctrine of the divinity of Man may have had a formative impact on the later divinization of the great Calcutta saint, Rāmakṛṣṇa, himself. We have already encountered the mysterious Vaiṣṇava pundit and secret Tāntrika, Vaiṣṇavacaraṇ, who took Rāmakṛṣṇa to meet many Tantric groups in the Calcutta area. A Kartābhajā master himself, Vaiṣṇavacaraṇ introduced Rāmakṛṣṇa to the belief that the guru is not only to be worshiped as divine (which most Tāntrikas believe) but is the Supreme Divinity embodied in *single historical individual*. As Kripal suggests, the notion of Rāmakṛṣṇa as a divine Avatār may itself have been appropriated from the Kartābhajās' Tantric belief in the divinity of Man, and specifically the divinity of *a* man, the supreme Kartā.

> Vaishnavacharan's truth that God could be worshipped . . . in man (or a man) was picked up by Ramakrishna and the disciples and transformed into something new. . . . His disciples, perhaps ignorant of the doctrine's Tantric origins in Vaishnavacharan's Kartābhajā community, listened enthusiastically as Ramakrishna told them about God's play as man. . . . *What began as a Tantric truth, rooted in the mystico-erotic practices of Vaishnavacharan's Kartābhajā sect, was transformed into a theology of incarnation.*[44]

Rāmakṛṣṇa's divine status, as God-made-Flesh, would also appear to have had an even more direct relation to Christianity. As Kripal suggests, it was at least in part an attempt to provide a kind of "Hindu answer to Christ"—a divine incarnation for a new Hinduism which could meet the challenge posed by the West.[45] Although Rāmakṛṣṇa would surely be the most famous and most successful of the various Hindu answers to Christ, it is likely that the Ghoshpara Kartā was one of the earliest and most original.

Rather remarkably, out of this seemingly chaotic mixture of diverse elements, the Kartābhajās were able to construct a relatively coherent—and, apparently, extremely successful—religious tradition, one especially well adapted to the shifting context of colonial Bengal. "Even today the Kartābhajās remain the most important among the folk religions," Cakravartī comments, "Such a religion, which could so intensely provoke the adherents of other faiths, must certainly have had something original about it."[46] If this is a bricolage, however, it is one with a keen subversive edge: for even as the Kartābhajās pilfer elements from each of these traditions, they also clearly distance themselves from and remain highly critical of all of them. If they legitimate themselves with elements adapted from mainstream Vaiṣṇavism, they also reject the orthodoxy of the Gauḍīya tradition, what they regard as its "Brahminization" or reintroduction of caste hierarchies, and they also clearly attacked and poked fun at the Vaiṣṇavas' excessive asceticism and denial of the body—indeed, those "so-called ascetics are nothing but lumps of flesh, given to dreams of coitus."[47] Likewise, if they appropriate elements of Islamic mysticism, they also reject the authority of the shariah and the Koran, and if they incorporate certain pieces of Christian faith, they also delight in making fun of the "missionary-brokers," with their "packets made in England." In short, this is much less a process of "syncretism" than one of (to use Roland Barthes's terms) "stolen language" or "robbery."[48]

The Janus-Faced Self: The Social Ideals and Secret Lives of the Kartābhajās

The secret offers . . . the possibility of a second world alongside the manifest world; and the latter is decisively influenced by the former. (Georg Simmel)

More than simply a tactic of religious appropriation and bricolage, however, the practice of secrecy also played a key role as a *social strategy* or a way of life; in fact, secrecy is the Kartābhajā's basic attitude to the world, by which he can preserve the outward facade of an exoteric, public social self while living the hidden life of an initiated disciple, freed from the usual burdens of caste and labor in the mainstream world. Ultimately, the *sādhaka* aims to cultivate two separate identities, two distinct selves, and to lead a kind of "double life." He must maintain a perfectly orthodox and acceptable identity in the mainstream social order and caste system while cultivating a secret inner Self, which is radically autonomous, spiritually powerful, and freed from all social norms. The former is called the *vyavahārik* (the conventional, social, or exoteric self), and the latter the *paramārthik*—the supreme Self, which is essentially divine, transcending all social laws or dualities of purity and impurity. According to one of the most often quoted Kartābhajā sayings, *lok madhye lokācār, sadgurur madhye ekācār;* translated loosely, this means "among conventional worldly society, follow conventional practices; but in the company of the True Guru, there is just one practice [namely, Kartābhajā *sādhanā*]."[49] Among common men or ordinary bestial souls (*jīva*), the Kartābhajā observes exoteric social conventions and religious institutions; according to the Mint Sayings, "If one is upright in political affairs, the Religion of Truth will be manifest" (STP 63). Yet in his inner private life, he is beyond all laws.

This duality between the esoteric and the exoteric had, of course, long existed among the Tantric traditions, particularly in the Sahajiyā schools of Bengal; maintaining both an "official" or social self and an unofficial, liberated Sahajiyā self, "the personality of the Vaiṣṇava-Sahajiyā was somewhat schizophrenic."[50] However, it would seem that the Kartābhajās articulated this duality with a clarity that is virtually unprecedented. The Kartābhajā strives to develop "a dual personality," to "live a secret life, without violating social norms" and thereby to "maintain the facade of a social man."[51]

> The Sahaja remains like one blind in the daylight, his eyes are opened in the night and his true life begins at night. In the daytime he has to do conventional things, to observe the rules of caste and pay respect to the Mallik, the Missionary and the Brahman . . . and abide by their orders. But he becomes the true man at night in the secret societies. . . . There they pay no heed to the rules of caste and social relations.[52]

Hence, the ideal Kartābhajā is neither an ascetic renunciant nor an ordinary, worldly, or "deluded householder" (*māyābik-gṛhastha*); rather, he is a dual character, a "householder-fakir," who simultaneously lives in the exoteric world of domestic life, business, or trade and in the esoteric world of Sahajiyā *sādhanā* and secret ritual.[53] Unlike the mad, wandering minstrels, the Bāuls—with whom they otherwise have a great deal in common—the Kartābhajās do not reject exoteric society, to live as nomadic outcasts. Rather, they "subvert it from within," as it were, by maintaining the outer facade of social conformity: "The Bāuls say they have died to the social world. Like the dead, they follow no further social duties. . . . But in the Kartābhajā sect, devotees don't deny social laws. Having become 'dead while living,' they continue to follow the worldly householder life with its rules and laws."[54] In this way, as Chatterjee comments, the Kartābhajās opened up a new "private sphere" in which those who were discontented or alienated from the dominant social order could find a new kind of identity and communal relationship, along with a new freedom and power: "[A] distinction has been innovated between the *vyavahārik*, the practical social aspect of the life of the devotee and the *paramārthik*, the supreme spiritual aspect. The former . . . marked the ground of inevitable compromise and surrender to the dominant norms of society and the latter the secret preserve of autonomy and self-assertion."[55]

The history of the Kartābhajā tradition is filled, even to this day, with many examples of such dual identities or split personalities. In my own experience among contemporary Kartābhajās in Bengal, I have encountered many such Janus-faced Mahāśays, who maintain two discrete selves: one public, exoteric, orthodox persona, and one secret Tantric persona. One of the two living claimants to the title of Kartā is a good example; outwardly he earns a respectable, though modest, living as an accountant in downtown Calcutta, even while, privately, he is a strong believer in the most esoteric Sahajiyā techniques, such as the practice of *parakīyā rasa*, kuṇḍalinī yoga, and various other secret rites.[56]

However, perhaps the most striking and most famous example of this dual identity is the mysterious figure of Vaiṣṇavacaraṇ—one of Rāmakṛṣṇa's most important gurus, who first introduced the saint to the "Kartābhajā bitches" and the innermost secrets of Tantric practice. Exoterically, in his outward public life, Vaiṣṇavacaraṇ was a highly respected pundit and a scholar of Vaiṣṇava scriptures, considered one of the greatest authorities on bhakti theology and highly regarded by Rāmakṛṣṇa and his followers:

> Among the pundits of Calcutta at that time, Vaiṣṇavacaraṇ was very well known. He recited the *Śrīmadbhāgavatam* in a beautiful voice, and was famous among the lower classes. That's why the master, Māthur Bābu and Brāhmaṇī all listened to his words. . . . His devotion to God and his subtle knowledge of the philosophical texts . . . had raised him up as a leader in the Vaiṣṇava community. . . . Whenever some religious question arose, the Vaiṣṇava community . . . depended on him.[57]

Yet esoterically, in his private life of ritual practice, Vaiṣṇavacaraṇ was also a Kartābhajā master, who was intimately familiar with the darkest and most secret Tantric circles of the Calcutta area, and who practiced *sādhanā* of "a very secret type." Above all, he was known to engage in the most difficult and dangerous sexual rites with female partners:

Taking a woman is their method of practice,
but how many men in a million are capable of such a practice?
The Master said this path is not easy—
The woman must become a hijṛā, the man must become a khojā,
then they will be Kartābhajās; otherwise, they will not.
At every step the practitioners fear falling.
Vaiṣṇavacaraṇ was a devotee of this path . . .
There were many male and female practitioners in that sect;
Very secretly they used to meet together
and practice, initiated by the master.
Vaiṣṇavacaraṇ practiced the erotic *bhāva*.[58]

In sum, Vaiṣṇavacaraṇ was an exemplar of the Kartābhajās' two-faced ideal of the true spiritual hero—a man who combines both the outward, orthodox and the inner-heterodox or Tantric personas in a single identity: "He seems to have lived two lives," Kripal comments, "Such a dual personality, incorporating both the right handed and the left handed traditions . . . made him an especially capable leader of a local Tantric sect, the Kartābhajās."[59]

A "Folk Rāmmohun Roy?" The Kartābhajās and the Social Reforms of Nineteenth-Century Calcutta

> Just see: there are thirty-six castes and four social classes; but He [the *Sahaja Mānuṣa*] accepts none of them.
> Among all castes, what caste is He? He bears the seal of Man. (BG 115; II.62)

In the context of early nineteenth-century Bengal, amidst the changing politics of early colonial rule and the rise of various indigenous reform movements, the teachings of the Kartābhajās represented a fairly radical and highly controversial social ideal. Not only did they accept men and women of all religious sects, but they also transgressed boundaries of caste and social status, freely inviting Brahmins to sit side by side with outcasts or share food with harlots and leather workers. Within the restricted sphere of esoteric ritual and ecstatic gatherings, at least, the Kartābhajā path opened the possibility of an alternative social field, beyond the usual burdens of caste, labor and trade. "What they offer," as Partha Chatterjee comments, "is a congregational space defined outside the boundaries of the dominant religious life, outside caste society or the injunctions of the shariah."[60]

According to the Kartābhajā teaching, all human beings are, in their innermost nature, identical with the absolute reality: the pure, natural, spontaneous reality of Sahaja. In Sahaja, there is no caste, no good or evil, no distinction between any of the forms or events of the phenomenal world: "There is no division between human beings. . . . The infinite forms in every land, all human beings . . . all things subsist within Sahaja, in the Self nature" (BG 32; II.59).

In this land no one is a stranger to anyone—
and look, in this land, 800, 000 districts are united!
   See all the subjects dwelling under the Emperor and the Minister;
in this world, everyone's filled with bliss!
They appear to be high or low class men
but this is only an illusion—they're all equal;
whether Hindu or non-Hindu, they all worship God.
   He who has good or bad reputation in the three worlds,
in this land, brother, receives no special treatment.
Look: united in Love,
all these animals, birds, men and living beings,
are overwhelmed with the ecstasy of Love! (BG 93; II.61)

Thus, as Gopal Krishna Pal explained to the *Bengal District Gazetteer* in 1910, that is why the Kartābhajā tradition is the true "Religion of Man": for it honors all human beings equally, and offers new status to the downtrodden and oppressed: "All members stand on the same footing and distinctions based on caste, wealth, etc. are not recognized, so that a person of however low a social status he may be . . . is accepted as the spiritual guide by those who are socially his superiors. . . . It is this highly liberal and democratic character of our sect . . . which induces outsiders to join our ranks . . . degraded humanity finds a cordial welcome and ready recognition."[61]

Even the more skeptical observers of the nineteenth century seem to have been impressed by this apparently humanistic and egalitarian side of the Kartābhajā tradition. Throughout the popular literature of nineteenth-century Calcutta, we read accounts of the famous Ghoshpara Melā, where men and women of all castes and religions gathered together to eat the same food. "We were amazed," the *Saṃvāda Prabhākara* reported in 1848, "For Brahmans, Śūdras and non-Hindu classes make no distinctions regarding their own food, and eat and drink here together; nowhere before had I seen or heard such a thing!"[62] As Cakravartī suggests, the frequent debate over the Kartābhajās among Calcutta's upper classes gives us clear testimony of just how radical and controversial a social movement they represented in nineteenth-century Bengal: "From all these descriptions, one gets a picture of social life in 19th century Bengal. . . . The Kartābhajā religion had created an unstoppable revolution amidst the caste-based social order."[63]

Indeed, the Kartābhajās have often been compared—both by contemporaneous observers and by modern scholars—with the social reforms taking place among Calcutta's upper classes, such as the Brāhmo Samāj. Not only did some of the most prominent reformers of Calcutta such as Śaśīpad Bābu, Nabīncandra, and Vijaykṛṣṇa take an active interest in the Kartābhajā faith, but, as Nabīncandra suggested, the Kartābhajās were perhaps the first men in Bengal to preach the harmony of religions and the brotherhood of mankind: "I could see that Rāmśaraṇ Pāl himself was the first one to feel the 'harmony of scriptures' or unity of religions. He taught that all religions have one foundaiton, and he was the first to spread the idea in this land, which is torn by sectarian divisions. All religions, all practices are true."[64]

In more recent years, some enthusiastic scholars such as Tushar Chatterjee have even hailed Dulālcāṅd as a kind of "folk Rāmmohun Roy." Even as Rāmmohun and his disciples were undertaking their reforms among the elite classes of Calcutta, combatting the evils of caste, championing the cause of women, calling for a "moral regeneration of society," the Kartābhajās of nearby Ghoshpara were spreading their own kind of universal, humanistic faith. Promising to grant admittance to "all sorts and descriptions of people. . . . for the worship of the Eternal, Unsearchable and Immutable Being,"[65] the Brāhmo Samāj was founded in 1828—at almost precisely the same time that the songs of the *Bhāver Gīta* began to circulate. Indeed, more than one scholar has tried to find evidence that Rāmmohun Roy himself not only knew of the Kartābhajās but in fact spent time in Ghoshpara and even drew some of the inspiration for his own religious and social reforms from the Kartābhajā ideals. Chatterjee even goes so far as to argue, not only that Rāmmohun was only very much interested in the Kartābhajās, but that the Kartābhajā religion, "with its noble humanistic teachings . . . should be regarded as the popular foundation for the Brāhmo religion of Rāmmohun."[66]

Now, there is no doubt that Rāmmohun was very interested in many diverse religious sects, and it is quite plausible that he might have visited Ghoshpara from time to time (his own guru Hariharānanda lived close to Ghoshpara, in Chakdoha village, and was undoubtedly familiar with the Kartābhajās).[67] However, the claim that the Brāhmo movement was inspired by the Kartābhajā teachings seems rather grossly exaggerated, to say the least. What seems far more likely, I would suggest, is that the elite reform movements such as the Brāhmo Samāj and the lower-class religious groups like the Kartābhajās reflect two parallel—but two different and widely divergent—responses to the changing environment of early colonial Calcutta, which appealed to two different strata of Bengali society. After all, as most recent authors have shown, the progressive ideals circulating among Calcutta's upper classes generally had little relevance to or impact on the ordinary lower classes of the Black Town: "The vast majority of the population of Calcutta was entirely unaffected by them," P. J. Marshall concludes.[68] Moreover, the inspiration for lower-class esoteric movements such as the Kartābhajās would seem to have been quite radically different from that of Rāmmohun. The Kartābhajās for the most part cared little for the new moral and educational standards of the Brāhmos, the rationalism and scientific advances of modern Europe, or the ideal of a "Golden Age" of a pure, monotheistic Hinduism embodied in the Vedas and Upaniṣads. On the contrary, they drew their inspiration from the rag-clad, wonder-working madman Āulcāṅd, from ecstatic devotional practices, and from the mystic teachings of the "Songs of Ecstasy": "Rāmmohun was a rationalist, and established his ideals on the rational religion of the Upaniṣads. . . . But the Kartābhajās became a tremendous irrational force, based on the miraculous deeds of Āulcāṅd. This was the complete opposite of Rāmmohun's religious ideal."[69]

The Kartābhajās, I suggest, represent not so much a lower-class version of the reforms taking place among Calcutta's upper classes but, rather, a kind of "darker underbelly" of colonial Calcutta, on the margins of the so-called Bengal Renaissance. Indeed, if recent scholars of the European history have begun to speak of a "Darker vision of the Renaissance," or even a "Counter-Renaissance"—that is, a continuing underworld of magical, occult and irrational forces which went against the grain of rationalism, science and social progress[70]—so too we might think of the Kartābhajās as a kind of "counter-Bengal-Renaissance," a mystical and esoteric cult made up of the poorer, uneducated lower classes who were largely untouched by the reforms of the upper classes. At the same time, however, we might also say that the Kartābhajās engaged in an ingenious appropriation of many of the ideas circulating among the wealthy, educated elite of Calcutta. Like the Brāhmo Samāj, they offered a universal, nonsectarian, caste-free Religion of Man, embodying more liberal attitudes toward women and lower classes. Yet the Kartābhajās also popularized and democratized these ideals, transferring them to the level of the lower classes, and taking them to more radical extremes:

> Beyond the . . . reforms of the respectable classes lay a sub-culture of popular religion which found adherents among the city's lower orders. . . . Running parallel to the bhadralok community's attempts to reform society, this underworld of plebeian religion often went far beyond these reforms.
>
> Brahmans, Sudras, and Yavanas sat together at the *Kartābhajā* festivals and ate the same food—a practice which even the bhadralok reformers did not follow publicly.[71]

The Religion of "Man" or the Religion of "a" Man? Guru Worship and the Status of the Mahāśay

O my Guru, you are the Guru of the World. (Mint Saying, no. 137—STP 64; III.137)

From its very origins, it would seem, there has been a certain tension and basic ambivalence at the heart of the Kartābhajā tradition. On the one hand, there is the ideal of the unity of humankind, the presence of the Supreme reality within every human body, the freedom from caste and class; on the other hand, there is the worship of a single human body—the Kartā—as God Incarnate, and the worship of a small set of gurus, the Mahāśays, as embodied divinities, worthy of supreme adoration. According to the root mantra given to every Kartābhajā initiate: "O Lord, at your pleasure I walk and speak; what you cause me to speak, I speak; whatever you give me I eat; Without you I could not remain even a moment. The Guru is truth, and falsehood is sorrow."[72] Or, as said in another Kartābhajā song:

The Guru is the root of the primordial tree
he pervades the three worlds
worms and insects, the dead and the living
there is no place without him.[73]

A variety of observers—both Bengali and European—have noted this seeming contradiction. The respected folklorist Sudhīr Cakravartī, for example, describes his own encounter in Ghoshpara with a middle-age Mahāśay named Trailokya Mahanta. Surrounded by fawning female disciples, who waited on his every desire and worshipped him as a living divinity, Trailokya appeared to feel quite deserving of his own god-like status: "First one disciple poured water on Mahanta's head with a gesture of reverence and combed his hair, and then ran oil through his top-knot. Then she wiped the sweat off his face with a cloth and fanned him. . . . I had never seen such a thing before in my life!"[74] As Trailokya explained, "the relation of Guru to disciple is truly like that of man to woman" (i.e., like the relation of the husband and lord of the household to his subservient and obedient wife, who worships him as the "Kartā" [master] and "deity" of the household).

In his historical novel about the Kartābhajās, the famous Bengali novelist Gajendra Kumār Mitra offers a wonderful description of this ambivalence and seeming contradiction within the tradition. As Nistāriṇī—the middle-age wife of a Kartābhajā disciple—bitterly complains, it seems that in this religion, only one "man" can truly be called a "Man" (*Mānuṣa*): "These people seemed to give a different meaning to the word *Mānuṣa*. Previously, Nistāriṇī had understood by *Mānuṣa* a two legged being who could speak, who held a job, who cooked and ate; but their use of the word was completely different. It seemed that only one person was the *Mānuṣa:* the Maśāy, or Guru. No one else was a *Mānuṣa*. 'To hell with this!' Nistāriṇī muttered behind her husband's back."[75]

In the course of my own fieldwork, I frequently had to struggle with this contradiction myself. During my visit to Ghoshpara, for example, I interviewed one of the two living Kartās—a man who ardently defends the Kartābhajā tradition as the Religion of Man and the divinity of all human beings. Much to his embarrassment, in the course of our conversation, an elderly female devotee suddenly threw herself at his feet, groveling and weeping, praising him as the Supreme Deity. Later that day, I asked him about this apparent contradiction: "If this religion is the worship of Man, and if God dwells in every human being, why do Kartābhajās only worship the Guru as God? Why don't you worship all men as God?" At that he paused for some time and said carefully, "that is a very good question. But it's a very complicated matter. It takes a great deal of time to understand such things. Ask me about this again later." For some reason, I don't think I ever will get a satisfactory reply to this question.[76]

Indeed, as we will see in more detail in chapter 7, more than one observer has pointed out that the role of the Kartā and Mahāśay is not unlike that of a Zamindār in the traditional revenue system of rural Bengal. Like the Zamindār, the Kartā stands as a "middleman" between God and man, and even as a "revenue collector" between the soul and its spiritual Proprietor. In this sense, many argue, the Kartābhajā tradition bears a closer resemblance to the medieval feudal system than it does to the reformed ideals of Rāmmohun Roy:

> Some authors have enthusiastically called this sect's founders "folk Rāmmohuns." . . . But within the hierarchy of their sect, the succession of the Kartā, Mahāśay and Barāti is reminiscent of the rule of the medieval Zamindār . . . and the oppression of the poor peasantry. Surely, in the comfort and relaxed enjoyment of the Kartās, which comes without effort from the earnings of the poor Barātīs, there is no sign of any social consciousness.[77]

This ambivalence and apparent contradiction, which lies at the heart of this Religion of Man, is one we will encounter many more times as we delve deeper into this tradition.

What's in it for the Women? Women in the Kartābhajā Tradition

> Woman is the root of the primordial tree. Who would exist without woman? Just consider semen and menstrual blood: the body of Woman is the vessel of the world. From woman, all creation occurs. (Manulāl Miśra, *Bhajanatattva Prakāśa)*

> The majority of the dupes of the sect are women who readily pay the small tax that is demanded of them for the sake of securing long life to their husbands and children. (Jogendranath Bhattacharya, *Hindu Castes and Sects)*

Finally, in addition to its more general function as a social strategy, secrecy has also long played a critical role in the Kartābhajā tradition as a *sexual strategy*—as a means for men and women to interact in new ways within an alternative, esoteric space of gender, distinct from their usual roles as males and females in mainstream society. Particularly for women, it would seem, the realm of secrecy offers new opportunities for freedom and power, for new independence beyond their usual subordinate roles in the exoteric world; yet at the same time, it can also create new possibilities for their servitude and submission. Since the early nineteenth century, observers of the Kartābhajā tradition have been especially struck by the fact that a large proportion of its following—in many accounts, by far the majority—were women. As the *Saṃvāda Prabhākara* reported in 1848, "Among the participants, 14/16 are women."[78] Though these figures are quite probably exaggerated, it is undeniable that women have always played a prominent role in this tradition. In one recent survey of the Kartābhajā Mela, for example, it was found that 301 out of 381 of those interviewed were women, and of these, 184 were widows, and 55 barren wives.[79] As Akṣaykumār Datta suggested in his account of 1870, it was largely due to the efforts of the female disciples—who would come and go "secretly" in other homes to make new converts—that the Kartābhajās grew and spread: "Very secretly [*gopane gopane*] this movement has become very powerful. . . . The majority of its following are women. Secretly and without their husbands' knowledge, they enter the inner chambers of many homes and increase the number of disciples."[80]

Indeed, one of the primary reasons that certain Bengali intellectuals and Brāhmo reformers such as Nabīncandra or Śaśīpad Bābu began to take an interest in the Kartābhajās was precisely because of their seemingly more liberal, even "modern" attitude toward women. The *Somaprakāśa*, reported in 1864 that:

> Because of shame and fear for the family reputation, few women in this society have the courage to move freely outside the home; but here, because of their devotion to the Kartā, these women can sit freely with many strange men without shame. . . .
>
> According to the Hindu śāstras and convention, women have no freedom. They must always be dependent on their fathers, husbands or sons; but in the Kartābhajā sect they enjoy great freedom.[81]

However, the Kartābhajā women were also just as commonly attacked and ridiculed by the upper-class Bengali society, decried as whores, bitches, senile old women, and sluts. As Rāmakṛṣṇa's biographer, Rāmacandra Datta described them, the Kartābhajā women led a "repulsive lifestyle, worse than that of prostitutes."[82] In the eyes of many observers, the free interaction between the sexes and the new independence given to women was precisely what led to the eventual corruption and decadence of the Kartābhajās: "The number of women is three times that of men; this is because the current of immorality has become very strong. . . . Now many men and women come here to commingle, which has been the cause of the downfall of this religion."[83]

Like the Kartābhajās' social ideals, then, the role of women in this tradition must be understood in relation to the changing role of women in colonial Calcutta, particularly under the impact of the Bengal Renaissance and the reform movements such as the Brāhmo Samāj. Indeed, the "women's issue" was one of the most hotly debated questions among Calcutta's *bhadralok* community. In the eyes of most European authors, the poor treatment of women was commonly seen as one of the most primitive features of Indian culture, and one of the primary obstacles to its social development. Thus, among the more progressive Bengalis of the nineteenth century, improvement of the condition of women, female education and the reform of laws regarding women (*satī,* widow remarriage, etc.) were identified as the most needed reforms of Indian society: "Rammohun chose the Hindu woman as his 'proletariat.' . . . He saw in her depressed condition the root cause of social immobility in India."[84] According to Chatterjee:

> The women's question was a central issue in the most controversial debates over social reform in 19th century Bengal—the period of its so-called Renaissance. Rammohun Roy's fame was largely built around his campaign against the immolation of widows. Vidyasagar's around his efforts to legalize widow remarriage and abolish polygamy.[85]

Unfortunately, as Ghulam Murshid and other critics have pointed out, the new freedoms given to women in the nineteenth century were primarily motivated not so much by a desire for sexual equality but, rather, by deeper interests among the male *bhadraloks*: it was often more a matter of emulating European norms and accelerating the process of modernization than of the actual empowerment of women: "To exploit them in their traditional roles as mothers and wives and to cope with the fashions of the day which . . . were imitations of the English, men allowed them only as much freedom as was necessary for their modernization."[86] Hence, while empowered and liberated in some ways, "the new woman was subjected to a *new* patriarchy."[87]

Before passing judgment on the women of the Kartābhajā tradition, however, let us first examine the various roles that women have actually played in this tradition—as gurus, as common devotees, and as sexual partners.[88]

The Guru-Mother or Mā Gosāiṅ

The most respected and most prominent role for a woman within the Kartābhajā sect is that of a female guru or Mahāśay, called Mā Gosāiṅ. Not only is the Mā Gosāiṅ or "spiritual Mother" considered equal in status to the male Mahāśay, but she is also revered as an incarnation of Satī Mā herself, bearing all of the Divine Mother's own miraculous powers. Throughout the nineteenth century, in fact, the apparent freedom, authority, and relative autonomy of the Mā Gosāiṅ appears to have generated intense controversy throughout the Bengali community. Some scholars have gone so far as to suggest that Satī Mā herself was perhaps the very first women in India to assume the leadership of a religious movement, thus serving as an icon for the empowerment of women in roles of religious authority: "Prior to Satī Mā, women . . . could engage in spiritual practice, but they could never lead a religious movement . . . Satī Mā was the first woman in history who assumed the authority of guru and undertook a vow to spread the Kartābhajā religion."[89] Whereas this claim is clearly overblown and probably historically inaccurate, it does seem to be the case that the Kartābhajās offered new roles for religious authority to women of nineteenth-century Bengal. As Cakravartī suggests, the Mā Gosāiṅ had unusual new opportunities to rise in status and capital—both social and economic—by gathering disciples and mediating between the barātī and the Kartā:

> [One] reason for the popularity of the Kartābhajās is social and economic. The families of the Mahāśays . . . .enjoyed great respect and wealth. In the Kartābhajā sect there was a great opportunity for the Mahāśays to advance by attracting new members. The female promoters were very active in this respect. Throughout the inner chambers of various homes of Calcutta, Mā Gosāiṅs used to come and go freely, spreading their religion.[90]

Even today, in the course of my fieldwork I have encountered a number of very powerful and highly respected Mā Gosāiṅs both in Calcutta and in the surrounding countryside. One of the most striking of these is a highly controversial and charismatic middle-aged woman of Taltola, north Calcutta. Because of her supposed supernatural powers and her claims to have worked several healing miracles among her devotees—including curing blindness—this Mā Gosāiṅ has attained a widespread and rather scandalous reputation. In 1980, for example, she created something of a furor throughout the Calcutta area when she supposedly used her *siddhi* to heal a mute woman. Even today, her home in Taltola remains the center of one of the liveliest Kartābhajā followings in all of Bengal.[91]

Whores, Barren Wives, and Widows: The Common Devotee

By far the majority of the women involved in worship of the Kartā, however, are much more ordinary, largely illiterate and uneducated, primarily "exoteric" devotees, many of whom suffer from some sort of sorrow, illness or need. Indeed, as many observers described them in the nineteenth century, the Kartābhajā devotees were thought to consist primarily of harlots, widows, outcasts, beggars, and others on the fringes of respectable society—mainly "bitches" or "whores" as Rāmakṛṣṇa described them. "The number of prostitutes is greater than that of women of good family," the *Saṃvāda Prabhākara* reported in 1848.[92] As Sen suggests, the Kartābhajās offered these largely poor and illiterate women new opportunities for freedom and status which they could never have found in mainstream society: "Even now, in hundreds of villages like Ghoshpara, in the darkness of night, the free mingling of men and women goes on. . . . Three fourths of them are women, and among the women, five eighths are widows. . . . They could never experience such freedom in high class society. The Brahmans were terribly opposed to the freedom of women. . . . But here there was no such restriction. Women could freely sit wherever they liked."[93]

Perhaps even more attractive to the female devotees, however, were the miraculous and magical aspects of this tradition. With her promise of supernatural deeds, the gift of sons to barren mothers, the figure of Satī Mā has long been especially attractive to women afflicted with some physical or emotional suffering. By bathing in the sacred Hīmsāgar pond and tying up a stone in the sacred pomegranate tree, it is believed, a barren woman will receive Satī Mā's supernatural grace and be blessed with a son, while a child-widow will have all her sorrows removed. As such, we find numerous accounts of female disciples immersed in ecstatic devotion before the image of Satī Mā and the Kartās, drowning in waves of joy, flailing about in divine intoxication, or rolling around on the ground in throes of spiritual madness: "They cry out and sing in waves of bliss, like the Gopīs. One moment they cry out to the two Ṭhākurs [Kartās], the next, they offer homage to the Guru's name and shout cries of joy. . . . Or again, they remain motionless and cry, sunk in devotion."[94] Other accounts describe female disciples engaged in the service of the Kartā or Mahāśays, whom they revere as incarnate divinities. As the *Somaprakāśa* reported in 1864, the Kartā Īśvaracandra lay surrounded by fawning female devotees, who waited on his every desire, serving him as the Gopīs serve Kṛṣṇa in the eternal Vṛndāvana: "The present Kartā, Īśvarabābu, lay on a bed, while women sat on all four sides, some massaging his feet, some rubbing his body, offering food to his mouth, some putting oil on his limbs, some putting garlands of flowers around his neck. It is said that some of the devotees perform the Kṛṣṇa-līlā. The Kartās steal the women's clothing and climb a tree, while the women pray to them from the base of the tree."[95]

The Flower of Limited Usefulness: Female Partners in Sexual Rites

The most controversial role for women within the Kartābhajā sect—and the one that has aroused the most scandal and debate—is that of partners (*sādhikās* or *bhairavīs*) in esoteric sexual rituals. In the field of Tantric studies as a whole, it would seem, this has long remained one of the least understood and neglected of problems.[96] On one side, since the first discovery of the body of texts called "Tantras," Orientalist scholars have long been horrified and repulsed (though also often tantalized and fascinated) by the role of women and the use of sexual intercourse as a religious ritual.[97] On the other side, in more recent years, a number of more sympathetic authors have argued that the Tantras represent a much-needed affirmation of the female and an empowerment of women in new roles of spiritual authority. As the most outspoken recent proponent of this more positive view, Miranda Shaw, puts it, Tantra "offers not a mode of exploitation but of complemenarity and mutuality. . . . Tantric texts encourage a sense of reliance on women as a source of spiritual power."[98]

Unfortunately, it is extremely difficult if not impossible to discover what real living women have to say about their role in such practices. Most Kartābhajās today will either deny completely that any Tantric sexual rituals are performed or else, while acknowledging their existence, will refuse to discuss them in detail. Although we do have one or two firsthand accounts of some Bāul, Śākta, and Sahajiyā *sādhikās*—such as the amazing series of interviews with female consorts conducted by Bholanath Bhattacharya in the 1970s[99]—no one to date has been able to interview a Kartābhajā *sādhikā* who will discuss the role of sexual rites.

Still, the Kartābhajā songs (as well as a few more agreeable male Kartābhajā gurus) do have quite a lot to tell us about the role of women in sexual rituals. The *Bhāver Gīta* itself makes this fairly clear:

Intense sexual love (*ati rati*) arises between a man and a woman.
. . . In *Sahaja*, he is the husband of the chaste wife.
The accomplished *sādhaka* and his consort in practice
are united without division, like a limb to a body. (BG 48; II.68)

Moreover, we do have a number of firsthand accounts by male observers—both within and without the community—which describe the role of the *sādhikās*.

Among the most striking of these is Rāmakṛṣṇa's encounter with the "Kartābhajā bitches." As his biographer Ramchandra Datta comments, "their way of life is of a kind so repugnant that I am unable to reveal it to the public"—and this repugnance was due primarily to their use of sexual rituals.[100] On one occasion, under the supervision of his Kartābhajā guru, Vaiṣṇavacaraṇ, Rāmakṛṣṇa was taken among a circle of Kartābhajā women. According to their judgment, however, Rāmakṛṣṇa was still too immature and naive to engage in the more advanced sexual rites:

> There is one opinion that holds that one should take a woman in mystical practice. Once someone took me into a group of Kartābhajā bitches. They all came and sat down near me. When I began to address them all as "Mā" they began to talk among themselves, "This one is just a beginner. . . ." A young woman sat down near Vaishnavacharan. When asked, Vaishnavacharan said, "Hers is the nature of a little girl."[101]

In sum, the image of the Kartābhajā *sādhikā* that we find these accounts is one of a forward, rather aggressive, and even somewhat mischievous woman who is not afraid of either seducing or ridiculing young men such as Rāmakṛṣṇa.

As one respected Kartābhajā guru, Advaita Candra Dās, explains, the female partner is crucial to the highest stages of Kartābhajā practice: She serves as the necessary "spiritual assistant" or even "alter ego" of the male *sādhaka*, and deserves to be revered as such: "If one can understand the nature of sexual union, he can know the power of the Self. The female is the 'half self' of the male, the assistant in spiritual practice; woman is always to be worshipped and honored;" ultimately, "the Sahajiyās see the reflection of the universe within women."[102]

According to Kartābhajā metaphysics (largely adapted from the Vaiṣṇava Sahajiyā tradition), the male and female partners are the finite embodiments of the supreme male and female principles, the cosmic Puruṣa and Prakṛti, or Śrī Kṛṣṇa and his eternal consort Rādhā. At the origin of all things, the primordial Self, Puruṣa, wished to know and enjoy himself and so created Prakṛti from himself. In their eternal erotic embrace, all creation took place: "The Supreme Self or Śrī Kṛṣṇa dwells within this very body. Originally, He was alone. . . . For the sake of tasting *rasa* he divided himself into Puruṣa and Prakṛti. This Prakṛti was created for the sake of coition. Its basis lies within the menstrual fluid (*raja*) itself. This *raja* is the root of both sexual pleasure and creation."[103] Hence, in order to "undo" creation and return to the primordial unity of the Supreme Self, the male must unite with his female *sādhikā* and reverse the cosmogonic process itself.

To be a true Kartābhajā *sādhikā*, however, the female must not be just any ordinary woman; she cannot be a common, worldly partner, given to lust and sensual desires. Rather, she must be pure and wholly untouched by common sensual lust. As the *Bhāver Gīta* declares, "this is the task neither of the adulterous lover (*vyabhicāriṇī*) nor of the chaste wife (*satīnārī*); the practice of the Sahaja kingdom is of a wholly different sort" (BG 115). As Dās explains, the kind of partner required is one who is enurely free of lust, who can engage in intercourse without the desire for base, carnal pleasure—like Ramī, the famous washerwoman-lover of the poet Caṇḍīdās: "The adulterous lover is tainted by the sent of lust; and the chaste wife is also tainted by the scent of lust. Apart from these two, however, there is another type of woman who is free of the scent of lust. She alone can be taken in this practice."[104] As one Kartābhajā song instructs the *sādhikā*, she must be of such quality that she can even violate the laws of marriage and caste, even engage in adultery, without showing a trace of carnal desire:

Keep this secret love in secrecy;
and accomplish the work of the heart.
. . . Pay no attention to the Vedas or Vedānta.
You will still be a chaste wife; you won't be an adulteress, under the control of no one,
Even though you become unchaste and abandon your family, worrying and worrying;
Even while seeing another's husband, with passion like radiant gold,
you will still follow the commands of your own true husband.
Swim in the ocean of impurity,
let down your hair, but don't get wet and don't touch the water! (SE IV.12)

So, too, the kind of union involved here is not ordinary sexual intercourse motivated by material desires for sensual pleasure. Tantric *sādhanā* is quite explicitly a kind of "inverted" sexual act, which deliberately transgresses the normal laws of marriage and caste and which even reverses the normal act of coitus itself. Paradoxically, the highest form of union is said to take place not within the vagina of the female but, rather, *within the body of the male himself.* Using the technique of *vajrolī* or the reversal of the flow—what Wendy Doniger O'Flaherty has appropriately dubbed the "fountain pen technique"—the male hopes to suck both the male and female sexual fluids back out of the female and into his own body.[105] Then, once he has absorbed the female principle, the male *sādhaka* can realize the presence of the divine Prakṛti within his own body. Indeed, as Manulāl Miśra tells us, he must "become a woman."[106] Finally, once he has realized the eternal womanly within himself, he no longer has need of an actual female partner: he can now actualize the union of Puruṣa and Prakṛti within his own body: "First, one must cultivate devotion with a female companion . . . and develop the Body of Ecstasy [*bhāva-deha*]. Then one must arouse the arrested semen, and prepare it in the Piṅgalā vein. . . . As a result of practice with a female partner, the Female Nature arises within his own body. Once he has attained the female nature, an actual female partner is no longer needed. The *sādhaka* himself experiences the female nature."[107]

Even within the Kartābhajā songs and texts themselves, then, we can see a profound tension at play. At the same time that they proclaim the glories of the female, the power of femininity, and necessity of women in ritual practice, they also give clear priority to the male. The union and liberating bliss which they describe always occurs within the male partner, within his own divinized androgynic body. The goal here does not seem to be an egalitarian kind of union but, rather, a hierarchical one. Just as the male principle (Puruṣa or Kṛṣṇa) generated the female (Prakṛti or Rādhā) from himself to create the universe, so, too, the goal of *sādhanā* is to reabsorb and reassimilate the female back into the male. As is the case in many other pan-Indian Tantric traditions, "The feminine partner is used as a means to an end which is experienced by the yogin himself."[108] Even while she may be temporarily empowered and divinized in esoteric ritual, outside the secret confines of *sādhanā*, her subordinate place in the social order is seldom questioned—on the contrary, "The social inferiority of women is even a necessary presupposition for the liberating antinomianism of Tantric *sādhanā*."[109] The question of what happens to the female once she has been used to arouse the divine energy within the male, is, to my knowledge, never asked. Indeed, according to the well-known Sahajiyā metaphor, she is simply the "flower" from which the "bee" (i.e., the male yogin) collects the honey (the sexual fluid), and which he then casts aside: "When the honey is collected, the flowers are of no use to the bees"[110] Or according to a song of Caṇḍīdās, "Just as the traveler walks over the road to arrive at his destination, so in the culture of love, the devotee should . . . take a woman"; in other words, as Bose comments, "As soon as the object is realized there is no necessity of women any longer."[111]

Empowerment or Exploitation? The Renegotiation of Sexual Power

In short, it would seem that the role of women in Kartābhajā sexual rituals is not a matter of simple "empowerment" or "exploitation." Rather, it appears to be a complex *renegotiation and reconfiguration* of the power relations between males and females, in which both parties derive certain benefits (although to different, often unequal, degrees). Within the context of esoteric ritual, the female is indeed "empowered" with divine authority and worshipped as an embodiment of the Goddess, as Prakṛti or Rādhā incarnate. However, if the female is empowered through ritual, this power is usually narrowly circumscribed and confined to the field of secret practice. Ultimately, the limited and temporary empowerment of the female serves, in Foucault's terms, to *optimize* and intensify the superior power of the male.[112] For it is, finally, the male who achieves the union of male and female principles within himself, who experiences the ecstatic bliss of liberation within his own divinized body.

A similar tension between "empowerment" and "exploitation," it would seem, characterizes the role of women within the Kartābhajā sect as a whole. Whereas the figure of the Mā Gosāiṅ did open up certain new roles for female leadership and spiritual authority, it also appears to have offered new opportunities for the Kartās and Mahāśays to manipulate women for their own interests—as sources of income, or as tools in sexual rituals. In any case, it is undeniable that the Kartābhajā leadership has become quite wealthy in large part by playing on the needs of many uneducated poor women, above all barren wives and widows. Ironically, despite their otherwise tremendous differences, the Kartābhajās do seem to share this fact with the reforms taking place among the upper classes and *bhadraloks*: if women were given new kinds of freedom and authority, they were still constrained by overarching male interests, and in many ways "subjected to a *new* patriarchy."

Conclusions: The Kartābhajās as a "Counter-Bengal-Renaissance"

With its unique religious and social ideals, it would seem, the early Kartābhajā tradition opens up an invaluable window onto the life and popular culture of Bengal's lower classes at the turn of the nineteenth century. Whereas the majority of past scholarship has focused on the lives of the wealthy, educated upper classes, the leaders of the Brāhmo Samāj and the Bengal Renaissance, the Kartābhajās give us a fascinating insight into the lives of those "lower orders" who were ignored or even repressed and ridiculed by the upper-class reformers. Indeed, although they had once been praised by some of the most progressive minds of the nineteenth century, the Kartābhajās soon came under bitter attack by the more conservative upper classes of the day. Such a powerful lower-class movement, which rejected caste, denied the Vedas, and engaged in deliberate violations of laws of purity, began to appear more and more as a dangerous and potentially subversive cult. "The reasons for such controversy surrounding the Kartābhajās are several," Cakravartī comments, "thousands of people entered this religion, which greatly upset the Hindu community of Calcutta. They wanted to put a stop to it."[113]

Rather than a "lower-class reflection" of the Bengal Renaissance led by a kind of "folk Rammohun Roy," the Kartābhajās are thus perhaps better understood, to use Hyram Haydn's phrase, as a kind of "counter-Bengal-Renaissance." They reflect an underworld of secrecy, ecstatic devotion, miracles, and magic—in short, of "*irrationalism*"—which spread regardless of the sober rationalism of the Brāhmos. Emerging in response to the changing economic and social events, the Kartābhajās transformed many aspects of the older Tantric traditions, adapting them to the needs of a new historical era. Thus we may call the Kartābhajās a kind of "popularized Tantra," insofar as they appropriated and transformed key elements of the esoteric Sahajiyā tradition—such as the concept of *Sahaja*, the denial of caste, the divinity of Man and the human body, the role of women—to create a more popular movement which appealed to the poor lower classes of Calcutta and the surrounding countryside. This new "Religion of Humanity," in short, offered new forms of status, authority and symbolic capital to those who were most deprived of actual economic capital.

As we see most clearly in its social ideals and in the case of women, however, this was also a highly ambivalent and not always entirely profitable form of capital. For it also brought with it the potential for new forms of inequality and oppression within the Kartābhajā hierarchy itself. If this was indeed a Religion of Humanity, it would seem that certain human beings—and in most cases, certain *men*—profited far more from it than others.

Part II

THE POWER OF SECRECY

Esoteric Discourse and Practice

3

The Language of the Mint

Secrecy and Esoteric Discourse in the Kartābhajā Tradition

gupta je mukta se, be-parda byabhicāriṇī.
[the one who is secret is liberated; the one who is manifest (outside the veil) is an adulteress] ("Mint Saying," [*Ṭyāṅkśālī Bol*], no. 66—STP 121; III.66)

There is a secret key to understanding [these songs]. . . . Revealing that key to anyone who is not a Kartābhajā is for them the supreme "heresy." This is their version of "Free Masonry." (Nabīncandra Sen, "Ghoṣpāṛār Melā")

In the following three chapters, we begin to delve into the most esoteric, most hidden dimensions of the Kartābhajā tradition, as we explore the use of secret discourse and bodily practice. The tactics of concealment had certainly long been a part of the Sahajiyā and other Tantric traditions of Bengal; indeed, it is not insignificant that the oldest vernacular literature in Bengal, the songs of the *Caryāpadas,* are composed in the coded discourse of *sandhābhāṣā* or intentional language, with its elaborate use of enigmatic imagery, strange metaphors, and riddles.[1] It would seem, however, that the tactics of secrecy assumed a new and more central importance amidst the changing circumstances of the early colonial era. In the face of foreign political rule and the shifting moral standards of indigenous reform movements, the Sahajiyā schools began to cultivate the techniques of secrecy in ever new and more ingenious ways.[2]

Perhaps nowhere is this increasing and ever more elaborate use of esoteric language more apparent than in the cryptic songs of the Kartābhajās and in their own unique form of *sandhābhāṣā,* which they dubbed—rather appropriately, I think—the "Language of the Mint" (*ṭyāṅkśālī bol*). Composed at a critical moment in the history of Bengal, at the dawn of the nineteenth century, amidst the shifting values of the Bengal Renaissance and on the outskirts of the imperial city of Calcutta, the Kartābhajā songs are saturated with bizarre imagery and disconcerting paradoxes, deliberately intended to confuse, befuddle and discourage the uninitiated outsider. According to a favorite Kartābhajā saying, "don't speak about your practice with just anyone; keep it to yourself with great caution."[3] As Chakrabarty comments, "A casual reader may not feel tempted to read these songs, which sound like gibberish. . . . If one carefully analyzes these songs one would find one or two statements fraught with meaning. Such statements lie hidden like needles in haystacks."[4] Indeed, the Kartābhajā songs would seem to offer us one of the most acute examples of Tantric *sandhābhāṣā* and among the most striking illustrations of esoteric discourse and its deeper roles within its social context.

Most of the large body of scholarship on Tantric *sandhābhāṣā,* it would seem, has tended to treat this esoteric discourse rather simplistically, analyzing it in terms of its supposed "hidden content," as if it were a kind of "code language" concealing a singular and ultimately knowable susbtance.[5] As I shall argue in the case of the Kartābhajā Mint Sayings, however, esoteric discourse is much more fruitfully examined, not in terms of its professed "hidden content" but, rather, in terms of *forms and strategies*, the tactics and manuevers through which it operates in specific social and historical contexts. After briefly outlining the form and content of these Mint Sayings, I then delve into the tangled hermeneutic problems involved in trying to make sense of such cryptic utterances, offering my own reading, based on a modified version of Bourdieu's model of symbolic capital. Finally, I engage the even stickier and more difficult problem of secrecy as it is played out in firsthand field research, as I reflect on my own conversations with various Kartābhajā gurus and my attempts to gain access to "secret truths" as handed down by the living oral tradition.

In the process, I grapple concretely with the methodological impasse which I presented in the introduction—namely, the epistemological-ethical double bind, the question of *how* one can know a secret and, supposing one can, *if* one should reveal it. As I suggested earlier, it may well be true that we can never know with certainty the real substance of a secret, but we can still say a great deal about its forms and strategic functions. Secrecy is thus better understood not in terms of some elusive hidden content but instead as a particular strategy, a calculated means of concealing and revealing certain information or practices. In Bourdieu's terms, secrecy transforms a given piece of knowledge into a scarce and highly valued resource, the possession of which in turn bestows a form of symbolic capital, status, or prestige on its owner. This is, however, a specifically "illegal" or "black market" kind of capital—which can be exchanged only within a highly restricted social field (e.g., esoteric ritual), and which elevates one's status only with an alternative social hierarchy (e.g., the lineage of the secret society). Yet, at the same time, this element of danger only makes the secret appear all the more desirable in the eyes of the initiate, and all the more awesome and powerful to the outsider. Indeed, it was in large part their very hiddenness that invested the Kartābhajās with such an aura of awesome, dangerous power, with a radical freedom overstepping the boundaries of mainstream society (though ironically, we will see, this would later become among the primary reasons for their infamy and ill repute in the exoteric world).

Coinage for the Poor: Esoteric Discourse in the Kartābhajā Mint Sayings

These Mint Sayings are neither for the Marketplace nor for wealth; they are only for the Poor. (Mint Saying, no. 123 (STP 66; III.123)

Money, more than any other form of value, makes possible the secrecy, invisibility and silence of exchange . . . money's formlessness and abstractness makes it possible to invest it in the most varied and remote values and thereby to remove it completely from the gaze of neighbors. (Georg Simmel, *The Philosophy of Money)*

Since the time of H. P. Śāstrī's discovery of the cryptic songs of the *Caryāpadas* there has of course been a fairly sizable body of scholarship on the subject of *sandhābhāṣā*.[6] Unfortunately, however, most past scholarship has offered what seems to me a superficial and simplistic analysis of the role of *sandhābhāṣā* as a form of esoteric discourse. Most often, it is simply assumed that it functions either (1) to offer symbols or metaphors for profound mysteries which cannot be expressed in ordinary literal language[7] or (2) to conceal the esoteric practices of Tantrics from the eyes of the uninitiated, who would find them immoral or illegal. "There were many reasons for the Vaiṣṇava Sahajiyās to keep their practices hidden," as Hayes suggests, "Most people in Hindu society were conservative when it came to issues of sexuality and the Sahajiyā practices frequently involved violations of caste. . . . They lived in constant danger of social condemnation by the Hindus and harassment by the Muslim authorities."[8] In either case, *sandhābhāṣā* is regarded more or less as a kind of "code language." In his classic work on yoga, for example, Eliade presents *sandhābhāṣā* as a sort of Morse code in which there is a simple one-to-one correspondence between each term and its underlying content. Thus, according to Eliade's esoteric lexicon, *vajra* = *liṅga* = *śūnya* (emptiness); *ravi* or *sūrya* (sun) = *rajas* (menstrual blood); *candra* = *śukra* (semen); *samarasa* = coitus = immobility of thought = arrest of semen, and so on.[9]

As such, most past approaches have fallen into precisely the same epistemological and ethical double bind that we discussed in the Introduction. The basic (and I think erroneous) assumption is that there must be some singular and determinate "hidden meaning" corresponding to each esoteric symbol. In the process, most scholars have ignored the *extreme indeterminacy and radical polysemy* of secret language. As Rahul Peter Das and Saktinath Jha have argued in the case of the Bāul songs, for example, there is often a tremendous plurality of interpretations of even the most basic esoteric practices. Most scholars, Jha suggests, have assumed that the famous Bāul image of the "four moons" (*cāri-candra*) simply refers to the act of consuming the four bodily products of semen, menstrual blood, urine, and feces. Yet as Jha has shown, the actual interpretation of the four moons differs radically among actual Bāul practitioners and can be understood in at least a dozen different, often contradictory ways, many of them having little relation to the conventional scholarly interpretation.[10]

As I hope to show in the case of the Kartābhajās' songs and their highly unusual "Mint Language," the role of *sandhābhāṣā* is far more profound than a simple code language used to conceal socially objectionable practices; rather, it has more profound strategic role as a means of *creating and exchanging valued pieces of knowledge,* as a discursive strategy which endows certain information with an aura of mystery, power, and symbolic value.

As a whole, the songs of the Kartābhajās stand out as among the most idiosyncratic, confusing, maddeningly difficult, and profoundly esoteric—and yet also as among the most unusual and original—subjects in the history of Bengali literature. Attributed (probably falsely) to Dulālcāṅd (a.k.a. Lālśaśī), who is said to have recited them orally to his four chief disciples, the songs of the *Bhāver Gīta* or *Śrī Juter*

Pada are in many ways much like those of their spiritual cousins, the Bāuls: relatively simple and unsophisticated in their language, they are fraught with profound esoteric significance and laden with seemingly impenetrable layers of strange imagery, jarring metaphors, and disquieting contradictions. No less an authority than Sukumār Sen praised the unique importance of the *Bhāver Gīta*, which represents both a highly unusual form of Bengali song and an influential body of mystical imagery; indeed, he even goes so far as to compare the songs of the *Bhāver Gīta* with those of Rabindranath himself.[11] Like the Kartābhajā sect as a whole, the songs of the *Bhāver Gīta* are a fascinating mixture of urban and rural, traditional and modern styles, combining the metropolitan forms of the *vaiṭhakī* or "parlour" songs of nineteenth-century Calcutta with the rustic language of village Bengal (see SE part I).[12] Yet rather strikingly, they remain to this day one of the least understood and neglected subjects in the study of Bengali literature. This neglect is not, however, terribly surprising, given the profoundly esoteric and deeply encoded nature of these cryptic songs. As the literary historian D. C. Sen elegantly put it, the songs of the *Bhāver Gīta* are much like the songs of birds—mysteriously beautiful yet generally unintelligible:

> The songs are composed in a very simple, beautiful form . . . which expresses deep philosophical truth, but which cannot be understood by anyone apart from initiates. . . . Even though the language is simple, it is highly enigmatic. . . . Just as we can't understand the songs of birds, so too, we can't understand these songs, but still our hearts are touched by their obscure beauty.[13]

Scattered throughout the Kartābhajā songs and the verses of the *Bhāver Gīta,* like precious jewels of hidden truth, the "Mint Sayings" are a body of short phrases, bizarre aphorisms, strange riddles, and often seeming gibberish. In the first decade of this century, the Mint Sayings were collected into a list of some 204 short cryptic utterances and published by the Kartābhajā theologian Manulāl Miśra in his major work, the *Sahaja tattva prakāśa* ("The Revelation of the Essence of Sahaja," STP 57–71; SE III). Most of the Mint Sayings will probably appear, to those outside the Kartābhajā fold, largely nonsensical, queer, and contradictory: "[A]t the root is secrecy [*gopanatā*]. To those outside the sect, they tell nothing at all, but they simply confuse them with riddles."[14] But to those within the fold, these strange Mint Sayings—though perhaps not entirely *meaningful* in a semantic sense—become an extremely precious, rare, and valuable source of symbolic power.

Now, first we should ask why these strange esoteric utterances are called the "Language of the Mint" and what the significance is of the image of "coinage" here. On the one hand, this is quite probably related to the historical context in which the Kartābhajā songs were composed, in the early and mid-nineteenth century; this was in fact precisely the same time that the colonial government in Bengal was trying to standardize and regularize the hitherto chaotic array of different kinds of coinage (cowry shells, old Mughal coins, French arcot, the Company's silver coins, etc.). During the 1830s—precisely the same time that the Kartābhajā songs were composed—the Company's program of coinage reform resulted in the establishment of the silver rupee as the standard coin in Bengal. Finally, in 1831, the Company built the famous "New Mint" in downtown Calcutta, where the British "first started to strike coins in its own name without reference to the Mughal Emperor in Delhi."[15]

But still more important, as I argue later, the importance of these Mint Sayings lies precisely in the *production* of value: the creation of valuable and exchangeable pieces of information. As Miśra explains in his introduction to the Sayings, these secret teachings are a kind of "coinage for the poor [*gorib*]," a source of power and wealth for those who are most needy and neglected by mainstream society: "These Mint Sayings are neither for the Marketplace nor for wealth; they are only for the Poor" (STP 66; SE III.123). Let us first survey a brief sampling of these Sayings and then make some effort to fathom their meaning and purpose (because there is no apparent linear continuity from one Saying to the next, I have chosen a sampling of the most representative and interesting of them [STP 57–71; SE III.3–20]):

3. The name of Man is a "Jest" [*Tāmāśā*]; the name of his work is *Sahaja* [the "innate" or "natural" state of supreme Bliss]. His form is variegated.
4. One must remember the stage when he collected cakes of cowdung . . .
23. One need not taste a hot chilli in another man's mouth.
34. With respect to one's motive, bathing in a scum-covered betal-grower's pond is better than bathing in the Ganges.
46. If one dies alive, he'll never have to die again.
50. I am not, you are not. He is.
69. If you work zealousy amidst the rubbish of the house, a pile of garbage can become a mass of fine essence [*sāra*].
85. I wish to become a Poor Man; if one attains the true condition of Poverty, there is supreme happiness.
105. Everyone is the wife of the Husband, and everyone knows the Husband's name. But if one does not enjoy Him sexually [*sambhoga kare*], the love is mere hearsay.
116. . . . No matter who you haggle with, there are still crocodiles in the Ganges; and a cat is still just a fat tiger in a forest of Tulsi trees.
124. The command of the Divine Mouth is: "the Poor belong to me, and I belong to the Poor."
132. He who is born as a maggot in excrement still dwells in excrement, even if he is seated in heaven.
133. If one lives in the kitchen, what will happen? He'll have to walk around carrying the stench of the place.
136. All jackals make the same sound.
184. The name of the land of one's [true] Mother and Father is the "Poor Company."
189. When one pulls the hair, the head comes along.
204. One can engage in moneylending with little wealth; but if there are debtors, the Moneylender dies. Thus, one must engage in Moneylending with great discretion.

Finally, there is perhaps the most famous and most well-known (though generally least understood) of the Kartābhajā secret sayings: "The woman must become a *Hijṛā* [a man who has had his genitalia removed][16] and the man must be a *Khojā* [a eunuch or impotent man]; then they will be 'Kartābhajās.'" Having outlined the historical context and form of the Kartābhajā's esoteric discourse, let us now turn to the more formidable task of trying to make some sense of these cryptic statements.

Extreme Indeterminacy: Interpreting the Kartābhajā Secrets

Can just anyone understand *Sahaja*? this is not an affair of spoken words; you must sit inside the unenterable room and keep this knowledge hidden far away! (BG 414)

From even this brief sampling, we can see that the Kartābhajās' esoteric discourse leads us into the most difficult snarls involved in every hermeneutical quest for meaning. Not only are there are a wide variety of radically divergent interpretations among contemporary scholars, but even among later Kartābhajā commentators and gurus, there is rather enormous difference of opinion as to the meaning of these cryptic sayings. As one famous nineteenth-century observer, the poet Nabīncandra Sen, described them, the Kartābhajās keep their teachings secretly encoded, much like the European Freemasons: "One Kartābhajā sang some of their religious songs for me. . . . I couldn't understand a word of it! The words were indeed Bengali, but the meaning could not possibly be understood! There is a secret key to understanding them. Revealing that key to anyone who is not a Kartābhajā is for them the supreme "heresy" [the English word is used here]. This is their version of "Free Masonry" [again the English word]."[17]

Like Nabīncandra, I encountered a similar frustration in the course of my own study of the Kartābhajā songs. Not only is it extremely difficult, as we will see in the next section, to gain access to and speak to Kartābhajā practitioners today, but even among the known historical texts, and even among those gurus who *will* speak openly, we encounter a tremendous variety of different, often contradictory interpretations of the same "Secret truths." Take, for example, the key Mint Saying—which is one of the most often quoted—that "the woman must become a *hijṛā* and the man a eunuch." Now, first we should note how very peculiar the first half of this statement is: for, typically, a *hijṛā* refers to a particular kind of male who has had his penis and testicles removed; the *hijṛā* then becomes part of a semireligious community of men who dress as women and often engage in homosexual prostitution.[18] In the course of my own textual research and fieldwork, I have encountered (at least) the following eight different interpretations:

1. According to the more conservative or "orthodox" interpretation, like that of the recently deceased Kartā, Satyaśiva Pāl, this phrase simply means that the

Kartābhajā must be extremely chaste and pure, as austere and sexless as a eunuch.[19]

2. In complete contrast, according to the more "esoteric" interpretation, this phrase means that the Kartābhajā disciple must be capable of the most difficult Tantric ritual of sexual intercourse, but do so without giving in to mere sensual lust. This paradoxical and dangerous feat is said to be like "making a frog dance in a snake's mouth," "bathing in the ocean without getting your hair wet," or like a woman becoming a *hijṛā*.[20]
3. For others, this statement has a more spiritual and mystical meaning: it refers to the ultimate state of divine union and bliss—a kind of "spiritual androgyny"—in which the Kartābhajā experiences both male and female principles within his own body.[21]
4. For some, it means that both male and female must be symbolically "feminine," passive and receptive in relation to God, who is the only true "Male" in the universe.[22]
5. And for still others, it simply means that the Kartābhajā must go beyond all dualities altogether—to the "formless state," beyond male and female, beyond body and spirit, beyond good and evil.[23]
6. Rather strikingly, at least a few have interpreted this sentence quite literally, taking it to mean that the Kartābhajā must really be a *hijṛā*—that is, part of a special community of castrated males, who dress as women and are involved in homosexual prostitution (as Rāmakṛṣṇa's biographer, Rāmacandra Datta described them, their "repulsive lifestyle is worse even than that of prostitutes"[24]).
7. Some suggest that the "meaning" of this statement is not fixed or singular, but rather varies depending on the disciple's capacity and level of initiation.[25]
8. Finally, I should note that, in the course of my interviews with several gurus, I ran into the rather frustrating problem of self-contradictory and changeable interpretations, receiving one answer on one occasion, and a completely different answer on another occasion, or in a different setting).

Figure 3.1 illustrates how these different interpretations might be outlined.

In sum, what we encounter in the problem of secrecy is an especially acute example of what Ricoeur calls the "conflict of interpretations" and "indeterminacy of meaning," which is inherent in every discourse. For every text and every utterance is subject to multiple, divergent readings in different social and historical contexts, to a constant process of rereading and reinterpretation within every group of readers. Hence the meaning of a given text is never fixed but is always in process, always being made and remade, deconstructed and reconstructed: "To interpret is to appropriate here and now the intention of the text . . . the intended meaning is not the presumed intention of the author but rather what the text means for whoever complies with its injunction."[26] As literary critics such as Roland Barthes have shown us, the meaning of any utterance is always profoundly *contextual*, its significance derived more from the social and historical context in which it is *read or received* than in the original intention of its speaker: "the ability of a text to make sense depends less on the willed intention of the author than on the creative activity of the reader . . . a text's unity lies not in its origin but in its destination."[27]

I. Conservative or "Orthodox" Interpretations

- **I.A.** The male and female must be totally chaste and pure, free of all sensual desire
  - **I.A.1.** The disciple must achieve an inward state of "spiritual androgyny," in which he experiences both male and female principles within his own body
  - **I.A.2.** The Kartābhajā must go beyond all dualities altogether—to the "formless state," beyond male and female, beyond body and spirit
- **I.B.** Both male and female devotees must become symbolically "feminine," that is, passive and receptive in relation to God, who is the only true "Male" in the universe

II. Esoteric or "Tantric" Interpretations

- **II.A.** The Kartābhajā disciple must be capable of the most difficult Tantric ritual of sexual intercourse—but do so without giving in to mere sensual lust
  - **II.A.1.** The male Kartābhajā must "become like a woman and engage in intercourse with a woman"; he engages in sexual rituals with a female partner in order to awaken and unite with the feminine power within himself
  - **II.A.2.** The "meaning" of this statement is not fixed or singular but, rather, varies depending on the disciple's own capacity and level of initiation
- **II.B.** The Kartābhajā *really* is a *hijṛā* or eunuch

Figure 3.1. Divergent interpretations of the Kartābhajā Mint Saying, *"strī hijṛā puruṣ khojā, tabe habe kartābhajā"* (The woman must become a hijṛā and the man must become a eunuch, then they will be Kartābhajās).

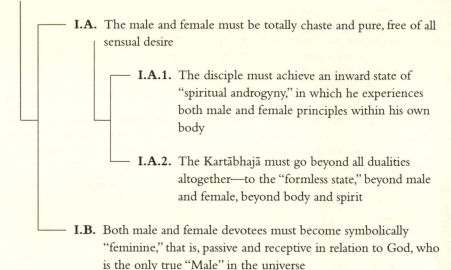

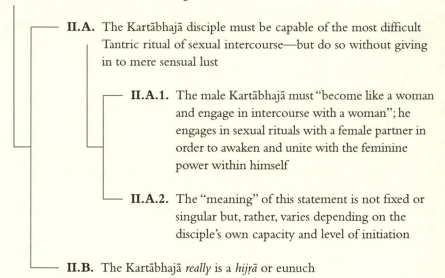

Precisely because of its intentionally ambiguous and mystifying character, esoteric discourse is perhaps among the most extreme cases of this basic hermeneutic problem: It is subject to a kind of "maelstrom of interpretations." Because it is so obscure, so deliberately hidden, a secret utterance may be given radically different meanings depending on its context—depending on which guru is interpreting it, to whom he is revealing it, in what context, at what stage of initiation, in which historical period or social milieu he is speaking, and so on. Hence, it is *not* simply the case that secret discourse is semantically "empty" or devoid of *any* content—a kind of "McGuffin" to use Hitchcock's metaphor.[28] On the contrary, we might say that it has *too many meanings*; it is capable of bearing an enormous variety of interpretations. Secret discourse, in short, is *extremely indeterminate and radically contextualized*. It is in this sense perhaps more like what Roland Barthes calls the "degree zero signifier"—"the pure sign that means *everything*," the "sign to which *all meanings* can be attributed."[29]

So the question remains, if we have not undergone initiation at the hands of a guru—and in fact even if we *have* undergone initiation—how can we make any sense of these deliberately confusing and obfuscating statements? Now, it may well be true that I can never know the ultimate referent of these statements (and it may even be true that there is no single, ultimate referent), but I *can* examine the metaphoric forms and discursive strategies through which they are transmitted—the tactics of disguise and dissimulation, of simultaneous revelation and obfuscation. Most important, I would identify the following four strategies:

1. *"Advertising" the secret: The dialectic of lure and withdrawal.* The first and most basic strategy is the "advertisement" of the secret—the claim to possess very precious, rare, and valuable knowledge while partially revealing and largely concealing it. For a secret is only worth anything if someone *knows* that an individual has a secret. As Bellman suggests, this is the very paradox of secrecy: Secrecy is based on a "do-not-talk prescription," which is contradicted by the fact that "secrecy is a sociological form constituted by the very procedures whereby secrets are communicated."[30]

In the case of the Kartābhajās, we have the rather ironic phenomenon that teachings which are supposed to be dangerous and powerful have also been *published*, distributed publicly, and made fairly readily available in the printed form of *Bhāver Gīta* or Miśra's collection of "Mint Sayings." As Miśra himself openly declares: "Out of compassion for the poor, lower class people . . . Dulālcāṅd revealed these most secret teachings. . . . In this precious treasury (of Mint Sayings), many valuable meanings are contained within each word." Yet the deeper *meaning* or significance of these truths is always held in reserve, kept only for initiates, and ultimately the highest-level initiates. As Miśra continues, "But He revealed . . . these most secret practices in a very cryptic form. Not everyone can understand the meaning of these secret teachings."[31] The Supreme reality of *Sahaja*, the *Bhāver Gīta* repeatedly tells us, cannot be communicated through ordinary language and must not be revealed to the uninitiated exoteric or "bestial man" (*paśu*): "Never speak of this openly to anyone!" the reader is regularly warned (BG 153; II.85). Yet, rather ironically, the Kartābhajās constantly, even obsessively, refer to their possession of secret knowledge—albeit in roundabout or sidelong ways, gesturing indirectly by means of "hints, symbols or enigmas" (*praheli, ābhāsa*): "One must understand through shadows" the *Bhāver Gīta* sings, "Know, in an hint, what its nature is—public exposure is impossible, but a trace of it is possible" (BG 48;

II.68). In sum, the advertisement involves a skillful dialectic of *lure and withdrawal*—the interplay between the promise of awesome secret knowledge and the continuous (perhaps infinite) *deferral* of revelation. The "true" meaning or "real secret" is always reserved for the *next* meeting, the next stage of spiritual attainment. As one self-proclaimed Kartābhajā guru enthusiastically announced to me, "*I know many secret things I can tell you*!"[32]

2. *Hierarchalization of truth and controlled access to information.* The second of these strategies is to construct a graded hierarchy of levels of "truth" and then to restrict access to these truths by means of initiation. As Barth observes, "If you seek to *create* highly valued information . . . you must arrange worship so that few persons gain access to these truths."[33] Although the Mint Sayings themselves can be obtained in printed form by more or less anyone, whether initiated or not, the meaning and value of these odd statements is strictly guarded and accessible only through the teachings of an authoritative guru. Thus, like most esoteric organizations, the Kartābhajās have constructed a complex hierarchical system of initiations. The sect as a whole is organized according to a basic tripartite hierarchy, consisting of the Kartā (the "Master," identified as Lord Kṛṣṇa incarnate), the Mahāśays (the regional gurus with authority over a given village or locale), and the common *barātīs* (ordinary disciples). The *barātīs*, in turn, are further divided into the common or "gross" (*sthūla*) exoteric devotees, at the lower levels of basic devotional teachings, and the truly "Poor" (*kāṅgāl*) esoteric disciples, who are initiated into the most profound and powerful secret practices. And finally, within the class of the "Poor," there is yet another hierarchy of degrees, according to one's level of spiritual attainment and knowledge: these consist of the four progressive stages of (a) the *pravarta* or beginner; (b) the *sādhaka* or "practitioner"; (c) the *siddha*, the accomplished or perfected disciple; and finally (d) the *siddher siddha*, the perfect of the perfect, who has attained the highest state of cessation (*nivṛtti*) or "living death" (*jyānte marā*) in which the individual self is annihilated in the intoxicating madness and ecstasy of Sahaja.[34] The hierarchy thus looks something like this:

- I. Kartā (God Incarnate)
- II. Mahāśay (regional Guru)
- III. Barātī (disciple)
  - A. The "Poor" (*kāṅgāl*) or esoteric disciples
    1. *Nivṛtti* ("extinction") or *Siddher siddha* (the most perfect of the perfect), attainment of divinity and supreme bliss
    2. *Siddha* ("perfect"), the stage of lesser gods
    3. *Sādhaka* (practitioner)
    4. *Pravarta* (novice, beginner)
  - B. The "coarse" or exoteric (*sthūla*) disciples

At each of these stages, as he advances in devotion and skill in esoteric practice, the disciple is entrusted with more and more of this secret knowledge. As one anonymous reporter described this system in his study of the Kartābhajās in 1881, "The practices of the Kartābhajās are conducted in secret. Their secrets can only be revealed according to the class of the disciple. Gradually, as he rises to higher and higher grades, the disciple gains authority to learn the most profound secrets."[35]

For example, an ordinary Kartābhajā novice is first entrusted only with simple teachings, such as the initiatory mantra given on first entry into the cult: "O sinless Lord! At thy pleasure I go and return! Not a moment am I without thee. Save me, great Lord."[36] The most profound pieces of secret information can be entrusted only to the most advanced disciples, who have attained the final stages of liberation and "extinction" (*nivṛtti*) in the divine abyss of Sahaja. These include, for example, the references to the supreme condition of "living death" (*jiyānte marā*)—"If one dies alive one never dies"—or the realization that everything that exists, including the human body, are pervaded by and united with God—for example, "I am not, you are not; He is." Above all, the most precious and guarded of the Mint Sayings are those dealing with erotic metaphors (e.g., "Everyone is the wife of the Husband. . . . But if one does not enjoy him sexually, the love is mere hearsay"), particularly those that contain references to esoteric Tantric rituals or the use of intercourse as a sacramental act .

To make matters all the more complicated, the same statements may often be given different, even contradictory interpretations at different stages of initiation. Take, for example, the Mint Saying, "the woman must become a Hijṛā and the man a eunuch; then they will be Kartābhajās." As one of the two living Kartās explained to me, this statement has an ordinary, exoteric meaning for novices and lower-level initiates: It means simply that the Kartābhajā must have restraint over his or her senses and desires, he or she must be like a "eunuch," chaste and pure. For the more advanced and developed initiates, however, this statement has a far more profound esoteric meaning: It refers to the ultimate state of divine union and bliss—a kind of "spiritual androgyny"—in which man and woman are united as one, both experiencing the supreme nondual unity of male and female within themselves.[37] In short, ascending the esoteric hierarchy is much like peeling an onion, each layer of which is deconstructed and negated as one proceeds beyond it. And it is just this progressive unveiling, this constant peeling of the layers of secrecy, which ensures that the power and value of the secret as a form of "capital" always remains intact. As a *self-reproducing form of wealth,* this capital only continues to increase and grow, becoming ever more awesome and valuable as one ascends in rank and status.

3. *The skillful use of obscurity: Mumbo jumbo with exchange value.* The third of these strategies we might call the intentional and systematic use of ambiguous language. Secrecy is thus a key part of what Bourdieu calls the process of "misrecognition" or mystification, the "modalities of obliqueness and opacity, which endow certain persons with the mysterious aura of power, prestige, or legtimate authority."[38] As Robert Thurman suggests, Tantric discourse very often involves a kind of "skillful use of obscurity" or "deliberate use of ambiguity in the control of religious ideology."[39] For example, sayings such as "All jackals make the same sound" or "there are crocodiles in the Ganges; but a cat is only a fat tiger in a forest of Tulsi trees" seem to carry little clear significance but appear to be intentionally confusing and deliberately opaque. And others—such as "when one pulls the

hair, the head comes along," or "If one lives in the kitchen . . . he'll have to walk around carrying the stench of the place"—seem to be little more than relatively innocuous and rather banal pithy aphorisms.

However, if many of these statements appear nonsensical, pointless, or even completely absurd, this is surely only another part of that mechanism which transforms ordinary words into rare, precious, esoteric knowledge. As Lindstrom suggests, "nonsense" plays a powerful role in the "information market" precisely because it points to something mysterious, unknowable, and awesome; as a kind of "mumbo jumbo with exchange value," it allows the speaker to circulate a highly valued utterance without really revealing anything: "This opaque nonsense is an important discursive procedure that permits people to seem to be revealing knowledge while maintaining its secrecy and its continuing exchange value. . . . People suspect that nonsense, were it to be plumbed successfully, might reveal itself to be powerful information. . . . Discursive nonsense permits a spokesman to circulate knowledge and at the same time maintain the secret."[40]

4. *Semantic shock and extreme metaphorization.* The fourth of these strategies we might call (borrowing Paul Ricoeur's phrase) the power of "semantic shock"—namely, the effect that deliberately jarring, unusual, weird, or even offensive juxtapositions of words have on their audience. As Ricoeur suggests, this "shock effect" is seen above all in the case of a good metaphor, in which two different semantic fields are suddenly brought together in a new and unexpected way: The result is a temporary suspension or even "destruction" of the ordinary semantic function of ordinary language, with a flash of new insight which forces us to think of things in a new and unexpected way. "It is the 'semantic shock' engendered by the coming together of two different meanings which produces a new meaning. Imagination . . . is the power of metaphorically . . . forging an unprecedented semantic pertinence."[41] Indeed, by temporarily shattering the usual system of reference, by suspending the common function of language, a powerful metaphor has the potential to reshape our vision of the world itself, to open up a new world of meaning and insight—in Ricoeur's words, to "remake reality." It is just this kind of semantic shock, I think, which occurs in the Kartābhajās' excessive use of strange metaphors and bizarre symbolism—maggots born in excrement, scum-covered ponds, eunuchs and androgynes, stinking fruits, cakes of cow dung, and so on. They seem to delight in particular in contradictions or disquieting paradoxes (e.g., "the woman must become a *hijṛā*"—a male who has had his genitalia removed). As in the case of a good metaphor, the purpose of these odd images is not so much to communicate information as to jar or shock their listener. As Ricoeur puts it, "The strategy of metaphorical discourse is aimed not at facilitating communication or improving the efficacy of argumentation, but rather at challenging and even shattering our sense of reality through reflective redescription."[42]

The Kartābhajās' use of esoteric discourse, however, goes far beyond even Ricoeur's concept of semantic shock and the "destruction and remaking of language." For the Kartābhajās aim at actually shattering their experience of reality, of annihilating dualistic conceptual thought and immersing the self into the infinite bliss of Sahaja. The deeper function behind these bizarre statements and paradoxical language is not simply a literary exercise or a code language to be deciphered on an intellectual plane: It is a soteriological technique, whose aim is precisely to shatter and deconstruct ordinary ways of thinking and viewing the world, to thrust the initiate into an ecstatic mystical experience. This nondual, suprarational state of Sahaja can only be described by paradox and absurdity—like being "dead while alive," like "bathing in the sea of nectar without getting your hair wet." By reflection on these seemingly irrational phrases, together with techniques of meditation and yogic discipline, the initiate is led into the "paradoxical situation," as Eliade calls it: the state in which the ordinary conceptual structures and categories by which we carve up reality are suddenly shattered and transgressed: "*Sandhābhāṣā* . . . seeks to project the yogin into the paradoxical situation. . . . The semantic polyvalence of words substitutes ambiguity for the usual system of reference in ordinary language. This destruction of language contributes . . . to breaking the profane universe and replacing it with a universe of convertible and integrable planes."[43]

But at the same time, in addition to this soteriological goal, the deliberate use of shocking or offensive imagery also has an important role within the linguistic market. For it also works effectively to intensify the symbolic value of a given piece of secret information: It maximizes the aura of danger, the *sexiness* and power that surround a particular statement, making it appear all the more awesome, mysterious, and potentially dangerous. This is above all the case in those statements using explicitly erotic imagery (e.g., references to esoteric sexual practices or the ritual of *parakīyā* love), which violate normal social conventions and religious boundaries, and which are even regarded as immoral or illegal in the eyes of mainstream society. According to one key Mint Saying (STP 66; SE III.121), "The one who is secret is liberated; the one who is outside the veil is an adulteress." Indeed, as the Kartābhajās sing in the *Bhāver Gīta,* "I'm afraid to speak of it, brother, lest whoever hears it be scared *be scared shitless!*"

Black Market Symbolic Capital: "Coinage for the Poor"

Just as one must protect his wealth and possessions from thieves, O Beloved, so too, Devī, one must protect this Kula worship from ordinary bestial men (*paśus*). O Devī, Kula ritual should always be kept secret, as a woman does not reveal her pregnancy by her lover. The Vedas, Purāṇas, and Śāstras display themselves like prostitutes, but this wisdom is secretive like a daughter in law. (*Kulārṇava Tantra;* XI. 82, 85)

Discourse is doubtless a form of capital, invested in symbols; it can be transmitted, displaced, accrued or lost. (Michel de Certeau, *The Writing of History*)

The net result of these various discursive strategies, these tactics of restricted access, deliberate obfuscation, or metaphoric shock, is precisely the *creation of value*:

Together, they serve to transform a given piece of ordinary information into a rare, highly valued resource or precious commodity. And precisely because secret discourse is extremely indeterminate and radically contextual, its "value" does not lie in its content or substance but, rather, in its *exchange*. Like money or coinage, secret discourse is something which is always (whatever its content) to be *exchanged,* to be transmitted from guru to disciple, from insider to outsider, from higher-level initiate to lower-level initiate. Hence, to possess this rare, mysterious, potentially dangerous knowledge is to possess enormous status, prestige, and "symbolic capital." As Manulāl Miśra himself explains in his introduction to the "mint sayings," this language is called "the Mint" precisely because, like a coinage mint, it creates highly valued objects, which must be carefully hidden within the vault of esoteric discourse.

> *The essential meaning of Ṭyāṅkśālī (the Mint):* . . . In order to give a taste of pure bliss to human beings sunk in delusion, the compassionate Dulālcāṇd, savior of the poor and lowly, revealed the Sahaja path. . . . [But] he expressed these most profound teachings and deeply secret practices in a very brief form. . . . Not everyone can understand the true profound essence of all these things. All the divine teachings that have flowed from Dulālcāṅd's mouth like supreme nectar are called *Ṭyāṅkśālī*. For, just as, by means of the Mint—that is, the device by which coins are fashioned—gold, silver, etc., are sealed and can be stored up in vast amounts, so too, in this precious treasury, many valuable meanings are hidden within each word.[44]

This is, however, no mere ordinary coinage, no mere wealth for the greedy and powerful men of the marketplace; rather, we are told, it is specifically a *coinage for the Poor,* a form of wealth and power for the weak and disadvantaged. As we read again and again in the Mint Sayings:

I wish to become a poor man; if one attains the true condition of Poverty, there is supreme happiness. (STP 64; SE III.85)

These Mint Sayings are neither for the Marketplace nor for wealth; they are only for the poor. (STP 66; SE III.123)

The name of the land of one's [true] Mother and Father is the "Poor Company." (STP 69; SE III.184)

As such, this Mint Language or "coinage for the Poor" played a series of important roles within the specific social and historical context of the Black Town of Calcutta in the early colonial period. First, it opened up the possibility of an "alternative social space" or what Bourdieu has called a *"free market of linguistic exchange."* Creating a new arena for discourse and social interaction, concealed from the dominant social order, it opened a new space in which poor, lower-class individuals could find a temporary freedom from the burdens of caste and labor in mainstream society. As Miśra himself explains in explicitly "economic" metaphor, the Kartābhajā's esoteric language opens up a new, secret marketplace (*gupta hāṭ*)—the Marketplace of Truth (*satyahāṭ*) or the Market of Bliss (*ānanda-hāṭ*). Concealed from the eyes of the rich and powerful, this is a market in which the poor lower orders (*kāṅgāl, gorib lok*) can attain vast new wealth and spiritual commodities:

> *Mānuṣa-cāṅd's Marketplace of Truth* [*satya-hāṭ*]: In this marketplace there is nothing but the buying and selling of pure love. The genuine disciples, Sādhus and saints grasp the scales of truth and engage in True business in this markteplace. . . . No merchants come here intoxicated with greed. . . . This is only a marketplace of the poor [*kāṅgāler hāṭ*]. When one engages in buying and selling in this marketplace, there is never any loss, and all one's desires are fulfilled; one can become rich in infinite wealth. . . . In this market of bliss, there is no distinction between kings and subjects, rich men and poor men.[45]

In this sense, esoteric discourse operates in a way not entirely unlike "slang." As Bourdieu suggests, slang is an intentionally deviant form of discourse, which is exchanged and understood only within a specific context, among a particular group of insiders. Hence it offers an alternative kind of distinction, communal identity, and symbolic capital, particularly for those groups that are marginalized or deprived of actual capital in mainstream society (racial and ethnic minorities, poor working classes, etc.). It is thus "the product of the pursuit of distinction in a dominated market. It is one of the ways in which those individuals . . . who are poorly endowed with economic and cultural capital are able to distinguish themselves."[46]

The Kartābhajās, however, take this a good deal further than the mere use of slang. Indeed, as we have already seen (chapter 2), they seek not only to create an alternative social space or "free market" of social exchange but also to create two separate identities, two distinct "selves." In the external world of society, he or she lives a "conventional" (*vyavahārik*) or exoteric life, in conformity with the laws of caste and religious orthodoxy, but in the inner life of the Kartābhajā sect, he attains an "ultimate" or "supreme" (*paramārthik*) identity, transcending normal social restrictions and orthodox religion. With a kind of dual or schizophrenic personality, the Kartābhajā could thereby "respect social norms and perform duties maintaining a traditional facade, while secretly worshipping the Kartā."[47]

Still more important, the possession of this secret information, and the progressive exchange and accumulation of the coinage or "capital" of the Mint Sayings, offers the initiate the opportunity to ascend an alternative social hierarchy—to attain what Winston Davis calls a kind of *"upward religious mobilty."*[48] For, like all forms of capital, secret knowledge is not mere wealth which is stored up and hoarded; rather, it is a *self-reproducing* form of wealth, which grows in mystery and power as one ascends the esoteric hierarchy. The further one advances in knowledge of these Mint Sayings, the more layers of hidden meanings he unpeels in each secret word, and the higher he rises in initiatic status, the more his symbolic capital accumulates interest and generates more capital. As one former Kartā, Satyaśiva Pāl, explains, the disciple rises successively through the degrees of initiation until he reaches the highest, the most powerful—and also the most dangerous, even deadly stage—of knowledge, which is possible only for the rarest of individuals: "One after the other, one must rise through the levels (of initiation). The final stage is very difficult, for there is no food, no pleasure, no sleep, no eyes, no ears, no worldly thoughts. . . . Then he will be dead while living [*jyānte marā*]. If there is a single mistake, there is a possibility of destroying the body. That's why this stage is not permitted for everyone. Only one in a million can perform this practice."[49] Thus, as the Kartābhajā apologist, Gopal Krishna Pal, explained to the *Bengal District Gazetteer,* the Kartābhajā path offers a rare opportunity for poor and downtrodden individuals on the bottom of the social ladder to attain new levels of "distinction." By ascending this alternative, hierarchy, by increasing the capital of their secret knowledge, even the poorest man may rise in status and power above those who are, in exoteric society, his betters: "a person of however low a social status . . . is accepted as the spiritual guide by those who are socially his superiors. *Thus persons who had no status in society find . . . vast opportunities for distinguishing themselves.*"[50]

Meetings With Remarkable Madmen: Sex, Secrecy, and Censorship among Contemporary Kartābhajā Gurus

Look, [Caitanya-Āulcāṅd] has come in the form of a Madman—
Does He who makes such mischief commit any sin?
Unless you frolic with that Madman, you can't dispel the darkness!
You can easily find deliverance from the hand of time—
For anyone who is intimately joined with this Madman,
becomes a Madman himself—and so dissolves himself [in Madness]!
. . . Brother, unless you become mad yourself, then, if you suddenly see the Madman, how will you recognize Him? (BG 149; II.12)

If the problem of secrecy as found in historical texts presents us with a profound ethical and epistemological double bind, then this dilemma is only multiplied a hundredfold when we begin to deal with real living practitioners of esoteric traditions.[51] Following the advice of authors such as Douglas Brooks,[52] I do believe that the scholar of an esoteric tradition such as Indian Tantra has a responsibility to consult not only the textual tradition but also, whenever possible, the living oral tradition as handed down by initiated practitioners. I do *not,* however, believe that access to a living oral tradition resolves either the ethical or the epistemological problems of secrecy; on the contrary, as I quickly discovered in the course of my own research in West Bengal and Bangladesh, it only compounds and intensifies them.

Between the years 1994 and 1997 I encountered and interviewed a variety of Kartābhajā gurus—among them, a female miracle worker and charismatic leader of north Calcutta, a dancing folksinger of rural Nadia district, a variety of minstrels and beggars of Bangladesh, a self-proclaimed wandering "madman" (*pāgal*), and two separate individuals both claiming the title of "Kartā" (the supreme Incarnation of God in human form).[53] In the process, I also encountered the full spectrum of attitudes toward secrecy and toward my inquiries into their mysteries, ranging from hostility and suspicion to extreme enthusiasm and almost too ready cooperation. Indeed, I was even approached by one colorful character—the same one who claimed to be a Kartābhajā master in possession of "many secret things" to tell me—who later turned out to be an imposter. Having heard that a rich Western scholar was looking for Kartābhajās, it seems, he took advantage of the situation by presenting himself to me as a repository of profound esoteric knowledge.[54] In sum, I quickly realized that the problem in the study of secrecy is neither simply "unlocking the secret" nor simply determining which (if any) of the innumerable secrets, mystic interpretations, and cryptic meanings is to be believed and which (if not all) are simply dissimulations, false trails, and disguises. Rather, it is a more subtle problem of understanding *how they function strategically* in specific contexts and in relation to specific interests.

Among the many Kartābhajā disciples whom I met, two in particular—one, an older *guru* from rural Murshidabad, and the other, one of the most prominent leaders of the tradition in north Calcutta—seemed to represent the two extreme poles in the study of secrecy: on the one hand, strong distrust, with a deep reluctance to reveal the secret; on the other, extreme openness, with a strong interest in revealing secrets. These extremes became all the more intense as I delved into the touchy subjects of Tantric sexual rituals and the meaning of disturbingly cryptic Mint Sayings such as "the woman must become a *hijṛā*. . . ."

A Poor Wandering Madman

Brother, understand through hints and symbols [*ābhāse*]. (BG 97)

One of my first and most instructive encounters with a Kartābhajā guru occurred in the small village of Ghoshpara (the sacred center of the tradition, located about 15–20 miles north of Calcutta) with a rather gruff and surly old fellow, whom I shall call here Kāṅgāl Mahanta.[55] It was with Kāṅgāl that I first came to appreciate the real frustrations and difficulties involved in the study of secrecy—that is, the problem of a religious practitioner who does not seem to want to tell anything, or at least not anything comprehensible.

Claiming to be 90 years old but appearing to me to be closer to perhaps 50, Kāṅgāl Mahanta is a mysterious and highly respected guru originally from the district of Murshidabad (though when I asked him about his home, he simply replied, "I have no home; I'm just poor wandering madman [*pāgalāmi*])." In appearance, Kāṅgāl seemed much like the wandering minstrels and holy "madmen," the Bāuls, who are identified by their ragged dress, their long beard and hair tied in a topknot, and their deliberately bizarre, crazy often antisocial and offensive behavior. Like the Bāuls, Kāṅgāl seemed to take a certain pride in speaking and acting in as unconventional and incomprehensible a manner as possible. However, like all of the most powerful and authoritative Kartābhajā gurus, he was also profoundly respected and revered, held in high status, precisely because of his mysterious, inscrutable character, and his possession of awesome esoteric knowledge.

Kāṅgāl was in fact a master at the art of metaphor, allegory, and symbolic disguise—a fact that became particularly evident when I tried to press him on the question of Tantric sexual rituals. When I initially raised the question, he immediately engaged in a long and complicated metaphorical exposition, using an amazing variety of weird natural and worldly imagery (water, plants, flowers, coconuts, geese, floods, boats, and a great deal of imagery drawn from the world of the marketplace). He began to tell me, for example, of the very origin of the Universe, when God (Nirañjana) sent the primordial flood to fill the precosmic Void; upon the ocean formed by the flood, there appeared seven islands, with seven heavens and seven hells. And at the very bottom of the ocean, within the lowest of the seven hells (Rasātala) there arose a single banian leaf, which contained a magnificent jeweled altar; and upon this jeweled altar lay a single Seed (*bīja*, also Semen); and within this Seed lay the secret Jeweled City, the city of radiant splendor.

When I pressed him as to the meaning of this mythic allegory, he told me that he was willing to explain at least *some* of it to me—though he could not reveal *everything*. The image here is that of the human body itself, which is a mirror and microcosm of the entire universe. The seven islands are the seven cakras, or spiritual energy centers, which, according to most Indian yogic systems, are believed to lie along the axis of the spinal column, and the jeweled city floating on the banian leaf is the innermost place of the Heart, the core of the self, wherein dwells the Man of the Heart (*Maner Mānuṣa*).

Most of this mythic imagery and Kāṅgāl's explanation was not entirely new to me, nor did it strike me as particularly "esoteric"; most of it I recognized from the songs of the *Bhāver Gīta* and from other printed texts.[56] Moreover, though I found this interpretation interesting, I quickly realized that Kāṅgāl was in fact leading me ever further into the labyrinth of metaphor and mystification, ever further away from the answer to my question. So I decided to interrupt his increasingly complicated narrative and attempt to redirect the conversation back toward the problem of Tantric sexual rites. Unfortunately, my questions were only answered by yet another long, rambling series of metaphors and symbolic digressions—this time, an extended metaphor using the imagery of merchant ships sailing on the rivers and streams to the wharfs of the seven cities to sell their imported goods.[57]

Now, although these kinds of metaphors and allegories are surely not meaningless, it became increasingly evident that Kāṅgāl was using them as a means of avoiding or circling around my original question, appearing to answer it with profound and mysterious statements while in fact not telling me anything tangible at all about what I had asked him. He had still skillfully managed to avoid saying anything about Tantric sexual practices (we will examine these metaphors and symbolic images, along with their possible meanings, in closer detail in the following three chapters).

In frustration, I tried to question him about the well-known Kartābhajā saying, which I analyzed earlier, "the woman must become a *hijṛā* and the man a *khojā*. . . ." As soon as I mentioned this saying, Kāṅgāl made a rather surprised face and an "ooph" sound, saying only the following: "This one is very *marmāntik*" (*marmāntik* is a difficult word to translate, meaning something like heart-rending, in the sense of deeply profound, essential, awesome, or powerful). At first, he seemed quite unwilling to tell me anything much about the meaning of this phrase at all. It was simply too powerful and potentially too dangerous. However, when I asked him whether or not this phrase was in fact a reference to sexual practices or to actual physical relations between men and women, he replied, rather hesitantly, "Yes, conjugal union is also a valid path. For, in order to reach the stage of Spiritual Love (*prema*), there is need of Lust (*kāmer darkār āche*); lust is the fuel which drives us to Love."

Still not entirely satisfied, however, I continued to press Kāṅgāl on the topic, and pointed out to him that many Kartābhajā disciples, including the former (conservative and orthodox) Kartā, fiercely oppose the use of sexual rituals or anything smacking of "Tantra."[58] "Many Kartābhajās I have met, and even your own former Kartā, have said that the Kartābhajā path is completely opposed to the practice of sexual rituals. Is this true?"

He hesitated and looked uncertain for a moment, then replied firmly, "Yes, what the Kartā says is always true."

Increasingly puzzled by his apparent inconsistencies, I asked, "But doesn't that completely contradict everything you have just told me? I thought you had just said that *maithuna* is a part of the Kartābhajā path, and that lust (*kāma*) is necessary in order to arouse the experience of true love (*prema*)?" By this time, however, I could see that Kāṅgāl's patience was wearing increasingly thin, and that he was quite clearly annoyed that I had caught him in a seeming contradiction. He paused for some time, and then, looking me sharply in the eye, asked, "How old are you?" "27," I replied. "Have you married?" he asked, bending still closer to my face his eyes piercing deeply into my own. When I said no, he let out a big "humph" and scoffed: "Well, in that case, I can say nothing more to you! What can you know about such things if you don't even have a woman of your own?"

Rather puzzled, I sat quietly for a moment and then, with a smile, replied, "Well, in that I case, I guess I'll have to get married." At that, all of Kāṅgāl's disciples burst out laughing and seemed quite pleased; Kāṅgāl himself, however, only seemed all the more annoyed at the entire affair.

Secrecy as Advertising and Good Public Relations

Know, in a hint [*ābhāse*], what its nature is.
Public exposure is impossible, but a taste of it possible. (BG 48; II.68)

If I experienced some frustration and disappointment in the case of Kāṅgāl Mahanta, I encountered quite the opposite problem in the case of another older guru of northern Calcutta, whom I shall call here Kṛṣṇacandra Devamahanta.[59] Indeed, here I discovered the problem of a guru who seems almost *too* anxious to tell a scholar a secret, almost too ready to say whatever he thinks one might want to hear—even if he is not entirely sure what he's talking about.

A man of about 40 years, who (in his exoteric public life) works in downtown Calcutta, Kṛṣṇacandra occupies an important place in the contemporary Kartābhajā hierarchy. As one of the living descendents of the Pāl family, Kṛṣṇacandra is the leader and spokesman for one of the main factions within the sect today. In contrast to the more conservative and orthodox group, centered in Ghoshpara, Kṛṣṇacandra's faction is considered more liberal, more unorthodox, and immersed in the more controversial, esoteric aspects of the tradition. Moreover, Kṛṣṇacandra appears to have taken it upon himself to try to reinvigorate and revitalize his tradition, to counteract its rather sad decline in this century, and to restore it to it the power and prestige it once held in the nineteenth century. He is thus the leader of a group of other like-minded gurus and the editor of a journal explicitly designed for this project.

Hence, it is not entirely surprising that Kṛṣṇacandra was delighted to discover a young Western scholar interested in studying and writing about his tradition. Nor is it surprising that he was quite happy to tell me as much about his tradition as he could—including its most esoteric, most hidden, and potentially "dangerous" aspects. Even upon my very first visit to his home, he assured me that he had many secret and hidden things (*gupta, rahasya jiniś*) he could tell me. Not only did he direct me toward several gurus in the remote areas of rural Bengal, who, he promised, would provide me with the innermost details of Kartābhajā secret ritual, but he was also enthusiastic about sharing with me whatever esoteric knowledge he himself possessed. In fact, I quickly came to the conclusion that Kṛṣṇacandra had a vested interest in making sure I knew that his tradition did indeed possess esoteric, ancient, mysterious—and therefore *precious and valuable* secret teachings. And this became all the more apparent as soon as the question of economic capital entered the equation.

When I told Kṛṣṇacandra, for example, that I had been trying to locate one old and rare edition of the *Bhāver Gīta* (dated 1870), which was supposed to be preserved somewhere in old Calcutta, he assured me that this valuable and highly esoteric text was in fact in his possession. It had been his father's and was kept in a special room in another part of his home. Excited, I asked if I might see it, and he immediately said yes of course—but not today, it would be inconvenient for him to locate it and bring it out just then; I would have to come back another day, and he would be happy to show it to me then. However, after making several long and unpleasant trips up to northern Calcutta, I came to the conclusion that I was never going to see this elusive text and that quite probably this text did not exist. But, of course, whether or not he actually did own it, Kṛṣṇacandra's *claim* to own this rare book was also, like all claims to the possession of secret information, a claim to status, prestige, and symbolic (and perhaps economic) capital.

On the other hand, however, Kṛṣṇacandra was quite happy to discuss at some length the more difficult and most esoteric Kartābhajā spiritual techniques, which are inherited from the esoteric Sahajiyā traditions of Bengal. According to Kṛṣṇacandra, these methods, being potentially dangerous if misused by untrained souls, are supposed to be reserved only for the most advanced initiates under the close supervision of a guru.[60] These include fairly elaborate methods of breath control, the means of awakening the "Serpent Power" (*kuṇḍalinī*), the technique of retaining the semen and raising the it to the top of the head, and various other Tantric and yogic practices.[61]

Encouraged by Kṛṣṇacandra's apparent openness, I decided to venture a series of probing questions regarding the role of Tantric sexual rites, and specifically the meaning of the Mint Saying, "the woman must become a *hijṛā* and the man a *khojā*. . . ." Again, to my surprise, I found him more than willing to speak to me about this highly controversial and sensitive topic. When I asked him if Kartābhajā disciples engage in secret Tantric practices involving sexual intercourse, he replied, "There are many paths. Sexual union is also a path." I then raised the objection that many more conservative Kartābhajās are utterly opposed to Tantric sexual rituals, arguing that the true meaning of the "*hijṛā*" or "*khojā*" is one who is utterly chaste and pure, as sexless as a eunuch. "I do not agree with this interpretation," he replied, "Most outsiders and even the majority of disciples cannot understand this saying. The practice of conjugal love is also a path. But it is a very hidden one. It is not to be discussed openly."[62]

Here Kṛṣṇacandra had recourse to the now familiar argument that there are many different levels of truth which apply to different human beings depending on their stage of spiritual development and moral quality. The more conservative interpretation represents the lower, exoteric or outward level of truth, which pertains to less advanced devotees who are simply not capable of rising to the higher levels of truth. For them, it is far safer to remain at the lower levels of conventional devotional practice. However, for the most advanced souls of the strongest character and purest morals, *maithuna* or sexual union with another man's wife can also be used as the quickest and most expedient (though potentially most dangerous) path to liberation.

I then asked Kṛṣṇacandra the rather perplexing question of just how it was that he was able to discuss such esoteric and controversial matters with an uninitiated outsider like myself. After all, aren't these private rituals and esoteric practices precious and valuable, and are they not potentially dangerous if entrusted to someone like me who has not received the proper instruction, moral preparation, and spiritual training? This question seemed to trouble him for a moment, and he paused for some time before responding: "I can tell you the general nature of these matters, that is true. But I cannot tell you the details. For that kind of *śikṣā* [instruction] there is need of *dīkṣā* [initiation]. Thus, I can tell you that conjugal love is also a path to discovering the Man of the Heart; I can tell you that there are many Masters today who follow this path. But I cannot tell you the inner workings of this path, the specific techniques and particular methods."[63]

Now, although their attitudes toward the discussion of what is "secret" varied tremendously, both Kāṅgāl Mahanta and Kṛṣṇacandra would appear to share a number of common strategies or tactics. Many of these are the same kinds of tactics we encountered previously in the textual materials and in the Language of the Mint—though they are rendered all the more complex and tangled by direct interaction with a living guru. These strategies include (at the very least) the following:

1. *Advertisement*—that is, the claim to possess precious, rare, and valuable knowledge while simultaneously partially revealing and largely concealing it.
2. *Sexiness*—the claim to possess knowledge which is not only valuable but also potentially dangerous, transgressing normal social and religious boundaries, and regarded as immoral or illegal in the eyes of mainstream society.
3. *Lure and withdrawal*—or the continuous dialectic between the promise of awesome secret knowledge and the continuous (perhaps eternal) *deferral* of the revelation of the secret; that is always reserved for the next meeting, the next stage of initiation, the next level of spiritual attainment.
4. *Hierarchalization* of truth—or the construction of a graded system of insiders and outsiders, degrees of initiation, and levels of knowledge, which can be used to explain away or get around apparent contradictions and inconsistencies (e.g., some teachings are for novices and some only for the highest initiates).
5. *The skillful use of obscurity*—or the deliberate use of ambiguity, digression, incompletion, and systematic obfuscation.
6. *Metaphoric shock*—or the skillful use of metaphor, allegory, symbolism, and, above all, the use of deliberately shocking, strange bizarre, or offensive metaphors.

All these tactics (what we might call the "haggling strategies" in the marketplace of secrecy) have the function of maintaining both the value and the scarcity of the concealed information, thereby assuring that the secret remains a key source of status and symbolic capital.

Conclusions: The Quest for Capital amid a Dominated Marketplace

In sum, for the largely poor and lower-class individuals who made up the majority of the Kartābhajā following, the use of this strange secret discourse or Mint Language could (and in many ways still can today) serve as an effective source of symbolic power: It could function both as a new source of prestige, status, or capital within an alternative social order or "free market" of linguistic exchange and also as a means of resisting or contesting the capital of the dominant classes in the mainstream order.

As we will see in the following two chapters, this power of secrecy as a source of capital only becomes all the more intense as it is played out in the Kartābhajās' skillful use of metaphoric language (particularly the language of the marketplace and the "Company") and in their more concrete physical practices and bodily techniques. However, as a specifically "black market" kind of capital—a symbolic good exchanged only within an aysymmetrical and "dominated marketplace," to use Bourdieu's terms—the symbolic goods of the secret society also represent a profoundly ambivalent kind of power. Indeed, as we delve further into the Kartābhajās' esoteric discourse and practice, we will find that this "coinage for the poor" can also often become a dangerous liability for its owner.[64]

4

The Poor Company

Mercantile Discourse and Its Deformations in the *Bhāver Gīta*

That which encompasses the thirty-six castes and the four classes,
bearing rule over the sixty cities—that is the Poor Company.
. . . Look—thirty-three million men have united
and sit, paying honor to that Company—the Poor Company.
When it puts its seal [on the merchandise], it will be honored by everyone.
(BG 161; II.5)

Throughout our discussion of the Kartābhajās, we have noted that much of their enigmatic language and songs are saturated with the imagery of the marketplace—the competitive, often ruthless world of trading and wholesaling, brokering and moneylending, profit and loss. Now we need to explore this imagery in more detail, looking more closely at the specific forms and the deeper implications of this rather striking use of mercantile terminology.[1] In the previous chapter, we examined the general features and formal structure of the Kartābhajās' unique Language of the Mint, with its various discursive strategies aimed at producing rare and valuable pieces of knowledge. In this chapter, we engage the more specific *metaphoric strategies*, the particular kinds of images and symbolic patterns, which they employ in order simultaneously to conceal and reveal, mask and disclose their esoteric teachings to their audience. As Debendranāth De observes, the Kartābhajā songs are for the most part in continuity with the older tradition of Tantric coded discouse or *sandhābhāṣā*, with its use of queer enigmas, riddles, and contradictory metaphors, but what is particularly unusual about these songs, and what distinguishes them from earlier Sahajiyā literature, is their specific *choice* of metaphors—namely, those drawn from the world of the marketplace: "The Kartābhajās are Sahajiyās. That's why in their songs many statements appear concealed in riddles. . . . However, in their effort to conceal their meanings in riddles there is widespread use of the metaphors of business, trade, buyers, shopkeepers, the Company, import and export, profit, etc."[2]

Now, the use of mercantile imagery is surely not without precedent in the world of Bengali literature. As early as the fifteenth-century *Caṇḍīmaṅgal*, in Rāmprasād Sen's hymns to Kālī, and even in Vaiṣṇava devotional texts such as the *Hāṭ Pattan*, the imagery of moneylending, taxation, and trade had often been used to express the transactions and exchanges of mortal life. And later in the nineteenth century, even Rāmakṛṣṇa would make an ironic and parodic use of the language of business to describe the troubled lives of lower-middle-class babus laboring in the mercantile and government offices of colonial Calcutta. Indeed, as we have seen, the marketplace is perhaps even the "worldly metaphor" *par excellence*.[3]

Yet what *is* unique about the Kartābhajā songs is, first, the remarkable extent to which they make use of economic discourse: indeed, as Chakrabarty observes, "Roughly 70 percent of the songs of the *Bhāver Gīta* refer to such business terms as Company merchants, agents, brokers, traders, porters, stockists, indigo traders, invoice, trade mark, etc."[4] Second, these songs are also among the first—and, to my knowledge, among the only—religious songs in Bengal to make explicit use of imagery drawn from the East India Company and the capitalist discourse of the European merchants. In addition to "invoices" (*inbhāis*), "contracts" (*koṇṭrakṭ*), "platoons" (*palṭan*), "money" (*mani*), and various other English terms, we even find the company (*kompānī*) employed as a key metaphor for the Kartābhajā tradition. Whereas the old company of the mainstream Vaiṣṇava tradition had become worn out and corrupt, filled with thieving brokers and swindling moneylenders, the Kartābhajās had come to found a "Poor Company" (*gorib kompānī*) or a "Mad Company" (*pāgal kompānī*), offering genuine spiritual goods to its followers. In short, this "Platoon of the Poor"—composed mainly of poor laborers, petty shopkeepers, and porters in the lower rungs of the market hierarchy, and often in the servitude of the *real* company—achieved a rather audacious appropriation of the imagery of the marketplace and its owner, the company, itself.

In the sections that follow, I examine the Kartābhajās' unique use of mercantile imagery, first in the general metaphor of the "marketplace of the world," second, in their unusual use of terminology drawn from the East India Company, and finally in their ingenious appropriation of the metaphors of the "Poor Company" and the "Mad Company." Now, if I focus primarily here on the economic dimensions of the Kartābhajās' esoteric songs, this is by no means intended to be a kind of "vulgar economism" or a simplistic reduction of religious language to material interests. Quite the contrary, I argue that social agents are not only capable of deploying religious myths and rituals in order to express more concrete economic or political motives (as the members of the subaltern studies have so clearly shown us)[5] but, at the same time, *religious actors are* also *capable of appropriating very "secular," economic, and political discourse while transforming it into a profound bearer of deeper religious or spiritual ideals.*

As I wish to suggest, esoteric discourse functions here as a skillful and playfully subversive strategy—a unique variety of what James Fernandez calls the "metaphoric strategies" which comprise much of social life. Not only do metaphors help us, as cognitive psychologists such as Lakoff and Johnson have shown, to organize our world, providing the basic image-schemas and models by which we construct reality[6]; more important, as Fernandez suggests, they also help to construct human identities and integrate social groups. In groups such as the syncretist Bwiti movement among the Fang, for example, metaphor is one of the key devices used to integrate the individual with the social collective—to "return to the whole." It is, moreover, one of the basic tropes used to situate or elevate individuals in "quality space"—to find a meaningful, valued status in the social structure, or to "move up in the world."[7]

In contrast to Fernandez, however, I would emphasize not simply the integrative and unifying effect of metaphor but also its potentially *subversive* and disruptive use—its role, not simply as a means of social cohesion and "returning to the whole" but as a means for dominated or marginal groups to parody, criticize, or challenge the dominant order. The Kartābhajās' use of the metaphors of the marketplace and the company, I would suggest, is a classic example of what de Certeau's calls the various "tactics of consumption," by which dominated subgroups can "subvert the dominant culture from within."

> Submissive, and even consenting to their subjection, the Indians nevertheless made of the rituals, representations and laws imposed on them something quite different from what their conquerors had in mind; they subverted them not by rejecting . . . them but by using them with respect to ends foreign to the system they had to accept. . . . Their use of the dominant social order deflected its power, which they lacked the means to challenge. . . . The strength of their difference lay in procedures of consumption.[8]

It is precisely these sorts of "procedures of consumption" that we will explore in what follows.

The Marketplace of the World and the Bazaar of Love

When you deal in the market of the world
you think you buy rich rubies, diamonds, pearls—
you really only buy brass beads, my friend.
. . . "My house," "my goods"—like this our days go echoing by.
We eat the poison of our possessions, and when wealth is lost we weep.
What good will weeping do when lost, my brother?
(Lālan Fakir, Bhaṭṭācārya, *Bāṅglār Bāul o Bāul Gān*, no. 63)

Unlike many earlier Bengali authors, such as Rāmprasād Sen, the songs of the Kartābhajās make little use of agrarian or Zamindāri terminology drawn from the village and countryside of rural Bengal; indeed, even when the "Zamindār" does appear in the Kartābhajā songs, he is typically cast as a symbol of the "foolish man," that is, the adherent of other sects, "whose wealth is plundered by his corrupt officials."[9] The songs of the Kartābhajās are instead very much *urban* songs, songs of the marketplace, which are filled with the imagery of the lively business of colonial Calcutta and Dhaka.

The marketplace (*hāṭ, bājār*), we have already seen, was a critical knot in the complex flow of power and the exchange of social and economic resources during the rapidly shifting era of eighteenth-century Bengal (see chapter 1). Political power required that a Nawab, Rājā, or Zamindār have intimate relations with and authority over the marketplace, which represented a nexus of commercial trade, finance, social life, and religious worship alike. Hence, the market appears throughout many eighteenth-century Bengali religious texts and social commentaries as a key metaphor for worldly power, political dominance, and official authority. During the colonial era, as Sudipta Sen argues, the marketplace became an even more critical center of power and authority, as the British company sought to undertake a progressive "conquest of marketplaces"—a systematic effort to regulate, control and more effectively administer these key economic and political focal points of Bengali society.[10]

Yet simultaneously, the image of the marketplace could also become a potential source of subversion and critique of the dominant order. As Mikhail Bakhtin suggests, the marketplace holds a unique place in most cultures. As a realm of social interaction which transcends most ordinary social barriers, it brings together men and women of all classes in a common sphere of exchange, allowing an unusual freedom to speak frankly and critically: "The marketplace . . . was a world unto itself. . . . All performances in this area, from loud cursing to organized show . . . were imbued with the same atmosphere of freedom, frankness, and familiarity. . . . The marketplace was the center of all that is unofficial: it enjoyed a certain extra-territoriality in a world of official order and ideology; it always remained 'with the people.'"[11] So, too, as Ranajit Guha has shown in his study of peasant resistance in colonial Bengal, the marketplace was also a special site of criticism and subversion, a realm where the lower classes could speak out and criticize the dominant order or the lives of the wealthy upper classes. Because it represents a place "where people gather regularly and *en masse* for trade and . . . folk entertainment," the marketplace always represented a potential threat to the ruling powers: "the bazaar was clearly identified in colonialist thinking with the origin and dissemination of rumor and subversive discourse among the lower classes."[12]

This ambivalent status of the marketplace—as both a center of power and as a potential site of contestation and critique—also holds true on the religious plane. Not only was the marketplace a key metaphor for political dominance, but it was also used in many cases as a metaphor for religious dominance and spiritual authority. Among the most remarkable uses of this market metaphor in a religious text appears in a curious work attributed (probably falsely) to the famous Vaiṣṇava poet, Narottam Dās, entitled *Hāṭ Pattan* (The Foundation of the Marketplace). Indeed, Śrī Caitanya himself is transformed into a kind of "holy businessman," who has founded the spiritual Marketplace of the Vaiṣṇava tradition in order to distribute the commodities of love, song, and prayer throughout the world:

When the boat set sail over the waters of love,
some clung on, eager to reach their destiny.
. . . A market and post were set up by the quay,
and the flag went up, a warning to the sinful.
Storehouses of four *rasas* in every direction,
secured all around with the name of Hari.
Guards sat chanting and chanting that name
One could buy or sell in this market at will.[13]

Caitanya's chief disciples are then appointed as the various agents and brokers of this market—Nityānanda becomes the ruler, Mukunda a clerk (*mutasuddī*), Advaita a scribe (*munśī),* and Gadādhar a treasurer (*bhāṇḍārī*), while Narahari Dās is transformed into a flirting courtesan[!]. The host of devotees flocking to the holy bazaar become the merchants and traders, selling their divine merchandise of songs (*kīrtan*) in praise of Kṛṣṇa.

The image of the marketplace, however, could also be given a far more critical and subversive edge: Indeed, it could also be used by lower-class or deviant sects such as the Kartābhajās as a negative and critical image. As Sen points out, the songs of the Kartābhajās often invert and subvert the image of the "official marketplace," cynically depicting it as a world of illusion and suffering, a realm of thieving, chicanery, and greed:

> In contrast to the appropriation of the market as a lordly domain in Narottama's narrative . . . in the songs of other sects—particularly ones that question or subvert kingly rule or prescribed religious leadership—the marketplace appears as a classic metaphor for material illusion in mortal life . . . The songs . . . of the cryptic Kartābhajā sect . . . talk about wandering human souls deluded by the labyrinth of marketplaces:
>
> "Those who wander among mankind seeking the easy abode
> can never find its path or even its address
> for in this earth, endless cities, bazaars and markets
> are laid by a trick of māyā—a rule of fate, the player."[14]

For the Kartābhajās, then, the image of the marketplace appears to function on two levels simultaneously: on both a very practical socioeconomic level, and on a more symbolic religious level. First, in its more concrete economic and political sense, the image of the "bazaar of the world" (*bhava-bājār*) has direct implications, describing the actual lives of men and women laboring in colonial Bengal. It serves as a source of critique and commentary on the lives of the poor lower orders of the slums and bazaars of the Black Town:

All the merchants engage in business in the Bazaar of this World.
Those who toil, in accordance with the law, don't have even an ounce [of
 wealth],
while those who engage in business, holding the surplus of trade,
happily take their profits and make some more purchases.
And when a break [in the trade] occurs, they give the beggar a handful!
 (BG 267; II.38)

Like many popular lower-class songs of nineteenth-century Calcutta, the Kartābhajā songs take great delight in poking fun at the life of common people in the marketplace—the "thieving brokers," the rapacious moneylenders, the cheating merchants with their crooked scales, and the poor porters and petty merchants struggling against debt and fraud. In one rather remarkable song, the author ironically laments the pathetic state of his countrymen, who have given up their land and their labor to the hands of foreigners. Even though castrated (*khojā*) and humiliated by British rule, they still try to ape the manliness (*mardānā*) of their masters, and still hope to mimic the foreign merchants in their business dealings:

Brother, no one can understand all these funny things!
They've been deluded, they've abandoned the milk and cream, and wander about, chewing husks of grain—
The Rājā of Bengal himself admits it!
Angrily tugging at his beard!
The Nawab dismisses and appoints his Ministers.
I could say such things too—if I smoked enough dope [*gāṅjā*]!
The laborer can understand nothing apart from his work;
for he never knows the taste of anything else.
. . . You people of this land are all eternally deluded!
Brother, how can you display the manliness of another [i.e., the British], if you yourself have been castrated [*khojā*]?
. . . Brother, for whose sake does all the traffic in this land take place?
Now no one can remember any other life!
. . . They're like tiny fish floundering in a handful of water,
Just seeing their affairs, I feel ashamed (BG 182; II.30)

In this respect, the Kartābhajā songs are not unlike many of the songs of Lālan Shāh and other Bāul poets. As Śaktināth Jhā suggests, the Bāuls often use the imagery of the bazaar and the sorrows of the poor Bengali merchant to describe the sad fate of those who seek happiness in the world of money and material wealth. Just as so many petty shopkeepers and traders were reduced to tremendous debt and abject poverty as the British capitalists and wealthy moneylenders progressively took control of the marketplace, so, too, the mortal human soul wanders in the endless debt and poverty of this mortal realm of *saṃsāra:*

> The *hāṭ* and *bājār* are mentioned again and again in the songs. . . . The East India company monopolised control over business in this era, and many small merchants had to take loans from Moneylenders or big businessmen, then lost their wealth and fell into poverty. . . . The metaphor of the wealth and inheritance of the small merchants becoming exhausted appears many times in these songs. . . . Because of thievery or disasters, the small merchants fell into poverty. . . . The Fakir religion is their last refuge.[15]

So too, we might also compare the Kartābhajā songs with the teachings of Rāmakṛṣṇa, which were also directed toward a similar kind of dislocated urban mercantile audience in colonial Calcutta. As Sarkar has argued, Rāmakṛṣṇa often spoke in ironic and satirical terms of the pathetic lives of the poorer and lower-middle-class babus, particularly the cakris or clerks, who toiled slavishly in the mercantile and governmental offices of colonial Calcutta.[16]

In the Kartābhajā songs, however, even more scathing observations are directed toward the rich and the greedy men of the marketplace, those who profit most and inflict the most suffering on others—above all, the moneylenders (*mahājan*), brokers, and middlemen (*dālāl, pāikār*). As Banerjee has shown, the poor lower classes of Calcutta often used poetry and song to complain of the sorrows of their laboring existence, as well as to mimic, criticize, parody, and ridicule the wealthy elite culture of the day. Throughout their popular ballads, we hear about the greedy and pretentious middle-class babus who have risen to new status by riding on the coattails of the company: "The earliest specimens of urban folk culture can be found in the humorous doggerels and proverbs, jokes and rhymes about contemporary society. . . . The rat race among English traders and Bengali banians to make fortunes . . . was a target of raillery on the part of the lower orders."[17] As we see in the following song, the author laments the sad fate of the poor shopkeeper who has signed everything away to the rapacious moneylender, and is now reduced to the status of a mere porter:

Will the Headman of the Porters protect you,
when the Moneylender's men come to arrest you for your debts?
Then you'll suffer everything!
What's overdue is recorded in the Money-lender's account book—
. . . We've all written our names in the Moneylender's book—
We became merchants and returned with all our assets—
the wealth of the money lender, together with the profits.
But even in the winning of earnings, there will be utter poverty—
I see that you've lost your profits and suffered everything! (BG 217; II.34)

Even more mercilessly, however, the Kartābhajās delight in poking fun at the treacherous brokers or middlemen, who run back and forth between the European traders and the indigenous merchants,[18] taking every opportunity to swindle the buyers and customers alike:

There's a great deal of thievery going on amongst these Brokers!
They bring so much of the farmers' goods, I see,
constantly, saying, "Oh! Oh!," they go from street to street—
and so many merchants and customers do business!
The Broker comes among them and sets up his flag—
And then he hides away the fine new merchandise, and makes an amicable settlement for himself! (BG 269; II.36)

Everything was overwhelmed with madness of the Brokers, and everything became corrupt!
Whenever someone wants to buy something, they ask "how [good] is it?"

The Brokers say, "it's genuine," but give them the fakes!
I hear that wherever I go, this sort of business goes on.
. . . The wretched Brokers have become a terrible nuisance!
while throughout the seven cities, the Shopkeepers consider their fate!
(BG 267; II.38)

Yet, on the other hand, in addition to its more concrete, real-life social and economic implications, the imagery of the marketplace also serves as a *religious weapon* and a tool for sectarian critique. As Sen suggests, it is powerful means of criticizing dominant religious organizations such as mainstream Vaiṣṇava tradition, which is depicted as corrupt, wealthy, and filled with thieves. We have already seen (chapter 1) that the Kartābhajās reinterpreted the key passage of the *Caitanya-caritāmṛta,* which states that "the rice remained unsold in the marketplace"; for the Kartābhajās, this means that the old marketplace of the Gauḍīya Vaiṣṇava lineage has become corrupt and self-serving, while the goods of bhakti and love are no longer being offered to the poor, lower-class devotees. Thus there is need of a new marketplace—the secret marketplace (*gupta hāṭ*) of the Kartābhajās, where the spiritual goods of love and devotion can still be purchased. So, too, as Ramakanta Chakrabarty explains, much of the mercantile imagery in the songs of the *Bhāver Gīta* is really a humorous and ironic attack on the orthodox Vaiṣṇava Gosvāmis. These wealthy and corrupt gurus are nothing more than greedy "brokers" middlemen, or traders (*dālāls, pāikārs*), surrounded by their agents and bailiffs, who have "become abnormally rich and have lost interest in spiritual culture."[19] "The so-called guardians of the divine order are absolutely worthless. . . . The world is full of false doctrines and false preachers. Mere brokers are posing as wholesalers."[20] Meanwhile, the Kartābhajās direct equally disparaging remarks toward the various other sects and faiths competing within the religious marketplace: "There are numerous small traders (insignificant sects). But these small traders are mostly bankrupt. . . . The spiritual market is full of commodities."[21] On the other hand, the Christian missionaries, who were among the Kartābhajās' foremost rivals in this marketplace of souls, are branded as "worthless market brokers, holding some packets made in England [*bilāter ek pakeṭ hāte phirteche bhārāte*]."[22]

In contrast to this world of misery, poverty, and treachery in the Bazaar of the world, the *Bhāver Gīta* praises the miraculous world of the *Prema-bājār,* the Bazaar of Love, which is the spiritual path of devotion. Lord Kṛṣṇa himself had come to this world in the form of Caitanya to found this wondrous Bazaar of Love, where the most amazing merchandise from all lands is available, where even the lowly and destitute are freed of their poverty:

Once this *Rasika* [Kṛṣṇa] came to the red city of Gour [as Caitanya].
He made the people weep and freely revealed the face of the Moon.
. . . Look—the desires of all men's hearts have been fulfilled.
So many Poor Men have become rich!
. . . Those who engage in business within the Bazaar of the *rasa* of Love

take the Government Merchandise to the wholesale merchants again and again.
Some put the goods into boxes and determine the weight,
and some go to the marketplace and joyfully engage in business [*byāpār karteche*]!
Twelve months a year they deal in import and export.
. . . The Bazaar is filled with so many kinds of things!
If there were any lack in this land,
He would return once again.
He has made everyone full of delight and free of poverty! (BG 247; II.56)

The true devotee is thus the one who has abandoned the "marketplace of the world" (*bhava-bājār*), and has instead chosen to work in the "wondrous factory" (*ājab kārkhānā*) in this bazaar of love, where he becomes a "merchant" (*dokāndār*) of true "spiritual commodities" (*māl*) (BG 41ff., 364–65). His "capital" (*jamā*) is the capital of honor and devotion, which he pays to the true Proprietor (*Mālik*) and ruler of the universe, namely, Caitanya in his newly incarnate form as the Kartā: "poor people have been spiritually enriched. . . . The spiritual market is full of commodities."[23] In this true, spiritual marketplace, ruled by the just and fair Rājā, there is no need for brokers, middlemen, or moneylenders (i.e., for Vaiṣṇava Gosāiṅs or Christian missionaries); business goes along freely and easily, without taxes or tariffs, as we see in the following songs—which are in fact the first songs of the oldest known Kartābhajā manuscript (KG 1):

Let me tell you a funny story about a King!
In his city, all along the road are rows and rows of merchants.
In the city-center there's a bazaar,
with the special seal of the Royal House.
Twelve months a year there's buying and selling, importing and exporting
whether the weight of the tares in the warehouse is little or great.
. . . [The king] never takes gifts, taxes or tariffs,
That's why there are so many merchants [*mahājan*]—they all revere him.
He waives all the taxes on the waterways.
. . . No one has need for brokering, commissions or such tactics [*dālāl dasturi jārijuri*]!
If there was exemption from the gifts, taxes and tariffs,
how was it prevented?
That indeed was Love!
The tax upon the waterways was waived;
So I'll go and dwell in that land!
There is no brokerage or commission;
for all that ostentatious show is false!
Look—Śaśī appears amidst the company of merchants! (BG 54; II.39–40)

In sum, the Kartābhajās' use of the the market metaphor serves as a clever double-bladed weapon: On the one hand, in the social and economic sense, it really does describe the rather unhappy lives of many poor men and women living in the slums and bazaars of Calcutta, with their dreams of a new, liberated bazaar, free of thieving brokers or treacherous moneylenders. On the other hand, in the religious sense, it also serves the purpose of criticizing the mainstream Vaiṣṇava tradition (represented in classic texts such as Narottam's "Foundation of the Marketplace"), while offering the vision of an alternative spiritual marketplace: the secret marketplace or Love-bazaar of the Kartābhajā path.

The Coming of the Company and the Arrival of the Wondrous Merchandise from Abroad

A commodity appears at first sight an extremely obvious, trivial thing. But analysis brings out that it is a very strange thing, abounding in metaphysical subtleties and theological niceties. . . . The mysterious character of the commodity form consists simply in the fact that the commodity reflects back the social characteristics of men's own labor as an objective characteristic of the products of labor themselves, as the socio-natural properties of things. (Karl Marx, *Capital*)

Listen all! How wonderfully did the God of heaven take cane in hand and topee on head, and come as merchants to the settlement at Calcutta to the joy of the people of Bengal! (Rāmprasād Mitra, village bard, second half of the eighteenth century)

Even more striking than this use of the imagery of the marketplace—which is in itself not unusual in the realm of Bengali literature—is the Kartābhajās' repeated and extensive use of the English term "company" (*kompānī*). In a long series of highly enigmatic songs (BG 65–67, 116–123, and 154–161), the Kartābhajās sing of the arrival of the British company's ships, weighted down with all their wondrous merchandise, creating a tremendous spectacle in the Bay of Bengal. Indeed, they even provide a vivid account of the fighting between the French and the British fleets and the glorious triumph of the English company.[24]

A delightful Merchant is coming upon the ship,
with so many wondrous things, creating a great splendor!
He has sent the news to this office:
They want a thousand and one ships.
Everyone will guess at what the merchandise might be!
And with them, I think, a fleet of one or two thousand will go!
The English and French, with great splendor,
were all detained at the wharf from their water-route,
Look—the French, fighting and fighting with the English,
have finally been subdued!
Just see, by the grace of God, a great wave has washed up over the deck!
All the danger has been dispelled.
The way has been opened,

and they're coming with all their wondrous, fine merchandise!
On each of their ships there will be a host of wealth.
. . . They have brought a ship loaded with merchandise, brother,
Look: while light still remains, they go upon the water,
O, what a beautiful display of excellent merchandise they've shown us!
O what pomp and display is on each ship!
. . . It seems as if they've built an incredible city upon the water!
Lalsasi says, "they've built a wondrous city upon the water!" (BG 117; II.22)

Having recounted the glorious victory of the British fleet over their adversaries, the author then proceeds to enumerate all the wondrous goods borne on the company ships. Describing in elaborate and endless detail all the tantalizing commodities or "cargo," which the company ships have brought, the author seems at first overjoyed by the splendid wealth of the foreign merchants. Never before has he ever seen such amazing and magnificent things—indeed, on seeing such a massive display of commodities and material wealth, the author even dreams of becoming a "broker" (*dālāl*) for these amazing goods:

The Company's ship is coming!
I just heard about it in the bazaar.
In each and every shop there's whispering—
Put down your newspaper [*nius pepār*],
you'll get to hear what's really happening!
. . . If anyone can act as the broker [*dālāl*] for even a single item of merchandise,
he'll become the owner of infinite wealth!
In the homes of the merchants of this city,
first we hold a [secret] counsel.
And Śaśī the *Rasika* thinks there will be much buying and selling! (BG 65; II.16)

Hey look—the ships of the Company are coming, with all their sails erect;
in the middle of the bay, what a spectacle is seen!
And so many still remain in the water.
They came and shouted the news at the top of their voices—
They'll come and unload in the city!
. . . Now various excellent merchandise can be seen,
They'll go to the warehouse and take the foreign goods.
Whatever one wishes will be there!
This import from abroad is no trifling stuff,
we know, for all these goods are marked with foreign labels.
If the permit for these imported goods is genuine,
Then and there I will purchase them.
And Śaśīlāl says, "Look, he floats in the ocean of *rasa*!" (BG 65; II.17)

There's various merchandise in the Warehouse [*āṛate*];
I stood up and came to see immediately.
No one could describe it—
I stood before it, amazed and perplexed.
How could I estimate its value, brother?
. . . There are so many shopkeepers—Sikhs, Armenians and Moghuls.
The Company is calling out [the inventory] on the shelves and rows,
Opening the bags that are marked, they calculate the invoices [*inbhāis*] on each item.
Everyone comes and goes [in this warehouse], but no one goes out anymore on the street!
Guns, pistols, old and new fashions on both sides,
knives and many fine trinkets,
and in a separate storeroom, various things from China.
Pictures, hanging lanterns, and mirrors of various types,
and how much candy, sugar and fruits—
Oh, how bright and sweet-smelling they are!
And Śaśī thinks, "There will have to be a Broker for all these things"!
(BG 66; II.18)

But what are we to make of all this elaborate imagery of the company and the seemingly endless enumerations of the miraculous foreign goods borne on the company ships? Is this a kind of Bengali version of a *Cargo Cult*? Is it, like the Melanesian cults, a sort of mythical retelling of "the mysterious arrival of European goods under colonial rule, and . . . the apparent contradiction between the wealth of the Europeans . . . and their own poverty"?[25] Once again, I would suggest that this imagery of the company functions on two levels simultaneously, both historically and spiritually, as both a socioeconomic and a religious commentary. On the concrete, historical level this is surely an actual account of the what was really happening at the ports and trading centers of colonial Calcutta: the rather overwhelming arrival of merchandise never seen before—often described as "treasure" in other contemporary literary and newspaper accounts (see chapter 1).[26] Moreover at least one or two Bengali authors of the early nineteenth century, such as Rāmprasād Mitra, had praised the arrival of the British company as a kind of "divine dispensation"—a final victory over the old crumbling Muslim rule, which would bring new order, justice, and prosperity to the land. As Mṛtyuñjaya Vidyālaṅkāra described it in his *Rājāvalī* of 1808, the company appears as the "force of divine will," which "vindicates dharma": "The Company . . . flying the flag of dharma, had gone to battle with the promise to defend those under its protection . . . The Company rules by divine will in order to protect its subjects."[27]

The Kartābhajās' description of the company, however, is an ambivalent and at times quite negative one. Not only has the company has brought with it a host of remarkable merchandise and foreign treasures, but it has also brought new possibilities for exploitation, impoverishment and oppression in this marketplace of the world. As the *Bhāver Gīta* laments:

O, how wonderfully funny you are!
You've quit your business, and now, I see, you're paying homage to the Porters
in the marketplace and at the wharf!
I see no shortage [of porters] in the service of the Company.
. . . So freely, I know, you had abandoned all your wealth,
wandering and searching throughout the entire Company—
that's why you break your back working here!
Your name is written in the account books of the Company Warehouse—
so why don't you sign on the top of the account book?
O, how many imported goods the Company has!
Surely you know that the weight is little, and not great—
But suddenly that cheating porter says that what is little is great!
You had come to work as a merchant in this land,
but when that business failed, you found a lot of work
in this market and bazaar.
And now the Porters, both petty and great, all control you!
Now no day is without joy!
Their pleasure grows by the hour!
You've labored for the Company for so long a time—
and Śaśī Lāl laughs and says, "oh, see how manly you are!" (BG 215; II.31)

Like the more general image of the marketplace, the imagery of the "company" is not simply a concrete social and historical commentary; rather, it too also has direct religious implications, as a commentary on the mainstream Vaiṣṇava tradition and the rise of the Kartābhajās. In certain songs, in fact, the authors make it clear that this strange language of the "company" is in fact a metaphor for the birth and spread of the Gauḍīya Vaiṣṇava tradition itself. The coming of the company ships refers to the coming of the Vaiṣṇava community, following in the wake of Caitanya, which has brought a wealth of "spiritual commodities" to the people of Bengal. In the following song, for example, we find a clear description of the arrival of Caitanya and his two companions, Nityānanda and Advaita Ācārya (the "Three Madmen"); at the same time, however, this song also plays ingeniously off the dual meaning of the words *Gorā*—meaning both "Fair Skinned" (an epithet of Caitanya) and "an Englishman"—and *kompānī*—meaning both a community in the general sense and the actual British East India Company (BG 415). Hence the phrase *Gorā Kompānī* carries the remarkable double entendre of the "Company of Caitanya"—which has come from over the ocean of the world bearing its host of spiritual treasures—and the "company of Englishmen"—who have come across the ocean with their wondrous ships full of material commodities:

The three Madmen[28] have become intoxicated with this humorous spectacle!
The single path and the single emotion of all three is Love.
Their meeting took place in India.
When he proclaimed the supreme Name of Hari,
. . . Nityānanda, by hook or by crook, created a great hubbub!
Having experienced the waves of love,
with horns, handclapping and drums,
many more got up and danced with him!
This Kali age has been blessed—
so hear of this wondrous thing, brother!
Govinda, his mind filled with bliss, assumed that Name of eternal joy: "Gour Nitāi."
When He became Caitanya, in the form of Gour ["fair-skinned"], a delightful thing occurred!
. . . Just look—a Fair-skinned Man [*gorā*: Caitanya or an Englishman] has become overwhelmed with love—
he's utterly maddened!
The Fair-skinned One has been destroyed, hewn down, and falls to the ground!
And the Company has shown the proof of it throughout the streets!
Those Three who came together as one and drowned this land [in *rasa*]—
are themselves the Fair-skinned Company [*gorā kompānī*]—but what do I know of them?
. . . Brother, abandon the idea of duality and contemplate the eternal Caitanya!
Become non-dual and remain united with Caitanya! (BG 415; II.8)!

In short, it would seem that the Kartābhajās have ingeniously appropriated the language of the company and the marketplace of commodities in order to describe the initial advent and spread of the Gauḍīya Vaiṣṇava tradition. With its wealth of "spiritual commodities, imported from abroad," the Vaiṣṇava company promises the eternal wealth of salvation.

The Poor Company: A Company of Madmen

The name of the land of one's [true] Mother and Father is the "Poor Company."
(Mint Saying, no. 184—SE III.184)

However, having recounted the various wonders of the company, the songs of the *Bhāver Gīta* later go on to lament the eventual corruption that eventually crept into the company and destroyed it. Because the leaders of the "company" were corrupt and immoral, they led the Vaiṣṇava tradition into a state of "spiritual bankruptcy."[29] They reintroduced Brahminical hierarchies into a tradition which was supposed to be anti-Brahminical; and so now, "The rice husked by the

Gauḍīya Vaiṣṇavas remains unsold in the market." "Once the Company [Gauḍīya Vaiṣṇavism] was very rich. But its porters were extremely poor. They starved and begged but the kings and emperors, who controlled the Company, were worthless men, given to robbery."[30]

The company of the Vaiṣṇava tradition has now become polluted, filled with thieves and corrupt officials who swindle their poor followers. Throughout the *Bhāver Gīta*, the author laments his own sad fate in the world of business. He has toiled for years in the marketplace under the company, but he has accumulated only debts. "I conducted business eight million times; but see, my troubles have not left me!" So now he sings, "I want no more of the wage-book, brother;" "I no longer wish to engage in all this business" (BG 216; II.33).

Yet, even though the company became polluted with the foul smell of thievery and immorality, its original nobility and purity have still been preserved, as it were, "behind" the old company. It was preserved secretly, esoterically, by the Kartābhajās (BG 159; see chapter 6). In place of the old, corrupt company of the Vaiṣṇava tradition, the *Bhāver Gīta* proclaims the birth of a New Company—a "good mannered" or "distinguished" (*ādab*) company, which is none other than the Kartābhajā community. "Out of the ruins of the company a new company was made."[31] As the *Bhāver Gīta* explains, the crazy Fakir Āulcāṅd—called the Poor Wretched Madman (*becārā kṣepā*)—has come and restored the original company founded by the three madmen—Caitanya and his two disciples, Advaita and Nityānanda. For the true company is only fulfilled when the fourth madman, Āulcāṅd, joins the original three madmen and so "completes the cycle."[32] In this true company, the just Guru does not rob his poor devotees but, rather, brings them a host of "spiritual commodities" and a new kind of "capital." For "a genuine guru is the real 'capital' of the devotee."[33]

Here we begin to see the deeper, more powerful implications behind this use of the "company" metaphor: The Kartābhajās appear to be playing, intentionally and explicitly, off of older Gauḍīya Vaiṣṇava texts such as the "Foundation of the Marketplace" and its more orthodox use of the image of the bazaar. For the new company of the Kartābhajās has been founded to replace and restore the old, corrupted "marketplace of love" originally founded by Caitanya. In other words, just as the British East India Company had arrived from across the ocean in order to displace the existing Hindu and Muslim political and economic structures, so, too, the new company of the Kartābhajās has arrived on the ocean of love in order to displace and supplant the thieving merchants and brokers of the old Vaiṣṇava community.

This new company, however, is also a rather deviant and playfully subversive one. Unlike the wealthy, corrupt, brahminically dominated company of the Vaiṣṇava Gosāiṅs, this is a Poor Company (*gorib Kompānī*) or platoon of the poor,[34] which draws its members from the needy, the lower classes, women, and the sick. This company of the poor, they claim, is one truly free of caste distinctions, welcoming men and women of all classes and faiths as equals.[35]

Brother, I do indeed call that Company "Poor":
for whenever and whatever comes to pass, they accept it without excuse—

even the touch of poison!
What shall I say about that Poor Company?
They do what has never been done before!
. . . If the house of *your* Company presents itself as wealthy,
then many good things may come to light.
But look at those who are in *my Poor* Company—
when anyone hears this brilliant Name, they are enchanted!
Even though, brother, apart from a broken old stair, there's nothing else to be seen in that house! (BG 220; II.3)

Whereas the old company pays respect to the rich and the powerful, the fat merchants, and Rājās, the Poor Company pays homage to the beggars and outcasts. In this true Company of the Poor, the most needy, the most downtrodden are elevated to the highest state, counted as equal to Rājās and Bādshāhs, to Nabābs and Ministers.

That which encompasses the thirty-six castes and the four classes,
bearing rule over the sixty cities—that is the Poor Company.
. . . Look—thirty-three million men have united
and sit, paying honor to that Company—the Poor Company.
When it puts its seal [on the merchandise]
it will be honored by everyone! (BG 161; II.5)

Ten, twenty, thirty Poor men gather together and form one Company [*kompānī*].
. . . Look, in this kingdom, if someone's born in the house of a merchant,
and is completely infatuated by wealth,
we call that man a "Rājā," brother.
But one who sits with a broken begging bowl in his lap,
everyone calls the [true] "Ruler" of the land!
Those whose bodies are emaciated by famine,
we consider the Princes and Ministers!
Look—they all have a means of escape: they cannot really be called "Poor."
He who has a great amount of capital in hand, which instantly grows sevenfold,
and then goes throughout the seven cities, beating his drum,
brother, we call "great."
But he who at no time has had any riches,
who possesses no wealth at all—he is the [true] Lord of the three worlds!
He who knows no *tantras, mantras* or meditations,
I count as a [true] holy man and sage!
Lālśaśī says, none of them has ever seen [actual] "poverty." (BG 218; II.1)

Look, the starving and poor people who wander about with begging bowls,
have you heard?—they are counted as Great Kings, Nawabs and Ministers!

All the weak, illiterate and low-life people
are [truly] the great holy men and the rulers of the three worlds.
Don't call them "poor men"—Consider them great men!
They see no [real] "poverty" in the entire threefold world. (BG 219; II.2)

It is only within this Poor Company that the disciple receives the sacred seal or stamp (*niśānī*)—the mark on his invoice (*inbhāis*)—which assures him that his spiritual merchandise is genuine. Indeed, just as the British East India Company sets its seal on its merchandise and the official stamp of its Mint upon its silver coins,[36] so too, the Kartābhajā company places its seal on its secret teachings, which assures that they are the genuine goods and not the cheap fakes and imitations of the other guru-rice-merchants in the spiritual marketplace.

There are so many imported and exported things—but whose seal is on them?
Lālśaśī says, "whose seal is on the invoices [*inbhāis*]?"(BG 160; II.4)

I'm examining everything, front and back—
Apart from [the Company's] seal, everything else is fake!
Brother, no one examines the merchandise itself; that's why there are seals upon it!
Look, 33 million men have united
and sit, paying honor to that Company—the Poor Company.
When it puts its seal [on the merchandise, it will be honored by everyone!
. . . [Suppose there is] 100% foreign silver or gold:
If sixty men take and divide it up, it becomes adulterated [diluted to 15/16]
But when they put the seal of this "Poor Company" upon it,
then, by that very seal, it becomes 100% again in the form of a Sikka coin!
(BG 161; II.5)

Again, what we seem to find here is a skillful twofold strategy of parody and critique: on the one hand, they are cleverly poking fun at and criticizing the "old company" of the mainstream Vaiṣṇava lineage, which has become wealthy and corrupt, but on the other hand, they would also seem to be speaking about the *real* company—"Hon'ble John Company"—and its treatment of the poor lower-class laborers. Whereas the bosses of the "rich Company" punish their employees, throwing any thieves into prison, the "Poor Company" has mercy on the lowly and downtrodden, forgiving those who steal out of need. "In the good name of the Company, all things move. That's why no one's ever engaged in thievery. Even if someone is accused of theft, he is freed from sin immediately!" (BG 161; II.2).

If someone commits a theft in *your* Company,
when the Magistrate catches him, he sends him to prison.
Even if the verbal evidence is weak,
still, he'll easily be hanged upon the scaffold!
It seems that that your Company has some respect—

for otherwise, how could the Magistrate give such a command?
But that would not be tolerated by this Hon'ble *Poor* Company!
Just seen the fun within my Poor Company—it's rather strange!
The Emperor [in my Company] gives no commands; the king punishes no one.
If someone, in need of money, commits a theft in this land,
the Company freely gives him infinite wealth.
Then and there his poverty disappears,
and he no longer covets anything!
Lālśaśī says, "thus the thief Ratnākar became the sage Vālmīki!" (BG 220; II.3)

In a still more striking juxtaposition of metaphors, however, this Poor Company is also proclaimed as the Mad Company (*pāgal Kompānī*), or the Company of the Land of Madness. The leader of this company is the poor wandering fakir, the mad beggar Āulcāṅd, who has now usurped the throne of the kingdom and engulfs the land in the Rule of Madness:

I'm struck with amazement, seeing this funny thing!
The throne of this kingdom is empty—
Ten office clerks have gathered together—
and have placed a Madman [upon the throne]!
All the people are saying, "What will happen? Alas! What will happen?"
When He sits upon the throne and acts as Magistrate for this land
for what actions, at whose command, shall we offer obeisance?
Look: the announcement has come: a Fakir has displaced the Ministers!
(BG 276; II.14)

This great madman has intoxicated the members of the Company, driving them insane with devotional ecstasy, and turning them into poor wandering lunatics like himself:

Don't you know the news about the land of Madness?
You won't dislike the craziness of the Madman, you know!
Look—He has come in the form of a Madman
. . . In this country, there is one Company comprised of ten Madmen!
(BG 149; II.12)

Look—one madman, two madmen, three madmen, a Festival of Madmen![37]
I can't understand this play of madness!
the uproar of all this madness!
People say, what is this terrible commotion they're making?
Struck with wonder, one can understand their ecstasy.
You say that many excellent, wonderful things are happening in this land.
They naturally occur, twelve months a year.
The land is filled with *rasa*!

Seeing that wonderful thing, the people go mad!
. . . Lālśaśī says, "in this land, Madness is the rule!" (BG 150; II.13)

Conclusions: Capital and Its Deformations

All commodities have a social use and a cultural meaning . . . Commodities are cultural signs. They have been invested by the dominant culture with meanings, social connotations. . . . Because the meanings which commodities express are socially given—Marx called commodities "social hieroglyphs"—their meaning can also be socially altered or reconstrued. . . . Things are imprinted with new meanings and values which expropriate them . . . and relocate them. (Stuart Hall et al., *Resistance through Rituals*)

It may indeed be tempting, given their long and elaborately detailed accounts of the marvelous Company from abroad, with its shiploads of "wondrous merchandise," to read the Kartābhajā songs as a simple kind of mimicking or aping of their wealthy foreign masters. We could for example interpret this as something like a Melanesian Cargo Cult—as an attempt not only to provide a mythical explanation for the arrival of European wealth and commodities but also magically to appropriate it for the natives themselves. For example, as Arjun Appadurai describes the Cargo Cult phenomenon:

> The symbolism of the mysterious arrival of European goods has to do with the distortion of indigenous exchange relations under colonial rule . . . and the apparent contradiction between the wealth of the Europeans . . . and their own poverty . . . It is no surprise, given their sudden subjection to an international economic system of which they saw only the mysterious aspects, that their response was . . . to seek to replicate what they regarded as the magical mode of production of these goods. . . . The symbolism of these movements constitute not just a myth about the origin of European commodities but an attempt ritually to replicate . . . the modalities of European life. This is the significance of the use of European military forms, speech forms, titles, and so forth.[38]

I would argue, however, that this striking use of mercantile terminology and the language of the "company" is not simply a passive assimilation or a jealous mimicry of the prevailing economic forms; rather, following the lead of anthropologists such as Comaroff, Sahlins, and Taussig, I would suggest that it represents a far more active *appropriation and transformation*. As Sahlins has persuasively argued, money and commodities are never simply dead, lifeless signs without social significance; rather they are always invested with symbolic meaning, embedded in social relationships, and organized by a cultural logic.[39] However, precisely because they have an implicit cultural and symbolic value, commodities can also be appropriated, as signs, by many different competing factions within a given society. The commodity is not exclusively a sign of bourgeois capitalist ideals; it can also be appropriated or "stolen" by marginal, deviant groups, and transformed into a sign of resistance. As Hebdige comments in his discussion of punks, mods, and other subcultures in England, such ordinary commodities as safety pins, dog collars, and hats can become powerful agents of subversion: "Commodities are open to a double inflection: to 'illegitimate' as well as legitimate uses. These humble objects can be *magically appropriated, stolen, by subordinate groups and made to carry 'secret' meanings:* meanings which express, in codes, a form of resistance to the order which guarantees their subordination."[40]

This subversive appropriation of money and commodities is particularly evident in the case of pre-capitalist and colonized peoples. As Taussig suggests, not only do pre-capitalist cultures tend to interpret the colonial presence in terms of their own indigenous myths, symbols, and traditions, but they often appropriate and reinterpret the forms of Western economics, commodities, and even capitalism itself, thus "transforming fetishization while subjecting it to a paganism that will capture it."[41] Similarly, as Comaroff has shown in her study of the South African Zionist movement, the native culture did not merely acquiesce passively to British colonial domination; rather, they *actively appropriated, transformed, and turned to their own advantage* a number of key symbols drawn from European culture—including the symbolism of money and capital—as "captured bearers of alien power:" "Conquered and colonized societies . . . were never simply made over the European image. . . . Their citizens struggled . . . *to deploy, deform, and defuse imperial institutions*."[42] In a similar way, I would argue, the Kartābhajā gurus appropriated and transformed certain key elements of the company and the marketplace of colonial Calcutta, turning them to their own advantage in an esoteric society. In so doing, they offered their low-class peasant and urban followers a new kind of spiritual company, with a new kind of capital and social status.

In sum, the Kartābhajās' use of the company metaphor would appear to function as an ingenious means of killing two birds with the same stone, of subverting two opponents at the same time. It is a weapon turned on both their economic and political enemies (i.e., the British) and their religious enemies (the Gauḍīya Vaiṣṇava tradition), which plays the one off of the other while undermining both. Much of their following, we have seen, *really was* composed of the "Poor Company"—that is, the porters, petty traders, and shopkeepers working under or in the service of the British Company hierarchy. But by turning the "Hon'ble Company" into the Mad Company and the Poor Company, they have also playfully subverted the authority of the ruling power in Bengal, the very same ruling power whose social and economic policies had most negatively affected the poor lower classes who made up the majority of the Kartābhajā following. At the same time, however, they have also turned this into a powerful religious weapon. By turning the metaphor against the "old company" of the orthodox Vaiṣṇava community, they have used it to attack their own greatest rivals within the spiritual marketplace of nineteenth-century Bengal.

As we will see in chapter 7, however, this use of economic discourse also bore with it some less admirable and more negative possibilities as well. For a metaphor, as Lakoff and Johnson aptly point out, not only helps us to organize a given realm of experience or understand a given domain of phenomena; like the narrow Enlightenment definition of the "human body as a machine," or the capitalist definition of "labor as a resource," a metaphor also inevitably tends to constrain us, to place limits on the ways in which we can experience the world, and thus to become oppressive and constricting: "political and economic ideologies are framed in metaphorical terms. . . . A metaphor in a political or economic system, by virtue of what it hides, can lead to human denigration."[43] So, too, the Kartābhajās' use of the economic terminology and the imagery of the company bore with it some more negative and oppressive conequences: It allowed them to build up a very lucrative "company" of their own, with their own, often highly asymmetrical and extractive hierarchies of power.[44]

5

Secret Bodies

Physical Disciplines and Ecstatic Techniques

The essence of Love consists of nectar.
The supreme nectar is the Body which is free of lust.
. . . The Eternal Body—who and where is it?
One can see only a shadow of it.
. . . With the movement of the Seed, your desires are eternally fulfilled.
And with the dawn of the moon, the Body becomes like an ocean of *rasa*.
(BG 43; SE II.54)

The role of secrecy in the Kartābhajā tradition is not, however, limited to esoteric discourse and the transmission of coded knowledge; it is also a profoundly experiential affair, rooted in the esoteric traditions of Sahajiyā yoga, meditation, and ritual. "*Sahaja* is not attained through the repression of the body," as one Kartābhajā disciple explains, "but in an innate, spontaneous way. . . . The path to attaining the supreme Essence is the physical method of Tantric yoga."[1] Like their cryptic esoteric discourse, however, the ritual and meditative practice of the Kartābhajās is deemed something dangerously powerful which must be performed only in solitude and secrecy, in the dead of night, hidden from the eyes of the outside world. As the recently deceased Kartā, Satyaśiva Pāl, explains, borrowing the phrase of Rāmakṛṣṇa, true spiritual practice is performed "inside the mosquito net":

> Midnight is the best time to practice. . . Rāmakṛṣṇa said, "practice inside the mosquito net. . . . *Sādhakas* are of various kinds. *Sāttvik sādhanā* is secret; the *sādhaka* practices in secret; when ordinary people see them, they think they're meditating inside the mosquito net. *Rājasik* practice is external; one wears a rosary around the neck and an ochre robe, carrying a gold, crystal-studded garland. It's as if he's wearing a sign board." Such outward show of worship is completely rejected by the Kartābhajās.[2]

Like esoteric discourse, moreover, esoteric practice is perhaps best understood not simply in terms of its basic contents or substances—its ritual forms or disciplinary techniques—but more important in terms of its *strategic role*, as a means of constructing individual and social identities, defining status and value within a symbolic hierarchy. Hence, if esoteric *discourse* offers the disciple a new source of status and capital within an alternative market of social exchange, esoteric *practice* in turn offers a new physical identity, a new body, incorporated into an alternative social body. And if secret discourse is a tactic which transforms certain knowledge into a rare, valuable commodity, which is the source of tremendous symbolic power, so, too, secret practice is a tactic which transforms the ordinary human body and its gross physical elements—(the bodily fluids, the semen and menstrual blood, etc.)—into profound symbolic resources and the source of a new, alternative identity. In sum, we will find that not only can the substances and processes of the human body be used to integrate the individual body with the greater social body or body politic, as so many anthropologists and sociologists have shown us[3] but also, as more recent authors such as Jean Comaroff and Caroline Bynum have argued, the symbolism of the body can be appropriated and manipulated by dissident, marginalized, or oppressed individuals in order to resist and subvert the status quo, or to gain new power and freedom beyond the constraints of the dominant social order and the body politic.[4]

In this chapter, I argue that the Kartābhajās' esoteric practices and ecstatic techniques involve a key strategy of deconstructing and reconstructing the human body. Their aim is to dismantle or dissolve the ordinary socialized body of the initiate, along with the conventional social hierarchy itself, and to create in its place a new, divinized body, which is in turn *reinscribed* into an alternative social hierarchy, with its own relations of authority and power.

I begin with a brief discussion of the relationship between the body and the social body in mainstream Bengali culture, as well as the ritual sacraments (*saṃskāras*) used to inscribe the physical body into the greater Bengali social hierarchy. I then discuss the role of initiation and bodily practice within the Kartābhajā tradition, as it serves to deconstruct the conventional, socialized body and to create in its place an alternative, liberated body. Finally, I examine the Kartābhajās' attempt to construct not simply an alternative body but an entire alternative identity or secret self—the "supreme" or ultimate identity (the *paramārthik* self), which is at once freed from the bonds of labor and servitude in the exoteric social hierarchy while at the same time it is inscribed into a new hierarchy of power within the Kartābhajā sect itself. The Kartābhajā *sādhaka*, in sum, embarks on a symbolic journey through the "marketplace of the world"—the mundane world of labor and servitude under the rule of the masters of the workplace—to the inner City of the Heart, where he is subject only to the spiritual "master," the Kartā or guru himself.

The Body and the Social Body: Constructing the Socialized Self in Traditional Bengali Culture

> The habitus as the feel for the game is the social game embodied and turned into a second nature. . . . The habitus [is] society written into the body, into the biological individual. (Pierre Bourdieu, *In Other Words*)

The human body, as Mary Douglas rather elegantly puts it, "is always an image of society. . . . The relation of head to feet, of brain and sexual organs . . . express patterns of hierarchy. . . . Bodily control is an expression of social control."[5] The form, substances and processes of the physical body serve, in most cultures, as the most basic raw materials for the construction of a socialized individual and for the incorporation of that individual into the greater hierarchy of the social body or body politic. As Foucault remarks, "Power relations have an immediate hold upon it; they invest it, mark it, train it, torture it, force it to carry out tasks, to perform ceremonies, to emit signs."[6] Through various "techniques of the body," such as gesture, dress, diet, walk, the individual body is *"inscribed"* with the codes and ideals of the social body, so that it "embodies" the values of the greater body politic. As Bourdieu puts it, the "political mythology" of the social order is "made flesh" through the *habitus*—the bodily disposition and largely prereflective behavior of actors within their social environment, their gesture and deportment, their ways of talking and moving: "Symbolic power works . . . through the control of bodies. . . . Bodily hexis is political mythology realized, *embodied* in a permanent disposition, a durable way of standing, speaking, walking and thereby feeling and thinking."[7] This bodily discipline works above all through the mechanisms of ritual, religious disciplines and "spiritual exercises." It is precisely through such disciplines that the body and its habitus come to be impressed and informed by the structures of the greater social body.

> There is a link between the body and . . . *"esprit de corps."*. . . If most organizations—the church, the army, political parties—give such a place to bodily disciplines, this is because obedience is belief and belief is what the body grants even when the mind says no. . . . Bodily discipline is the instrument *par excellence* of domestication. . . . Thus is explained the place that all totalitarian regimes give to bodily practices which, by symbolizing the social, contribute to somatizing it. . . . "Spiritual Exercises" are bodily exercises.[8]

During situations of colonial rule, it would seem, the body often assumes a new and even more critical role. As a number of recent postcolonial critics have pointed out, the physical body itself—that is, the skin color, hair texture, body shape, or language—is always among the most immediate and most important signs of "difference" and "Otherness" between colonizer and colonized. In most cases, moreover, the body is identified as the clearest sign of the inferiority and primitiveness of the latter: "The difference of the colonial subject by which s/he can be othered is felt most immediately in the way in which the superficial differences of the body . . . are read as indelible signs of their natural inferiority."[9]

However, precisely because the body is the primary locus of otherness, difference, and domination, it is also potentially the most important site of struggle, subversion and resistance: "The body . . . has become the literal site on which resistance and oppression have struggled, with the weapons being . . . the physical signs of cultural difference . . . as the symbols and literal occasion of the power struggles of the dominator and dominated."[10] The same body which is the locus for the inscription of colonial power and capitalist discipline can also be transformed into the supreme source of resistance, struggle, and liberation.[11]

This intimate relationship between the individual body and the social body is nowhere more clear than in the world of Bengal (and that of India as a whole): "The form of the body is a symbol, and its symbolism in the highly symbolic world of traditional India was very potent indeed."[12] As Ronald Inden and Ralph Nicholas have shown, Bengali society has traditionally been imagined in the form of a physical organism or a social body, which is held together by bonds of love and common bodily substances, shared between individual bodies. Through the ten *saṃskāras,* the "sacraments" or "life-cycle rites" (marriage, first impregnation, baptism, initiation, etc.), each individual body is progressively transformed and assimilated into the greater totality of the social body. One's bodily substance, in short, determines one's proper rank and status within the social hierarchy; "The moral code for . . . a particular caste or clan is . . . imbedded in the bodily substance shared by the members . . . and inherited by birth."[13] Through *saṃskāras,* the fluids and substances of the individual body are transformed in order to unite it with the greater body of the community. "Every *saṃskāra,*" write Inden and Nicholas, "is a transformative action that refines and purifies the body, initiating it into new statuses and relationships by giving it a new birth. A *saṃskāra* removes defects from the body... by immersion, aspersion, sprinkling, touching parts of the body . . . anointing and feeding with special substances."[14]

Thus, the most important of the *saṃskāras*—particularly marriage (*vivāha*), first impregnation" (*garbhādhāna*), and "procreating a son" (*puṃsavana*)—center primarily around the bodily substances of semen, menstrual fluid, milk, and blood, manipulating these substances in order to construct a socialized bodily identity. *Vivāha*, in particular, is considered the most important means of defining caste and rank in Bengali culture, for it ensures the proper union of individual bodies within the greater social order. "The marriage of man and woman . . . makes their previously unrelated bodies the same body."[15] When joined through a proper marriage, the male and female are believed to share the same bodily fluids, the same blood, tears, and sexual fluids. Therefore, an improper marriage threatens the whole delicate balance of the social hierarchy, bearing "the capacity to ruin the entire order of jātis in the community . . . the improper combination of coded bodily substances entailed the improper combination of worship and occupational substances as well."[16]

So, too, the second and third *saṃskāras* also center around bodily fluids, though now in relation to procreation and the hope for a male child. Both sacraments use fluid symbolism in order to influence the conception of the fetus, hoping subtly to alter its composition and determine its gender. According to traditional Bengali beliefs (a variation on more widespread Indian beliefs) every body is made of a combination of hard and soft elements: the hard bones and nerves, the soft skin and blood, and, most importantly, the hard male semen and the soft female uterine blood. Semen and menstrual blood are each formed through a complex series of bodily transformations, which begins when food is transformed into blood, blood into flesh, flesh into fat, fat into marrow, and marrow into semen *(śukra, bīja)* and uterine blood (*ārtava*). A child is created by the mingling of blood and seed within the womb, a predominance of male seed producing a boy, and a predominance of female blood producing a girl. Thus, the second and the third *saṃskāras* work on these fluids in the hope of influencing their flow and thereby ensuring the birth of a male child. In the rite of first impregnation (*garbhādhāna*), for example, the husband touches his wife's navel and gives her a drink from the five products of the cow; so, too, during the rite of procreating a son (*puṃsavana*), the wife must drink symbolic "seminal foods," such as yogurt with lentils and barley seeds in order to "increase the seminal portion of her child." The birth of a healthy male child is thus crucial to the Bengali social order, for it is the physical embodiment of the union of husband and wife—"it concretely embodies their one body relationship."[17]

As Glen Hayes has shown, the Vaiṣṇava-Sahajiyā Tantric tradition also developed a series of rituals which work on the fluids and processes of the individual body—perhaps what we might call a series of "alternative sacraments" or esoteric *saṃskāras*. Like the conventional Hindu *saṃskāras*, the Sahajiyā rituals work on the substances of the body in order to re-form it and reintegrate within a greater social community or family—the lineage of the Sahajiyā tradition. And yet, these esoteric or alternative sacraments are designed to create not an orthodox social body but, rather, an alternative, spiritualized, and divinized body, the *siddha-deha* or *aprakṛta deha:* "Just as the ordinary Hindu passes through rites of passage [*saṃskāras*] in the physical body . . . so too the Vaiṣṇava-Sahajiyā undergoes a series of transformations between each subtle-body container . . . both the Vaiṣṇava-Sahajiyā and the traditional Bengali systems use . . . states of bodily existence to indicate participation in the sacred."[18] Beyond Hayes, however, I would argue that the Sahajiyās do not simply adapt the traditional *saṃskāras* passively and unreflectively; rather, they intentionally *manipulate and transform* them, often inverting them, in order to create an alternative body within an alternative hierarchy—an esoteric social body. For, as Bynum has argued in her work on the use of body symbolism among medieval women mystics, "marginal and disadvantaged groups" can also "appropriate society's dominant symbols in ways that revise and undercut them."[19] Or, as Comaroff suggests in her study of body-symbolism in the South African Zionist movement, human beings are not simply condemned mindlessly to reproduce the norms and values of the domiant social body; rather, "*the human imagination is independently reflective and exists in a dialectical relationship with the very . . . forms which give it life.*" Thus, if the substances and processes of the body can serve as the most basic symbols of the social order, these same substances can also be manipulated and transformed by dissident or marginalized groups in order to challenge, resist, or subvert that same social order.[20] This is nowhere more apparent than in the case of the Kartābhajās, who aim to achieve not only a new bodily identity but with it a new communal identity or social body. Their "alternative sacraments" do not seek to create a socialized body, incorporated into the conventional social and economic order, but, on the contrary, to *deconstruct and destroy* the conventional social body and to create in its place a new autonomous, secret body, liberated from the dominant world of caste and labor.

The Secret Body: The Deconstruction and Reconstruction of the Body in Kartābhajā *Sādhanā*

Like that of most esoteric traditions and secret societies, Kartābhajā practice begins with the fundamental act of initiation (*dīkṣā*)—an act intended to put to death and deconstruct the ordinary physical body and socialized self and to give birth to a new, esoteric identity, integrated within the alternative family of the Kartābhajā lineage. Once the guru whispers the secret mantra into his ear—the mantra "Guru Satya" or "the Guru is Truth," which he is strictly enjoined "never to repeat to anyone"[21]—the initiate dies in his worldly, exoteric identity and is reborn in a new, esoteric identity, shifting from the world of established social structures into a new role within the secret society (the *kula,* "family" and *parampara,* "lineage"). Here, the initiate gains a new Mother and Father—the Mā Gosāiṅ and the Mahāśay—as well as new spiritual brother and sisters—the *gurubhāi* and *gurubon*—in this alternative "company." According to the "Mint Sayings," "If one is not born in the house of his [true] Mother and Father [the Guru and Mā Gosāiṅ], he will not be upright in his conduct;" for "The name of the land of one's Mother and Father is the 'Poor Company'" (STP 59, 69).

Once his old exoteric identity has been destroyed and a new esoteric self conceived in its place, the *sādhaka* may begin to engage in the more profound and powerful disciplines of the upper levels of the Kartābhajā path. Like their esoteric discourse, the Kartābhajās' esoteric practice derives much of its symbolic efficacy from a strategy of *hierarchalization*—the restriction of access to certain rituals and techniques by a graded series of initiations. As we have seen earlier (chapter 3), the Kartābhajā order is divided fundamentally into two levels of disciples-the gross or exoteric and the "Poor" or esoteric—and the latter class is in turn further divided into the four hierarchical grades of *pravarta, sādhaka, siddha,* and *siddher siddha.* Each of these stages then has its own set of rituals and meditative practices, corresponding to the qualifications of the initiate. As Satyaśiva Pāl, explains, this hierarchical system begins with the more basic practices of invocation of the Name of Kṛṣṇa, and then gradually progresses through the techniques of *prāṇāyāma* (breath control), the awakening of Kuṇḍalinī (the serpent power), and the penetration of the *cakras,* until one reaches the highest, most esoteric, most dangerous practices of the *siddher siddha.*

> [Remembrance of the Name] is the first stage of practice. . . . One must practice remembrance of the Name for a determined period and specific number of times. Later, he will need more concentration, using the techniques of *Prāṇāyāma*, the awakening of the Kuṇḍalinī and the penetration of the six *cakras* . . . One must rise successively through each of these levels. The final stage is very difficult. . . . If there is a single mistake, there's a possibility of destroying the body. Only one in a million can perform this practice . . . Thus, the succession of Kartābhajā path is: *pravarta (sādhu), sādhaka (satī), siddha (sūra) and nivṛtti (mahat/siddher siddha).*[22]

For the majority of the "gross" or common (*sthūla*) disciples, in the lower ranks of the Kartābhajā hierarchy, esoteric practice is limited primarily to the weekly meetings or "gatherings of love" of (*premānuṣthāna*). "Held in the strictest secrecy," these involve the communal singing of Kartābhajā songs and the sharing of food in explicit violation of caste distinctions.[23] In their most intense forms, as the singing and dancing reached the height of power, these gatherings were designed to culminate in a state of spiritual intoxication and devotional ecstasy, with the spontaneous display of the symptoms of divine madness—tears and laughter, writhing on the ground, trembling with joy, etc. As Datta described it in his account of 1870, "Their primary practice is the 'Gathering of Love.' By means of the repetition of mantras and the gathering of love, they progressively manifest the signs of ecstasy, such as tears, horripilations of joy, laughter, trembling, gnashing of teeth and so on."[24] Within the esoteric space of the Kartābhajā gathering, lost in this state of devotional ecstasy and madness, the devotee is temporarily liberated both from the conventional social world in exoteric society, and from the restrictions of the ordinary socialized body itself.

But for the more advanced initiates, the "essential" (*marmik*) or truly "poor" (*kāṅgāl*) disciples on the higher stages of the path, Kartābhajā practice is essentially a private and solitary affair, a practice focused on the individual physical body itself; its aim is not simply to liberate the individual body from the conventional socal world but actually to transform, re-create, and divinize the body itself.

Cosmo-Physio-Economics:
Bodily Cosmography and Subtle Physiology

Like most Tantric schools, the Kartābhajās follow an ancient Indian tradition of *dehatattva* or the doctrine of *bhāṇḍa-brahmāṇḍa*—the conception of the human body as a microcosm, which reflects all the elements of the macrocosm: "All things and all events lie within this microcosm of the human body (*e bhāṇḍa brahmāṇḍete*)" (BG 33; II.59). The human body possesses its own inner geography and elaborate interior landscape, its own sun and moon, rivers and mountains, and an elaborate subtle physiology of nerves (*nāḍīs*), channels, and energy centers (*cakras*). The aim of *sādhanā* is to journey through this inner cosmos, to reach the seat of the indwelling Man of the Heart, or *Sahaja Mānuṣa*.

Like the fundamental life-cycle rites of traditional Bengal, much of the Kartābhajās' bodily cosmology and physical practice centers around the mystery of the sexual fluids, semen (*bīja, bindu, śukra*), and menstrual blood (*raja*). Identified with the supreme male and female principles of reality, Puruṣa and Prakṛti or Kṛṣṇa and Rādhā, the semen and uterine blood are the very particles of the absolute which lie hidden within each human body. As the vessel of the supreme self, or Sahaja Mānuṣa, the semen is believed to reside within the highest of the seven cakras of the subtle body, the 1,000-petaled *sahasrāra* at the crown of the head. As in virtually all Indian Tantric, alchemical, and yogic schools, the semen is, as David Gordon White comments, "the raw material and fuel of every psychochemical transformation. . . . The tantric practitioner undergoes transformations through which a new superhuman and immortal body is conceived out of the husk of the mortal biological body."[25] In the *Bhāver Gīta*, the semen or *bindu* is described as the cosmogonic seed which orignally fell from Nirañjana's forehead into the ocean of Māyā to create all things, and it now lies as the hidden spark within every human being, concealed in the form of the Sahaja Mānuṣa at the top of the crown. Hence the retention of the seed (*bīja rakṣaṇa*) is critical to spiritual practice and the shedding of semen the greatest sin for the *sādhaka:*

Look—from His Forehead, the seed fell from his skin into the bottomless waters.
Then a Fisherman came and bound it within the net of Māyā.
Brother, know for certain that within that [net of Māyā] lie both birth and death.
. . . Brother, within that Seed, upon that ocean, lies Life—
and I have abandoned all my friends to search for that thing!
. . . Upon [that ocean] lies a Great Jewel of a Man—
That jewel is an invaluable treasure, like the seed within a seed!
But no one can retain it without good companions [i.e., spiritual practitioners]
If there are good companions, then when you grasp this thing it will not be lost.
Keep it with great control, gazing upon this ray of light within the Inner Chambers! (BG 414; II.74)

Conversely, the female principle of Prakṛti or Śakti, embodied in menstrual blood, lies within the lowest of the cakras, the *mūlādhāra,* at the base of the spine. However, in order to taste the joys of love, the Supreme Self descends from his seat in the crown for three days each month—corresponding to the menstrual period in women—and dallies with his divine consort in the place of the *triveṇī* or the meeting-place of the three central veins of the subtle body (*Iḍā, Piṅgalā and Suṣumṇā*). As the *Bhāver Gīta* describes him, he's like a royal goose swimming with his beloved lady goose amid the great sea of nectar.

As a wondrous Royal Goose, He has plunged into the waters and floats upon them
Swinging and swaying, He dallies in union with his beloved Lady Goose
And I see the dawn of both the wondrous full Moon and Sun together!
From time to time He appears upon Her Lotus, in order to adorn her in splendor! (BG 413; II.81).

A contemporary guru, Advaita Dās, explains this complex biocosmological system thus:

> Engaged in divine play, the One Supreme Essence, enjoys *rasa* in the form of two bodies. For, just as the essence of woman lies in menstrual blood, so too, that of man lies in semen. And just as the union of menstrual blood and semen is the cause of procreation, so too it is the root of the erotic *rasa*. At the highest point of the body

there is a thousand petalled lotus which is the seat of the Supreme Self, who exists in the form of semen. He cannot enjoy *rasa* unless He unites with Prakṛti in the form of menstrual blood. That's why, during the three days of the menstrual flow, He comes down from His seat on the Lion's throne. . . . During these three days, He frolics in bliss.[26]

Like most other Tantric schools, the Kartābhajās also commonly imagine the female principle using the old yogic image of the "serpent power," Kuṇḍalinī. Lying coiled at the base of the spine in the *mūlādhāra cakra*, Kuṇḍalinī is Śakti in her unconscious state, separated from her eternal lover, Puruṣa. In the *Bhāver Gīta*, however, all this is described with a rich fabric of mythological imagery, using the figure of the 100-headed serpent Vāsuki, who lies in the lowest of the seven Underworlds, Rasātala, guarding a great jeweled altar:

At the bottom of the bottomless ocean, amidst a single stream, lies Rasātala:
And within it, I see with my own eyes, their lies a jeweled altar!
Above, below, within, on all sides
Vāsuki, with three thousand eyes, guards it in all directions (BG 298; II.75).

He who is the great Wealthy Man [*Dhanī lok*],the Author of the Primordial Book of all that is, finite or infinite
lies within the ocean, upon this jeweled altar
He is without form—above, below, or in the middle.
. . . He is seated with the heart, filling it to excess! (BG 299; II.76).

All this mythical imagery has direct reference to the interior landscape of the human body itself. The rivers and islands are the veins (*nāḍīs*) and energy centers (*cakras*) of the subtle body; Rasātala, the lowest of the seven hells, is the *mūlādhāra* or root *cakra*; the great serpent Vāsuki is the coiled Kuṇḍalinī who sleeps within the *mūlādhāra*; the Rich Man upon the jeweled altar is indwelling divine self, the Maner Mānuṣa, seated on the altar of the heart. A later commentator on the *Bhāver Gīta*, Rājnārāyaṇ Caṭṭopādhyāy, explains:

Within the body there are seven heavens and seven hells. Among these, *Rasātala* is the lowest. There lies a foundation, upon which . . . there is a wide vein named the Brahmanāḍī. Within that vein, upon the lotus of the heart, there is a jeweled altar called the Svādiṣṭhāna. This is the seat of the Supreme Self. . . . It is the seed-bearing flower which pervades all things. Just as Vāsuki holds up the earth with his head so too, in Rasātala, that is, below the navel, the serpent Kuṇḍalinī is the basis of this bodily universe. 3000 subtle veins arise from this and pervade the entire body.[27]

The aim of *sādhanā* is therefore to reunite the divine male and female principles, to achieve the ideal union of semen and menstrual blood within the individual body. Through the use of both meditative imagination and physical rituals, *sādhanā* proceeds as a kind of mystical marriage, or, rather, an internalization and alchemical transformation of the ordinary process of marriage. It is a marriage which deliberately *reverses and inverts* the normal *saṃskāras* of marriage and impregantion, by reversing the normal flow of bodily fluids, specifically semen and menstrual blood. In some cases, this "esoteric marriage" and mystical union involves actual physical intercourse between the male *sādhaka* and his consort who are symbolically identified with the divine couple Kṛṣṇa and Rādhā (though as we will see in chapter 6, there is a great deal of controversy within the tradition as to whether this should involve intercourse solely with one's own wife [*svakīyā*], or with another man's wife [*parakīyā*]).

Intense sexual love [*ati rati*] arises between a man and a woman;
In *Sahaja*, he is the husband of the chaste wife.
The accomplished *sādhaka* and his consort in practice
are united without division, like a limb to a body. (BG 48; II.68)

As Advaita Dās explains this passage: "He must first cultivate devotion with a female companion, and gradually develop the Body of Ecstasy (*bhāva-deha*). Then, he must arouse the arrested semen, and prepare it within the *piṅgalā* vein. Thus natural sexual lust is transformed into supernatural love."[28] In short, as we read in one of Manulāl Miśra's cryptic songs, the key to this secret Sahaja practice is precisely the alchemical transmutation of the act of physical intercourse (*rati*) itself—a transmutation of base lust (*kāma*) into the supreme desire (*mahākāma*), the pure, divinizing elixir of love (*prema*),

Within the Thousand petalled lotus, the name of Perfect Conjugal Love is
inscribed.
White, blue and yellow, this Love is like milk.
If one can retain the seed, lust will be conquered.
The seed, like milk, is mixed with lust.
But if it becomes free of lust, I'll enter the gate of erotic play! [*vilāsa*]
The cause of this amourous play lies within the power of lust itself;
The secret *Sahaja* love is a strange new kind of devotion! . . .
When desire [*kāma*] becomes free of desire [*akāma*], the Great Desire
[*Mahākāma*] arises;
Engaged in this Great Desire, I'll reach the eternal realm! (STP 127)

In other cases, however, this process takes place solely within the body of the individual *sādhaka* himself, in a kind of internalized sexual union. According to Advaita Dās, the female partner is first used to arouse the Kuṇḍalinī and to control the semen, but once the male *sādhaka* has accomplished this, he can in fact unite the male and female principles within himself. Because every human being contains both male and female principles, both *Puruṣa* and *Prakṛti*, the *sādhaka* can assume the role of the female Prakṛti or Rādhā herself, and so enjoy an erotic union with Kṛṣṇa-Puruṣa within his own body. (Thus, as we saw in chapter 2, the female partner is ultimately only a useful tool, which can be dispensed with in the higher stages of the path.)[29] Using difficult techniques of breath control and meditation, the *sādhaka* must then awaken the slumbering Kuṇḍalinī and raise her upward through the central channel of the subtle body, the *suṣumṇā nāḍī*. Piercing each of the six *cakras*, Kuṇḍalinī will at last reach the 1,000-petaled lotus at the top of the head, wherein lies the Supreme Self, the Sahaja Mānuṣa or true, inner "guru." Here, in a kind of internalized, spiritual orgasm, the divine male and female principles are united within the *sādhaka*'s own body:

> The Guru dwells within the Sahasrāra, above the six cakras.
> He is united with his Śakti, always filled with bliss
> . . . Sit with a pure mind and stay fixed gazing at the form of Brahma.
> Look within: the dalliance of the *iḍā* vein is on the left side of the body;
> within it moves the *prāṇa*-wind.
> The *suṣumṇā* vein is the true essence of the *sādhaka*; grasp that stream within the lotus vessel.
> Kuṇḍalinī is the depth of consciousness which pierces the *nāda-bindu*.
> . . . Always remain within that chamber—like a Madman [*unmadī*], engrossed in bliss
> But you must flee the finite world, and cross over the universe.
> . . . Yogeśvarī [Kuṇḍalinī] said, "when you awaken me, you'll reach the City of Bliss.
> Taking hold of the supreme Śiva, the [finite] self will grasp the Supreme Self![30]

Amidst this internalized pan-somatic orgasm, a reign of nectar showers down from the *sahasrāra* throughout the entire body, transforming the gross physical body into the radiant, immortal spiritual body, the *aprakṛta deha* or *siddha deha*.[31]

The Merchant of Love on the Seas of Desire: The Voyage to the City of the Heart

Although these basic Tantric practices and bodily techniques are not particularly original in themselves, what *is* unique about the Kartābhajās' bodily system is (once again) its the highly unusual use of economic and mercantile imagery. Not only do these songs, as we have seen in chapter 4, employ the imagery of commerce to describe this mortal world and the path of spiritual practice, but they also use it in an "internalized" sense to describe the inner workings of the body and the techniques of physical *sādhanā*. As I have tried to summarize it in table 5.1, we can discern at least three interrelated, alloformic levels of symbolism: those of the cosmos, the body and the marketplace. The disciples of the older Vaiṣṇava Sahajiyā schools, for example, had embarked on a metaphoric journey of "boating upon the Crooked River"—a journey through the veins and channels of the subtle body to reach the Sahaja Mānuṣa within the Heart.[32] For the Kartābhajās, on the other

Table 5.1 The Cosmo-Physio-Economic System of the Kartābhajās

Pre-Cosmic Plenum-Void (*Śūnyabhar*) (BG 124–25)		
Cosmos	*Body*	*Marketplace*
cosmic ocean (BG 124, 159)	the womb (BG 130ff.)	the Hidden City (BG 130ff.)
seven underworlds, Rasātola (the lowest of the underworlds) (BG 159)	the lowest cakra, the *Mūlādhāra*; the seat of the sleeping Kuṇḍalinī serpent or Vāsuki (BG 298)	The primordial Warehouse (*ārat*) (BG 124)
dry land, earth	the physical body (the "throne" (BG 150ff.) or the merchant ship (BG 298)	the Bazaar of the world (*Ālambājār, bhava-bājār*) (BG 124ff., 8–15)
floods, typhoons, and other dangers on the ocean of the world (BG 8-15)	the "enemies" of the six senses	brokers, moneylenders and thieves
seven heavens, seven islands and seven oceans (BG 299)	the *nāḍīs* and the seven *cakras* (BG 289–89)	the Company ships and merchant vessels sailing on the seven rivers and streams (BG 298, 65–70)
the king or zamindār	the ego or finite self (the King)	the Rāja or Mālik, owner of the Bazaar
the Sahaja land, heaven, the eternal Vṛndāvana	100-petaled *Cakra* (or the Lotus of the Heart) (BG 190)	the Company Fort (BG 160ff.)
Viṣṇu or Kṛṣṇa floating upon the banyan leaf (BG 143ff.)	*Maner Mānuṣa, Sahaja Mānuṣa, Pāgal, Kṣepā*	the Magistrate of the Hidden City (BG 130–38) or the Rāja of the Company
the incarnation of God as Man (Caitanya, Āulcānd)	the appearance of the *Maner Mānuṣa* in the Triveṇī (*mūlādhāra cakra* or menstrual flow in woman) (BG 414)	the coming of the Company (BG 60ff.); being sent to trade in the Bazaar of the World (BG 130ff.)
the return of Man to heaven	catching the *Maner Mānuṣa;* uniting the male and female principles and returning to the Lotus in the crown (BG 415)	attaining the Jewel which pervades both the Hidden City and the Bazaar of the World (BG 138–39)

hand, the journey through the *nāḍīs* and *cakras* now becomes the voyage of the "merchant ship" laden with treasure, through the "Bazaar of the world" in search of the mystical City of the Heart—a voyage which entails a remarkable combination of cosmogonic, physiological and economic terminology, and an ingenious fusion of Sahajiyā bodily practice with the imagery of merchant trade under the East India Company.[33]

The Supreme Self, or Sahaja Mānuṣa, as we've already seen, is often described as a kind of wondrous "Wealthy Man" (*dhanī*) (BG 298–9), or a "Businessman" who sets up a business office (*Kuṭhi*), protected by the "Company's Fort" (probably Fort William) with its canons, bullets and guns (BG 307–9; II.71–2). Here, in this secret office, he engages in debt and credit, in buying and selling and merchant exchange.

Just see the Primordial Ocean, at the limit of the seven oceans.
Beneath it, the *Sahaja* Man has come and built an Office.
He has raised the flag, inlaid with so much gold lace.
When I think of it, my mind is dumbfounded; how can I describe it?
This, brothers and friends, is the ocean of *rasa*, the City of Eternal Bliss!
(BG 307: II.71)

Brother, amidst heaven, earth, hell and the forty worlds,
where is His Office [*kuṭhi*]?
Now show me, brother, where they've built the Company's Fort.
Surely, there is a flag planted upon it.
How far does the moat around it stretch?
How many guns and supplies, and how many soldiers are there? (BG 160; II.4)

So, too, the inward search for the Sahaja Mānuṣa becomes the voyage of a merchant ship, "bearing salt, sugar-cane and other goods," as it "crosses the seven rivers" in search of the mysterious city of Rasātala (BG 298–99). According to one very old Kartābhajā song recorded by Datta in 1870, this is the merchant ship of the human body, equipped with its ten oarsmen (the five sense organs [*jñānendriya*] and five physical organs [*karmendriya*] and six men at the ropes (the passions), captained by a great Merchant of Love (the Self) and his bailiffs (the five elements):

Who is this who has crossed over to dry land?—some *Rasika*!
there are ten oarsmen, and six draw the ropes
Even if one knows him, he can't truly know him.
He travels in bliss—and Oh, how many rows of followers go with this Rasika!
There is a boat filled with treasure,
and within it dwells a Merchant of Love [*premer mahājan*] and five bailiffs [*couki*].[34]

In some of the Kartābhajā songs, this voyage of the merchant ship takes on even more explicit Tantric connotations. As we see in the following song collected in the "Saṅgīta Mālā," this is now the thinly veiled metaphor for the Tantric act of sexual intercourse, in which the male enters the vagina—the treacherous Triveṇī, or meeting place of the three rivers (Ganges, Yamuna, Sarasvati), which are identified with the three veins of the subtle body, the *iḍā, piṅgalā* and *suṣumṇā*. The "merchandise" borne on this ship is clearly the male semen, which he is in danger of "unloading" prematurely amid these dangerous, deadly waters:

Filled with desire, I sailed my ship upon the Triveṇī canal
in the reverse direction, in the face of the ebb tide;
the rudder did not touch the water.
Among the terrible shoals there is an inlet
and within it there is a crooked stream bearing a blue lotus.
But due to a foul wind, I could not cross it;
the boat of desire unloaded its merchandise!
. . . Sweat falls, hanging on my beard—Alas, I die!
the cable holding the rudder is cut, and the boat sails off-kilter!
. . . Alas I die! The treasury has fallen into terrible danger![35]

The ultimate goal of this inward voyage on the merchant ship of the body is to reach the secret place of the heart, the inner city of the self. If he can successfully bear his precious cargo of "sugar-cane and salt" through the seven rivers of the subtle body, if he can avoid "losing his merchandise" in the treacherous waters of desire, the *sādhaka* will reach the innermost altar of the heart, whereupon dwells the great rich man, the Sahaja Mānuṣa:

What's the use of delaying?—Go now, set sail upon your ship!
We remained on the banks of the Ganges, waiting for our companions;
. . . [Bearing] my salt and sugar-cane, I gradually crossed over the seven primordial rivers.
. . . I came like a flickering flame into this mortal world.
I was a flame within that [world of death]; but there was a terrible wave upon the seven primordial oceans;
no one, not even the helmsman, brother, could quickly cross over it!
. . . At the bottom of the bottomless ocean, amidst a single stream, lies Rasātala
And within this ocean, I see with my own eyes, there lies a jeweled altar!
He who is the great Wealthy Man, the author of the primordal book of all that is, finite or infinite,
lies within the ocean, upon this jeweled altar
He is without form—above, below, or between.
He bestows deliverance; but He's very difficult to grasp; For He is the vessel of delight! (BG 298, 299; II.75, 76)

The Hidden City (ḍhākā sahar) and the Bazaar of the World (ālam bājār)

The buying and selling of Love occurs in the Bazaar of Love, within the Hidden City! (Anonymous Bāul song)

Perhaps the most striking use of this cosmo-physio-economic imagery, however, appears in one unusually long series of songs from the *Bhāver Gīta* (BG 130–50;

II.44–50), which use the extended metaphor of merchant trade and travel between the "City of Dhaka" (*ḍhākā sahar*) and "Alam Bazaar" (*ālam bājār*).[36] Now, both Dhaka and Alam Bazaar are of course real places, the latter being an important center of trade within the old city of Dhaka (which still exists today). As the author sings, he had once made the long and difficult journey to the city of Dhaka in order to meet the Magistrate (*Hākim*), only to receive the command to go to Alam Bazaar and engage in business:

I went alone to the city of Dhaka, brother.
I saw the Magistrate, and he commanded me, "go to Alam Bazaar."
I've come here at his command.
. . . Brother, I had to travel far from the place where I had been before.
Gradually I became very thin,
and as the days passed, my state fell into ruin. . . . (BG 130; II.44)

Indeed, no one can remain in Dhaka City!
. . . There, all coming and going is regulated.
. . . All the people, with their dwelling places in Alam Bazaar,
in eight million forms, engage in trade within the city.
. . . And how much accounting goes on in just a few hours! (BG 132; II.46)

On one level, these songs are surely descriptions of real events in Bengal of the nineteenth century, and it is by no means unlikely that the author and his audience were themselves engaged in just this sort of mercantile exchange. On a deeper esoteric level, however, these songs also have far more profound mystical implications. For the author soon makes it clear that the "city of Dhaka" does not refer simply to a literal geographic locus; rather, it is also the metaphorical "Hidden" or "concealed" (*ḍhākā*) City—a term which also appears in Bāul songs as a metaphor of the womb and the prenatal state of the fetus.[37] So too, *ālam* is a Perso-Arabic term for the "world" itself and thus refers to the *bhava-bājār or* marketplace of the world, so often described in the *Bhāver Gīta*. To be sent by the magistrate's command from the Hidden City to the Bazaar of the World is thus to be forced from the blissful prenatal state within the mother's body into the endless suffering of the mortal body in the realm of *saṃsāra:*

Brother, I see the Bazaar of the World [*ālambājār*] is a very funny place!
Again and again, everyone comes and goes because of his own selfish interest.
There's nothing like these people!
Even when they feel terrible suffering,
they forget that suffering and feel happy.
And yet I too wish to come very often to this land!
. . . As I watch these funny things, I'm amazed!
Some have come to be Emperors;
Some have come with a begging bowl in hand;

Some, while begging, attain the Emperor's throne!
And some abandon the Emperor's life altogether and become fakirs!
(BG 134; II.48)

The aim of the spiritual path and bodily practice is thus to journey through and beyond the bazaar of the world, to search for and attain the "precious gem" or resplendent jewel which alone can bring liberation. This invaluable gem, we soon discover, is none other than the Sahaja Mānuṣa, who dwells at the innermost core of the human body, resting "within the lotus of the Heart itself!" (BG 133; II.47). Lying as the secret center within every human body, this gem is beyond all social distinctions, penetrating the entire universe, and encompassing both the Hidden City and the Bazaar of the World:

Brother, the splendor of that Gem does not lie in its color [*varṇa*, also "social class"]:
The color arising from that Gem is itself its own manifest radiance.
What more can I tell you, brother?
Within it lies the Hidden City [*ḍhākā sahar*].
. . . The City lies within the Jewel—
That's why in that land the splendor is unending!
. . . Look—the Jeweler is the Origin of the three worlds and the oceans.
And, Oh, how many qualities He has created with the brilliance of this gem!
. . . That Jewel pervades the ten directions,
both the inner and outer, both the conventional world and the Hidden City
(BG 139; II.50).

In sum, the journey from the Hidden City through the bazaar of the world to the secret place of the heart is really the summation of this whole complex cosmo-physio-economic system: to sail upon the company ships, to cross the manifold rivers and streams, to search for the treasured jewel—all this is a fascinating allegory for the journey through the world of *saṃsāra* in search of the priceless treasure of the divine self; and, on a still more esoteric level, all this is in turn an allegory for the journey of the individual *sādhaka* through the interior landscape of the human body, through the cakras and veins, ponds and lotuses of the subtle organism, in search of the Maner Mānuṣa within the lotus of the heart.

Living Death (Jyānte Marā): The Attainment of Extinction and the Birth of the Liberated Body

He who dies alive never dies. (Mint Saying, no. 46—SE III.46)

He is dead while alive, he is the best of men. He experiences the ultimate state [*mahābhāva*]: he has reached the farthest shore. (*Sahajiyā Sāhitya*, attributed to Caṇḍīdās, SS 21)

The final aim of this esoteric practice, and the final goal of this long journey through the Bazaar of the World to the inner city of the heart, is nothing less than the supremely paradoxical state beyond all dualities: a state which can only be described as "extinction," "cessation" (*nivṛtti*), or "living death" (*jyānte marā*), in which the finite self is annihilated and dissolved amidst the ecstatic bliss of the Self. The concept of "living death," it is true, had long been used in the Sahajiyā tradition of Bengal; however, the Kartābhajās would appear to have combined it with certain Sufi ideals, such as the command to "die before you die." Just as the final goal for the Sufi is the paradoxical state of "annihilation " (*fanā*) and "subsistence" (*bakā*) in God, dead to the self and alive to the supreme Self, so, too, the final aim of Kartābhajā practice is to attain the contradictory state of *nivṛtti*—death to the transient mortal world and eternal life in the ultimate reality. As Lālśaśī sings:

Brother, do not become full of sorrow and lose the Essence [*vastu,* i.e., the Semen]—
If you don't know the true Essence, brother, you can't plunge into this delight!
. . . Brother, see with your own eyes—
And even as you look, you'll become dead while alive [*jiyānte marā*]!
With great effort, grasp that Man [of the Heart], and abandon all the delusions of the [finite] man![38]

However, this highest stage of practice is also extremely difficult and dangerous. If performed incorrectly, if even a single trace of selfish lust taints his devotion, the *sādhaka* will destroy himself. And that is why, as Satyaśiva Pāl warns, these bodily techniques must be reserved only for the very few, most advanced and morally pure of initiates: "The final stage is very difficult, for there is no food, no pleasure, no sleep, no eyes, no ears, no worldly thought. . . . Then he will be dead while living [*jyānte marā*]. If there is even a single error, there is the possibility of destroying the body. That is why this stage is not for everyone. Only one in a million can perform this practice."[39]

If, however, the initiate can successfully achieve this difficult state, this Living Death becomes a new birth—the birth of the new, liberated, and wholly autonomous body, called the *siddha deha* or *aprakṛta deha.* The finite mortal body, which is subject to the burdens of caste, labor, poverty, and oppression, has been annihilated and in its place the infinite, eternal body, is freed from all the bonds of the ordinary social and economic world.

The essence of Love consists of nectar.
The supreme nectar is the Body which is free of lust.
. . . The Eternal Body—who and where is it?
One can see only a shadow of it.
Oh holy man, with the taste of this ecstasy,
that nectar flows within the lotus of the heart.

With the movement of the Seed [*bindu*, semen] your desires are eternally fulfilled.
And with the dawn of the moon, the Body becomes like an ocean of *rasa*.
(BG 43; II.54)

In this final stage of annihilation and rebirth, the Kartābhajā is utterly beyond all laws and social norms, enjoying the divine, ecstatic, intoxicated, and yet supremely "natural" state of *Sahaja*. He or she is "not required to abide by any sectarian convention" but has transcended all known laws amidst the intoxicating ecstasy of Love: "The Siddha is a normal social being. But the inner man is like an active volcano throbbing with tremendous love of God. . . . Nivṛtti is the stage of man's nonduality with the greatness of God. At this stage the Kartābhajā is *jiyānte marā,* or unliving."[40]

As I wish to suggest, this central importance of the body among the Kartābhajā and other non-Brahminical sects in the eighteenth and nineteenth centuries is inseparable from the social and political situation of the time. It is an attempt on the part of marginalized, discontented individuals to regain power over their physical selves, which had been alienated by a rapidly changing social and economic order. For, as Dick Hebdige points out, if dominated subcultures "possess little else, they at least own their own bodies. If power can be exercised nowhere else, it can at least be exercised here."[41] Throughout the small "deviant sects" of colonial Bengal, Partha Chatterjee has recently argued, the human body provided precisely this kind of site for resistance and struggle. As a "strategy devised within a relationship of dominance and subordination," the ritual transformation of the body was an attempt to construct an alternative identity: a secret and autonomous bodily self, beyond the outer public self and freed from the bonds of an oppressive social order and economic system:

> The deviant cults . . . are fundamentally concerned with the body. The Sahajiyā cults practice forms of bodily worship that do not respect the *śāstra* or *shari'ah*. But they can be conducted only in secret . . . and propagated only in the language of enigma. . . . There is underlying it all the attempt to define a claim of proprietorship over one's own body, to negate the daily submission of one's body to . . . the dominant dharma and to assert a domain of bodily activity where one can . . . disregard those demands.[42]

This secret body achieved thorugh *sādhanā* is therefore nothing less than a new physical identity—one that gives concrete form and substance to the Kartābhajā's new social identity or "secret self" which we have encountered previously. As we saw in chapter 2, entry into the Kartābhajā tradition allows the initiate to cultivate a kind of "dual personality" and to "live a secret life."[43] On on hand, he can maintain conventional socially acceptable exoteric identity—the *vyavahārik* or ordinary self, bound to "inevitable compromise and surrender to the dominant norms of society"; yet simultaneously, on the other hand, he can construct a secret and supremely liberated Ultimate Self—the *paramārthik* self, which represents "the secret preserve of autonomy and self-assertion."[44] Engagement in the higher stages of Kartābhajā physical practice, however, takes this ideal of a secret identity yet a step further. It aims to give birth not just to a hidden social identity but to a whole new secret corpus or spiritual flesh, which incarnates and embodies this supremely liberated *paramārthik* self.

In sum, regardless of their precise "content," both esoteric discourse and esoteric practice involve a set of similar, though clearly distinct, strategies or tactics, which have a similar role as a source of symbolic power and capital.

1. Like esoteric discourse, secret practice rests on a strategy of *hierarchalization* and restricted access to ritual practices. The secrecy surrounding certain rituals or yogic techniques only intensifies their mystery, awe, and power and only enhances the prestige of the initiate as he or she rises in the esoteric hierarchy.
2. This practice involves a strategy of appropriation and alchemical transformation: Kartābhajā practice adopts many of the basic forms, symbols, and ritual structures of mainstream society—(the symbolism of the Bengali *saṃskāras* or life-cycle rites of birth, marriage, procreation, etc.). Kartābhajā *sādhanā*, however, adapts and transforms the life cycle rites in the service of an alternative social hierarchy.
3. Specifically, this *sādhanā* involves a deliberate *inversion* or *reversal* of the normal bodily processes of procreation and birth: The usual flow of body fluids must be turned around and redirected, in order to create not an ordinary "socialized body," part of the conventional social order, but, rather, an inner secret body, freed from the mainstream social body. Thus, *by reversing and "rechanneling" the flow of body fluids, the sādhaka also rechannels the "flow of power" within the social organism.*
4. At the same time, like most Tantric *sādhanā*, this involves a deliberate strategy of *transgression* and the *skillful use of impurity*—the intentional manipulation of substances which are normally considered impure or defiling (in this case, semen and menstrual blood). As Mary Douglas aptly observes, "The danger risked by boundary transgression is power. The vulnerable margins . . . which threaten to destroy order represent the powers inhering in the cosmos. Ritual which can harness these . . . is harnessing power indeed."[45]
5. Finally, this practice involves *the skillful use of metaphor* to disguise and transmit these practices. Esoteric practice is described, quite strikingly, using the imagery of commerce and trade: It is the business of the Bazaar of Love, or the journey of the merchant ship through the bazaar of the world in search of the "Hidden City."

Thus, just as secret *discourse* serves to transform ordinary language into a powerful source of value and symbolic capital, so, too, secret *practice* transforms the ordinary human body and its elements into profound bearers of symbolic power. And just as the Kartābhajās' unique form of secret discourse functions as a sort of "coinage for the poor," a source of capital and wealth for those who are normally deprived of economic and social capital, so, too, the Kartābhajās unique form of "bodily economics" has a similar function: It aims to transform the "economic body" of the initiate itself, to free him from his ordinary life of toil in the marketplace of the world (*bhava-bājār*) and send him on a journey on a new merchant vessel, sailing to the Marketplace of Love (*prema-bājār*) within the City of the Heart.

Conclusions:
The Reinscription of the Body into an Alternative Social Hierarchy

Through esoteric practice, with its systematic deconstruction and re-creation of his own physical body and identity, the Kartābhajā *sādhaka* can achieve at least a limited kind of freedom from the bonds of labor, caste, and poverty amidst the marketplace of the world. As we see in the case of Kartābhajā masters such as Vaiṣṇavacaraṇ, he can cultivate a powerul, even ominous secret body and secret identity, even within and behind the outward facade of his orthodox self in the exoteric seocial body. However, if this new spiritual body is in one sense liberated from the conventional hierarchy of power in mainstream society, it is also clearly inscribed within a *new* hierarchy—the esoteric hierarchy of the Kartābhajā lineage itself. So, too, if the ordinary socialized body is deconstructed, and if the hierarchies of exoteric society are temporarily dismantled, this is by no means a matter of pure antinomianism; on the contrary it is the necessary prerequisite to the incorporation of the body into an alternative social hierarchy, with its own structures of power and subordination.[46]

The new spiritual body which the Kartābhajā *sādhaka* hopes to achieve is itself incorporated into the true divine and deified body—the body of the Mahāśay, which is believed to be the physical incarnation of the divinity. As Satyaśiva Pāl, puts it, "They regard the Guru as non-different from the Supreme Lord [*Parameśvara*], and accept the body of the Mahāśay . . . as the Body of the Deity [*dever śarīra*]."[47] And if each guru or Mahāśay is an incarnate divinity, then the Karta or supreme guru is none other than the original Puruṣa himself—the supreme person who contains all the forms and structures of existence within his own physical form. Not unlike the supreme Puruṣa of the Vedas, his body is the alloform both of the cosmos and of the Kartābhajā's esoteric society itself, comprising all the hierarchal grades of the Kartābhajā lineage.[48] When he undergoes initiation and practice, the disciple in fact signs over his own body to the "ownership" of the Kartā, who is the true "Proprietor" (*mālik*) of each of his disciples' bodies: "the human body is bestowed by the Kartā as the dwelling place of the disciple, as the house in which the living soul resides."[49] Just as a Zamindār or Mālik "owns" the land and homes of his tenants, so too, the Kartā, the "Master or Boss," owns the bodies of his disciples. As one promininent Kartābhajā guru, Advaita Dās, explains this ideal, "In reverence for the Guru, the disciple surrenders his body . . . [N]othing remains of his own power . . . The living soul dwells within its house. It is for the sake of dwelling in this house that they surrender to the Guru."[50] As we will see in chapter 7, this relationship of proprietorship or "landlordism" not only demands the complete subordination of the disciple to the guru but, still more strikingly, also demands its own "rent" or "tax"—the "corproreal taxation" which the disciple must pay for the privilege of occupying his body with his soul.[51]

In short, even as the Kartābhajā *sādhaka* is liberated from his ordinary life of toil and servitude under the *māliks* and *kartās* in the marketplace of the world (*ālambājār*), he is assimilated into a new "spiritual corporation," employed in the service of the true "Boss" or Kartā within the marketplace of love.

Part III

THE LIABILITY OF SECRECY

Secrecy as a Source of Scandal and Slander, Elitism and Exploitation

6

The Stinking Fruit in the Garden of Love

The Kartābhajās and the Ambivalent Role of "Tantra" in Colonial Bengal

The Kartābhajā religion is currently being practiced.
This too is a path for reaching God—
But this path is a very filthy [*noṅgrā*] one.
Just as there are various doors for entering a house,
by some doors one enters the front room;
and by some doors one can enter the inner chambers.
But there is a separate door for the Sweeper [*methar,* the cleaner of filth, i.e, the latrine door]
The dirty path of the Kartābhajās is of this sort.
Their habit is practice with a female partner.
This is a very difficult matter for weak human beings.
Particularly in this Kali age, the minds of men
are naturally attracted by women and money.
At every stage, the Master gave the instruction: beware of women and gold.

(Akṣaykumār Sen, *Śrī Śrī Rāmakṛṣṇa Puṅthi)*

If the tactics of secrecy and concealment can offer powerful new sources of status, freedom, and capital, they nevertheless often bear much less desirable consequences for their possessors. In the following chapters we begin to explore the more negative and problematic aspects of secrecy—its *liabilities* as a cause of scandal and censorship from outside the esoteric tradition, as well as a source of elitism and exploitation within the community itself. Above all, in the case of the Kartābhajās, the practices of secrecy became deeply entangled in the larger and more controversial discourse surrounding "Tantra" in nineteenth-century Bengal.

The category of "Tantra," it seems, has long held a deeply ambivalent role in both the Western and the Bengali imaginations. Infamous for their use of sexual practices and their explicit violation of caste, the Tantras have been a continuous source of mixed horror and fearsome power of both moral repugnance and tantalizing allure. Once regarded by European Orientalist scholars and conservative Indian elites as the most degenerate corruption of the Hindu tradition,[1] the Tantras have in our own time been celebrated as a much needed liberation of sexuality, a glorification of the human body, or an empowerment of women.[2]

Yet this basic ambivalence surrounding Tantra appears to have been particularly acute during the period of colonial rule in Bengal, under the impact of European ideals, Victorian morality, and the indigenous reform movements of the Bengal

Renaissance. Not only is the term "Tantrism" itself—as a singular, abstract category applied collectively to a large and highly diverse body of texts and traditions—largely a product of European Orientalist scholars of the nineteenth century, but within the colonial imagination, Tantrism was quickly identified as the very worst and most degenerate aspect of the Indian peoples under imperial rule.[3] Embodying the most extreme example of all the worst tendencies inherent in the "Indian Mind," Tantrism could be said to represent the *extreme Orient*, the most Other, the quintessence of all the idolatry, polytheism, and licentiousness that was believed to have corrupted Hinduism in modern times. For if the Orientalist scholars had identified the Golden Age of Hinduism with the noble, rational religion of the Vedas, they identified the Tantras as its worst and most depraved corruption in the modern age. "Tantrism is Hinduism arrived at its last and worst stage of development," as Sir Monier-Williams put it; in the Tantras, the noble classical tradition of the Vedas had become, "exaggerated and perverted," mixed together with such "terrible and horrible things" as "sanguinary sacrifices and orgies with wine and women."[4]

Correspondingly, among the educated Hindu society of Bengal, there appears to have been a growing sense of embarrassment or repugnance toward anything smacking of Tantra and an increasing desire either to sanitize, repress, or eradicate any such phenomena: "Tantric traditions were being made more respectable through excisions, and at times suppressed altogether . . . as stricter ideas about gentility developed in the shadow of Victorian norms."[5] As Stewart suggests, many traditions such as the Vaiṣṇava Sahajiyās faced increasing persecution throughout the colonial period. Progressively forced "underground," ever deeper into the realm of secrecy and occultation, the Sahajiyās were therefore forced to develop new and more ingenious methods for concealing their practices from the eyes of the outside world.[6]

As perhaps the most important later branch of the Sahajiyā tradition in nineteenth-century Bengal, which emerged at a critical historical moment and key geographic locus, the Kartābhajās stand out as among the most intense examples of this growing ambivalence surrounding the subject of "Tantra" during the colonial era.[7] Since its origins, the Kartābhajā tradition has been pervaded by controversy and scandal, centering largely around the question of Tantric sexual practices—above all, the practice of *parakīyā* love, or intercourse with another man's wife. Throughout the newspapers and popular literature of nineteenth century, the Kartābhajās are ridiculed for their decadent morality and their fondness for women, wine, and pleasures of the flesh. In the words of Rāmakṛṣṇa, quoted above, the Kartābhajā path was considered a kind of "back door," an underground or unclean way of approaching God. It is a secret door (*guhya dvāra*) and a "filthy path" (*noṅgrā path*), which can only be described with the metaphor of the door of the *methar,* the "cleaner of filth and night soil"—that is, the "latrine door." Though this too may be a path to God, the one who goes by this path "gets very filthy."[8]

In response to this sort of attack, the Kartābhajās appear to have felt a growing embarrassment about anything smacking of "Tantra" and so made an increasing effort to conceal, censor, or repress any such phenomena. Throughout the highly cryptic Kartābhajā songs, we find frequent references to Tantric sexual practices, though disguised only in the most bizarre symbolism and obscure metaphors. The practice of *parakīyā* love, for example, is described with the rather striking image of the "*stinking fruit in the garden of love*"—a fruit which, though originally pure, became corrupt and "foul smelling," and so had to be uprooted by the "Good-Mannered Company" (*ādab kompānī*) of the Kartābhajā sect (BG 154ff.).

In the course of my analysis, I borrow some insights from James Scott, Sue Jansen, and others who have examined the role of censorship in social discourse. On the one hand, censorship or the enforced suppression of certain discourse or practice is always among the most effective tools of those in power. As the "knot that binds power and knowledge," it is the means by which the dominant classes ensure that they remain in control of the information that gives them authority and power. And yet as Scott points out, censorship—in the form of self-censorship, or the strategic encoding of discourse—is also among the most effective "arts of resistance" or weapons of the weak. It is a key strategy through which dominated groups continue to transmit their message in the concealed form of a "hidden transcript" or off-stage discourse, which eludes and subverts the discourse of the dominant classes.[9] In the Kartābhajā songs, we find two distinct kinds of self-censorship at work simultaneously—both a tactic of *deodorization* and a tactic of *disguise*, both an attempt to eradicate Tantric sexual elements and an attempt to conceal or mask them in new and more creative ways.

After a brief summary of the history of the debate surrounding *parakīyā* love in the Vaiṣṇava and Sahajiyā traditions, I then examine the rise of the Kartābhajās within the context of colonial Bengal and their highly enigmatic songs describing the "stinking fruit" of *parakīyā* love. Finally, to conclude, I suggest that this basic ambivalence at the heart of the Kartābhajā tradition opens up a number of larger questions for the study of Tantra in Bengal. First, it demonstrates the ways in which Tantric traditions are deeply rooted in real social, political, and cultural conditions and the ways in which these traditions change historically, creatively adapting in the face of changing circumstances. Second, it raises the critical question of *censorship*—the central ambivalence surrounding Tantra and the constant attempts to mask, suppress, or eradicate any elements smacking of scandal or immorality. Last, and perhaps most important, the Kartābhajās also raise the question of the very definition of Tantra itself—that is, how certain groups come to be identified (or attacked) as "Tantric," and how the term *Tantra* has come to be constructed in the popular and scholarly imaginations. Ultimately, I hope, the rather striking case of the Kartābhajās can help us to reimagine the category of Tantra in a more useful way in contemporary discourse.

Illicit Love, Human and Divine: The Problem of *Parakīyā* Love

Look—the ways of Love are endlessly devious!
The milkmaids are charmed, but they cannot charm Him [Kṛṣṇa].
. . . At the touch of that *rasa*, there is madness!
That Gallant lover is the supreme *Rasika*,
with terrible cunning from beginning to end.
Busily engaged in *Parakīyā* love, He charms them with a single glance.
(BG 52; II.82)

Within the Vaiṣṇava tradition of Bengal, there is a long and rather torturous history of debate surrounding the question of *parakīyā* love, or sexual intercourse with another man's wife. Initially, this problem arose as a theological question regarding the relationship between Lord Kṛṣṇa and his amorous companions, the Gopīs or cowherd maidens: Was Kṛṣṇa's love affair with the Gopīs a (seemingly immoral and improper) *parakīyā* relationship, or was it in fact in some sense a proper *svakīyā* relationship? If the former, then how do we explain the fact that Kṛṣṇa (i.e., God) could violate the conventions of morality and social order?

Even among the first disciples of Caitanya, this had posed a sticky and embarrassing problem. In the works of Rūpa and Jīva Gosvāmin, for example, we find all sorts of theological gymnastics aimed at proving that the love affair between Kṛṣṇa and the Gopīs was actually not an adulterous *parakīyā* relation; on the contrary, because Kṛṣṇa is ultimately the true husband of all women, this was in fact a pure *svakīyā* relation (indeed, in his *Lalita Mādhava*, Rūpa even went to so far as to depict an actual marriage between Rādhā and Kṛṣṇa in Dvārakā).[10] In the *Caitanya-caritāmṛta,* on the other hand, Kṛṣṇadāsa Kavirāja attributed the *parakīyā* doctrine to Caitanya himself, on the grounds that the sentiment for another man's wife actually strengthens the intensity of emotion (*parakīyārase strī bhāver ullāsa*).[11]

In the seventeenth and early eighteenth centuries, a growing number of Vaiṣṇavas, such as Jīva's own disciples, Śrīnivāsa and Śyāmānanda, and after them, Yadunandana Dāsa, began to promote the *parakīyā* doctrine as the true inner meaning of Kṛṣṇa's relationship to Rādhā. The *svakīyā* doctrine, they held, is merely an outward, external meaning intended for "superficial people" (indeed, Yadunandana even attributes the *parakīyā* view to Jīva Gosvāmin himself).[12] Finally in 1717, this controversy came to a head and resulted in an open debate among Vaiṣṇava pundits at the court of the Nabāb Jāfāra Khān in Murshidabad. After intense argument, it is said, Śrīnivāsa's descendant, Rādhāmohana, led the Parakīyā-vādins to victory over the Svākīyā-vādins. Henceforth, the Gauḍīya Vaiṣṇava community reached a consensus that—from the theological point of view, at least—the *parakīyā* doctrine represents the correct understanding of the relationship between Kṛṣṇa and his Gopīs. For it is precisely because the Gopī is willing to abandon all, to forsake her own husband, to transgress the law, for the sake of her Lord, that she demonstrates the highest form of bhakti.[13]

However, it was not long before the Tantric Sahajiyās appropriated this theological point, reinterpreted it, and used it as a means of legitimating their own ritual practices. Now the doctrine of *parakīyā* refers not simply to the illicit love affair between Kṛṣṇa and his Gopīs but to the illicit sexual relations between male and female practitioners—who are themselves ritually identified with Kṛṣṇa and Rādhā. "To the Sahajiyās, the *parakīyā* doctrine is more than an interpretation of a textual passage. If Kṛṣṇa's *līlā* was with *parakīyā* women, the *parakīyā līlā* is what men must emulate."[14] Like Rādhā and Kṛṣṇa, who are willing to abandon all social conventions because of their intense love for one another, the Sahajiyā too must be willing to violate any taboos and transgress any boundaries of caste or *śāstric* injunction in order experience the liberating bliss of true love [*prema*].

> If there is no *parakīyā* there can be no birth of *bhāva*. It is in fear of separation that grief and passionate longing grow. To *svakīyās* there is no fear of separation . . . and without longing there is no *prema*.[15]

> In *parakīyā* there is real passion [*rāga*] and the profound joy of *rasa*. In *svakīyā* there is no *rasa* but merely a semblance of it.[16]

Not surprisingly, however, this more literal or physical interpretation of the *parakīyā* doctrine was quickly and unanimously condemned by the more conservative mainstream Gauḍīya Vaiṣṇava community. "The orthodox tradition promotes celibacy or . . . sex within marriage. The *parakīyā* mode is only for Rādhā and Kṛṣṇa *not* for devotees."[17] According to a text attributed to Narottam Dās, attacking those who misunderstand and abuse this key distinction, "They can't understand the difference between the practice of lust and the practice of love. They can't separate the poison from the nectar. Calling it love, they are maddened with lust and perish. . . . They regard themselves as Kṛṣṇa and their consorts as Rādhā and engage in sexual intercourse. This is the surest road to hell."[18]

If the problem of *parakīyā* love has a long and controversial history in Bengal, this controversy appears to have become all the more acute during the late eighteenth and nineteenth centuries, as British colonial power and European morality began to penetrate Bengal, and as a variety of indigenous reform movements begn to spread among the Western-educated Indian elites. Above all, it appears to have become caught up in the broader controversy surrounding the category of "Tantra" and the use of sexual intercourse as a form of religious practice. As Padoux has shown, it was largely during the colonial period that Orientalist scholars first began to construct the abstract category of "Tantrism" itself, as a singular, unified, and homogenous body of texts and traditions. Indeed, the category of Tantrism would seem to have formed a key part of the broader Orientalist project of imagining India as a whole. Within the Orientalist imagination, as Ron Inden has argued, the world of India was progressively constructed as the quintessential "Other" of the West; conceived as an essentially passionate, irrational, effeminate world, a land of "disorderly imagination," India was set in opposition to the progressive, rational, masculine, and scientific world of modern Europe.[19] And "Tantrism," it would seem, was quickly singled out as the darkest, most irrational core of this Indian mind—the "disease" which had infected the pure, rational monotheism of the Vedas, signaling the progressive decay of Hinduism in the modern times. The "nonsensical extravagance and absurd gesticulations" of Tantric ritual, as the respected Orientalist H. H. Wilson, laments, "have now become authorities for all that is abominable in the present state of Hindu religion."[20] By the late nineteenth century, the category of "Tantrism" had become infamous throughout the European scholarly and popular imaginations alike, universally condemned as something "too abominable to enter the ears of man, and impossible to reveal to a Christian public" (William Ward),[21] as a cult of "nudity worshipped in Bacchanalian orgies which cannot be described" (Talboys Wheeler),[22] as "an unattractive cult of magic, dominated by sexual ideas and expressing power in terms of violence and cruelty" (W. H. Moreland),[23] or simply as "an unlimited array of magic rites drawn from the most ignorant and stupid classes" (J. N. Farquhar).[24]

Not surprisingly, we find throughout the nineteenth century a growing sense of embarrassment among the Indian upper classes, and an increasing effort either to censor or to suppress such unpalatable phenomena as Tantrism. On one hand, as we see in the case of the *Mahānirvāṇa Tantra*—which most scholars agree is almost certainly a product of the late eighteenth century—there was a clear attempt to present a more "sanitized," rational, and "Vedāntic" kind of Tantra, purified of the more offensive magical and sexual elements.[25] On the other hand, as we see in the case of Western-educated Hindu reformers such as Rāmmohun Roy and his followers in the Brāhmo Samāj, the Tantras have now been singled out as the clearest sign of all the polytheism and idolatry that had infected and corrupted modern Hinduism. Following the lead of the European Orientalists, Rāmmohun and his fellow reformers looked back to the noble, rational religion of the Vedas as India's Golden Age, while they despaired of the modern "Age of Kālī" in which the perverse rites of the Tantras ran rampant. Steeped in "idol worship, superstition and the total destruction of the moral principle," Tantrism had come to represent, in the eyes of most educated Indian elites, a "horrendous and debased form of religion and a radical departure from the authentic Hindu tradition."[26]

An even more acute example of this growing embarrassment surrounding Tantra is the great Calcutta mystic Śrī Rāmakṛṣṇa. As Kripal has shown, Rāmakṛṣṇa was a man filled with "shame disgust and fear" about his own sexual inclinations and profoundly torn in his relation to Tantra, particularly in its sexual aspects. A thing of "almost limitless and terrifying power," Tantra was for Rāmakṛṣṇa at once seductive, awesome, and alluring yet also surrounded with an aura of obscenity, scandal, and corruption. Throughout the writings of Rāmakṛṣṇa's disciples—who were in most cases even more embarrassed than their master about these scandalous affairs—Tantric phenomena appear only in the most "censored and bowdlerized" form, "buried beneath a mountain of pious ink," or else excised altogether.[27]

So, too, within the Vaiṣṇava community of Bengal, we find throughout the nineteenth century increasing efforts to purge or sanitize the tradition of any remaining Sahajiyā or Tantric elements. Perhaps the most powerful among these reformist movements was begun in the middle of the nineteenth century by the enigmatic British civil servant and Vaiṣṇava convert, Bhaktivinod Ṭhākur (Kedarnāth Datta, 1838–1914), and his son son Bhaktisiddhānta Sarasvatī (d.1937), the founder of the highly conservative movement of the Gauḍīya Maṭh. According to the Gauḍīya Maṭh's reading of Vaiṣṇava history, Bhaktivinod and his disciples had come forth largely in order to combat the perversions introduced by the Tantric Sahajiyās and their distorted, disgustingly literal interpretation of *parakīyā* love: "The religion initiated by Chaitanya had lost its ecstatic zeal and came to be identified with one of its offshoots, the Sahajiyā sect . . . The Sahajiyās integrated Tantric aspects in their practices, ritual sexual intercourse being primary . . . Vaishnavism was almost abandoned by the educated section of people . . . Most of the Vaishnava followers lost their high standard of morality. . . . In this context Bhaktivinod burst upon the scene."[28] As Bhaktivinod explains, many of the evils and social maladies of the modern era are directly related to the decline in moral values and the misunderstanding of basic Vaiṣṇava teachings, such as the true nature role of *parakīyā* love. "It is the duty of Krishna's devotees to serve Him with this erotic transcendental love," Bhaktivinod argues, "But he who, taking the role of Krishna, tries to imitate His amorous lila is doomed to hell forever. Those who are cunning, deceitful and lascivious commit such offense."[29] So, too, Bhaktivinod's son, Bhaktisiddhānta (who was perhaps even more conservative and reactionary than his father) fiercely rebukes those "gross and horrible" Sahajiyās who abuse the glorious pastimes of Kṛṣṇa by interpreting them in a literal physical sense: "[A] considerable number of persons have been misled in trying to follow the preachers of the religion of unconventional spiritual Amour. . . . Many pseudo-preachers make use of the teachings of the Bhagavata for condoning illicit carnality. These preachers are a great nuisance and come under the penal classes of the Civil Law for safeguarding decency and morality."[30]

In the face of this increasing scrutiny and criticism, as Stewart has argued, the Sahajiyā schools were progressively forced deeper into the underground realms of secrecy and silence. Not surprisingly, it was during this same period that the Sahajiyās began to cultivate the arts of encryption, dissimulation, and discursive disguise in ever new and more imaginative forms:

> The encryption of the Vaiṣṇava Sahajiyā texts begins in earnest during the period of . . . Muslim dominance and becomes the norm in the British colonial period. Even then the movement does not appear to have gone 'underground' until the 19th century, when the British exert full control over the delta . . . [W]ith the growth of colonial power, the Sahajiyās began to feel pressure to become more invisible than ever, not simply to obscure their rituals, but to transform their *rahasya* into the truly secret, in a Western sense.[31]

As we will now see, however, this growing ambivalence surrounding Tantric sexual practices is perhaps nowhere more apparent than in the case of the Kartābhajā tradition.

The "Good-Mannered Company" (Ādab Kompānī) and the "Foul Smelling Fruit": The Kartābhajās and the Problem of *Parakīyā* Love

In the Kali age, people are deluded by ignorance, therefore the desire for the five M's is the religion of this era; and for this reason the Kartābhajā teaching has secretly become very powerful in this land. (Rāmcandra Datta, *Tattvasāra)*

While deeply rooted in the older Sahajiyā and other Tantric schools of medieval Bengal, the Kartābhajās also appear to represent a changing moral attitude within the Sahajiyā tradition—above all, they reflect a growing awareness of the problematic role of sexual practices and the category of "Tantra" as a whole. Indeed, not only did they hail themselves, as we have already seen, using the stolen British the title of the "Poor Company" (see chapter 4), but they also often called themselves by the profoundly ironic title of the *ādab kompānī*—the "Good Mannered Company" or the "Courteous Company." A Perso-Arabic term of respect and honor, *ādab* is used to refer to the finest qualities of the aristocratic and "distinguished" wealthy classes, along with the "norms of refined behavior and taste," or the "generally acknowledged modes of dress, interpersonal behavior and deportment."[32] Initiated into this "Distinguished Company," sealed with a contract under the rule of the just *bādshāh* (the Kartā), the disciple may engage in the true business of the "bazaar of love" (cf. BG 41–45):

The land has been secured with a contract [*konṭrakṭ*].
There's an Emperor [*bādshāh*] in this land,
and beneath him is the Good-mannered Company [*ādab kompānī*].
Let me tell you the nature of this Landlord's estate:
There are four castes—Brāhmaṇs, Kṣatriyas, Vaiśyas, and Śūdras—
He came with fine merchandise to join all four together.
It's said that the Emperor of this land kept his merchandise hidden.
He came and gave initiation to the Proprietors of this land:
he taught them about calculations and prices, profits and gifts.
Those ten gathered together, received ownership and made a Contract!
(BG 265; II.6)

Like most earlier Vaiṣṇava Sahajiyā literature, the songs of the Kartābhajās are filled with a variety of highly erotic imagery and references to esoteric sexual practices. However, given the particularly sensitive social and historical milieux in which they emerged, and given the kind of severe criticism they faced from the upper-classs *bhadralok* community, the Kartābhajās only mention such practices in the most ambivalent, compromised, and equivocal terms, concealing them behind extremely tangled and confusing veils of symbolism, metaphor, and the secret discourse of *sandhābhāṣā*. Throughout the Kartābhajā songs, we find classic Tantric erotic metaphors such as "throwing away the poison and drinking the nectar" (separating *prema* from *kāma* in the act of love), "making the frog dance in the serpent's mouth" or "swimming the ocean without getting your hair wet" (i.e., engaging in intercourse without ejaculating).[33] Like the Bāuls, the Kartābhajās often use the imagery of the "Royal Goose dallying with his beloved Lady Goose" and the "bees drinking the nectar of the lotus"—metaphors commonly used to refer to the act of sexual intercourse and the union of the male semen with the female menstrual fluid (BG 415; II.81).[34] And as we have already seen (chapter 3), perhaps the most well-known and most infamous of all the Kartābhajās' esoteric sayings is their very cryptic "root mantra," the odd little phrase: "meye hijṛā puruṣ khojā, tabe habe Kartābhajā (the woman must become a Hijṛā, and the man must become a Khojā; then they will be Kartābhajās")—a saying that is understood by many, both within and without the tradition, to be a reference to Tantric sexual practices and, specifically, to the paradoxical act of enjoying sexual union without feeling even a trace of base, sensual desire.

However, the most controversial of all the Kartābhajā songs are those that refer to the Sahajiyā practice of *parakīyā* love—a practice which, we have already seen, had become an object of increasing scandal and debate during the colonial era. The question of *parakīyā sādhanā* appears numerous times throughout the Kartābhajā songs—but always in the most obscure, confusing, and apparently contradictory forms.[35] The most important of these is a long series of some fourteen songs of the *Bhāver Gīta* (BG 148–61). Indeed, it is these very songs which our author is afraid to reveal to us—"lest we be scared shitless!" (BG 159; II.89).

All these songs employ the central metaphors of the "Madman" (*khepā, bāul* or *pāgal*), "the Company" (*kompānī*), the "Fruit Garden" (*meoyār bāgān*), and the "foul-smelling fruit" (*bodboi phal*). In a curious mythological narrative, which combines the imagery of plant life and gardens with the "moats and canons" of Fort William and the East India Company, our author tells us that the Divine Madman had a wondrous fruit tree, with the power to intoxicate and enchant anyone who tasted its fruit. Because no one on earth could reach the fruit of this tree, however, the Madman planted a magical garden in the heavens, protected within the confines of the "Company's Fort," with all its canons and guns (almost surely a reference to Fort William in Calcutta).[36] And then, out of his wish to delight and madden the world, he distributed the fruit throughout the world, giving it to the "men of the company" and making them all madmen like himself.

No one can reach the wondrous fruit of that land.
That's why the Madman will return and plant the fruit in heaven,
and as it bears fruit, He'll distribute it throughout the world.
Whoever receives and tastes that fruit,
while tasting it, will forget everything else!
. . . There's an ocean surrounding this wondrous place.
Upon it, the fruit garden was born.
. . . There's a wondrous place within a Fortress,
where there are canonballs and bullets, canons and guns.
Brother, this wondrous place is what you have sought.

Out of desire for awakening, you get a whiff of it.
Lālśaśī says, "at His command, the soul becomes a Mad Bāul! [*khepā bāul*]."
(BG 153).

The referents of these complex metaphors are, for the most part, relatively clear and have been explained by a number of later commentators.[37] As one former Kartā, Satyaśiva Pāl, explains, the madman here is the divine madman, Caitanya, who was secretly reborn in the form of Āulcāṅd; the "company" is the Vaiṣṇava community following in the wake of Caitanya, and secretly continued by the Kartābhajās; the fruit garden is the "garden of love [*prema*]," or the realm of spiritual practice and devotional worship; and finally, as the *Bhāver Gīta* itself tells us quite explicitly in the last song of the series, the wondrous and mysterious "fruit tree" which is planted in this garden is none other the practice of *parakīyā rasa* itself (BG 159; II.89).[38]

Initially, in the first several songs, the author presents *parakīyā rasa* as a positive, even necessary practice; it is the sweet fruit planted in the garden of love by the divine madman Caitanya-Āulcāṅd, a fruit that delights and intoxicates all the men of the Company:

A great splendor arose within this garden of sweet fruit,
and look—the men of your Company come running, maddened with the sweet smell!
To those who have eyes to see it,
the Madman will give this fruit to taste.
Having tasted it, they'll be enchanted by the Madman,
and follow behind Him like a bull led by the nose!
. . . When that Company of yours becomes [like] my Madman,
they'll be able to taste this fruit.
When they get it, they'll feel the Ecstasy [*bhāva*] of madness.
Becoming connoisseurs in that taste [*rase rasika*],
they'll engage in a wondrous play!
. . . That Madman said, "I'll distribute this sweet fruit throughout the world!
I'll make a deep stream in the earth,
I'll make everyone speak one language,
enchanting them with this fruit, with the greatest fun!
And now the whole universe will drown in the waves of Love!"
The Madman himself will remain plunged within [the ocean of love];
And the Company will come and float [upon the waves of love] to its heart's desire.
Lālśaśī says, "That Madman [*khepā bāul*] can do whatever he pleases!"
(BG 154; II.86)

However, as the *Bhāver Gīta* goes on to tell us, there's something not quite right with this *parakīyā* fruit; indeed it begins to give off a strange "foul smell" (*bodboí*), which seems to overpower anyone who inhales it. Not only does it intoxicate those who taste it with its marvelous joy and bliss, but it also seems to become rather addictive and self-destructive:

Look, now you're paying homage to that Madman;
You know nothing impure.
That's why I'm telling you: We never want to smell that fruit;
but you've lost yourself in the fragrance of that fruit, brother.
Now you can't stand anything else—
But never speak of this openly to anyone! (BG 153; my italics)

Therefore, to save ordinary devotees from becoming totally corrupted by sensual lust—by addiction to sexual intercourse and even "enjoyment of menstrual blood"—the "Good-Mannered Company" (*ādab Kompānī*) was forced to "uproot the garden," fruit, roots, and all.

Previously, at the dawn of the Fourth Pralaya [i.e., the beginning of the Kali Yuga]
"The Darkness which Destroys Doubt" [i.e., Caitanya] suddenly came to this shore.
I don't know how he became so beautiful!
He created the garden of *Parakīyā Rasa.*
There was no end to the field of night.
But brother, a foul smell arose within it, you know.
Yet with great effort, the supreme, Virtuous One preserved [the garden].
When the Good Mannered Company got wind of that foul smell,
they uprooted the garden, roots, flowers and all.
If the Good Mannered Company had not gotten wind of that smell,
then everyone, the highest and the lowest, would have gone crazy—
eating menstrual blood, sleeping together!
After this happened, the Garden remained empty. (BG 159; II.89)

Nonetheless, even though the garden of love has had to be uprooted and destroyed, still, the wise madman was able to preserve this garden in another form. In a series of cryptic passages, we are told first that the madman rebuilt this garden, not on earth, but instead "in heaven" [*ākāśe*], and later, that he preserved this garden "secretly," beyond the sight of mainstream society, and, as it were, *behind* the old garden of fruit:

When the Company uprooted this garden of fruit,
The Madman himself went to see and evaluate it.
There was some foul-smell within it.
He rebuked all those who desired it.
Did the Company have the strength to bear that foul smell?
And seeing it, He himself was driven Mad!
He said, "I'll rebuild that [Garden] in heaven!"

Lalśaśi says, "I'll delight the Company with the Fruit of that Garden!"
(BG 155; II.87)

Even now, behind that fruit garden, the Company continues;
Lālśaśī says, "behind that fruit garden, the Company is continuous!" [*meoyār piche kompānī abirām*]. (BG 159; II.89)

Now that we have briefly traced the origins of the Kartābhajās and their highly enigmatic songs, let us turn to the more formidable task of interpreting these cryptic songs—or at least sorting out their multiple, conflicting readings and interpretations. As we will see, there are in fact many different and contradictory ways to construe this striking image of the "Company" and its stinking fruit—some which would eradicate this foul smell altogether, and some which would more skillfully mask it behind more palatable aromas.

"Deodorized Tantra": Sex, Secrecy, and Censorship in the Kartābhajā Tradition

When one becomes free of the scent of lust, he attains the Gopī-bhāva.
(*Vivarta Vilāsa)*

What we encounter in this long and rather curious metaphoric narrative of the "stinking fruit," I would suggest, is a powerful illustration of the problems of censorship and repression, as well as the corresponding tactics of self-censorship, encryption, and symbolic disguise to which censorship inevitably gives rise. As the "knot binding power and knowledge," censorship is always at work in some form in the social field, governing what can be said, expressed, or even thought: "a mechanism the powerful use to tighten control over people or ideas that threaten to disrupt established systems of order."[39] However, as Scott argues, the tactics of enforced silence are also just as frequently exercised by dominated groups themselves, upon their own utterances, in the form of self-censorship. As one of the most common "arts of resistance" or the weapons of the weak, this systematic editing of one's own discourse can be a powerful means of communicating potentially dangerous or subversive information while staying within the boundaries of the official law. Not unlike "prudent opposition newspaper editors under strict censorship," dominated and marginal groups must learn how to exploit all the loopholes, ambiguities, and lapses "in order to convey their message in oblique form without being silenced altogether."[40] The art of self-censorship thus demands the complex and ingenious use of concealed, encrypted language—a technique of "writing between the lines"—designed to pass by the censors while still transmitting its message in covert form to its intended audience.[41] And the more severe the censorship imposed by the dominant political order, as Freud so insightfully reminds us, "the more thorough the disguise and . . . the more ingenious the means employed to put the reader on the track of meaning."[42] Within the Kartābhajā tradition, however, these efforts at self-censorship appear to have taken two different forms—on one hand, a tactic of deodorization, and on the other, a tactic of disguise.

On one side, throughout the later nineteenth and early twentieth centuries, the more conservative leaders of the Kartābhajās have sought to defend their tradition against charges of licentiousness, often bending over backward to sanitize and eradicate any trace of the "foul stench" of Tantric immorality. In J. E. H. Garret's *District Gazetteers* of 1910, for example, we find a stirring defense of the Kartābhajā faith by one particularly outspoken devotee named Babu Gopal Krishna Pal. Far from a decadent and degenerate Tantric cult, Pal argues, the Kartābhajā religion is the true "Religion of Man," equal in its noble humanism and moral purity to the reformist movements like Rāmmohun's Brāhmo Samāj itself.[43]

Even more reactionary and apologetic defenses of the Kartābhajā faith, however, emerged in response to the question of *parakīyā* love. For example, one of the most respected and revered of the Ghoshpara Kartās, Satyaśiva Pāl Devamahanta, offers a highly conservative—indeed *ultra-conservative*—interpretation of Kartābhajā practice. In his long commentary on the songs of the "Stinking Fruit," Pāl argues that the Gauḍīya Vaiṣṇava community had initially embraced the doctrine of *parakīyā* love—but solely on the *theological* plane, as the relationship between Kṛṣṇa and Rādhā, and thus most emphatically *not* between actual men and women. However, this doctrine was then misunderstood and corrupted by later followers (i.e., the Tantric Sahajiyās) and therefore had to be uprooted by the "Good Mannered Company" (i.e., the Kartābhajās). In its place, Āulcāṅd, as the new incarnation of Caitanya, planted a new garden, which was the doctrine of *svakīyā* love. At present, Pāl suggests, the true and authentic Kartābhajās believe solely in the most orthodox, most conservative doctrine of *svakīyā* love—on *both* the human *and* on the theological planes. Thus, in a rather remarkable hermeneutic maneuver, Pāl claims not only that the Kartābhajās are free of all scandal and licentiousness but, in fact, that they are even more orthodox and conservative than the mainstream Gauḍīya Vaiṣṇavas themselves!

> The Kartābhajā religion is strongly opposed to the Parakīyā doctrine. It is based upon the Svakīyā doctrine. . . . In the Kali yuga . . . Lord Kṛṣṇa descended into this world and became incarnate in the form of Caitanya. He created the garden of Parakīyā love. That garden was pure and spotless . . . But before his entry into the city of Puri, a foul smell arose in this garden . . . People misunderstood the pure Parakīyā rasa and began to engage in immoral practices. . . . When Caitanya, in the form of Āulcāṅd, saw that the people were practicing immoral acts, he went mad. . . . He reproached everyone who desired it. Then he said, "I'll create a new fruit garden," and he began to spread the Svakīyā doctrine in a new form in Ghoshpara.[44]

This, according to Pāl's reading, is the basic meaning of the Kartābhajās' rather infamous and controvesial root mantra, "Meye hijṛā puruṣ khojā, tabe habe

Kartābhajā." Far from bearing any kind of Tantric sexual implications, this means on the contrary that the man and woman must be utterly chaste and pure, free of all carnal desire, in complete control of the senses.[45]

Yet on the other side, in complete opposition to this strategy of "deodorization" or denial of Tantric sexual practices, there is also the strategy of "disguise," or the more skillful concealment of such objectionable elements. Side by side with this more conservative interpretation, there have always been a variety of Kartābhajā disciples who have strongly advocated Tantric practices and the use of *parakīyā* love as a religious sacrament—though only behind the thickest veils of secrecy. Even the great twentieth-century Kartābhajā theologian and systematizer, Manulāl Miśra, the most important Kartābhajā author after Dulālcāṅd, offers a highly esoteric Tantric interpretation, comparing Kartābhajā practice to the illicit love affairs of Vidyāpati and his illicit lover, Lachīmā: "Let me tell you about this conjugal love [*rati*]: through this love, Rādhāṅga Rāy . . . enjoyed a woman and became the Conqueror of Death. And Vidyāpati too engaged in this love. . . . The young girl Lachīmā was endowed with all virtues; Vidyāpati joined with her in Sahaja Love, very secretly [*ati gopane*] . . . . Become a woman, brother, and engage in this practice with a woman. Remain in secrecy and practice this love!"[46]

Even today one can find a variety of gurus throughout old Calcutta and the rural hinterlands of Bengal who still defend the more esoteric and controversial Tantric side of the tradition. One of the most learned and most repected living Kartābhajā gurus, Śrī Advaita Candra Dās of Shyambazar, northern Calcutta, for example, interprets the same passage of the "Stinking Fruit" in an explicitly Tantric sense, as referring to literal sexual practices. The deeper meaning of this song, in Dās's reading, is that *parakīyā* sexual practices (in the Tantric Sahajiyā sense) were originally taught by Caitanya-Āulcāṅd; however, because they were abused by self-interested, false devotees and misunderstood by the exoteric Vaiṣṇava tradition, they had to be removed from the mainstream Vaiṣṇava community. Nevertheless, these practices have in fact still continued behind the fruit garden—that is, *secretly, esoterically*, beyond the sight of exoteric, worldly minded men and solely within the esoteric realm of the Kartābhajā sect. In this interpretation, the "foul smell" simply refers to the presence of selfish lust (*kāma*) which must be purified and transformed if true love (*prema*) is to emerge through the practice of *parakīyā*: "The practice of *parakīyā rasa* is very difficult. There must not be even a trace of lust in the *sādhaka*." The true partner in Kartābhajā *sādhanā* must be as pure and unsullied as Caṇḍīdās's untouchable washerwoman-lover, Rāmī—a woman who can engage in seemingly antisocial sexual relations, yet without bearing the foul odor of lust:

> The adulterous lover is tainted by the scent of lust, and the chaste wife [*Satīnārī*] is also tainted by the scent of lust; but apart from these two, there is another type of woman who is free of the scent of lust. She alone can be taken in this practice. . . . Thus, Caṇḍīdās praised Rāmī, the washerwoman, as his very life: "You are enjoyment without the scent of lust; She has the form of a washerwoman and the nature of a virgin; there is no scent of lust upon her."[47]

According to Dās's reading, this is the meaning of the key Kartābhajā metaphors of "sitting on the lotus without drinking the nectar," and "dallying with Lord Kṛṣṇa, without retaining any scent of him on one's body." These are both common metaphors used throughout the Sahajiyā and Bāul literature for the practice of sexual *sādhanā*. The Tantric yogin engages in sexual intercourse (i.e., sits on the lotus) without emitting his semen or enjoying physical orgasm (i.e., drinking the nectar): "There are two marks of the Sahaja condition. One is that the scent of Kṛṣṇa will not remain upon the body. The other is that the bee will sit on the lotus but will not drink the nectar. . . . He may have a female companion, but he will not drink the nectar. Even while remaining with a beautiful woman, he will never give in to lust."[48] The true *sādhaka* is the one who can engage in *parakīyā* love—who can taste the stinking fruit—and yet somehow avoid becoming stained by its foul smell—that is, avoid giving in to the madness of lust. In Dās's reading, this is the *real* and most esoteric meaning of the Kartābhajā root mantra, *meye hijṛā puruṣ khojā*. To become a *hijṛā* or a *khojā* does not mean simple chastity and abstinence but, rather, that one has the power to perform what is seemingly impossible, contradictory, or absurd—like making a frog dance in a snake's mouth or bathing in the sea of nectar without getting your hair wet, the true *sādhaka* can engage in sexual intercourse without giving in to lust and without shedding his semen.[49] In support of this reading, Dās then cites the following rather explicitly Tantric Kartābhajā song (which is, interestingly enough, not included in the official corpus of the *Bhāver Gīta*),

Keep this secret love in secrecy;
and accomplish the work of the heart.
Make the frog dance in the mouth of the serpent,
then you will be the king of *Rasikas*.
He who is skillful can thread a needle with the peak of Mount Sumeru.
If one can bind an elephant with a spider's web,
he will attain *rasa*.
. . . Pay no attention to the Vedas or Vedānta,
and don't drink the rasa of the Vedas.
You will still be a chaste wife; you won't be an adulteress,
under the control of no one,
Even though you become unchaste and abandon your family, worrying and worrying.
Seeing another's husband, with passion radiant like gold,
you will still follow the injunctions of your own true husband.
Swim in the ocean of impurity, let down your hair,
but don't get wet and don't touch the water.
. . . Be a cook, make the curry—but don't touch the pot![50]

One who dares to engage in such a difficult and dangerous practice, however, must always remain hidden and disguised from the eyes of common, exoteric, and worldly society: "This Sahajiyā practice, like other forms of Tantric practice, is secret. It cannot be revealed to ordinary people. Those who follow this path cannot tell anyone about it."[51] This, according to Dās, is precisely the reason that the songs of the *Bhāver Gīta* are so strange and confusing, so filled with bizarre metaphors and seemingly inscrutable, even nonsensical imagery. Their aim is precisely to mislead, confuse, and divert ignorant outsiders, who would only misunderstand and abuse these powerful and dangerous teachings:

> The bestial, common person is without authority and is forbidden from this practice. . . . Once they gain authority to engage in this practice, pure men have as their the duty to prevent others from engaging in this practice.
>
> Lālśaśī composed countless verses in the form of instructions for the method of *sādhanā* using *sandhā-bhāṣā*. . . . The method of Kartābhajā practice remains bound in great secrecy between the guru and disciple and is not knownto the majority. That is why most people cannot understand the methods of practice in this sect.[52]

Like the esoteric language of Tibetan Tantric texts, as Robert Thurman has argued, these deeply encoded songs would seem to involve a direct and explicit "skillful use of obscurity"—a discourse which is deliberately opaque, intentionally misleading, whose aim is not to clarify and enlighten, but rather to *obfuscate and confuse.*[53]

Not surprisingly, the conflict of interpretations surrounding the Kartābhajās is not limited to Kartābhajā devotees themselves but has also aroused tremendous debate in contemporary scholarship. Since the mid-nineteenth century until the present day, there have always been a wide range of scholars who regard the Kartābhajās as a basically Tantric sect, which has since its origins been shot through with sexual practices. As Tushar Chatterjee puts it, "it is observed from extensive field studies . . . that the Sahajiyā Tantrik tradition of orgiasticism has been in practice among the Kartābhajā sect all through."[54] Second, there are those who offer a more apologetic interpretation, regarding the Kartābhajās as a more conservative Vaiṣṇava sect, into which certain Tantric elements may have entered at a later date, as corruptions of an originally pure tradition. As Akṣaykumār Datta put it in 1870: "Perhaps the intentions of the founder were true, but his followers departed from the pure path. . . . The sin of sexual transgression occurred . . . and this has been the cause of their downfall."[55] Still others, like Ramakanta Chakrabarty, take a kind of middle-road view, describing the Kartābhajās as half Vaiṣṇava, half Sahajiyā, or as "conservative" Sahajiyās who practice only *svakīyā* sexual rites, while rejecting the more objectionable *parakīyā* rites.[56] Finally, some like Sudhīr Cakravartī suggest that there are in fact two separate and very different branches within the Kartābhajā tradition—one which follows more mainstream Vaiṣṇava practices, and another highly secretive branch, surviving primarily in the more remote areas of rural Bengal, which continues to engage in Sahajiyā sexual rites.[57]

My own opinion is that the Kartābhajā sect is now and has always been a highly pluralistic tradition, consisting of a wide range of conflicting factions. As we have already seen, the songs of the *Bhāver Gīta* themselves are almost certainly not the product of a single author but, instead, the rather messy and fragmented result of many decades of oral transmission and transformation which arose between the time of the oldest known manuscripts (1821–26) and their first printed editions in 1870 and 1882 (see SE part I). They quite clearly embody the voices of many different authors, probably holding many different and conflicting opinions. Thus there has always been intense ambivalence regarding Tantric elements within the tradition itself; indeed, we might regard the songs of the "Stinking fruit in the garden of Love" as a kind of agonizing process of self-reflection and internal debate over the history of the tradition itself—a kind of metanarrative or commentary on the troubling presence of Tantric elements within the Vaiṣṇava tradition itself.

This is, however, also an unusual sort of commentary or metanarrative, one which makes a striking use of the metaphor of the "company" itself. Whether we understand it as a tactic of "deodorization" or "disguise," I suggest, this rather weird appropriation of the company and its terminology is good evidence of just how acutely aware the Kartābhajās were of the changing social, political and moral context in which they emerged—namely, the early years of the British East India Company rule and the dawn of the new social ideals of the Bengal renaissance.

At the same time, however, it also shows that they had the ingenious skill (and rather remarkable audacity) to appropriate the image of "Hon'ble John Company" and to transform it into the "Good-Mannered Company" of the Kartābhajā tradition. As Scott suggests, not only are marginal groups capable of masking their dissent against the dominant order behind an elaborate web of elusive imagery and metaphoric disguise, but, often, they also disguise themselves in an even more ingenious way, by making use of symbols and metaphors drawn from the of dominant classes themselves. Black slaves in the American South, for example, often appropriated the prophetic symbols of Joshua and Moses in order to express their hope for freedom and the end of the white man's power; so, too, Filipino natives often adapted the Christian tradition of the Passion Play to convey a "general yet guarded dissent from elite culture," simultaneously conveying their resistance to the dominant colonial order while masking their dissent in the "acceptable" imagery of the colonizers and missionaries themselves: "What permits subordinate groups to undercut authorized cultural norms is the fact that a cultural expression by virtue of its polyvalent symbolism and metaphor lends itself to disguise. By the subtle use of codes, one can insinuate into a ritual, a pattern of dress, a song, a story, meanings that are accessible to one intended audience and opaque to another audience the actors wish to exclude."[58] So, too, I would suggest, at least part of the logic behind the Kartābhajās' use of the "Good Mannered Company" lies in a similar kind of clever appropriation and deformation of a key metaphor—a metaphor that masks their real activities, while simultaneously communicating them through the seemingly "legitimate" imagery of the Hon'ble Company itself. To borrow a phrase of de Certeau, we might think of this as a kind of symbolic "poaching" by which dominated groups can adapt and even hide behind the discourse of the dominant classes themselves; it is part of "a logic whose models go as far back as the age old ruses of fishes and insects that disguise or transform themselves to survive. . . . Everyday life invents itself by poaching in countless ways on the property of others."[59]

An Ugly Old Slut in a House Full of Rubbish and Dung: The Growing Scandal, Slander, and Suppression of the Kartābhajās in Nineteenth-Century Bengal

Unfortunately, however, it would seem that neither the tactics of "deodorization" nor "disguise" was terribly successful. The history of the Kartābhajā tradition in the late nineteenth and twentieth centuries is in fact a rather sad and ironic story of a brief period of success, fame, and power, followed by a long saga of scandal, slander, censorship, and a gradual decline into obscurity. It is the history of what was originally a small, highly esoteric "obscure religious cult," which grew into a large and popular religious movement, but which ultimately fell into increasing disrepute in large part because of its alleged Tantric rituals and immoral sexual practices. More than virtually any other of the small lower-class sects, the Kartābhajās were singled out in nineteenth-century Bengali discourse as the most depraved and dangerous example of these "deviant orders"—as a "degenerate form of the Tantric religion," or even as "*the foremost of the Aghora-panthīs.*"[60] "Everybody shuddered at the name Kartābhajā. The vices which they imbibed from the Tantriks became most prominent. . . . Kartābhajā became a term of ridicule."[61] As the Calcutta satirist, Kedarnāth Datta, described them in 1871, "According to a Kartābhajā saying, '*Meye Hijṛā Puruṣ Khojā, tabe habe Kartābhajā*'—but today this has become a source of ridicule among circles of wicked men. . . . Due to ignorance and lack of control over the senses, they abandoned the truth and sought the pleasures of the senses; the path of religion has become the path of irreligion."[62] Among the most intense (and humorous) of these many attacks was that of Dāśarathī Rāy, the famous Bengali poet, who mercilessly ridiculed the Kartābhajās for their alleged licentiousness, criminal behavior, and fraud. In Dāśarathī's scathing poem, "Kartābhajā," the Kartā himself is portrayed as nothing more than a kind of "dog in a rice husking room," a "ringleader among thieves," or an "ugly old slut in a place full of rubbish and dung."

They have a separate Tantra; abandoning the mantras of all other gods,
they are initiated by the Human mantra [*Mānuṣa-mantra*].
Religion is mixed up with all irreligion;
they turn every deed into the enjoyment of sensual pleasures!
In all their teachings there is deception and fraud.
. . . [In this sect] the murderous highwayman becomes a holy man.
The harlot becomes a woman of good family,
The chaste wife is no longer counted among her husband's possessions!

At each full moon dance, they sleep together.
. . . All the old whores [*māgīs*] who aren't yet dead enjoy conjugal relations;
Seeing this, I died in shame!
The young beautiful women all act as Gopīs and engage in the Līlā.
They smear perfume and sandal-paste, garlic and collyrium on the Kartā's limbs,

and exchange garlands with him
while the Kartā removes their clothing![63]

By the early twentieth century, the Kartābhajā tradition had dwindled to a kind of sad laughing stock, remembered primarily for its scandalous behavior, unworthy of serious scholarly attention, and "impossible to describe without offending the judgments of good taste."[64]

Conclusions: Imagining and Reimagining "Tantra" in Contemporary Discourse

To close, I would like to suggest that the question of sexual practices within the Kartābhajā tradition also raises much broader and more important questions in the study of Indian Tantra as a whole. Not only is it a striking illustration of how very deeply rooted are Tantric traditions within their specific social, cultural, and political contexts, and the many ways in which these traditions change and adapt in the face of changing history; at the same time, the "Good Mannered Company" of the Kartābhajās also demonstrates the often profound impact of colonialism, Western influence, and changing social values on Tantric traditions. The problems of secrecy and censorship have most probably always been integral to the Tantric traditions of Bengal, but they appear to have become all the more intense during particular social and historical contexts, such as the period of Muslim rule, or perhaps most acutely during the British colonial era.

Finally, and most important, I would also suggest that the rather unusual case of the Kartābhajās can also help us to reimagine and redefine the category of Tantra in contemporary discourse. For if, as Padoux suggests, the category of Tantrism is itself largely a modern Western creation, and one with an ambivalent and muddled history, can we still employ this term in a useful way? As I wish to argue, the category of Tantra, although deeply problematic and ambiguous, is also a potentially useful, and perhaps now unavoidable, tool for the understanding of certain aspects of South Asian belief and practice. Rather than a singular monolithic entity, however, Tantrism is perhaps much better understood as a product of the scholarly imagination, which we find it useful to employ as a tool or heuristic device. This is moreover a highly pluralistic, fluid category—to borrow a phrase from Jonathan Z. Smith, a "messy hodgepodge" or "heap of rubbish."[65] in the case of the Kartābhajās, we have found that this tradition clearly shares virtually every one of the ten features which, according to Brooks, are characteristic of those traditions that we can justifiably label "Tantric,"[66] and there are also many within the tradition itself who, even today, would readily identify themselves as *tāntrikas*. Yet, simultaneously, there are just as many, and probably far more representatives of the more conservative or "orthodox" side of the tradition, who would be deeply offended and shocked by the mere suggestion that they might have any association with the scandal, the smut, or the "foul stench" of Tantrism. Hence, the Kartābhajās present us with a telling reminder of just how problematic (though admittedly unavoidable) a category this remains in contemporary discourse.

Still more important, however, I would also agree strongly with Jeffrey Kripal and his recent work on Rāmkṛṣṇa. As Kripal argues, much recent scholarship has followed in the "reformist" and highly cerebral tradition of scholarship begun by Sir John Woodroffe, by limiting itself to abstract, philosophical Sanskrit texts while ignoring the more concrete social, historical, and political contexts in which Tantra is practiced.

> Scholarship on Tantra . . . is still working in the legacy of its founder, John Woodroffe, whose work was marked by profound philosophical . . . and moral biases and an apologetic designed to rid Tantra of everything that smacked of superstition, or scandal. Writing within this "Victorian" tradition, numerous scholars have attempted all sorts of mental gymnastics in a desperate effort to rescue the tradition from its stubbornly "impure" ways.[67]

What is most needed now is a study of Tantric traditions, seen neither as a seedy cabal of libertines nor as an abstract set of philosophical texts; rather we need to take these traditions seriously as living, embodied phenomena, with an enormous diversity of forms within their many social and historical contexts. We need, in short, to move beyond the abstract level of disembodied Sanskrit texts to examine these traditions in their most human, most ambiguous "lived compromises and contradictions."[68] Perhaps then we might move beyond the construction of Tantrism as the exotic "extreme Orient" and instead understand it as a concrete, historical—even if rather messy and problematic—category in the history of religions.

7

The Economics of Ecstasy

The Economic Hierarchy and Business Tactics of the Kartābhajās

You've come into this world, but you don't know the value of money [*ṭākā*]
Money is such a thing that it's virtually equal to Allah himself!
You will not find any sort of scale of measure like money in this universe.
. . . If I go to a holy man, I find that he too has money.
No one pays any respect to those who have no money.
And those who have thousands of rupees become king.
Even a murderer goes unpunished if he has enough money! (Pūrṇa Dās Bāul,
Bāṅglār Bāul o Gān)

Not only can the tactics of secrecy become an ironic liability and a source of attack from outside the esoteric community, but they can also become a liability from *within* the community, as the source of new forms of oppression in the hierarchy of the secret order itself. Indeed, if the Kartābhajās' rather ingenious use of secrecy could serve as a powerful source of status, value, and symbolic capital for many poor lower-class individuals who lacked such resources in mainstream society, we must nonetheless be wary of romanticizing this tradition, of naively idealizing it as a kind of noble force of resistance by the colonized and dominated against their oppressors. The practice of secrecy, in this as in most esoteric traditions, could also easily be turned into a *strategy of elitism and exploitation*—a means of obfuscating inequalities, constructing new hierarchies of power, or concealing more subtle forms of oppression. As Simmel long ago pointed out, secrecy is always among the favorite tools of the dominant factions at the top of the social hierarchy: It is the basic strategy of masking and mystification, which at once conceals the numerical insignificance of the elite while exaggerating their aura of power, awe, or mystery.[1] In the case of the Kartābhajās, it allowed the Kartā and his Mahāśays to construct an elaborate, highly asymmetrical hierarchy within the Kartābhajā community itself.

So, too, the Kartābhajās' skillful appropriation of mercantile discourse, economic terminology, and the imagery of the "company" also appears to have borne with it a more negative and less admirable side. Already by the mid-nineteenth century, the Kartābhajās had in fact developed an extensive and fairly sophisticated economic system of their own, with a lucrative system of regular taxation and revenue collection which in many ways reflects the traditional Zamindāri system of revenue collection in rural Bengal. It was in large part their very effective business strategies that allowed the leaders of this highly esoteric, so-called "obscure religious cult" to rise to the status of some of the most affluent religious figures of nineteenth-century Bengal. Their pursuit of status and symbolic capital, it seems, was closely related to their accumulation of real economic capital, land, and material wealth. As one recent author put it, the Kartās appear to have formulated "an effective plan for uniting religion and economics" or even a "commercial enterprise on the spiritual plane."[2]

This central ambivalence at the very heart of the Kartābhajā tradition—its simultaneously liberating and exploitative character—is nowhere more apparent than in the infamous Kartābhajā festival (*melā*) held each spring in Ghoshpara. As the most public and popular side of this tradition—what we might call the exoteric side of an esoteric tradition—the Ghoshpara Melā was widely discussed throughout nineteenth-century Bengal. It was notorious both because of the unusual degree of freedom from ordinary social constraints that it allowed and because of the seeming crass commercialism and vulgar profiteering that went on among its organizers. Like the uniquely liminal geographic space of the village of Ghoshpara itself, the Melā opens up what Bourdieu calls a "free market" of social exchange.[3] As an alternative social space, the Melā is a temporary event in which normal social boundaries and religious laws do not apply, a time when those who normally have little symbolic capital can suddenly rise to new status and social power. Very much a "carnivalesque" event in Bakhtin's sense, this is a time that normal social relations are turned topsy-turvy, when women, the poor, and the lower classes have a brief chance to be on top.

Yet at the same time, the Melā also has a very pronounced economic dimension, the primary beneficiaries of which are not the poor lower classes but, rather, the Kartās and Mahāśays. If it is a "carnival," it is also in many ways a case of commercial cooption, one of the primary functions of which is to extract revenue from poor and uneducated lower-class people. From the mid-nineteenth century to the present day this Melā has served as the Kartās' primary source of income and a central part of their broader "economics of ecstasy."[4]

Finally, with its complex organization and business practices, the Kartābhajā tradition also opens up a number of illuminating insights into the heterogeneous world of colonial Bengal, and perhaps into some broader questions of colonial studies as a whole. For the economic organization of the Kartābhajās reflects not only the important transformations brought about by the incursion of British capitalism and the East India Company but also the deeper continuities between precolonial and colonial economic structures. As we saw in chapter 1, Indian society was by no means suddenly and radically transformed by the presence of European capitalism. On the contrary, "there were many threads of continuity between precolonial India and the India of the East India Company."[5] On the whole, Bengal of the early nineteenth century was a complex mesh of competing factions in which "non-capitalist agrarian production and capitalist economic development were bound in a dialectical relationship."[6] It is precisely this complex dialectic of capitalist and pre-capitalist, indigenous and European structures that we find reflected in the Kartābhajā tradition.

Simultaneously, I argue, the Kartābhajās also give us some useful insights into the problems of "resistance" and "domination" within situations of colonial contact. As a number of recent critics have argued, much of the discourse on post-colonial theory has been hampered by a persistent tendency toward simplistic binarisms and static dichotomies: domination and resistance, colonial oppression and native struggle, and so on. Moreover, in their celebration of resistance and struggle, post-colonial studies often overlook the more subtle forms of *collusion and cooperation* between colonizer and colonized. By romanticizing the struggle of colonized peoples as noble champions of freedom against the expansion of global capitalism, they ignore the many ways in which the colonized often introduce new, in some cases equally oppressive, hierarchies of their own.[7] We need, as Kelly suggests, a more complex understanding of the colonial situation, emphasizing the ambivalent mixture of both resistance and accommodation. For what we find is often not a story of "victory for the colonized in resistance to colonial hegemony" but, rather, one in which "the heroes are flawed and their successes mixed with failures."[8] If the Kartābhajās strategically appropriate many elements of the dominant economic discourse, investing them with highly subversive new meanings, it would seem that its poor, lower-class members are also reinscribed into a new economic hierarchy, which serves primarily to benefit a small group of powerful gurus.

Corporeal Taxation: Hierarchy and Economic Exchange

Maheśvarī [Kālī] is my landlord, I am thine own immediate tenant.
Now I am subject, now am I free yet never have my dues been left unpaid.
. . . I am a tenant on the Mother's land, keeping a firm hold of the right plot, all dues paid.
Now by the strength of your name, I mean to continue to hold and also to make it rent free.
Prasād says, My rent is not a single cowry in arrears. (Rāmprasād Sen)

Despite the constant rhetoric of egalitarianism, universality and freedom for all castes, the Kartābhajā sect had by the early nineteenth century evolved into a complex, highly asymmetrical, and apparently rather lucrative economic hierarchy. Indeed, as Lincoln aptly points out, "Egalitarianism . . . is never a simple matter, there being a multitude of ways in which hierarchy may be reasserted, the most egalitarian of claims . . . notwithstanding."[9] Unlike most of the smaller esoteric sects of the day, the Kartābhajās quickly organized themselves into a graded hierarchical order, bound by a regular system of taxation and revenue collection. Clearly, the extraction of revenue and the close intermingling of religious and economic practices was by no means a new invention of the Kartābhajās. One need only look to Vaiṣṇava sects such as the Vallabhācārīs, who collected similar kinds of taxes from their devotees, or to ascetic sects such as the Dasnāmīs and Sannyāsīs of the eighteenth century, to see that business and spirituality have long gone hand in hand in Bengali religions.[10] What *is* unique about the Kartābhajās, however, is the remarkable degree of systematization they introduced, as they built up an effective economic hierarchy and an efficient system of annual taxation which in many ways mirrored the existing systems of land revenue in colonial Bengal.

Secrecy, as Simmel reminds us, is often one of the key elements in the construction of social and political hierarchy—the privilege of access to valued knowledge and information which separates the dominant from subordinate strata in every social order. As Elizabeth Brandt comments in her study of secrecy and social hierarchy in the Taos Pueblo community: "Knowledge is power in both a spiritual and secular sense and the use of power must be controlled. . . . Certain kinds of information are declared secret. . . . A major consequence of secrecy is the establishment of status hierarchies based on access to knowledge."[11] Indeed, like many secret societies across cultures, the Kartābhajās seem to have simultaneously opposed the existing social order and caste system, even as they created an alternative hierarchical order, in many ways *mirroring or mimicking* the dominant order itself. As Chesneaux points out in the case of subversive groups in China, "the secret societies were diametrically opposed to the [existing] order and its conventions. . . . Yet at the same time they set out to create . . . a system of rules as complete as the one they opposed. . . . They mirrored established society while constituting . . . the principal force of opposition and dissent."[12]

The Kartābhajās' spiritual-economic system is described even in the earliest known accounts of the sect—such as William Ward's account of 1816—and it survived even down to the most recent times—as we see in Sudhīr Cakravartī's report of 1986, or even in the apologetic works of contemporary devotees like Advaita Dās, in 1992.[13] As Banerjee points out, the Kartābhajās' unique religious terminology itself implies the economic interests of its leaders. As we have already seen, the term "Kartā" was used most commonly during this period to refer to the "boss" or "Head Man" of a mercantile office or business, and the Kartābhajās' term for their religious center in Ghosphara—the *Gadi*—is more commonly a term used for a "mercantile office," a "trader's seat," or "zamindār's throne" than for a religious site; as such, the use of the term was likely tied to the growth of small merchants and business offices in the expanding colonial center of Calcutta:

> The Kartābhajās have been traditionally using the term "*gadi*" for their religious headquarters. . . . The term *gadi* . . . beginning its journey from the comfortable seat of the local trader, graduated to the cosmopolitan world of Calcutta to become an epithet for the trading houses in the metropolis. . . . The choice of the word *gadi* . . . could reflect the desire to establish their headquarters as a religious ally of the commercial society developing in Calcutta and other trading centers of the colonial regime.[14]

Under the supervision of this Gadi, the Kartābhajā sect unfolded as an integrated spiritual-economic hierarchy. As we have already seen in chapters 3 and 5, the Kartābhajā order is traditionally structured according to three levels of *Kartā, Mahāśay* (regional Guru), and *barātī* (common disciple), and these three strata are in turn connected by a complex system of taxation and revenue collection. Each Mahāśay is instructed to offer the Kartā a full half of his annual income, and each Mahāśay in turn takes a fourth part of the earnings of the disciples within his particular district. Those who were too poor to pay in cash are told to lay aside a handful of rice every day for the sake of the guru. In this way, as we read in the account of the Calcutta newspaper, *Somaprakāśa*, the Kartā Īśvarabābu (the son of Dulālcāṅd) received some 10,000–12,000 *ṭākās* in revenue during the 1847 festival at Ghoshpara alone.[15] Unfortunately, as frustrated researchers such as Māṇik Sarkār and I myself have discovered, the Pāla family has been consistently unwilling to disclose its revenue income from devotees in more recent years.[16]

The principle behind this practice is the ideology of "corporeal taxation" or bodily revenue (*daihik khājanā*)—the belief that the Kartā "possesses" the body of each of his followers. Each initiate therefore has to pay a fixed "rent" for the privilege of occupying his body with his soul, just as he had to pay a fixed annual tax on his home: "Since the Kartā is the Owner (*Mālik*) of each disciple's body, you have to pay a rent for the fact that you are living."[17] As might be expected, this physioeconomic system was often criticized and disparaged by nineteenth-century observers like Jogendranath Bhattacharya, who compared it to the looting Mahratta raiders and their claim to a *couth* or a fourth part of their subjects' revenue: "To be ready with a pretext for exacting money from his followers [Rāmśaran] declared that he was the proprietor of every human body and that he was entitled to claim rent from every human being for allowing his soul to occupy his body. The idea is similar to . . . the Mahratta claim of *chouth* and has . . . served similar purposes. . . . To enforce his right . . . the Kartā appoints baillifs and agents for collecting his revenue."[18] However, this system has also been justified and defended by many contemporary, highly respected Kartābhajā exponents, such as Advaita Candra Dās, "*Bodily Revenue:* Out of reverence for the Guru, the disciple surrenders his body. . . . Nothing remains of his own power. His life is spent at the command of the Guru. . . . The living soul dwells within its house. It is for the sake of dwelling in this house that they surrender to the Guru."[19]

As Kumkum Chatterjee points out in her discussion of markets, economics, and political power in northern India, the practices of taxation and the payment of tribute have long played a central role in the construction of the greater "Social Body" and Body Politic. They are key mechanisms in the bonding of subject and ruler—a symbolic "incorporation" of the body of the subject into that of the monarch, who is in turn the representative of the Body Politic as a whole: "Tribute and gift-giving . . . served as an important bonding link between rulers and their subjects. . . . Tribute was regarded as the offering by the subject of his loyalty and subordination to the ruler. . . . Its aceptance by the monarch . . . signified the symbolic incorporation of the donor into the body of the recipient and . . . the body politic."[20] So, too, we have seen that much of Kartābhajā ritual and physical practice aims to deconstruct and re-create the body of the disciple, while simultaneously *incorporating* him into the divine bodies of his Mahāśay and Kartā (chapter 5); hence, the ritual offering of money, food, or other goods to the Kartā's Gadi is one of the central rites which symbolically enacts this incorporation, grafting the individual body onto the body of the Kartābhajā hierarchy itself.

In addition, this practice of "corporeal taxation" was supplemented with a series of other taxes, fees, and levees. As Chakrabarty summarizes this complex economic system, the Kartā's income consisted of four primary sources: (1) taxes collected from the common *barātīs* and the large percentage of the earnings of the Mahāśays; (2) a mandatory initiation (*dīkṣā*) fee for each disciple, which initially consists of the *Ṣolo ānā* mantra—which means both the "complete" *mantra*, and "costing sixteen annas"; (3) an additional *praṇāmī* fee (i.e., money offered at the time of making obeisance) for the privilege of protracting oneself before the Kartā and touching his feet; and finally there is (4) a *dāyika* or "mortgage" [or "indebtedness"] fee, an additional tax placed upon the body/house of the devotee as the "price of sin."[21] As we have seen previously (chapter 2), this last form of revenue, the *dāyika* or mortgage fee, quite probably shows the influence of Christian notions of sin, confession, and penance absorbed from the powerful Baptist missionary influence in Nadia district. Because the relationship between the Kartā and the sinner is conceived precisely in terms of a proprietor or businessman (*mālik*) and an agent or employee (*belik*) (BG 3), it is only fitting that the price for sin should be a monetary one.[22]

A "Permanent Settlement for the Soul?"

O my senseless heart,
You have failed to cultivate the human land.
How will you face the tax claims when the season escapes?
You have no balance to your credit at all. (Bāul song, Bhattacharya, *Songs of the Bards of Bengal*)

As more than one contemporary scholar has observed, this complex system of revenue collection and "mortgaging" appears to bear a rather suspicious resemblance to various older and more "secular" forms of taxation in Bengal. Given the enormous amount of marketplace imagery and the language of the *bājār* or *hāṭ* within the Kartābhajā songs, it is probable that this system is closely related to the system of market taxes and revenues which the Nawābs, Rājās, and Zamindārs collected from the various mercantile centers under their rule. As Sen has argued, it was these were crucial revenues which the British Company fought to appropriate, control, and regulate upon its own rise to power in Bengal.[23]

It is perhaps even more probable, however, that the Kartābhajās' corporeal revenue system was closely related to the traditional Zamindāri system of rural Bengal. As we have seen earlier, the first Kartā, Rāmśaraṇ Pāl, was a Sadgop (milkman) by caste and a cultivator by trade, who had married the daughter of the wealthy Zamindār, Govinda Ghoṣe, and thus inherited the latter's rich estate. It would appear that he adapted much of the Zamindāri system of taxation and land revenue into the structure of his movement. As Banerjee puts it, Dulālcāṅd and his successors set up nothing less than a kind of *religious Zamindāri*.[24] Even pious defenders of the Kartābhajā tradition, such as Advaita Dās, admit that this system of "corporeal taxation" does have clear similarities to the Zamindāri system: "The living soul dwells within its house. It is for the sake of dwelling in this house that they surrender to the Guru."[25]

A number of contemporary scholars have also compared the hierarchical structure of the Kartābhajā sect—with its Kartā, Mahāśay, and Barātī—even more directly to the hierarchical structure of the feudal system in Bengal—with its Zamindārs, Taluqdārs (intermediate landholder), and Raytadārs (peasant). Even though some enthusiastic supporters of the group, such as Nabīncandra Sen or Śaśīpad Bābu, had praised the Kartābhajās as a kind of folk version of Rāmmohun Roy and the Brāhmo Samāj, more skeptical authors agree that the Kartābhajā ideal of egalitarianism and universal humanism is rather superficial. Despite the constant rhetoric of egalitarianism and freedom for all castes, Sarkār argues, the Kartābhajā sect was based on a clear and nonegalitarian economic hierarchy:

> This recalls the feudal system of Bengal. This is so even if they spoke of "the highly liberal and democratic character of our sect." . . . In the hierarchy of the all-powerful Kartās, the influence of the feudal system is much greater than that of democracy. To these *Gadis* the starving, poor, peasants and homeless Barātīs give their accumulated earnings as "rent" to the Mahāśays; and a record of the rent is written into an account-book . . . Thus the economic disparity between the Kartā and the barātīs is analogous to that between the Zamindār and the tenant [*raytadār*].[26]

In the process, the family of Kartās was able to achieve a rather impressive "upward mobility" in the course of the nineteenth century, rising from a poor group of milkmen/farmers to an affluent landholding family. As Hitesranjan Sanyal suggests, Rāmśaraṇ and his family were part of a broader movement of upward social mobility taking place among the Gop castes of Bengal; the Sadgops or pure Gops were themselves a dissident offshoot of the traditional milkman caste, and many like Rāmśaraṇ had begun to rise from their traditional status to more lucrative roles as traders, government officials and even wealthy landowners. At the same time, as Banerjee points out, the Pāl family of Kartās also reflects a broader trend of upward mobility among many *nouveaux riches* entrepreneurs of nineteenth-century Calcutta: "The transformation of the Kartās . . . from the end of the eighteenth century was a religious parallel to the changes taking place in the contemporary socio-economic milieu during those crucial decades. Like Ramsharan Pal, many . . . in the commercial world of Calcutta arose from humble origins to become millionaires in the nineteenth century."[27]

However, it seems probable that the Kartābhajā hierarchy does not simply reflect the old Zamindāri system of precolonial Bengal but also embodies some of the changes in taxation taking place under the British Company toward the end of the eighteenth century. If we place this phenomenon in its historical context, we find that it closely parallels the British enforcemnt of new revenue systems, notably the

Permanent Settlement of Cornwallis in 1793—an event which occurred *almost simultaneously with the rise of the Kartābhajā sect.* As we have seen previously, the following of the Kartābhajās was drawn in part from those very peasant classes of rural Bengal which had suffered the most from the increasingly exploitative revenue system of the late eighteenth century. But, rather strikingly, the Kartābhajās in turn created their own system of fixed revenue and regular taxation—though now transposed onto the religious plane. In this seeming "Permanent Settlement for the Soul," it is not only the devotee's land but his very body and spirit which are subject to a standardized rent. In short, just as they had appropriated elements of capitalist discourse and mercantile terminology, so, too, the Kartābhajās appropriated certain structures of the revenue system of rural Bengal, investing them with new meaning and incorporating them into their own religious hierarchy.

Indeed, some scholars have even suggested that this semifeudal economic hierarchy not only paralleled but actually helped to *stabilize, reinforce, and preserve* the existing economic system at precisely that time at which it was most threatened by discontent and rebellion among the rural peasantry. It is ironic, but perhaps not accidental, that the Kartābhajā hierarchy became powerful in the district of Nadia—the home of some of the greatest peasant uprisings of nineteenth-century Bengal, including that of Titu Mir (1831), the Farazis, and the Indigo Rebellion (1860). Throughout Nadia and the neighboring districts of Bengal, early decades of the nineteenth century witnessed increasing demands imposed by the Zamindārs and increasing discontent among the peasantry (see chapter 1).[28] As Sarkār suggests, it is likely that the Kartābhajā hierarchy actually served to buttress the existing economic system in the face of a growing instability and chaos in rural Bengal: "The practice of Guru worship and the philosophy of the Kartābhajās was a means of keeping the Zamindāri system stable in Nadia, which was the main center of the Indigo Rebellion, the center of action of the Farazi sect, and the land of Titu Mir."[29]

Hence, we might well compare the organization of the Kartābhajās with other similar religio-economic hierarchies of colonial India—for example, that of the Bhuinyas (tribal peasantry) of neighboring Bihar, which Gyan Prakash has so lucidly described. Using Bourdieu's concept of "reproduction," Prakash suggests that the religious myths, spiritual hierarchy, and ritual practices of the Bhuinyas actually helped to reflect, reproduce, and re-create the economic hierarchy of the Bhuinya cultivators under the power of their *māliks* or landlords. In the ritual of their spirit cult, the Bhuinyas constructed a kind of metaphysical mirror and replication of the dominant economic hierarchy itself. At the same time, however, these were not mere static reflections but, rather, dynamic relations which had to be actively "*reproduced*" through the work of ritual in the Bhuinya spirit cults: "The Malik Devata represented the subordination of the Bhuinyas by landlords . . . [and] echoed the power of landlords over kamias based on land control. . . . Rituals were not mere executions of pre-existing rules. . . . Ritual practices were dynamic events in which social relations were actively reconstructed."[30] So too, it would seem, the economic and social hierarchies of colonial Bengal had in a variety of ways to be actively reproduced—particularly at a time when they were increasingly threatened by changing political forces, peasant insurrections, and agrarian violence. The Kartābhajās' ritual practices, spiritual beliefs—and above all their system of revenue collection—were perhaps among the key elements in this ongoing process of reproduction.

Carnival or Commercial Cooption? The Ghoshpara Melā and Its Economic Role

Formerly people used to be come to the festivals out of genuine devotion. They used to seek the essential Man of the Heart. . . . Now where are all these men? What do people seek now? Now they only seek excitement and pleasure. Everything has become a business. (An observer at the Pouṣ Melā, 1995, from Sudhīr Cakravartī, *Paścim Baṅger Melā*)

The primary occasion for the Kartābhajās' revenue collection takes place (even to this day) at the great festival held at Ghoshpara during the time of the Dol or Holi festival in the month of *Phalgun* (February–March). Among the many festivals and holy days of the Kartābhajās' sacred calendar,[31] this is the single most popular and important, still widely regarded as the one of the most famous of all the folk religious festivals of Bengal.[32] A massive, large-scale celebration, attracting many thousands of pilgrims, devotees, and curious tourists from all over Bengal and Bangladesh, the Melā represents the most "exoteric" or nonsecretive side of this tradition, the side turned toward the outside world, as it were. "Unlike the . . . secretive rituals of the initiated members of the Kartābhajā sect," Banerjee comments, "the rituals observed by the general run of pilgrims had always been of a demonstrative nature . . . with the hope of a cure for the various disabilities . . . from which they suffered."[33]

Throughout the newspapers and popular literature of nineteenth-century Calcutta, we find vivid descriptions of this notorious Melā, which had become a favorite topic of debate and controversy among the upper-educated classes. Like the Holi festival, the Ghoshpara Melā is a time for the collective gathering of several thousands of people, ecstatic celebration, and the temporary dissolution of normal social structures. My own experience of the Melā as it is survives today was something like a chaotic fusion of a Grateful Dead Concert and a Russian Easter Mass—a rather raucous event in which pious devotees fling themselves prostrate in the mud or flail wildly in spiritual ecstasy, wandering *yogis* and *tāntrikas* from all over Bengal display their supernatural powers, and groups of Bāuls gather to sing their mystic songs or share bowls of hashish—and all this amidst a maelstrom of Ferris wheels and merry-go-rounds, magic displays and carnival freak shows, street performers and musicians, and row upon row of shops selling every imaginable kind of food and merchandise.[34]

Up to the time of India's independence, the Melā used to occupy a large plot of land, half a square mile in size, drawing an estimated 50,000–100,000 devotees on each of its three days. Scattered throughout the area were some 3,500 trees, at the base of which each regional Mahāśay set up his Gadi (his "office" or "Zamindār's throne"). From this divine seat, each Mahāśay received the "bodily revenue" from each of the devotees under his charge, marked it down in an account book, and then passed along the appointed percentage to the Kartā. In addition, the Kartā and his family have also long received a variety of other taxes, gifts, and fees from the men and women who attend the festival—from the shopkeepers and vendors who set up their stalls, and from devotees, yogis, and holy men who set up their own personal holy seats or shrines. As the Calcutta paper, *Somaprakāśa,* described the Melā in 1864, "For three days in all directions people from various places, of various castes come together, and enjoy the festival with endless pleasurable activities such as eating together and singing. . . . In these few days the Pāl Kartā attains great wealth. As the Mahāśays gather the disciples from their various regions, the Kartā or Kartrī becomes present and many people make offerings."[35] In short, like all Melās in Bengal, the Ghoshpara Melā is also very much a *commercial affair*—as much an event for trade, buying, and selling, and a magnet for local merchants, as a pilgrimage site and religious event. Together with the *bājār, hāṭ,* and *gañj*, the Melā has thus been throughout the history of Bengal one of the primary forms of marketplace or central loci for the buying and selling of goods.[36] As a site of religious experience and spiritual authority, however, it is also a key locus for the buying and selling, bartering, and exchange of "spiritual goods," such as the mystical grace of Satī Mā and the healing powers of Āulcāṅd. [37]

Indeed, one of the key questions we must ask here is whether the Ghoshpara Melā represents a kind of liberation and empowerment for Kartābhajā devotees, which frees them from the burdens of caste and labor in mainstream society—a *carnival* in the Bakhtinian sense—or whether it is simply a means for a small group of people to make a few dollars—a *commercial cooption*, which only reinforces social hierarchies and economic inequities.

A Free Market of Social Exchange: Poor Man's Symbolic Capital

When a visitor makes the short journey from the crowded, noisy, chaotic streets of Calcutta to the beautiful, peaceful little village of nearby Ghoshpara, it is not difficult to see why this particular site would have attracted so many of the poorer lower classes of nineteenth-century Calcutta. Ghoshpara represents a kind of "alternative social space"—a social and cultural oasis, very close to, and yet outside and on the margins of, the vast, bustling city of Calcutta. Hence, Ghoshpara, and particularly its annual Melā, could serve as the ideal locus for an alternative "social marketplace," what Bourdieu has called a *free market* for social exchange, where the normal laws of caste, wealth, and status are temporarily suspended.[38] Like the free linguistic spaces of gossip or slang, the Melā opens an alternative social space on the margins of urban Calcutta, a space where poor oppressed classes of the city can escape the burdens of poverty and powerlessness, in a relatively free and unregulated social field. Or, to borrow James Scott's phrase, the Melā represents a "social space of relative autonomy," within which the "hidden transcript"—the unstated, secret ideas, desires, and complaints of the dominated classes—can find expression. As Scott suggests, these alternative spaces of the hidden transcript are most frequently found in the marginal, liminal areas—the rural areas, villages, and forests, outside the reach of official power: "The social location par excellence for the hidden transcript lies in the unauthorized and unmonitored secret assemblies of subordinates. . . . The heresy of Lollardy was most rife in the pastoral, forest, moorland and fen areas, where the social control of the church and the squirearchy did not penetrate."[39] Ghoshpara village, located on the rural fringes of the colonial center of Calcutta, on the margins between the city and the rural hinterland, would seem to have offered just this sort of alternative space and site for an alternative social transcript.

The most infamous element of this three-day festival—and the most hotly debated among the Calcutta elites of the nineteenth century—was the free mixing of individuals from all castes, all religions, and (most scandalous of all) both sexes. Not only did men and women from the lowest castes, both Hindu and Muslim, sit together and mix freely, but, much to the horror of the more conservative Hindus, they even shared the same communal feast and offered food to one another in flagrant violation of caste distinctions. As one reporter described his wonder at the Kartābhajās' seemingly antinomian eating habits: "We were amazed—for Brāhmaṇs, Śūdras and Yāvanas ignoring their respective food habits, eat and drink together here; we've never heard or seen such a thing anywhere before!"[40] As Banerjee suggests, this communal meal offered a rare opportunity for the poorer lower classes who comprised the bulk of the Kartā's following to escape the bonds of caste in mainstream society:

> The most significant feature of the community feast at the Ghoshpara fair was the shedding of all caste, religious and sex discrimination. . . . The feast . . . provided the lower orders mainly from the depressed castes, untouchables, Muslim peasants and artisans . . . with an opportunity of coming together. . . . Almost all contemporary records stress the predominance of these sections of the population at the fair. They enjoyed . . . equality with the more privileged segment which was denied to them in daily social existence.[41]

In traditional Bengal, as in most cultures, the material substance of food and the patterns of eating and feasting, as well as the seating arrangements and rules of etiquette that accompany them, are among the most basic ways of expressing larger social and political hierarchies. As Claude Lévi-Strauss, Mary Douglas, Marshall Sahlins, and other anthropologists have shown us,[42] food and the concomitant laws of etiquette and culinary technique are integral to the construction and reproduction of the social hierarchy itself. Elaborate laws and prohibitions surrounding food—what P. S. Khare aptly calls the "Gastrosemantics" of what foods may be eaten, how they are to be prepared, from whom one may receive food—are integral to the complex network of relations that comprise the social fabric. They form the key links between the cosmos and the human body, as well as between the structure of the individual body and the hierarchy of the social body.[43] As Lincoln comments: "Ritual etiquette and other strongly habituated forms of practical discourse . . . do not just encode and transmit messages, but they play an active role in the construction, maintenance and modification of the borders, structure and hierarchic relations that . . . constitute society itself."[44] Conversely, the explicit violation or transgression of the laws surrounding food and mealtime etiquette are also among the most basic ways of transgressing and deconstructing the hierarchies of conventional society as a whole:

> Society is characterized by hierarchy as much as by solidarity. Such hierarchies not only find expression though but are actively constructed and reconstructed in mealtime rituals by means of particularities of menu, portions, seating arrangements, order of service . . . Although such rituals most often serve as instruments of social replication . . . there exist other possibilities as well, during those . . . occasions when meals serve as the instruments with which alternatives are opposed to the established order.[45]

It is not surprising therefore that many conservative Hindus should have regarded the Kartābhajās' eating habits as not only polluting and impure but also potentially dangerous, as a subversion of the social order itself. The Calcutta poet Dāśarathī Rāy, for example, appears to have been quite horrified by the Kartābhajā' scandalous and deliberately transgressive attitudes toward food and the traditional laws of caste purity:

O say, who can understand them? Everyone's got a religious disease!
. . . There's no consideration of caste; ritual is empty; thirty-six classes come together.
Washermen, oilmen, and tanners, Bāgdīs and Hāṛīs, Brāhmaṇs and Kāyasthas,
Ḍoms and Koṭāls, all together eat the same food.
. . . They overturn all Hindu religion!
They don't believe in gods or Brahmins, they're the foremost of the *Aghorapanthīs*—
I can't stand to hear about all their deeds!
They put food into one another's mouth—Oh, Bravo! what good taste!
They consider this their *Mahāprasād*.
Then they gather up the remnants of rice and wipe their mouths with their hands.[46]

Miracles and Wonders: The Sacred Hīmsāgar Pond, the Dālim Tree, and the Divine Grace of Satī-Mā

> This religion is spread primarily among the uneducated society . . . Just as many quack doctors of the villages profess to cure the poor farmers living in tiny huts, so

too the leaders of Ghoshpara befriend the many poor sinners of Bengal. (Sarojnāth Mukhopādhyāy, *Śaratkumār Lāhiṛī o Baṅger Bartamān Yug*)

Next to the possibility for the free mixing of castes and ritual meals in deliberate violation of class boundaries, the primary attraction of the Ghoshpara Melā has long been the promise of various kinds of miracles, blessings, or gifts of physical healing. The primary public and exoteric rituals at the Melā center around two sacred sites believed to be infused with tremendous spiritual power and grace: the sacred pomegranate tree (*dālim*) and the holy pond called the "Hīmsāgar" (ocean of snow). After prostrating themselves at the foot of the pomegranate tree, pilgrims traditionally make a special vow (*mānat*) to Satī Mā, by tying up a stone in the tree and saying a prayer, begging the mother for her compassionate grace. As the *Saṃvāda Prabhākara* reported in 1848, "I saw many people falling to the ground at the base of the Darisva tree. . . . Many were terribly afflicted and oppressed . . . they had all come to be rescued from their lot, or in the hope of attaining their heart's desire. . . . Prostrating themselves before the holy tree, they paid homage, with sorrowful words like 'the Body of the Guru is the Body of Truth; we are all terrible sinners, free us from sin, etc.' "[47] No less popular is the ritual act of bathing in the Hīmsāgar pond—believed to wash the sinner of all his faults. As the newspaper *Saṃvāda Prabhākara* described the practice of confession and penance at Ghoshpara in 1848, this ritual is undertaken primarily by those afflicted by some need or misfortune—sickness, poverty, barrenness, and so on. To be freed of their maladies, however, they had to confess all their sins before the Kartā's agents, then immerse themselves in the sacred pond. All this, according to this reporter's rather vivid account, was accompanied by rather brutal punishments and beatings by the Mahāśays:

> Finally, they went to the pond named Hīmsāgar, a little distance from the temple. The sinners descended into the water, fell prostrate, before the officers of the Kartās, admitted their many sins and received remission. But if any of them showed any hesitation in expressing his sins, the officers made a roaring sound and, with terrible force, pulled them by their hair and forced them to admit their sins. Then the sinners immersed their bodies into the pond and were made free of sin.[48]

Finally, the bath in the sacred Hīmsāgar is typically followed by the ritual of *daṇḍikhāṭā*—the act of prostrating oneself repeatedly in the mud, slowly traversing the distance between the Hīmsāgar and Satī Mā's temple. As we see in many nineteenth-century accounts, this ritual was often of a "rather violent nature, involving both exhibitionist self flagellation and physical coercion by the Mahashayas and other agents of the Kartā."[49]

However, the most important figure in this more miraculous, magical, popular, and exoteric side of the Kartābhajā tradition—above all, among women devotees—is undoubtedly the figure of the Holy Mother, Satī Mā or Sarasvatī Mā. As Banerjee points out, the Kartābhajā Melā has throughout the late nineteenth and twentieth centuries come to center more and more around the miraculous figure of Satī Mā, who is famed above all for her supernatural power to cure illness and grant sons to barren women. Indeed, by the late nineteenth century she had come to assume the qualities of an Archetypal Mother Goddess or Universal Female Principle (*Ādyā Śakti*), as "stories of her miraculous healing powers spread far and wide. She was supposed to have cured the blind, the deaf and the dumb and made barren women bear children."[50] In his historical novel, *Āmi Kān Pete Rai*, based on the personal narrative of a real Kartābhajā Kīrtan singer of nineteenth-century Bengal, Gajendrakumār Mitra provides a wonderful account of this widespread belief in the miraculous powers of Satī Mā—above all, the faith that Satī Mā's grace could grant a male child to a barren wife, like the character Nistārinī:

> It was Sairabhī who first told Nistārinī about it. She said, "Listen, sister: I hear you visit the festival at Ghoshpara every year—why don't you make a prayer under the pomegranate tree and tie up a stone? I've heard that, after a bath in the Hīmsāgar pond, if one prays to Satī Mā and ties up a stone in the pomegranate tree, the prayer will be fulfilled. The Bābus of the Chatterjee family didn't used to believe all this; they made fun of it and called it foolishness. . . . But the second brother's wife . . . went there secretly. She got a result right away—within ten months she delivered a bright son! . . . She conceived for the first time twenty-three years after her marriage. . . . So why don't you go too and tie up a stone there? . . .
>
> Toward the end of the night Nistārinī saw a strange dream. She saw herself entering Satī Mā's chamber and praying desperately for a son. . . . At that moment, it seemed as if someone had grabbed her sari and pulled it, calling in a soft voice, "Mā." Startled, she looked up and saw a charming little boy, as beautiful as a lotus.[51]

Not surprisingly, this element of miracles and magical powers was also a favorite target for ridicule among Bengal's upper classes, who took no end of delight in poking fun at the ignorant superstition of the Kartābhajās. Swami Vivekenanda, for example, ironically compared the Kartābhajās' faith to that of the Christian Scientists in America: "Christian Science is exactly like our Kartābhajā sect: say 'I have no disease,' and you are whole."[52] J. N. Bhattacharya offers a particularly cynical account of the Kartābhajās' miraculous events, describing a rather appalling event in which a blind man is "magically cured" by the Kartā:

> The crowd was great but somehow [the blind man] managed to elbow his way through it and bring his case to the Kartā. Quite suddenly he was seized by some attendants and taken to the side of a tank. . . . He was laid on the ground and while holding him fast, some of them commenced to rub the sockets of his eyes with sand in the most violent manner. . . . They vociferiously enquired every now and then whether his eyesight was restored. Finding no other way of escape from the excruciating torture . . . the man gave an answer in the affirmative, and then there was a shout of "Shachi Mayi-ki Jai" . . . He was given something like the honor of a Roman triumph. He was borne in the air through the crowd with . . . the declarations that the blind man was restored his eyesight through the mercy of Shachi Mayi.[53]

An even more cynical account of the Kartābhajās' magical chicanery is presented by the Calcutta poet, Dāśarathī Rāy, in his satirical poem, "Kartābhajā." In Dāśarathī's humorous narrative, the Kartā deceives his followers into believing that he can relight the extinguished oil-lamps with the magic water of his hookah:

The Kartā smokes a great deal of tobacco—now listen to the reason:
. . . On the night of the *majlis*, he smokes tobacco all the time
. . . The hookah is not filled with water; instead he fills it with oil and blows into it.
No one else knows that the hookah is filled with oil.
When the oil of the lamps is extinguished, they call out "bring oil!"
The lights are nearly extinguished.
Then the Kartā fills the lamps with the oil from the hookah,
And at the Kartā's command, the lights are lit with the hookah water.
Seeing this, the young widows think it's a miracle.
"O Mā! he has lit the lamps with water from the hookah!"
. . . amidst this party of women, what wicked fraud he performs!
I wish I could give him a good thrashing!
Seeing and hearing all this, I've lost all patience!
But in the government of the Hon'ble Company,
I have no authority, so what can I do?[54] (see SEV)

"Spiritual Businessmen and Brokers" (Dharma-byabsāyī-dālāl)

Based in large part on its reputation as a locus of divine grace and miraculous healing, the Ghoshpara Melā has become a very lucrative source of income for a large number of other more "secular" characters and more explicitly profit-oriented entrepreneurs. There is in fact a large class of promoters who travel to various rural areas of Bengal, telling the poor and uneducated villagers of the wonders of Ghoshpara and inviting them (for a fee) to come to the great festival and resolve their various sufferings. Sudhīr Cakravartī has very aptly dubbed these characters spiritual "brokers" (*dālāl*) or "religious businessmen" (*dharma-byabsāyī*), who enter into the various villages of West Bengal and persuade the people that they need to go to the Melā in order to overcome their physical and economic afflictions: "There are thousands of people, uneducated, helpless, suffering from sickness, bearing the dead. . . . Concealed and unknown, many religious-businessman-brokers [*dharma-byabsāyī-dālāl*] come secretly to our villages. They lead all these helpless people here with their false promises and flimsy arguments."[55] Cakravartī describes one particularly striking example of an educated man who had been persuaded by a "religious broker" to come to the Ghoshpara festival for three years in order to cure his son's extreme hyperactivity. After three years, nothing had happened, and the man had become extremely disillusioned and angry—despite the broker's claims that the failure was simply due to a lack of faith on the part of this poor man:

> The boy is terribly hyperactive. I've been coming here for the last three years. I've fed him the earth of the Dālim tree, I've bathed him in the water of the Hīmsāgar. But nothing happened. What shall I do? . . . Everyone said, "you must cry to the Mother." One fellow told me I must come here for three years. . . . But what's happened? Nothing. That fellow snatched a lot of money from me. And now he's saying I didn't call upon Satī Mā. It's all worthless! What a charlatan![56]

Finally, in addition to the Kartās, Mahāśays, and the "spiritual brokers," a wide variety of other more secular individuals also profit enormously from the Kartābhajā Melā—namely, the hordes of shopkeepers, streetvendors, tradesmen, artisans, minstrels, and prostitutes who flock to Ghoshpara each spring. According to Sarkār's 1976 report, for example, the Melā attracted some 335 shops of various sizes, including tea stalls, restaurants, pan dealers, sweet shops, and a host of other merchants selling clothing and handicrafts. Together, they made an estimated profit of 131,691 rupees. Depending on the size of his business, each owner had to pay up to 350 rupees for setting up shop on the grounds, and an estimated total revenue of 7,869 rupees was deposited in the office of the Kartā.[57]

Carnival and Capital

All this raises the question, then, of what role the Ghoshpara Melā might have played in relation to the broader political structure of Bengali society in the nineteenth century: Was it a kind of carnival, in Bakhtin's sense of a subversive liberation from dominant social norms? Or was it simply a kind of social safety valve, which temporarily vented popular frustrations so that the dominant order could once again be established in an even stronger form—and which, ultimately, allowed a small group of individuals to profit handsomely on the deal?

There is, of course, a vast body of literature on the question of the carnivalesque, and above all on the question of its subversive or hegemonic function. On one side, there is Bakhtin's highly romantic view, which celebrates the carnival as a liberating inversion of social hierarchies, offering a rare opportunity for the disadvantaged classes to voice their criticisms of the rich and powerful, in a "a domain where the deference required before the lords and clergy did not apply." Like the world of the marketplace, Bakhtin suggests, the carnival is "the privileged site of anti-hegemonic discourse," and even a kind of "black mass of official values" which "encouraged forms of discourse excluded from the world of hierarchy: parody, ridicule, blasphemy, the grotesque, scatology."[58] A more recent version of this positive view is that of James Scott, who argues that carnivals, while not necessarily a source of revolution, provide an alternative social space in which the dominated classes can step outside and criticize the dominant order, and so imagine the possibility of a different world: "Carnival . . . gives a privileged place to normally suppressed speech and aggression. It was the only time . . . when the lower classes were permitted to make threatening gestures toward those who ruled."[59]

It is basically this more romantic and celebratory view of the "carnival" that Sumanta Banerjee adopts in his discussion of the lower-class festivals of nineteenth-century Calcutta. With their irreverent songs and "scatological liberties," their ribald satires of the upper classes and wealthy babus, the lower-class street festivals, Banerjee suggests, provided a small space of freedom amidst an oppressive urban environment. Like the medieval carnivals in Europe, they were "small scattered islands of time . . . when the world was permitted to emerge from the official routine under the camouflage of laughter": "Calcutta folk culture strove to defeat though laughter the gloomy seriousness that surrounded its economic existence and to transform it into a gay carnival. . . . These folk artists created a second world, a second life outside the official world of the respectable educated classes. They created an irreverent and iconoclastic world in opposition to the bhadralok world of strict rituals and stiff restraints."[60]

It is indeed tempting to try to understand the Ghoshpara Melā—with its creation of an alternative social space or free market and its promise of miraculous grace and supernatural power—as a similar kind of Bakhtinian carnival. Not accidentally, the Melā coincides with the traditional Holi festival, which itself is typically described as a "carnivalesque" event—as McKim Marriott puts it, a ritual occasion of seemingly "Dionysian values," during which the normal laws of society are temporarily suspended, traditional hierarchies are overturned, wealthy Brahmans are beaten by poor untouchables, and "insubordinate libido inundates all established hierarchies of age, sex, caste, wealth and power."[61]

On the other side, however, there are a number of more suspicious authors who argue that the "carnival" or ritual inversion is really not a force of social subversion or rebellion; on the contrary, it is more often a key mechanism of *social control.* As Max Gluckman and others have argued, the carnival only temporarily vents social tensions and frustrations, thereby allowing the social order to be reinforced in an even stronger form: "norms and hierarchies temporarily dissolve in symbolic inversions, moral license and generalized anti-structure, only to be reestablished when carnival is over."[62] Likewise, as Ranajit Guha has argued in the specific case of the Holi festival in India, this should by no means be regarded as a threat to or subversion of the dominant social order. On the contrary,

> Just as in Sanskrit grammar the injunction against any breach of rules is emphasized by the license allowed to deviant usage in the holiest of all texts, the Vedas . . . so too does the ritual inversion at Holi affirm the legitimacy of spiritual and social sanctions against nonconformity by condoning the latter on one prescribed occasion. Its overall effect is "the stressing, not the overthrowing of the principle of hierarchy . . . through reversal, a process whereby it *remains* the structural vertebra of village life."[63]

In the case of the Kartābhajās, it would seem that the Ghoshpara Melā probably did far more to reinforce and preserve, rather than undermine or subvert, the dominant social order. Indeed, with its very obvious economic hierarchy and revenue system, the Kartābhajā Melā appears to have been quite intimately entwined with the maintenance and reproduction of the existing socioeconomic order of colonial Bengal during one its most precarious moments.

Nevertheless, as Scott points out, carnivalesque phenomena such as this often carry a threat to, and represent a constant source of anxiety for, the dominant order. Although they may not inspire revolutionary violence, they do represent a continuous source of nonconformity and a persistent, though often subtle, corrosion of the dominant ideology. In most cases, the dominant classes do not in fact support or encourage carnivalesque events—as the safety-valve theory would imply—but rather fear them and try to suppress them: "The view that carnival is a mechanism of social control authorized by elites is not entirely wrong but it is seriously misleading. . . . If in fact the safety-valve theory guided elite conduct, one would expect elites to encourage carnival, especially when social tensions were running high. The opposite is more nearly the case."[64] It seems clear that the dominant upper classes of Calcutta most certainly did *not* view the Ghoshpara Melā as something beneficial to society or political order. On the contrary, they regarded it as a scandalous, subversive affair and a dangerous threat to the well-being of society—indeed, even more dangerous and potentially subversive than the traditional Holi festival. This was no doubt due largely to the turbulent political context of nineteenth-century Bengal. We must remember that the homeland of the Kartābhajās—Nadia, Khulna, the twenty-four Parganas, and neighboring districts—witnessed some of the most intense and violent peasant insurgencies, including Titu Mir, the Farazis, and the Indigo Rebellion. With its explicit rejection of social hierarchies, caste, and religious boundaries, and the massive gathering of poor, discontented, exploited peasants and laborers, the Kartābhajā Melā was, not surprisingly, a major source of concern for the dominant authorities of colonial Bengal.

My own opinion is that the Ghoshpara Melā—like many popular festivals and lower-class religious events—can be understood neither in terms of a simple Bakhtinian carnivalesque liberation nor a mere mechanistic "safety valve" for pent-up social tension. Instead, following the lead of Bourdieu and Foucault, I would characterize the Melā as an *alternative social space* or alternative field of power, in which existing power relations can be temporarily *suspended, renegotiated and reconfigured.*[65] As such, the role of the Melā is analogous to that of women in the Kartābhajā tradition as we have discussed it earlier. Women, we have seen, may indeed be "liberated and empowered" in one sense, but they are at the same time *reinscribed* into a new hierarchy, which serves primarily to *optimize and maximize* the superior power of the male (chapter 2). So, too, within the new social space of the Ghoshpara Melā, devotees are temporarily liberated from the normal hierarchies of mainstream society, freed from the burdens of caste and labor, and empowered with a new kind of spiritual authority; yet they are at the same time reinscribed within a new hierarchy, which serves primarily to benefit the superior power of the Kartā and his Mahāśays.

The "Poor" Company and the Opulence of Its Leaders: Corruption, Controversy, and Conversion in the Later Kartābhajā Tradition

The Master of the forty worlds is the "Good-Mannered Company."
So why do I hear you calling them the "Poor Company?"
. . . They've become the Masters of the world—
can you really call them "poor," brother? (BG 160; II.4)

Rather ironically, the elaborate system of taxation and the highly lucrative celebration of the Ghoshpara Melā allowed the leaders of this "Poor Company" of the Kartābhajās to become perhaps the wealthiest and most powerful of the smaller sectarian gurus of nineteenth-century Bengal. Not surprisingly, the Kartās also elicited the jealousy and antagonism of their rivals, the orthodox Vaiṣṇava leaders descending from the Gosvāmins: "No wonder the Ghoshpara pope grew affluent very soon. . . . The Brahmans and Vaiṣṇava gurus began a propaganda against them."[66] Indeed, despite their rhetoric praising the value of poverty and nonattachment to worldly goods, Dulālcāṅd and his sons built up an opulent *Rajbari* style mansion from which they managed their large landholdings and collected their revenues. As the missionary J. C. Marshman wrote, describing his visit to Dulālcāṅd's residence in 1802: "Dulal's handsome and stately house, exceeding that of many Rajas, and his garners filled with grain, all the gifts of his deluded followers, convinced us of the profitability of his trade."[67]

Not surprisingly, by the second quarter of the nineteenth century, many lower-class followers of the movement began to show a growing dissatisfaction with the wealth and power of the Kartās. The growing disparity between the spirituality of the Kartā's teachings and the apparent opulence of his lifestyle in turn led to the disillusionment of many of his poor, low-class devotees. Particularly in the years following Dulālcāṅd's death (1833), the Pāl family became a favorite target of ridicule throughout Bengali newspapers and literature, where they were satirized for their hedonistic lifestyle, loose morals, and the groups of fawning female devotees with whom they surrounded themselves. As one observer, Kumudnāth Mālik, lamented the sad decline of the Kartās into commercialism and greed, "Alas, the sport of time has led to the proliferation of *gadis* and . . . many external paraphernalia. There is no longer the devotion and love, the honesty, beauty and grace. . . . All that remains is the exhibition of pomp for money and the futile pretense of power to cure ailments by the magic of religion."[68]

Surely the most scandalous of all the Kartās was the son of Dulālcāṅd, Īśvaracandra (1813–1882), who was widely known for his opulent Zamindāri lifestyle and Rājā-like conspicuous consumption. "During his regime, the religious zemindari of Ghoshpara acquired some of the distinctive features of a typical decadent feudal family."[69] With an infamous reputation as a lecherous pervert with a special fondness for women and pleasures of the flesh, Īśvaracandra is described in contemporary reports surrounded by fawning women and deluded devotees. As the Calcutta paper, *Somaprakāśa* described him:

> The present Kartā, Īśvara Bābu, lies on a bed, while women sit on all four sides of him, some offering food, some massaging his body, and some spreading sandal paste onto his limbs. . . . It's said that the followers of this religion also perform the Kṛṣṇa-līlā of Vṛndāvana. The Kartās steal the women's clothing and climb a tree, while the ladies pray to them from the base of the tree. Moreover, the invocation of spirits, witchcraft , etc. are secretly practiced. . . . Many people join this movement simply out of selfish interest, for the opportunity to engage in wicked activities.[70]

Not only was he scandalized as morally degenerate, but Īśvaracandra was also said to have been briefly imprisoned in Calcutta's jail because of his licentiousness and fraudulent behavior. As Dāśarathī Rāy mercilessly ridicules Īśvaracandra in his scathing satire,

Their foremost Kartā-Bābu [Īśvaracandra] has become completely degenerate;
he's fallen wholly into sin!
The people of his house have corrupted him, everything has become a fraud.
His hoax has dissolved like water, and his hands have been bound.
There's no more display of trickery—for three years he's been in the Calcutta Jail!
. . . By means of their magical mantras, they delude people's minds.
. . . They show you something that looks like something else, saying lead is
gold!
Seeing their dazzling display, the people are easily amazed and blinded.
Just as a Magician's jugglery can alter the scales,
they can show you all things, but feed you nothing![71]

It is no accident that, in the early nineteenth century, a large number of lower-class members abandoned the movement and converted to Christianity. The missionary presence, as we have seen (chapters 1 and 2) had grown quite pronounced in Bengal during the late eighteenth and early nineteenth century, as the Serampore Baptists, Carey, Marshman, and their disciples began to preach actively in the area. The Kartābhajās, with their worship of a man as God Incarnate and their ritual meals free of caste distinction, seemed to the missionaries ideal candidates for conversion. Under the leadership of Rev. William Deer in 1835, the missionaries made a pronounced effort to spread the Bible among the Kartā's following in the villages areas of Nadia district in and around Krishnanagar.[72] By 1836, a number of the poorer Kartābhajās had grown disgusted with the hypocrisy of their gurus and began to turn to the messianic ideals of Christianity; finally, in 1838, a huge group of devotees, consisting of ten entire villages and some 400–500 persons, converted en masse: "According to Kartābhajā teaching, gurus were not supposed to be caught up in worldliness. . . . There can be little doubt, however, that Dulalchand . . . lived in considerable luxury. . . . Dulalchand's sons were . . . especially condemned by Bengali writers as not living up to the highest of moral standards. And this was precisely at the time the largest numbers of Kartābhajās were converted to Christianity."[73]

By the end of the nineteenth century, with their waning numbers and growing reputation for greed, materialism, and sensual indulgence, the Kartābhajās had become something of a laughing stock among the upper-class circles of Calcutta. As Dāśarathī, in his typically ironic style, depicts the final downfall and disgrace of the Kartābhajā,

The worship of the Kartā, one should know, is just so much jugglery;
and if one doesn't know this, his entire family could be deluded!
In this community there was a great devotee named Khudirām Caṭṭo.
. . . The Kartābhajā religion became Khudirām's great sorrow.
It was forbidden for all the people to assemble together;
and because he didn't heed that [prohibition], Khudirām experienced great sorrow!
. . . A number of people became greatly upset, and went to inform the Rājā's house.
The Rājā gave the command to fetch [Khudirām and his cohorts]
Crying and crying, they went along with the armed footman, trembling with terror
. . . They were punished by the Rājā and left his palace;
now they have shaven their beards and abandoned the Kartābhajā religion!
. . . The joys of the Kartābhajās have ended.
The leading Kartās have abandoned the temple.
They've realized this is the end and cut their long beards
Recently Khudirām was seen in the city of Pāṭuli.
In the name of God, what a disgrace!
The people of the village have made him an outcast.
This Brāhmaṇ has fallen into terrible troubles—
Alas, no one gives him anything; Oh, what terrible sorrow![74]

Conclusions: The Kartābhajās and the Colonial Situation

In short, what we find in the case of the Kartābhajās is an especially poignant illustration of both the power and the liability of secrecy—its potential as a source of status, prestige, and wealth and its potential as a source of exclusion, elitism, and, ultimately, the loss of that same status and prestige. Secrecy is, by its very definition, an *exclusionary tactic*—a mechanism for denying certain members of society access to valued information. It can be used not only by the marginalized and malcontented who wish to conceal themselves from their social superiors but also by the dominant factions *within* the esoteric society itself, as a means of consolidating their own power and mystifying their own status.[75] If the Kartābhajā leaders could claim their esoteric knowledge and mystical powers as their primary source of spiritual authority, they could also manipulate them as their primary source of economic capital and material income. Rather ironically, however, these very same claims to esoteric knowledge and mystical powers would also gradually become among the primary reasons for their eventual fall into *disrepute and loss of status* among Calcutta's more conservative upper classes.

At the same time, with their surprisingly lucrative business practices and economic organization, the Kartābhajās also offer some refreshing insights into the world of colonial Bengal. Indeed, they are a wonderful reflection of the real pluralism and dynamism of this pivotal moment in the history of British India. Rather than a passive reaction to an overwhelming colonial presence, the Kartābhajās represent a rich mixture of urban and rural economics, colonial and pre-colonial cultural forms, indigenous and foreign language, the mercantile imagery of the Company and the semifeudal hierarchies of the rural Zamindārs. At the same time, they also embody an ambivalent fusion of both complicity with and resistance to the dominant economic forces around them, a simultaneous collusion with and subversion of the indigenous and colonial elites alike.

As such, I would hope that this study might have much broader comparative implications for colonial and post-colonial studies, throughout South Asia and even cross-culturally. Following the lead of McClintock, Suleri, Kelly, and others, I would suggest that colonial situations such as this one cannot be understood in terms of either a simple passive assimilation to colonial hegemony or a simple noble struggle of the colonized against the imperial oppressor. Rather, they represent a complex *renegotiation*, which involves collusion and accommodation as well as subversion and resistance, entangled together in a "dense web of relations between *coercion, complicity, refusal, mimicry, compromise, affiliation and revolt.*"[76] The Kartābhajās provide a striking insight into this deeper ambiguity in the colonial context and may thereby help to break down the binarisms of colonizer and colonized, domination and subordination, that so often inform postcolonial theory.

8

The Progressive "Exotericization" and "Institutionalization" of an Esoteric Tradition

The history of the Kartābhajā tradition in the late nineteenth and twentieth centuries can perhaps best be described as the progressive "exotericization" and "institutionalization" of an esoteric tradition. It is the history of a once highly secretive, relatively small and marginal sect, deeply rooted in the Tantric schools of Bengal, which gradually adopted a successful exoteric or public dimension (most visibly embodied in the annual Ghosphara Melā) that eventually came to predominate and displace the more esoteric core of the tradition.

As we have seen, secrecy itself—as a specifically "black market" form of symbolic capital—carries both positive and negative possibilities: It may, on one hand, serve to enhance one's status and symbolic power (when one's secret knowledge is considered rare, valuable, powerful, and awesome), but it may also, on the other hand, threaten or undermine one's status (when that knowledge comes to be viewed by exoteric society as dangerous or immoral). Above all, with the mounting charges of sexual immorality and the seedy scandal of the Tantras, and with the progressive loss of respect among the upper classes, the esoteric roots of this tradition increasingly became a liability and embarrassment for its leadership. The "stinking fruit" of its Sahajiyā practices had to be driven ever deeper underground into the realm of censorship and concealment, ever further marginalized from the orthodox center of the tradition in Ghoshpara. Thus, as Nandī comments, even though the original core of the Kartābhajā tradition is the esoteric sādhanā of Sahajiyā Tantra, the majority of common or "gross" (*sthūla*) devotees today know only the most exoteric, popular and devotional side of the tradition:

> Even though we can plainly see the presence of Tantric practices or Sahaja Sādhanā in the *Bhāver Gīta*, these are not always followed by common practitioners. That's why many think that the Kartābhajās' esoteric bodily practices are the result of external influences. But this is not the case. Rather, with the influence of later history, a more devotional faith began to replace secret practices [*guhyācāra*]. . . . There are still some who continue to follow the secret rites. But their number is small. From the time of Dulālcāṅd and Satīmā, the number of devotees began to grow. Thousands of people started to come out of attraction to the greatness of Ghoshpara. . . . But among them there are probably none who follow the difficult path of Sahaja-Sādhanā.[1]

At the same time, as Sumanta Banerjee suggests, the Kartābhajā tradition of the late nineteenth and twentieth centuries also came to be progressively "institutionalized"—that is, slowly transformed from a loose and obscure cult centering around the mysterious mad Fakir, Āulcāṅd, to a well-organized, rather bureaucratic and popular faith centering around the miraculous healing powers of Satī Mā and the sacred hierarchy of the Mahāśays:

> The institutionalization was marked by (a) specifying a particular spot as the headquarters of the sect; (b) dynastic succession of gurus who claimed the authority of the first guru . . . (c) organized priesthood consisting of a network of preachers . . . (d) collection of money on a regular basis . . . (e) a repository of written texts . . . explaining the religion. The most interesting aspect of the institutionalization of the Kartābhajā sect is that popular interest in Ghoshpara has shifted form the egalitarian message of Aulchand to the curative rituals associated with Sati Ma. . . . The mother goddess has not only outlived her guru, husband and son, but has outshone all of them in popular tradition.[2]

Already by the late nineteenth century, in fact, the Kartāhajā hierarchy had grown so elaborate that it seems to have fractured under its own weight. Following the death of Īśvaracandra Pāl, it finally splintered into no less than four different factions and four separate Kartās—all claiming the status of the supreme Guru and the unique incarnation of God in human form (Figure 8.1).[3]

Nonetheless, in spite of this increasing exotericization, the deeper esoteric currents of the Kartābhajā tradition have continued throughout the more remote areas of rural Bengal and old Calcutta though often to the annoyance and embarrassment of the conservative leadership in Ghoshpara. Indeed, even one of the two living claimants to the title of Kartā confided to me that he practices a variety of Tantric techniques and that he recognizes the more objectionable Sahajiyā practice of *parakīyā* love as a valid spiritual path. In short, as Cakravartī suggests, there are today two different currents in the Kartābhajā tradition—one, a largely popular, devotional, and exoteric religion, led by the Pāl family in Ghoshpara, basically in line with more conventional Vaiṣṇava faith, and another, now much smaller, highly esoteric cult scattered throughout the rural areas of Bengal, and deeply rooted in the older Tantric traditions: "For some time two separate forms of Kartābhajā worship have been practiced. The first is pure and free of lust, following the teachings of Ghoshpara. The second form is a close branch of the Sahajiyās and engages in esoteric bodily practices."[4]

Almost from the beginning of the tradition, there have been a variety of deviant offshoots from the primary Kartābhajā body, rejecting the increasing institutionalization and exotericization of the Ghosphara Kartās and proclaiming themselves the true bearers of the most secret and mysterious essence of the Kartābhajā teaching. The first of these was founded by Kānāi Ghoṣe—who was initially said to have been the foremost of the twenty-two fakirs, but who eventually rejected Rāmśaraṇ Pāl's leadership and moved to the nearby village of Kancharapara to start his own sect. This group, called the *Satyasrota* (the True Current) or the *Gupta Kartābhajās*

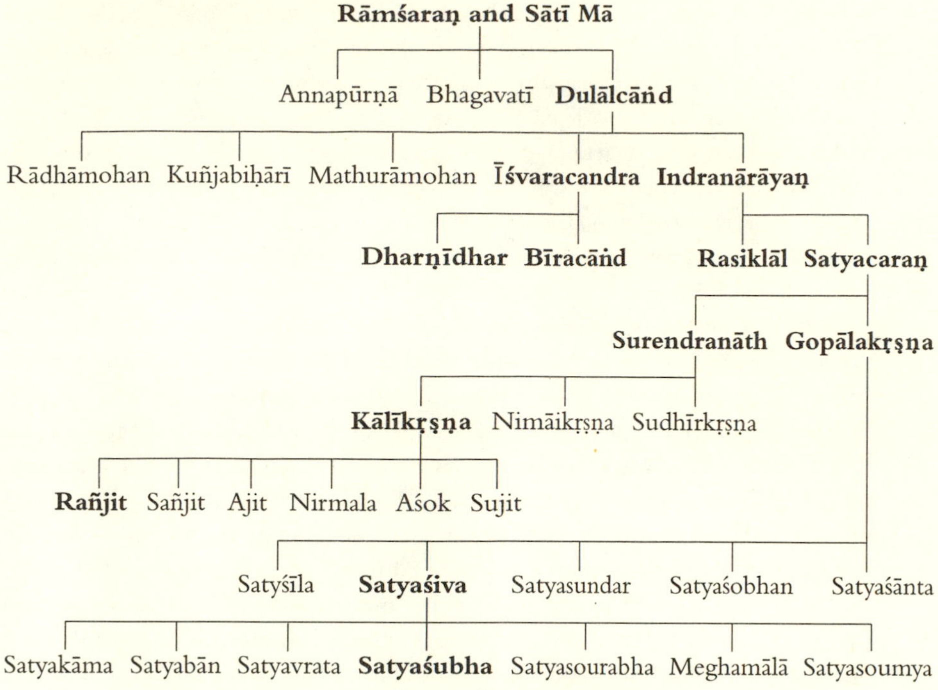

Figure 8.1 The Pāl Family of Kartās (names in bold indicate claimants to the title of "Kartā")

(the "Secret Kartābhajās"), still continues to regard itself as the true bearer of the deeper, "esoteric" side of the Kartābhajās, preserving it against the growing bureaucratization and dilution of this tradition among the Pāl family of Kartās.[5]

However, the most important of these offshoots of the Kartābhajās—or perhaps even its "sister sect"—is the smaller, more obscure and highly secretive tradition of the Sāhebdhanīs. Calling themselves literally, by the title "wealthy gentlemen" (*dhanī sāheb*), or even—given the highly loaded connotations of the term "Sāheb" in colonial Bengal—"the *Rich Englishmen*," the Sāhebdhanīs, like the Kartābhajās, take delight in playing on the titles and discourse of the dominant classes. According to some scholars such as Ratan Nandī and Tuṣār Caṭṭopādhyāy, the Sāhebdhanīs are in fact a subsect or offshoot of the Kartābhajās; according to others like Sudhīr Cakravartī, the Kartābhajās and Sāhebdhanīs are "two branches of the same tree." But in any case, like the Kartābhajās, the Sāhebdhanīs trace their origins to a mysterious, possibly fictional, Muslim ascetic (in this case named "Sāhebdhanī"), whose first disciple (one Dukhirām or Mulīcāṅd Pāl) then organized the tradition and instituted a hereditary succession of gurus. Their foremost poet and song writer, Kubir Gosāiṅ, is often cited together with Lālan Shāh and Dulālcāṅd as one of the three great folksingers of rural Bengal. Moreover, like those of the Kartābhajās, the songs of the Sāhebdhanīs make extensive use of imagery drawn from contemporary economic events in colonial Bengal, terminology drawn from the East India Company, the English railroad system, and the Indigo trade[6] (see SE IV for translations of Sāhebdhanī songs). On the whole, however, the Sāhebdhanīs are even more secretive than the mainstream Kartābhajā tradition, and generally much closer in their ritual practice and esoteric language to the Bāuls of rural Bengal (among their secret practices, for example, is the infamous "four moon" ritual (*cāri-candra*), which involves the consumption of the four bodily excreta of feces, urine, menstrual blood, and semen).[7]

Finally, to this day, throughout the more distant regions of village Bengal, in the districts of Bardhaman, the twenty-four Parganas, Murshidabad, and western Bangladesh, one can still find a number of older Kartābhajā gurus who have little connection with the more "orthodox" lineage of the Pāl family in Ghoshpara and continue to practice the most esoteric and more objectionable Sahajiyā techniques. As Śaktināth Jhā suggests in his study of the Kartābhajās of Murshidabad, the disciples of this and other rural areas are for the most part very different from the Ghoshpara tradition: They typically do not identify with the mainstream Gauḍīya Vaiṣṇava tradition—and in fact are often quite hostile to it—but are deeply tied to the more esoteric Sahajiyā, Bāul, and other Tantric schools.[8]

In the course of my own field research, I met a number of older Mahāśays from the more remote districts of old Calcutta and rural Bengal—such as the rather colorful and somewhat ill-tempered old fellow from Murshidabad, Kāṅgāl Mahanta, interviewed earlier—who continue to preserve the oldest, most esoteric Tantric side of the tradition. Indeed, Kāṅgāl Mahanta stands out as a striking illustration of the continuing power and symbolic value of exoteric knowledge, even in spite of—or perhaps *because of*—its potentially dangerous threat. I was, in fact, first introduced to Kāṅgāl Mahanta by one of the two living Kartās, precisely because of the old guru's reputation as a treasury of profound esoteric knowledge, as a master of the inner secrets of the *Bhāver Gīta,* and, above all, as an initiate deeply versed in the mysteries of Sahajiyā sexual rituals such as *parakīyā* love. Even today, it seems, the simultaneous danger and power, the outward repugnance and deeper lurid attraction of "Tantrism" and secrecy, survive within the Kartābhajā tradition.[9]

Conclusions and Comparative Comments

"Uninitiated Understanding"

But you *can't* get rid of secrets, Chief—Without secrets, we'd lose our cushy jobs!
(Secret Agent Maxwell Smart, *Get Smart*)

Interpretation is indefinite. The attempt to look for an original, unattainable meaning leads to the acceptance of a never ending drift or sliding of meaning. . . . Every object . . . hides a secret. Every time a secret has been discovered it will refer to another secret in a progressive movement toward a final secret. Nevertheless there can be no final secret. The ultimate secret . . . is that everything is secret. Hence the Hermetic secret must be an empty one, because anyone who pretends to reveal any sort of secret is not himself initiated and has stopped at a superficial level.
(Umberto Eco, *Interpretation and Overinterpretation*)

Within the highly idiosyncratic and today relatively unknown sect of the Kartābhajās, it would seem, we gain a surprising number of new insights into several much larger and more general questions. Indeed, this so-called obscure religious cult appears to have a great deal to tell us about some of the most difficult problems in the study of South Asian history and the History of Religions as a whole. Now that we have traced the more detailed social contexts and historical development of the Kartābhajās, with their surprising rise to power and their progressive decline into scandal and obscurity, let us zoom back out and review the larger implications of this study. In order of specificity, from the most narrow to the most general and comparative, these implications may be summarized as follows.

Implications for the Study of Colonial Bengal

On the most narrow historical level, our discussion of the Kartābhajās has opened up a rare and fascinating window onto the lives and religion of the "lower orders" of colonial Bengal. Whereas most past scholarship on nineteenth-century Bengal has concentrated almost entirely on the wealthier upper classes, the leaders of the Bengal Renaissance, and the various elite reform movements, a close look at the Kartābhajās presents us with a very different side of Bengali culture. If Rāmmohun Roy and his fellow reformers can be called the heralds of the Bengal Renaissance and modern era of India, then the Kartābhajās, led by their "folk Rāmmohun," represent one of the strongest examples of a darker undercurrent, going against the grain of the bhadralok reforms. As the "darker side of the Bengal

Renaissance," or even the "counter Renaissance," the Kartābhajās demonstrate the continuing power of magic, occultism, esoteric yoga, and miraculous powers among the poorer lower orders, running often in direct opposition to the sober rationalism of Calcutta's upper classes.

At the same time, the Kartābhajās also present a striking example of the complex nature of the colonial situation itself—its ambiguous mixture of pre-colonial and indigenous social and economic forms and the dynamic interplay of both collusion and subversion, cooperation and resistance, at work between the colonizer and colonized. With its unusual fusion of a semifeudal Zamindāri-style economic hierarchy and mercantile terminology drawn from the bazaars of colonial Calcutta and the business of the East India Company, the Kartābhajā organization is a composite, yet apparently rather lucrative, amalgam of pre-colonial and colonial structures, with a rich "admixture of capitalist and precapitalist forms."[1]

Still more strikingly, with their simultaneous subversive appropriation of mercantile discourse and their imposition of new, in some ways equally burdensome, hierarchies of taxation, the Kartābhajās also demonstrate the highly ambivalent status of the colonized and subaltern classes. This is, perhaps, a status which cannot be reduced to a simple binarism of domination and resistance. In one sense, it would seem, the Kartābhajās do indeed reveal the creative ingenuity and even subversive power of the poorer "lower orders," their ability to adapt, transform, and deform the discourse of the dominant classes, turning even the language of the British East India Company to their own advantage as source of esoteric meaning and power. In contrast to Bourdieu's rather top-heavy and pessimistic model of the social order, which tends to reduce human actors to "passive blocks of wood" who "mindlessly reproduce the dominant order," I have followed the lead of Michel de Certeau and others, by emphasizing the "tactical" ability of ordinary social consumers to manuever within, as well as to resist, thwart, challenge, and subvert, the dominant social order and the status quo.[2]

Thus, if I have in the course of this volume placed a great deal of emphasis on the role of mercantile discourse and its relation to the larger economic context of colonial Bengal, it has by no means been intended as a kind of "vulgar economism" or a simplistic reduction of religious actors and their creative products to the surrounding material circumstances. Quite the contrary, I have argued that social agents not only employ "religious" symbols, myths, and rituals in the service of political or economic ends (as the members of the Subaltern Studies Collective have shown us) [3]; still further, I have argued that *they can creatively appropriate, adapt, and deform seemingly "economic" and "political" symbols, transforming them into profound bearers of religious meaning and spiritual ideals.*

At the same time, however, I have also tried to avoid the overemphasis on the creative "agency" of colonized peoples and the romanticization of native resistance against foreign domination, which characterizes much recent post-colonial literature. Indeed, as Talal Asad and others have pointed out, this often exaggerated emphasis on native subjectivity is perhaps itself just a new and more subtle imposition of modern Western bourgeois notions of "agency" and the "autonomous subject" onto other cultures.[4] The Kartābhajās, as "flawed and fallible heroes,"[5] also clearly submitted to, colluded with, and cooperated with the dominant order around them, and they in turn introduced new forms of exploitation, in many cases mirroring, mimicking, or reproducing the existing indigenous and colonial structures of power.

In sum, to understand a group as rich and multifaceted as the Kartābhajās, we need to avoid *both* the extremes of a romantic celebration of native agency in its valiant struggle against imperial domination *and* that of a cynical commentary on the eventual cooption and collusion of native peoples with their foreign masters. To use Bourdieu's terms, what we have here (as in many colonial situations) is not a simple matter of domination or resistance; rather, it is often one in which "resistance" itself becomes a more subtle part of, or leads to new forms of, domination. Like speakers of "slang" in Bourdieu's analysis, the Kartābhajās may have found in their esoteric discourse and secret practices a source of freedom and empowerment beyond the dominant world of exoteric society; yet these same secret practices—with their use of dangerous, polluting or socially objectionable substances and their expression in often deliberately shocking or offensive language—would ultimately become for them a new source of scandal and ridicule in the eyes of the outside world. They were thus

> condemned to produce paradoxical effects which cannot be understood . . . within the alternatives of resistance or submission . . . When the dominated quest for distinction leads the dominated to affirm what distinguishes them, that is, that in the name of which they are dominated and constituted as vulgar, do we have to talk of resistance? . . . If in order to resist I have no other recourse than to lay claim to that in the name of which I am dominated, is this resistance? . . . Resistance may be alienating and submission may be liberating. Such is the paradox of the dominated.[6]

Implications for Tantric Studies: An Embodied and Historicized Tantra

Beyond the realm of Bengal studies and the colonial era, however, the Kartābhajās may also help us to rethink and reimagine the broader, pan-Indian category of "Tantra" itself. Largely the product of the Western imagination and Orientalist scholarship, the category of Tantrism is, as Padoux has shown, a highly problematic and poorly defined one in modern discourse. And the Kartābhajās—with their own profound ambivalence about the presence of "tantric" elements within their tradition—stand out as among the most telling examples of just how slippery a category this remains in modern academia. Nonetheless, as I have tried to argue here, it is still possible (and perhaps now unavoidable) to retain and redefine this category in a more useful way in contemporary discourse. Rather than a static, monolithic, clearly defined entity, Tantrism is probably much better understood as a very ambiguous, messy and problematic—though admittedly necessary—product of the scholarly imagination. If it is to continue to serve us as a useful scholarly tool or heuristic device for understanding a certain body of South Asian texts and traditions, then it is perhaps better understood not so much as a tidy and coherent historical object but instead as a J. Z. Smith-ean hodge-podge or "heap of rubbish" (see chapter 6).[7]

Still more important, following Jeffrey Kripal's lead, I have argued that we need to go beyond the highly abstract, philosophical, and almost entirely textual (primarily Sanskritic) studies that have dominated most recent scholarship on Tantra; instead, we need to look more closely at the living historical contexts in which those traditions we wish to call "Tantric" arise and function, the concrete material, economic, social, and political circumstances with which they interact. Emerging at such a key historical period and in such a central geographic locus, the Kartābhajās present us with an ideal opportunity to look at a "Tantric" tradition within a particualrly intense, rapidly shifting social and historical milieu.

As such, this study has been intended to provide an important complement to and development of earlier studies of the Sahajiyā Tantric traditions, like those of Edward C. Dimock and his students. Beyond an analysis of the basic doctrines and practices of a particular Tantric school, I have also tried to place the Kartābhajās concretely within their social, historical, and economic world, examining the complex ways in which they were at once informed by and yet also actively responded to this volatile cultural context. Indeed, as I have tried to show, the Kartābhajās demonstrate in striking detail just how problematic the very topic of "Tantrism" became in nineteenth-century Bengal, as it was not only defined and categorized but also singled out, attacked, and ridiculed as the very worst, most degenerate, and most dangous aspect of the "Indian Mind" itself. Although originally rooted in the older Sahajiyā and other Tantric schools of medieval Bengal, the Kartābhajās represent at least three profound transformations, which I have characterized as follows: (1) a "popularized" Tantra, which promoted itself explicitly as an "easy" (*sahaja*) path for the poor lower classes; (2) a "deodorized" Tantra, which came under increasing attack because of its alleged immoral Tantric practices and which in turn made increasing efforts to sanitize or cover over the more objectionable elements; and (3) a "commercialized" or "institutionalized" Tantra, which eventually built an elaborate financial organization and which, for a short time, became the most successful all Bengal's "minor sects."

What emerges from this historical and embodied approach, it would seem, is a different image of "Tantra" than the one we find in the highly philosophical, rather dry, and generally rather elitist Sanskrit treatises of Kashmir Śaivism, which today seem to provide the dominant paradigm for our academic definition of the subject. Instead, the Kartābhajās reveal a different, far less sophisticated or cerebral, far more earthy, human, and vital face of "Tantra"—a living and embodied, historically and culturally dynamic, but generally quite ambiguous and rather messy kind of Tantra, rooted in the lives and problems of real social agents amidst the shifting, often hostile and tumultuous forces of history and change.

Implications for the Study of Esoteric Traditions: Unitiated Understanding

Secret knowledge is deep knowledge (because only what is lying under the surface can remain unknown for long). Thus truth becomes identified with what is not said or what is said obscurely and must be understood beyond or beneath the surface of a text. Thus the gods speak . . . through hieroglyphic and enigmatic messages.

(Umberto Eco, *Interpretation and Overinterpretation*)

Finally, and most ambitiously, this volume has also been intended to open some new insights into the broader comparative topic of secrecy across cultures and throughout historical periods. If it is true that contemporary academia and modern Western culture as a whole are pervaded by what Eco calls the "syndrome of the secret"—a morbid preoccupation with the tantalizing regions of the forbidden and the occult, or a Hermetic desire to strip away the outer surface of the visible form so as to discover behind it a deeper, concealed meaning[8]—it is no less true that the problem of secrecy has long been woefully under-theorized and misunderstood in the history of religions. It is certainly true that many early historians of religions, such as Mircea Eliade or Kees Bolle, had been fascinated and even preoccupied by esoteric traditions, placing the mysterious, the hidden and the secret at the very heart of religious experience,[9] yet their work has generally had the effect of abstracting these esoteric traditions from their concrete historical and social circumstances, absorbing them into the more general and universalized experience of "Homo religiosus"—in short, of *mystifying* them still further. What I have tried to do here, on the other hand, is to examine the role of secrecy within its concrete social and historical contexts, to analyze its role as a form of symbolic power, as it is played out in real material, economic, and political contexts.

In so doing, I do not pretend to have resolved the epistemological and ethical double bind I posed at the beginning of this book; nor is this intended to be the only or always the best solution to the double bind of secrecy. Rather, it is offered as a new and hopefully more fruitful hermeneutic strategy—a methodological shift which takes as its focus not the ever-elusive substance of *the Secret* but, rather, the more visible forms and tactics through which *secrecy* operates as an effect or process. This shift allows us (1) to continue to say something intelligent about esoteric traditions without becoming mired in the endless quest for some elusive, ever-receding content and (2) to study other cultures in a critical and hermeneutically "suspicious" way, while remaining conscious and respectful of those aspects of their traditions which may be "off limits" to the uninitiated, uninvited scholarly observer.

Once we adopt the "formal" or strategic approach to secrecy I have outlined here, it is of course tempting to regard secrecy as a matter of mystification plain and simple, as pure form with *no* content—as a McGuffin in Hitchcock's sense, or a kind of Wizard of Oz phenomenon, in which, despite all the awesome smoke and mirrors, mystery, and magic surrounding the secret, the Wizard turns out to be nothing more than a confused and pathetic old man. As Goffman, for example, has argued, the awe generated by secret mysteries may in fact only conceal the underlying shame that there is no secret after all: "We have . . . a social coin, with awe on one side and shame on the other. The audience senses secret mysteries and powers behind the performance and the performer senses that his chief secrets are petty ones. As countless folk tales and initiation rites show, often the real secret behind the mystery is that there really is no mystery. The problem is to prevent the audience from learning this too."[10] As I have tried to show, however, it is typically *not* the case that secrets are merely semantically "empty" or devoid of content. On the contrary, the problem is more often that they *have too many meanings.* They are in most cases *radically polyvalent* and *indeterminate to an extreme degree.* Because of their deliberate ambiguity and systematic obfuscation, secrets can be given an enormous, virtually infinite range of interpretations and explanations, which shift and change in different contexts, by different exegetes, before different audiences, and in different performances. The secret is thus among the most acute examples of the problem we face in every hermeneutic encounter, in every attempt to make sense of religious data and in every ethnographic encounter: the inescapable polyvalence and indeterminacy of meaning that lies inherent in every symbol, every utterance, and every text.

This is not to say, then, that the study of the content of secrecy is a futile quest for some nonexistent entity (after all, *some* secrets are very real and very important). It is simply to say that in many, if not most, cases, it is more profitable to *shift our gaze* and examine secrecy in terms of its forms and tactics, as a specific discursive strategy and a mechanism for the production of symbolic value.

What this means, however, is that we must also be far more *modest* in our claims regarding esoteric traditions, and far more ready to admit that there is an awful lot we do not know and cannot say much about. We must, in short, accept the extreme indeterminacy inherent in the very nature of something that is supposed to be "secret." But again, this is only the most extreme and acute example of the limitations and problems inherent in *all* attempts to study other cultures, which many ethnographers have recently begun to recognize. As Clifford comments in his study of Marcel Griaule, we can no longer presume to have some kind of "initiatory" access to another culture, to penetrate its innermost "Secrets" and to represent them with perfect accuracy in our scholarship. Rather, we must acknowledge that both we and the other culture are inextricably bound to history, material circumstance, and social interests, which place profound limitations on our ability to understand one another: "Initiatory claims to speak as a knowledgeable insider revealing cultural truths are no longer credible. Field work . . . must rather be seen as a historically contingent dialogical encounter involving . . . both conflict and collaboration. . . . Ethnography seems condemned to strive for the encounter while recognizing the political, ethical and personal cross-purposes that undermine any transmission of intercultural knowledge."[11]

At this point, therefore, we are ready to summarize our reflections on the general problem of secrecy, which can be outlined briefly in the following theses:

1. Secrecy is best understood, not in terms of some alleged "hidden content"—which is at once (a) ultimately unknowable, (b) ethically problematic even if "known," and (c) radically polysemic, or subject to an enormous plurality of conflicting interpretations. Instead, secrecy is more fruitfully described as a unique type of *discursive strategy.*
2. Secrecy is thus part of the more general strategies of discourse which, as Lincoln has argued, are integral to the ongoing construction and deconstruction, support and subversion of the greater social order.[12] Yet unlike most forms of social discourse, such as those we find in more "public" media like myth, ritual, or classificatory systems, secrecy is a highly specialized discursive technique which is intentionally exclusive, inherently elitist, deliberately dissimulating, and willfully misleading.
3. As a discursive and rhetorical, strategy, secrecy functions to restrict access to certain knowledge, information, or behaviors, and to conceal certain ideas or actions from unwanted outsiders. But in contrast to mere silence plain and simple, secrets are structured in such a way that they can be *disclosed.*[13] For a secret is only valuable insofar as it can, at least potentially and partially, be revealed.
4. The general strategy of secrecy, in whatever its form, typically involves a number of basic rhetorical maneuvers, which operate simultaneously to restrict access to certain knowledge and to make certain that others know this information to be important and highly valued. The most significant of these maneuvers include the following:

    a. *advertising* the secret, or partial revelation and partial concealment
    b. the dialectic of *lure and withdrawal*
    c. *hierarchical access to* information
    d. the *skillful use of obscurity,* or the use of deliberate and systematic ambiguity
    e. *semantic shock*, or extreme metaphorization and the use of deliberately jarring, disconcerting, even offensive imagery

5. The net result of these maneuvers is to transform a given piece of information into a *scarce resource* or a rare (and therefore very often highly valued and desirable) commodity of knowledge and power within a given social formation.
6. The possession of this scarce resource in turn bestows a unique type of symbolic capital—in the form of status, prestige, or valued knowledge—upon its owner.
7. Unlike most forms of capital Bourdieu has described, the capital brought with secrecy is of a narrowly circumscribed nature, which can be accumulated and exchanged only behind closed doors, within the restricted confines of the secret society. Hence it might be thought of as a kind of black market capital—a dangerous or "illegal" form of power, which is valued, not in the mainstream social order, but solely within the esoteric community. Yet like other black market goods, such as drugs, pornography, or prostitution, the dangerous or illicit nature

of the secret often only increases its value, heightening its aura of transgressive power and erotic allure.

8. While operating most generally as a strategy for acquiring symbolic capital, secrecy typically involves a number of substrategies or supporting tactics. These include, among others:

   a. A *hermeneutic strategy*, or a particular way of rereading sacred texts and traditions, giving them a deeper, hidden meaning (see chapter 1).
   b. *A strategy of religious appropriation* and bricolage, or a means of poaching elements from a variety of traditions, weaving them into a new esoteric synthesis which transcends them (chapter 2).
   c. A *social strategy or way of life*—a means of living simultaneously in the exoteric world of mainstream society and in the secret world of the esoteric sect (chapter 2).
   d. A *discursive strategy*, or a way of manipulating language to create rare and valued pieces of information (chapter 3).
   e. A *metaphoric strategy*, or a particular means of using symbolism and imagery, which invests many common, "secular" metaphors, and even the terminology of the dominant order itself, with a variety of deeper hidden meanings (chapter 4).
   f. *A practical and ritual strategy*, or a means of manipulating the physical substances of the human body in order to deconstruct the ordinary socialized body and to create a new, divinely liberated secret body (chapter 5).
   g. A *strategy of deodorization and disguise,* which attempts to conceal and/or eradicate socially objectionable elements from the tradition (chapter 6).
   h. A strategy of *elitism and exploitation,* as a means of mystifying and legitimizing asymmetries of power within the community itself (chapter 7).

9. Like all discourse, secrecy is a strategy which may be used either to reinforce and support, or to undermine and subvert, a given social formation and hierarchy of power.[14]
10. On one side, secrecy is often a tool of the dominant classes and ruling elite, employed to mask, mystify, and obfuscate their own status and privileges. The possession of secret information is often a key part of the more general phenomenon of "authority" and the authorization of certain individuals with the power to speak and govern within a particular social formation. It is thus a part of the overall *authority effect*, as Lincoln calls it—"the whole theatrical array of gestures, demeanors, costumes, props and stage devices through which one may impress or bamboozle an audience."[15]
11. On the other side, secrecy may also be turned into a weapon of the dominated, marginalized, or disenfranchised classes, who wish to conceal themselves from or even to resist and subvert the existing social order. It is thus the privileged tool not only of radical political groups but also of marginal and disenfranchised individuals who hope to find an alternative source of status in an alternative social hierarchy.
12. As a specifically "black market," or illegal kind of knowledge, however, secrecy is an inherently ambivalent and potentially self-defeating strategy: It is often also a potential *liability* for its owner, who can always be accused of harboring danger-

ous, immoral, antisocial, or subversive information. Hence, secret societies are often among the first to be attacked and ridiculed for their alleged licentious or even revolutionary activities.

13. Tactics of secrecy therefore almost always go hand in hand with tactics of *censorship*—both from within and from without the esoteric community. Externally, secret organizations are often scrutinized, silenced, and suppressed by the dominant order as a potential threat to social stability and the status quo. At the same time, internally, secret organizations impose a variety of forms of *self-censorship*, strategies of disguise, and/or self-purification in order to conceal any more objectionable elements from the eyes of exoteric society.
14. Secrecy may also be turned into a strategy of *elitism and exploitation* within the esoteric organization itself. By its very exclusive character, secrecy lends itself naturally to the construction of new hierarchies, ranks, degrees, and levels of status, new kinds of asymmetries between masters and disciples, novices and adepts, as well as between men and women, high and low class or rich and poor.

Beyond the "Syndrome of the Secret": Comparative and Cross-Cultural Directions

Finally, it is also my hope that this approach and this modified version of Bourdieu's concept of symbolic capital might have some broader comparative implications for the study of secrecy in other cultures. Whereas most early historians of religions such as Eliade sought to compare esoteric traditions on the basis of the substance, building up phenomenological typologies of common symbolic forms, I would suggest that a more fruitful comparison would focus instead on the common discursive strategies employed in various secret organizations.

The Kartābhajās offer us a particularly acute example of the inherent ambivalence and duplicity of secrecy—namely, its potential role as either (and often both) a strategy of elitism or an "art of resistance," a tactic which may be deployed, like all discourse, both to support and reinforce, or to subvert and undermine, a given social or political arrangement. On one side, the example of the largely poor, lower-class, and socially disempowered Kartābhajā sect gives us some valuable comparative insights into the uses of secrecy among marginalized, disgruntled, deviant, or subversive groups. One might, for example, compare their tactics of secrecy, self-censorship, and disguise with those of poor and disenfranchized groups, such as Voodoo cults like the Bizango in Haiti; indeed, one might even compare these subversive uses of secrecy with the more radical strategies employed by overtly rebellious or revolutionary societies, such as the Mau Mau in Kenya or the White Lotus and Triad societies in China.[16]

Yet simultaneously, as the very ambivalent case of the Kartābhajās has shown us, the tactics of secrecy may just as easily be used by dominant elite factions, who wish to reinforce their own power and status within the social hierarchy. Here, we might fruitfully compare not only the more "elitist" of the Asian Tantric traditions—such as South Indian Śrīvidyā, Japanese Shingon, or Vajrayāna Buddhism—but also certain Indian Sufi orders such as the Chishtīya, which were for the most part highly elitist and aristocratic in orientation.[17] Going still further afield, we could also examine similar strategies of elitism and esoteric power in a variety of traditional or pre-industrialized societies, such as the Australian Aboriginal communities that Ian Keen has recently described. As in the case of the Kartābhajā hierarchy of Kartās and Mahāśays, the tactics of "deliberate mystification, systematic ambiguity, and misrecognition" are commonly deployed by senior adult males in order to preserve and reproduce their superior status over women and younger males. Even more striking examples of the inherently "elitist" role of secrecy can be found in some of the more conservative and aristocratic esoteric traditions of Europe, such as Renaissance Hermeticism, Kabbalah, and Freemasonry. As a number of recent scholars have shown, the secrecy and esoteric ritual of the Masonic lodge worked in most cases not to mask subversive and revolutionary agendas. Rather, not unlike the esoteric hierarchies of the Kartās and Mahāśays of the later Kartābhajā tradition, they often served to reproduce and reinforce the traditional status of the wealthy and powerful classes during precisely those periods in which they were most threatened by the changing forces of society and politics.[18]

Indeed, as Chesneaux acutely points out, even the most seemingly deviant and revolutionary of secret societies—such as the Triad, White Lotus, and other rebellious groups of China—very often reintroduce their own new hierarchies and asymmetries of power. Much like the Kartābhajās, they often re-create hierarchies of power within the secret society which *mirror, mimic, and reproduce* the hierarchies of the dominant social order itself.[19]

Finally, I would hope that we might also apply some of these insights more specifically to cases of secret societies under the unique conditions of colonial rule. As Andrew Apter and others have shown in the case of African societies such as the Yoruba, the role of the secret cult often becomes even more critical and highly volatized during periods of colonial occupation and native resistance. Not only does secrecy allow discontented native factions to remain concealed from their colonial masters and to organize collective resistance, it also invests them with that aura of danger, fear, and "savage mystery" that so often looms within the colonial imagination, with the seeming potential to subvert and unravel the very fabric of colonial rule itself.[20]

But as in virtually all esoteric traditions, the power of secrecy in traditions under colonial rule is also a highly changeable and unpredictable one. It is certainly true that many secret societies become radically polarized as a force of resistance to, and even violent rebellion against, a foreign colonial government, as we see in the case of the Mau Mau in Kenya or in the Revolutionary nationalist societies in twentieth-century Bengal. Yet, at the same time, many secret societies become enmeshed in a far more subtle and complicated pattern of *competition and rivalry* with colonial powers—a pattern that often involves strategies of both collusion and resistance, partial cooperation, and partial subversion of the imperial order. The Chinese Triad societies in colonial Malaysia, for example, became enmeshed in intense economic competition with European capitalists for dominance in business and trade, which involved an ambivalent and constantly shifting "dialectical interplay between induction and resistance," in which "the power relations between the state and the secret orders was subject to maneuver and strategic bargaining by the power agents on both sides."[21] In short, like the Kartābhajās, secret societies under the conditions of colonial rule often find themselves drawn into a dense web of maneuvers, recalibrations, and jockeyings for power, which can seldom be reduced to simple binarisms of hegemony and resistance.

Now, the "content" of the secrecy involved in all these various esoteric traditions is obviously radically different and very much determined by their specific historical and cultural contexts; however, my suspicion is that the *forms and strategies* through which secrecy operates—the tactics of metaphoric disguise, hierarchical access to information, deliberate obfuscation, the dialectics of advertising, lure and withdrawal, and so on—may well turn out to be strikingly similar across cultures and throughout historical periods.

Notes

Introduction

1. The term "esotericism" was first coined by Jacques Matter in 1828, *Histoire critique du gnosticisme et de son influence* (Paris: Levrault, 1828). See Antoine Faivre, "Introduction I," in *Modern Esoteric Spirituality* (New York: Crossroad, 1992), and "Esotericism," in *Encylopedia of Religion*, ed. M. Eliade (New York: Macmillan, 1986), v. 5.

2. See section "The Torment of Secrecy." See also Hugh Urban, "Elitism and Esotericism: Strategies of Secrecy and Power in South Indian Tantra and French Freemasonry," *Numen* 44 (1997), and Urban, "The Torment of Secrecy: Ethical and Epistemological Problems in the Study of Esoteric Traditions," *History of Religions* (1998): 209–48. For reviews of the academic study of secrecy, see Beryl Bellman, *The Language of Secrecy: Symbols and Metaphors in Poro Ritual* (New Brunswick: Rutgers University Press, 1984); T. M. Luhrmann, "The Magic of Secrecy," *Ethos* 17, no. 2 (1989); S. Tefft, ed., *Secrecy: A Cross-Cultural Perspective* (New York: Human Sciences Press, 1980).

3. Mircea Eliade, *Occultism, Witchcraft and Cultural Fashions* (Chicago: University of Chicago Press, 1976), 47–50; Kees Bolle, ed., *Secrecy in Religions* (New York: Brill, 1987); Antoine Faivre and Karen-Claire Voss, "Western Esotericism and the Science of Religions," *Numen* 42 (1995): 48–77. More recently, some better work on secrecy has come forth, which pays more attention to its social and historical contexts; see essays in H. Kippenberg and G. Stroumsa, eds., *Secrecy and Concealment: Studies in the History of Mediterranean and Near Eastern Religions* (Leiden: Brill, 1995).

4. Douglas Brooks, *The Secret of the Three Cities: An Introduction to Hindu Śākta Tantra* (Chicago: University of Chicago Press, 1990), ix.

5. The volume of Sanjukta Gupta, Teun Goudriaan, and Dirk J. Hoens, *Hindu Tantrism* (Leiden: Brill, 1979), for example, limits itself solely to Sanskrit materials and makes only brief inquiry into the social and historical contexts of these traditions. The large body of literature on Kashmir Śaivism includes André Padoux, *Vāc: The Concept of the Word in Selected Hindu Tantras* (Albany: SUNY, 1990); Paul Muller-Ortega, *The Triadic Heart of Shiva: Kaula Tantricism of Abhinavagupta in the Non-dual Shaivism of Kashmir* (Albany: SUNY, 1989); Mark Dyczkowski, *The Doctrine of Vibration: An Analysis of the Doctrines and Practices of Kashmir Shaivism* (Albany: SUNY, 1987).

More promising approaches to the living contexts of Tantra include Jeffrey J. Kripal, *Kālī's Child: The Mystical and the Erotic in the Life and Teachings of Ramakrishna* (Chicago: University of Chicago Press); Douglas Brooks, "Encountering the Hindu 'Other': Tantrism and the Brahmans of South India," *Journal of the American Academy of Religion* 60, no. 3 (1992), 405–36; David Gordon White, *The Alchemical Body: Siddha Traditions in Medieval India*

(Chicago: University of Chicago Press, 1996); Sarah Caldwell, *Oh Terrifying Mother: Sexuality, Violence and Worship of the Goddess Kālī* (New York: Oxford University Press, 1999), and most recently David Gordon White, ed., *Tantra in Practice* (Princeton: Princeton University Press, 2000).

6. Georg Simmel, *The Sociology of Georg Simmel*, ed. K. Wolff (Glencoe: Free Press, 1950), 345. For example, at both the 1995 and 1997 meetings of the American Academy of Religions, fine panels were held on the topic of secrecy in Tantric traditions, but among all the papers presented, there was virtually no mention either of the social and political contexts of secrecy or of the possible comparative implications of the topic. Jeffrey Kripal's paper at the 1997 meeting, which dealt with secrecy in the Rāmakṛṣṇa tradition and the various positive and hostile reactions to his work, is the only notable exception.

7. Padoux, *Vāc,* 31. "Not only do . . . theorists give different definitions of Tantrism, but its very existence has sometimes been denied. . . . But it so happened that it was in texts known as tantras that Western scholars first described practices different from those of classical Hinduism . . . so Western experts adopted the word Tantrism for that particular, and for them, repulsive aspect of Indian religion." André Padoux, "Tantrism, an Overview," in *Encyclopedia of Religion*, ed. M. Eliade (New York: Macmillan, 1986), v. 14, 271–72). John Woodroffe had also made this point long ago (*Shakti and Shākta* [New York: Dover, 1978]), 54. I have engaged the genealogy of Tantrism in Hugh Urban, "The Extreme Orient: The Construction of 'Tantrism' as a Category in the Orientalist Imagination," *Religion* 29 (1999): 127–46.

8. Muhammed Riāzuddin Āhmad, editor of *Islām Pracārak*, January 1903, cited in Debendranāth De, *Kartābhajā Dharmer Itivṛtta* (Calcutta: Jigasa Agencies, 1968), 88–89.

9. Samareś Basu (a.k.a. Kālakūṭa), *Kothāy Se Jan Āche* (Calcutta: De's Publishing, 1983), 25 (emphasis added). Kālakūṭa is a famous Bengali author who has written a number of novels about religious sects such as the Kartābhajās, Bāuls, and others.

10. Kripal, *Kālī's Child,* 29.

11. Lise McKean, *Divine Enterprise: Gurus and the Hindu Nationalist Movement* (Chicago: University of Chicago Press, 1996).

12. For a discussion of the historical sources, see chapter 1, section titled "The Secret Vṛndāvana." The primary text is the *Bhāver Gīta,* ed. Rameścandra Ghoṣe (Calcutta: Aurora Press, 1882); Here I use the recent edition of Śānti Rañjan Cakravartī (Calcutta: Indralekha Press, 1992). Other primary texts include Manulāl Miśra, *Bhāver Gīta Vyākhyā Saha Sahajatattva Prakāśa Vā Sanātana Sahaja Satya Dharmer Ādi Itihāsa* (Calcutta: Author, 1911), and Miśra, *Kartābhajā Dharmer Ādi Vṛttānta Vā Sahajatattva Prakāśa* (Calcutta: Author, 1925).

There are also two important personal accounts by Kartābhajā devotees: that of Babu Gopāl Krishna Pāl in J. H. E. Garrett, *Bengal District Gazetteers, Nadia* (Calcutta: Bengal Secretariat Book Stall, 1910), and that of Krishna Pāl in William Ward, ed., *A Brief Memoir of Krishna Pāl, the First Hindoo in Bengal Who Broke the Chain of Caste by Embracing the Gospel* (London: J. Offer, 1823).

Contemporary newspaper accounts include *Saṃvāda Prabhākara*, 18 Caitra 1254 B.S. [1848]; *Somaprakāśa*, 20 Caitra 1270 B.S. [1864]. Contemporary literary accounts include Dāśarathī Rāy, "Kartābhajā," in *Dāśarathi Rāyer Pāñcālī,* ed. H. P. Cakravartī (Calcutta: University of Calcutta Press, 1962); Nabīncandra Sen, "Ghoṣpāṛār Melā," part 4 of "Āmār Jīban," in *Nabīncandra Racanāvalī* (Calcutta: Baṅgīya-Sāhitya-Pariṣat, 1974), v. 3; and the biographies of Rāmakṛṣṇa, such as *Śrī Śrīrāmakṛṣṇa-Kathāmṛta* by Mahendranāth Gupta (Calcutta: Kathāmṛta Bhāban, 1987) and *Śrīśrīrāmakṛṣṇa-Līlāprasaṅga* by Swami Saradānanda (Calcutta: Udbhodan Kāryālay, 1986). Missionary accounts include William Ward, *Account of the Writings, Religion and Manners of the Hindus* (London: Black, Parbury and Allen, 1817–20); *Church Missionary Register* (June–Oct. 1839); James Long, *Handbook of Bengal Missions* (London: J. F. Shaw, 1848).

13. See chapter 2, section titled "The Janus-Faced Self," and chapter 4, section titled "The Poor Company—A Company of Madmen"; see also Ramakanta Chakrabarty, *Vaiṣṇavism in Bengal, 1486–1900* (Calcutta: Sanskrit Pustak Bandhar, 1985), 379–85.

14. For example, the missionary William Ward and the Orientalist H. H. Wilson, who were among the first authors to write about "Tantrism"—not to mention the father of modern Tantric studies, Sir John Woodroffe, a judge on the High Court of Calcutta. See William Ward, *A View of the History, Literature and Religion of the Hindoos*, v. 2 (London: Kingsbury, Parbury and Allen, 1822); H. H. Wilson, *Essays and Lectures on the Religions of the Hindus* (New Delhi: Asian Publishing, 1976 [1858]); and the many works of John Woodroffe, such as *Principles of Tantra: The Tantratattva of Śrīyukta Śiva Candra Vidyārṇava Bhaṭṭācārya Mahodaya* (Madras: Ganesh, 1960).

15. Rāy, "Kartābhajā," 665.

16. See, e.g., Saradānanda, *Śrīśrīrāmakṛṣṇa-Līlāprasaṅga*, v. 2, 22–23.

17. Brooks, *The Secret of the Three Cities*, 55ff.

18. BG 35–40. According to one Kartābhajā song, "The worship of the Kartā is a delightful thing! It is the true worship. Its whereabouts are not in the injunctions of the Veda—all those are but the business of thievery" (cited in Advaita Dās, *Ghoṣpāṛār Kartābhajā Sampradāya* [Calcutta: Rām Dās, 1983], 47).

19. On Kuṇḍalinī yoga, see Advaita Dās, *Saṅgīta o Darśana* (Calcutta: Cayanikā, 1992), 118–21.

20. The basic Kartābhajā belief is the identity of the chief guru or Kartā with God (Kṛṣṇa-Caitanya); however, Kṛṣṇa himself is only the personal manifestation of the nondual absolute reality, Sahaja (BG 47–50); cf. Dās, *Saṅgīta o Darśana*, 118–20; Chakrabarty, *Vaiṣṇavism in Bengal*, 371–75.

21. Like other Sahajiyās, the Kartābhajās believe in the identity of the name of Kṛṣṇa with the named, God himself and employ secret mantras as the most basic technique of initiation and *sādhanā* (see Satyaśiva Pāl, *Ghoṣpārār Satīmā o Kartābhajā Dharma* [Calcutta: Pustak Bipaṇi, 1990], 261–65).

22. "The Sahajiyā practice, like Tantric practice, is secret. It cannot be revealed to ordinary people. Those who follow this path cannot tell anyone anything about it." Dās, *Saṅgīta o Darśana,* 119. "The essence of the Kartābhajās has remained hidden in secrecy, in the Sahaja language. Their external forms, their rituals and their religious practices, are only manifestations of this Sahaja path." J. Cakravartī, "Kartābhajāner Rūpa o Svarūpa," in *Kartābhajā Dharmamata o Itihāsa,* v. 2, xvi.

23. The secret communal meal shared by members of all castes is one of the most infamous features of the Kartābhajā tradition, and the one most frequently commented on by contemporary observers. Cf. Akṣaykumār Datta, *Bhāratavarṣīya Upāsaka Sampradāya* (Calcutta: Karuṇā Prakāśanī, 1394 B.S.), 223–25. At least some Kartābhajās advocate the use of Tantric sexual rituals, often in violation of caste restrictions. Cf. Dās, *Śrī Satīmā Candrikā* (Calcutta: Firma KLM, 1986), 69–70.

24. For an account of the initiation rite, open to men and women of all castes and religions, see Datta, *Bhāratavarṣīya Upāsaka Sampradāya,* 223n; Chakrabarty, *Vaiṣṇavism in Bengal,* 365–67.

25. Padoux, *Vāc,* 40.

26. Dās, *Saṅgīta o Darśana,* 121.

27. De, *Kartābhajā Dharmer Itivṛtta,* 12.

28. D. C. Sen, *Bṛhat Baṅga: Suprācīn Kāl haite Plāsir Juddha Parjanta* (Calcutta: De's Publishing, 1993), v. 2, 893. Other scholars who identify the Kartābhajās as Sahajiyās or Tāntrikas include De, *Kartābhajā Dharmer Itivṛtta,* 7–10; Upendranāth Bhaṭṭācārya, *Bāṅglār Bāul o Bāul Gān* (Calcutta: Orient Book Co., 1981), 69–70; Tushar Chatterjee, "Some Observations on Guru Cult and Minor Religious Sects of Bengal," *Society and Change* (Jan.–March 1981): 207–11. As Bimalkumār Mukhopādhyāy concludes, "Among the sects spawned by the Sahajiyās, the Kartābhajas should be mentioned first and foremost. It is also the oldest" ("Pravartakakendrik Sahajiyā," in *Kartābhajā Dharmamata o Itihāsa,* v. 2, 1).

29. For example, the recently deceased Kartā, Satyaśiva Pāl, bends over backwards to prove that they are not Tantric (*Ghoṣpārār Satīmā,* 259–62).

30. See Sumanta Banerjee, *The Parlour and the Streets: Elite and Popular Culture in Nineteenth-Century Calcutta* (Calcutta: Seagull, 1989), 69–71.

31. See Hugh Urban, "The Poor Company: Economics and Ecstasy in the Kartābhajā Sect of Colonial Bengal," *South Asia* 19, no. 2 (1996), and Chakrabarty, *Vaiṣṇavism in Bengal,* 375–78.

32. Cakravartī, "Kartābhajāner Rūpa o Svarūpa," xxv.

33. "Calcutta's lower orders remained invisible to the bhadralok society. They found their way into newspaper columns only when they posed a threat to the economic and social comforts of the bhadralok." Sumanta Banerjee, "The World of Ramjan Ostagar the Common Man of Old Calcutta," in *Calcutta the Living City,* Vol. I, *The Past,* ed. S. Chaudhuri (Calcutta: Oxford, 1990), 80.

34. Chakrabarty, *Vaiṣṇavism in Bengal,* 375–78. See Rabindranath Tagore, "The Bāul Singers of Bengal," appendix to *The Religion of Man* (Boston: Beacon Press, 1961); Edward C. Dimock, *The Place of the Hidden Moon: Erotic Mysticism in the Vaiṣṇava Sahajiyā Cult of Bengal* (Chicago: University of Chicago Press, 1966).

35. When Rachel McDermott asked Sen's advice for her dissertation on Kamalākānta, he told her she should abandon it and study the Kartābhajās instead (personal communication, 1995).

The most important English scholarship includes Geoffrey A. Oddie, "Old Wine in New Bottles? Kartābhajā (Vaishnava) Converts to Christianity in Bengal, 1835–1845," *Indian Economic and Social History Review,* 32 no. 3 (1995); Chakrabarty, *Vaiṣṇavism in Bengal,* 346–84. Sumanta Banerjee, "From Aulchand to Satī Mā: The Institutionalization of the Syncretist Karta-bhaja Sect in 19th century Bengal," *Calcutta Historical Journal* 16, no. 2 (1994). The most important Bengali scholarship S. Mitra, ed., *Kartābhajā Dharmamata o Itihāsa* (2 vols.) (Calcutta: De Book Stores, 1976–77); De, *Kartābhajā Dharmer Itivṛtta*; and Ratan Kumār Nandī, *Kartābhajā Dharma o Sāhitya* (Naihati: Asani Press, 1984).

36. Apurna Bhattacharya, *Religious Movements of Bengal, 1800–1850* (Calcutta: Vidyasagar Pustak Mandir, 1981), 47; cf. Kripal, *Kālī's Child,* 223–25. "Why was there such intense opposition to and ridicule of the Kartābhajās? . . . The growing popular support of the Kartābhajās threatened and incited the orthodox Hindus." Sudhīr Cakravartī, *Gabhīr Nirjan Pathe* (Calcutta: Ananda, 1989), 65.

37. Cf. Sudhīr Cakravartī, "Kartābhajāner Rūp o Svarūp," xv; Tuṣār Caṭṭopādhyāy, "Ghoṣpārār Melā, Kartābhajā o Lālan," in *Lālan Sāhitya o Darśana,* ed. K. R. Hāq (Dhaka: Bangla Academy, 1976); for an account by a contemporary literary figure, see Sen, part 4 of "Āmār Jīban," 174–91.

38. Rameścandra Majumdār, ed., *Bāṅglādeśer Itihāsa,* 264–65, cited in De, *Kartābhajā Dharmer Itivṛtta,* 79.

39. Sudhīr Cakravartī, *Paścim Baṅger Melā o Mahotsava* (Calcutta: Pustak Bipaṇi, 1996), 161. "Calcutta's bhadralok society was quick to condemn the Kartābhajās as a religion of *itar* people and prostitutes who were promiscuous in their habits and violated the norms of Hindu religion." Banerjee, *The Parlour*, 69.

40. Nandī, *Kartābhajā Dharma,* 67. For accounts of the Ghoshpara Melā today, see Cakravartī, *Paścim Baṅger Melā*; and Māṇik Sarkār, "Ghoṣpārār Melā," in *Kartābhajā Dharmamata o Itihāsa*, v. 2.

41. For the most intelligent discussions of comparison in the history of religions, see Jonathan Z. Smith, *Map Is Not Territory: Studies in the History of Religions* (Chicago: University of Chicago Press, 1978), 240–64, and Smith, *Imagining Religion: From Babylon to Jonestown* (Chicago: University of Chicago Press, 1986); Fitz John Porter Poole, "Metaphors and Maps: Towards Comparison in the Anthropology of Religion," *Journal of the American Academy of Religion*, 54, no. 3 (1986). As Smith puts it: "Comparison does not tells us how things 'are' . . . like models and metaphors, comparison tells us how things might be . . . 're-described', in Max Black's term . . . comparison provides the means by which we 're-vision' phenomena to solve *our* theoretical problems." *Drudgery Divine: On the Comparison of Early Christianities and the Religions of Late Antiquity* (Chicago: University of Chicago Press, 1990), 52.

42. See Smith, *Imagining Religion*, introduction; Cristiano Grotanelli and Bruce Lincoln, "A Brief Note on (Future) Research in the History of Religions," *Center for Humanistic Studies Occasional Papers,* no. 4 (Minneapolis: University of Minnesota, 1985). "Religions should be studied as . . . social and historical entities, within their proper cultural context. They must be studied not only as phenomena that change . . . but as expressions of broader tensions within social configurations and . . . as vehicles of conflict."

43. Bruce Lincoln, "Theses on Method," *Method and Theory in the Study of Religion* 8, no. 3 (1996), 225.

44. See Pierre Bourdieu, *The Logic of Practice* (Stanford: Stanford University Press, 1981); Michel Foucault, *The History of Sexuality,* Vol. 1: *An Introduction* (New York: Vintage, 1978). I also use the work of de Certeau to criticize Bourdieu's often static and reified model of the social order. See Michel de Certeau, *The Practice of Everyday Life* (Berkeley: University of California Press, 1984).

45. In a lucid discussion, Martha Kaplan identifies three primary strategies used to analyze situations of colonial rule. The first, as we see in Sahlins's work, emphasizes the lasting importance of indigenous categories of meaning and native agency. The second, as we see in Eric Wolf's work, sees colonial power as an overwhelming hegemonic force that has forever changed the world of the colonized. The third, represented by Michael Taussig's work, sees the colonial space as a jungle or chaotic space of terror, which is neither indigenous nor colonial but an epistemic murk (*Neither Cargo nor Cult: Ritual Politics and the Colonial Imagination in Fiji* [Durham, N.C.: Duke University Press, 1995], 2–3). Kaplan's own approach, to which I would also subscribe, emphasizes both the creative agency of the colonized to make their own history and the dominant power of the colonial state to shape and constrain that history.

46. Jean and John Comaroff, eds., *Modernity and Its Malcontents: Ritual and Power in Postcolonial Africa* (Chicago: University of Chicago Press, 1993), xi-ii; cf. Jean Comaroff, *Body of Power, Spirit of Revolution: The Culture and History of a South African People* (Chicago: University of Chicago Press, 1985), 131, 236–38; Marshall Sahlins, "Cosmologies of Capitalism: The Trans-Pacific Sector of the World System," *Proceedings of the British Academy* 74 (1988); Michael Taussig, *The Devil and Commodity Fetishism in South America* (Chapel Hill: University of North Carolina Press, 1980).

I am also in basic sympathy with the members of the Subaltern Studies Collective; see R. Guha, ed., *Subaltern Studies: Writing on South Asian History and Society,* Vol. 1. (Delhi: Oxford, 1982); Partha Chatterjee, *The Nation and Its Fragments: Colonial and Postcolonial Histories* (Princeton: Princeton University Press, 1993).

47. The literature on postcolonial theory is obviously vast and rapidly growing; see, for starters, Homi K. Bhabha, *The Location of Culture* (London: Routledge, 1994); Franz Fanon, *The Wretched of the Earth* (New York: Grove Press, 1961); Edward Said, *Culture and Imperialism* (New York: Knopf, 1994); B. Ashcroft, G. Griffiths, and H. Tiffin, *The Empire Writes Back: Theory and Practice in Post-colonial Literatures* (London: Routledge, 1989), 33.

48. For good criticisms of postcolonial discourse, see Russell Jacoby, "Marginal Returns: The Trouble with Post-Colonial Theory," *Lingua Franca* (Sept.–Oct. 1995); Rosalind O'Hanlon, "Recovering the Subject: Subaltern Studies and Histories of Resistance in Colonial South Asia," *Modern Asian Studies* 22, no. 1 (1988): 189–224; Sara Suleri, *The Rhetoric of British India* (Chicago: University of Chicago Press, 1992); Anne McClintock, *Imperial Leather: Race, Gender and Sexuality in the Colonial Context* (New York: Routledge, 1995). McClintock suggests that postcolonialism is "prematurely celebratory and obfuscatory" and is "haunted by 19th century ideals of linear progress"; it reifies a singular, monolithic non-Western Other and in so doing masks subtle forms of *neocolonialism* (*Imperial Leather,* 13).

49. "Indians remained . . . active agents and not passive victims in the creation of colonial India. . . . There were many threads of continuity between precolonial India and the India of the East India Company." Bayly, *Indian Society and the Making of the British Empire* (Cambridge: Cambridge University Press, 1988), 5. See David Washbrook, "Law, State and Agrarian Society in Colonial India," *Modern Asian Studies* 15 (1981).

50. John Kelly, *A Politics of Virtue: Hinduism, Sexuality and Countercolonial Discourse in Fiji* (Chicago: University of Chicago Press, 1991), xiv. See Aiwa Ong, *Spirits of Resistance and Capitalist Discipline: Factory Women in Malaysia* (Albany: SUNY, 1987), 216–17. See also Talal Asad's criticism of the overemphasis on "agency" and the autonomous subject (*Genealogies of Religion: Discipline and Reasons of Power in Christianity and Islam* [Baltimore: Johns Hopkins University Press, 1993]).

51. The metaphor of the "bazaar of the world" (*bhava-bājār*) and the "bazaar of love" (*prema-bājār*) appear ubiquitously throughout the *Bhāver Gīta;* see BG 41–46; appendix II.1–56. For an excellent discussion of the use of the "market metaphor," see Sudipta Sen, "Passages of Authority: Rulers, Traders and Marketplaces in Bengal and Banaras, 1700–1750," *Calcutta Historical Journal* 17, no. 1 (1996).

52. A good deal of literature has been devoted to the definition of "secrecy" and its distinction from "privacy." Here I am following the model suggested by Edward Shils, as modified by recent theorists such as Carol Warren, Barbara Laslett, and Stanton Tefft. According to Shils, privacy is characterized by the *voluntary concealment* of information or behaviors, whereas secrecy is characterized by the *obligatory concealment* of information, with a prohibition attended by sanctions. Shils, *The Torment of Secrecy The Background and Consequences of American Security Policies* (Carbondale: Southern Illinois University Press 1956), 26–27. Warren and Laslett, on the other hand, distinguish privacy and secrecy not by the volition of their possessor but, rather, by their *moral or legal content.* Thus, privacy refers to information or behaviors that are morally and legally neutral (e.g., marital sex), whereas secrecy refers to those considered immoral or illegal by mainstream society. Then, within the realm of secrecy, Warren and Laslett further distinguish between (1) "private life secrecy"—or the concealment of behaviors that outsiders consider undesirable, immoral, or illegal (e.g., homo-

sexuality or child abuse); and (2) "public life secrecy"—which concerns primarily political secrecy by governmental agents (e.g., the CIA or FBI) directed against political opponents ("Privacy and Secrecy: A Conceptual Comparison," in *Secrecy: A Cross-Cultural Perspective,* ed. S. Tefft [New York: Human Sciences Press, 1980], 25–28; see Tefft's "Introduction" to the same volume).

53. I am indebted to Tony Stewart, both through his written work and numerous personal conversations over the last several years, for his insights into the "double bind" or "Gordion Knot" of secrecy. See his as yet unpublished manuscript, "Sex, Secrecy and the Politics of Sahajiyā Scholarship Or: Caveats from a Faint-hearted Student of Tantra (1990).

54. De, *Kartābhajā Dharmer Itivṛtta,* 17

55. Caṭṭopādhyāy, "Ghoṣpāṛār Melā," 133. As Maulavi Abdul Wali apologetically explained in his famous early account of the Bāuls and Faqirs of Bengal, he was ultimately unable to penetrate into the esoteric practices of these very guarded men: "The Faqirs would in no case meet me, the tracts written by them were all composed in their mystic language. . . . I despaired of adding to my scanty knowledge as to their abominable habits." "On Some Curious Tenets and Practices of Certain Class of Fakirs of Bengal," *Journal of the Anthropological Society of Bombay* (November 30, 1898).

56 I interviewed several dozen Kartābhajās from various parts of rural West Bengal and Bangladesh and had the opportunity to work closely with three higher-level gurus in Calcutta. After much deliberation, however, I have decided, out of respect for the privacy of my informants, not to use the real names of any living Kartābhajās in this book. Although some readers might feel this goes against my larger principle of "upfrontness" in the study of esoteric traditions, I cannot in good conscience name my sources without their informed consent—especially when I am dealing with subject matter that could potentially be quite damaging to their reputations. Although it is by no means an ideal solution to the ethical-epistemic double bind, I will therefore use pseudonyms wherever it is necessary to refer to individuals by name.

57. George Marcus and Michael Fischer, *Anthropology as Cultual Critique: An Experimental Moment in the Human Sciences* (Chicago: University of Chicago Press, 1986), 7–10. For discussions of these problems in recent ethnography, see James Clifford and George Marcus, *Writing Culture: The Poetics and Politics of Ethnography* (Berkeley: University of California Press, 1986); John and Jean Comaroff, *Ethnography and the Historical Imagination* (Boulder: Westview Press, 1990).

58. Clifford and Marcus, *Writing Culture,* 8.

59. For a good overview of the main approaches to secrecy—sociological, psychological, political, etc., see Bellman, *The Language of Secrecy,* ch. 1; Luhrmann, "The Magic of Secrecy"; Tefft, "Introduction," in *Secrecy*. For the major sociological approaches see Simmel, "The Secret and the Secret Society," 307–76; Phillip Bonacich, "Secrecy and Solidarity," *Sociometry* 39 (1976): 200–208; Barbara Ponse, "Secrecy in the Lesbian World," *Urban Life* 5 (1976): 313–38; Warren and Laslett, "Privacy and Secrecy," in *Secrecy.*

For the perennialist view, see René Guénon, *Aperçus sur l'initiation* (Paris: Gallimard, 1946); Frithjof Schuon, *Esoterism as Principle and as Way* (Bloomington: World Wisdom Books, 1986).

60. Simmel, *The Sociology of Georg Simmel*, 331.

61. According to Norman MacKenzie, there are nine primary types: (1) patriotic; (2) racial; (3) political; (4) economic; (5) civic; (6) religious; (7) military; (8) scientific; and (9) judicial. *Secret Societies* (New York; Holt, Rhinehart & Winston, 1967). Mak Lou Fong uses

R. K. Merton's sociological model of the five modes of role adaptation: conformity, retreatism, ritualism, innovation, and rebellion. *The Sociology of Secret Societies: Study of Chinese Secret Societies in Singapore and Peninsular Malaysia* (New York: Oxford, 1981), 11–12. For other typologies, see C. W. Heckethorn, *The Secret Societies of all Ages and Countries* (New Hyde Park: University Books, 1965 [1875]).

62. Tony Stewart, "Sex, Secrecy and the Politics of Sahajiya Scholarship," 41.

63. James Clifford, *The Predicament of Culture: 20th Century Ethnograhy, Literature and Art* (Cambridge: Harvard University Press, 1988), 67. On the problem of the "commodity economy" of anthropology, see George Stocking, *The Ethnographer's Magic and Other Essays in the History of Anthropology* (Madison: University of Wisconsin Press, 1992), 179–80.

64. Marcel Griaule, *Les Sao Legendaires* (Paris: Gallimard, 1943), 74 (emphasis added).

65. Marcel Griaule, *Methode de l'ethnographie* (Paris: Gallimard, 1957), 59.

66. Lamont Lindstrom, *Knowledge and Power in a South Pacific Society* (Washington: Smithsonian Institute, 1990), 200.

67. Among the few authors to grapple with the ethical problem are Kripal in *Kālī's Child* and Sisella Bok, *Secrets: On the Ethics of Concealment and Revelation* (New York: Pantheon, 1982); however, Bok's comments are largely limited to raising the major questions, offering very little in the way of concrete solutions. In the field of Tantric studies, Tony Stewart has tackled the problem in his essay, "Sex, Secrecy and the Politics of Sahajiyā Scholarship"; however, Stewart's conclusions are generally quite pessimistic about the prospects of a solution to the problem.

68. This is the approach adopted by most scholars of Jewish and Western esoteric traditions, such as Gershom Scholem, Antoine Faivre, H. Kippenberg, and G. Stroumsa, and so on. Cf. Gershom Scholem, *Major Trends in Jewish Mysticism* (New York: Shocken, 1961), 21–25; Faivre, *Modern Esoteric Spirituality*; Kippenberg, "Introduction," in *Secrecy and Concealment*.

69. See Dimock, *The Place of the Hidden Moon*, 39n; Padoux, *Vāc*; Sanjukta Gupta, *Hindu Tantrism*. (Londen: E. J. Brill 1979).

70. Among anthropologists, this is the approach adopted, for example, by Andrew Apter, *Black Critics and Kings: The Hermeneutics of Power in Yoruba Society* (Chicago: University of Chicago Press, 1992). For a good example of this "insider's" approach" to the Voodoo tradition, see Karen McCarthy Brown, *Mama Lola: A Vodou Priestess in Brooklyn* (Berkeley: University of California Press, 1991).

71. Miranda Shaw, *Passionate Enlightenment: Women in Tantric Buddhism* (Princeton: Princeton University Press, 1995).

72. Brooks, *The Secret of the Three Cities*, 6–7.

73. Even in his most work on the Siddha Yoga tradition, Brooks never really engages these issues. See S. P. Sabharathnam, Douglas Renfrew Brooks, Constantina Rhodes Bailly, William K. Mahony, Paul E. Muller-Ortega, Swami Durgananda, and Peggy Bendet, *Meditation Revolution: A History and Theology of the Siddha Yoga Lineage* (Agama Press, 1998).

74. Fredrik Barth, *Ritual and Knowledge among the Baktaman of New Guinea* (New Haven: Yale University Press, 1975), 7.

75. Barth, *Ritual and Knowledge*, 6. A similar case occurred among the Telefolmin peoples of New Guinea, who were about to lose a cult center to the construction of copper mines. To preserve their sacred lore, they invited an anthropologist to come and study materials which had formerly been kept strictly secret ("Prompt Assistance for Telefolmin," *Cultural Survival* 3 [Spring 1979]).

76. Edward Conze, *Buddhist Thought in India: Three Phases of Buddhist Philosophy* (Ann Arbor: University of Michigan, 1967), 271–73.

77. "A theoretical shift had been required to analyze . . . the manifestations of power; it led me to examine . . . the *open strategies and the rational techniques* that articulate the exercise of powers." Foucault, *The History of Sexuality,* Vol. 2. *The Use of Pleasure*, 6.

78. Bruce Lincoln suggests a similar shift in his study of "authority." Rather than a concrete entity, authority is best understood as a complex "effect" produced by a whole set of interdependent relations—the right speaker, the right context, the right time and place, the right props, and so on. *Authority: Construction and Corrosion* (Chicago: University of Chicago Press, 1994).

79. Bellman, *The Language of Secrecy,* 144.

80. Some scholars like Walter Burkert have suggested that the "secrets" of cults like the ancient Mysteries were really quite banale and meaningless; what was important was simply the fact that it was highly prized and could grant prestige ("Der Geheime Reiz des Verbogenen: Antike Mysterienkulte," in *Secrecy and Concealment,* 79–100). However, as Andrew Apter points out, even though it is tempting to dismiss secrets as mere "vehicles of deliberate mystification" or "manufactured illusions," this is ultimately inadequate for understanding the deeper power of secrecy: "The possibility that ritual vessels are semantically empty is intriguing but inaccurate. Cult members do divulge esoteric knowledge, circuitously, in fragments, under exceptional conditions . . . ritual symbols are neither aribitrary nor meaningless, but are indices of political power." *Black Critics and Kings*, 86.

81. Pierre Bourdieu, *Outline of a Theory of Practice* (Cambridge: Cambridge University Press, 1977), 178; see Bourdieu, "The Forms of Capital," in *Handbook of Theory and Research of the Sociology of Education*, ed. J. Richardson (New York: Greenwood Press, 1986), 252. "Symbolic capital is . . . economic or political capital that is disavowed, misrecognized and thereby recognized, hence legitimate, a credit . . . which in the long run guarantees economic profit." Bourdieu, *The Field of Cultural Production* (New York: Columbia University Press, 1994), 75.

82. Bourdieu, "The Forms of Capital," 252–55.

83. Bourdieu, *The Logic of Practice*, 123. "The transformation of any kind of capital into symbolic capital, a legitimate possession . . . is the fundamental operation of social alchemy" (ibid, 129).

84. See Bourdieu, "The Economics of Linguistic Exchange," *Social Science Information,* 16 (1977): 645–68, and *Language and Symbolic Power* (Cambridge: Harvard University Press, 1984), 77.

85. Luhrmann, "The Magic of Secrecy," 161, 137; cf. Bok, *Secrets*, 282: "Control over secrecy and concealment gives power."

86. Lindstrom, *Knowledge and Power in a South Pacific Society,* 119, xii–xiii.

87. Simmel, *The Sociology of Georg Simmel*, 337. "The secret operates as an adorning possession. . . . This involves the contradiction that what recedes before the consciousness of others and is hidden is emphasized in their consciousness; that one appears noteworthy through what one conceals" (ibid.).

88. "The practices we describe as economic in the narrow sense (buying and selling commodities) are a sub-category of practices pertaining to a specific field, the market. . . . But there are other sub-categories of practice which pertain to other fields, the fields of literature, art, politics and religion; these fields are characterized by their own properties, forms of capital, profit, etc. . . . Bourdieu does not wish to reduce all social fields to the economy . . . he wishes to treat the economy in the narrow sense as one field among a

plurality of fields which are not reducible to one another." Thompson, Introduction to *Language and Symbolic Power*, 15; cf. Peter Jenkins, *Pierre Bourdieu* (London: Routledge, 1990), 87.

89. Sen, "Passages of Authority"; and *Conquest of Marketplaces: Exchange, Authority and Conflict in Early Colonial North India* (Ph.D. diss., University of Chicago, 1994). On the Kartābhajā use of economic terminology, see Urban, "The Poor Company"; Chakrabarty, *Vaiṣṇavism in Bengal*, 378–80.

90. Comaroff, *Body of Power*, 5. See de Certeau, *The Practice of Everyday Life*, 59, 60; Jenkins, *Pierre Bourdieu*, 97; Craig Calhoun, "Habitus, Field, Capital," in *Bourdieu Critical Perspectives*, ed. C. Calhoun et al. (Chicago: University of Chicago Press), 69, 93–94. As John Fiske summarizes, "I find Bourdieu's work very productive, provided that we don't buy into . . . a rigid deterministic framework . . . his account is much too deterministic and doesn't allow enough for . . . social agents having to negotiate these multiple contradictions that . . . capitalism faces us with." "Cultural Studies and the Culture of Everyday Life," in *Cultural Studies*, ed. L. Grossberg et al. (London: Routledge, 1992), 166.

91. Recently, Bourdieu has briefly discussed the possibilities for symbolic resistance in the case of language use and linguistic exchange—for example, the use of "slang" and language which deliberately rejects legitimate, official linguistic forms (*Language and Symbolic Power*, 94–97).

92. As de Certeau argues, Bourdieu's concept of strategy remains oddly limited and restricted. For Bourdieu the strategies of a social agent are in most cases "unconscious" and not subject to intentional calculation; they are "the capacity for rule governed improvisation" which goes on beneath the surface of conscious agency. "The habitus is the source of these moves which are objectively organized as strategies *without being the product of a genuine strategic intention." Outline of a Theory of Practice*, 7. Thus, de Certeau concludes, "there is no choice among several possibilities, and thus no strategic intention . . . there is only an assumed world as the repetition of the past. . . . *Docta ignorantia*, therefore, a cleverness that does not recognize itself as such." *The Practice of Everyday Life*, 56.

93. "I call a strategy the calculus of force relationships which becomes possible when a subject of will and power (a proprietor, an enterprise, a city, a scientific institution) can be isolated from an environment. . . . Political, economic, and scientific rationality has been constructed on a strategic model. I call a tactic on the other hand a calculus which cannot count on . . . a spatial or institutional location. . . . The place of the tactic belongs to the other. A tactic insinuates itself into the other's place, fragmentarily. . . . The weak must continually turn to their own ends forces alien to them. . . . Many everyday practices (talking, reading, moving about, shopping) are tactical in character. And so are . . . many ways of operating: victories of the weak over the strong . . . clever tricks, knowing how to get away with things, hunter's cunning, maneuvers. . . . The Greeks called these ways of operating (*metis*)." de Certeau, *The Practice of Everyday Life*, xix.

94. de Certeau, *The Practice of Everyday Life*, xi-xii. For similar discussion of the tactics employed by ordinary "consumers," see the works of the British Cultural studies school, e.g., Raymond Williams, *The Long Revolution* (London: Routledge, 1961); Stuart Hall and Tony Jefferson, eds., *Resistance through Rituals: Youth Subcultures in Post-War Britain* (London: Routledge, 1993); Paul Willis, *Working Class Culture: Studies in History and Theory* (London: Routledge, 1979); L. Grossberg, C. Nelson, P. Treichler, eds. *Cultural Studies* (London: Routledge, 1992).

95. Bruce Lincoln, *Discourse and the Construction of Society: Comparative Studies in Myth, Ritual and Classification* (New York: Oxford, 1989), 5–7.

96. Foucault, *The History of Sexuality*, 101. "Two basic types of secret societies exist:

those that support the existing political leadership . . . and those that oppose the status quo. The first type . . . enables political leaders to deny outsiders access to the appropriate knowledge (inside secrets) that legitimizes their power . . . secret societies of the second type employ secrecy to protect their membership from punishment or deny their enemies knowledge of the . . . strategies (strategic secrets)." Tefft, "Introduction," in *Secrecy*, 14.

97. Wade Davis, *Passage of Darkness: The Ethnobiology of the Haitian Zombie* (Chapel Hill: University of North Carolina Press, 1988), 284. See also Urban, "Elitism and Esotericism."

98. *The Sociology of Georg Simmel,* 365. As Abner Cohen has shown in his study of Masonry among the Creoles of Freetown, membership in a secret society helps to reinforce the "distinctiveness" of elite culture, while providing the aura of profundity and power which mystifies their elite status: "Membership is taken as a privilege and Masons are proud of it. . . . Masonry [is] a mechanism for the development of the 'mystique' which marks their distinctiveness." *The Politics of Elite Culture: Explorations in the Dramaturgy of Power in Modern African Society* (Berkeley: University of California Press 1981). 124. See also Richard Schaefer, "The Ku Klux Klans' Successful Management of Secrecy," in *Secrecy,* 163.

99. Ian Keen, *Knowledge and Secrecy in an Aboriginal Religion* (Oxford: Clarendon, 1994), 254.

100. Lynn Dumenil, *Freemasonry and Americn Culture, 1880–1930* (Princeton: Princeton University Press, 1984), 30. A similar argument has recently been made by David Ownby and Mary Somers Heidhues in the case of Chinese secret societies: *Secret Societies Reconsidered: Perspectives on the Social History of Modern South China and Southeast Asia* (London: M. E. Sharpe, 1993), 5–10.

101. Douglas Brooks, *Auspicious Wisdom: The Texts and Traditions of Śrīvidyā Śākta Tantrism in South India* (Albany: SUNY, 1992), 188. See also Sanderson, "Purity and Power."

102. Brown, *Mama Lola,* 378–79. See also Tiryakian, "Toward the Sociology of Esoteric Culture;" E. J. Hobsbawm, *Primitive Rebels: Studies in Archaic Forms of Social Movement in the 19th and 20th Centuries* (New York: Prager, 1959); and Ponse, "Secrecy in the Lesbian World."

103. On the role of secret societies in the Nationalist Movement, see Leonard Gordon, *Bengal: The Nationalist Movement, 1876–1940* (New York: Columbia University Press, 1974).

104. James C. Scott, *Domination and the Arts of Resistance: Hidden Transcripts* (New Haven: Yale University Press, 1990), 4–5, 121.

105. Scott, *Domination and the Arts of Resistance,* 18, 12. "Every subordinate group creates . . . a hidden transcript that represents a critique of power spoken behind the back of the dominant. The powerful . . . also develop a hidden transcript representing the claims of their rule that cannot be openly avowed. . . . [T]he process of domination generates a hegemonic public conduct and a backstage discourse consisting of what cannot be spoken in the face of power" (xii).

106. On the topic of censorship, see Sue Curry Jansen, *Censorship: the Knot that Binds Power and Knowledge* (New York: Oxford 1988); Ilan Peleg, ed., *Patterns of Censorship around the World* (Boulder: Westview Press, 1993). There is large body of literature on freedom of speech and censorship, though primarily in Western political thought; the classic works include J. B. Bury, A *History of Freedom of Thought* (London: Oxford, 1913); George Putnam, *The Censorship of the Church of Rome and Its Influence upon the Production and Distribution of Literature* (New York: G.P.Putnam's Sons, 1967 [1906]).

107. Jansen, *Censorship,* 14, cf. 6–7.

108. Jansen, *Censorship,* 184.

109. Scott, *Domination,* 138–39.

110. Jansen, *Censorship*, 81–82. See Leo Strauss, *Persecution and the Art of Writing* (Glencoe: Free Press, 1952).

111. Sigmund Freud, "The Interpretation of Dreams," in *The Basic Writings of Sigmund Freud*, ed. A. A. Brill (New York: Modern Library, 1938), 223.

112. See Nicholas Dirks, *Colonialism's Culture: Anthropology, Travel and Government* (Princeton: Princeton University Press 1994), 15; Marianna Torgovnick, *Gone Primitive: Savage Intellects, Modern Lives* (Chicago: University of Chicago Press 1990). As Torgovnick puts it, "Primitives are our untamed selves, our id forces—libidinous, irrational, violent, dangerous" (8). On the fear of the "wild man" or savage in South America, see Michael Taussig, *Shamanism, Colonialism and the Wild Man: A Study in Terror and Healing* (Chicago: University of Chicago Press, 1987).

As Tefft comments, "In colonial situations secret societies often oppose the spread of foreign groups who compete with them. . . . Loyalty to the secret order insulates the membership and prevent them from making contact with foreigners who might undermine . . . traditional associations." "Introduction," in *Secrecy,* 55.

113. Valentine Chirol, *Indian Unrest* (London: Macmillan, 1910), 346. As Sir George MacMunn put it, "wherever political agitation assumes the most virulent character, there the Hindu revival assumes the most extravagant shapes." *The Underworld of India* (London: MacMillan, 1933), 156.

114. Lindstrom, for example, has studied the peoples of the South Pacific Islands, where there is a high value placed on protected domains of cultural knowledge: when faced with Western domination and anthropological scrutiny, these mechanisms of secrecy and silence often become even more elaborate and more protective of their cultural secrets. "Protected by marginal silence, resistant local modes of information persevere. . . . Silencing as a procedural tactic endeavors to protect local relation of conversational domination." *Knowledge and Power*, 196. For a good study of the changing shape of secret societies under colonial rule, see Wolfgang Kempf, "Ritual, Power and Colonial Domination: Male Initiation among the Ngaing of Papua New Guinea," in *Syncretism/Anti-Syncretism: The Politics of Religious Synthesis,* eds. C. Stewart and R. Shaw (London: Routledge, 1994), 110.

115. Sumit Sarkar, *An Exploraton of the Ramakrsihna Vivekanada Tradition* (Simla: Indian Institute of Cultural Studies, 1993), 45. On Rāmakṛṣṇa's ambivalence toward Tantra, see Kripal, *Kālī's Child*, passim.

116. Kripal, *Kālī's Child*, 24–25, 32. On the *Mahānirvāṇa Tantra,* see Hugh Urban, "The Strategic Uses of an Esoteric Text: *The Mahānirvāṇa Tantra*," *South Asia* 18, no. 1 (1995), 55–82.

117. Stewart, "Sex, Secrecy and the Politics of Sahajiyā Scholarship," 39.

118. The Bengali here is *atisāri hay*—literally, to suffer "morbid looseness of the bowels, diarrhoea, or dysentary."

Chapter 1

1. Edward C. Dimock Jr., trans. *The Caitanya Caritāmṛta of Kṛṣṇadāsa Kavirāja* (Cambridge: Harvard University Press, 2000), 981.

2. Personal communication, September 26, 1996.

3. "*Bāulke kahio; loke hailo Bāul; Bāulke kahio; hāṭe nā bikāy cāul. Bāulke kahio; kāye nāhik āul; Bāulke kahio; ihā kahiyāche Bāul.*" CC, Antya Līlā, 19.18–21; trans. by Dimock, *The Caitanya Caritāmṛta,* 981.

4. Nāth, commentary on CC, Antya, 19.18–21, v. 5, 652–53. According to Rādhāgovinda, a *praheli* verse is "one whose deeper meaning is secret."

5. "The Company [Gauḍīya Vaiṣṇavism] was very rich. But its porters were extremely poor. They starved and begged, but the kings who controlled the Company were worthless men given to robbery. Out of the ruins of the Company a new Company was made." Chakrabarty, *Vaiṣṇavism in Bengal,* 378, paraphrasing BG [1882] 124–26.

6. *De, Kartābhajā Dharmer Itivṛtta,* 25–26.

7. Interviewed at Dās's home in Calcutta, August 8, 1996.

8. Daniel Bloom, *Kabbalah and Criticism* (New York: Seabury Press, 1975), 125–26. See also Bloom, *A Map of Misreading* (New York: Oxford, 1975); Daniel O'Keefe, *Stolen Lightning: The Social Theory of Magic* (New York: Vintage, 1982). As Bloom puts it, "a reading, to be strong, must be a misreading, for no strong reading can fail to insist upon itself. . . . Interpretation is revisionism and the strongest readers so revise as to make every text belated . . . earlier and fresher than any completed text could hope to be." *Kabbalah and Criticism,* 125.

9. See Sen, "Passages of Authority," and *Conquest of Marketplaces.* On the market metaphor generally, see Bourdieu, *The Field of Cultural Production.* For a good example of the market metaphor in earlier Vaiṣṇava texts, see *Hāṭ Pattan,* in *Sāhitya Pariṣat Patrikā,* 1–2 (1908). On the Kartābhajās' use of market imagery, Urban, "The Poor Company."

10. See Amiya Kumar Bagchi, "Wealth and Work in Calcutta, 1860–1921," in *Calcutta: The Living City:* Vol. 1, *The Past,* ed. S. Chaudhuri (Delhi: Oxford, 1990), 212; and Sabyasachi Bhattacharya, "Traders and Trading in Old Calcutta," in *Calcutta: The Living City,* 203. As Śaktināth Jhā comments, "The East India Company monopolised the control of business in this era, and many small merchants had to take loans from Moneylenders, lost their wealth and fell into poverty. . . . Because of thievery or natural disasters, many small merchants fell into poverty." *Phakir Lālan Sāiṅ: Deś, Kāl Ebaṅg Silpa* (Calcutta: Saṃvāda Prakāśaka, 1995), 218.

11. Oddie, "Old Wine in New Bottles?" 329.

12. Bhuvanamohan Gaṅgopādhyāy, "Preface," in *Śrī Śrī Juter Pada* (Calcutta, 1298 B.S. [1891]), 3.

13. For this legend, see Miśra, *Kartābhajā Dharmer Ādivṛttānta* (KDA), 1–71.

14. See the classic work of Shashibhushan Dasgupta, *Obscure Religious Cults, as a Background to Bengali Literature* (Calcutta: Firma KLM, 1962), and Dimock, *The Place of the Hidden Moon.* For a good background on the cultural and economic context of the Vaiṣṇava, Sahajiyā, Bāul, and Sufi traditions during the Mughal era, see Sanatkumār Naskār, *Mughal Juger Bāṅglā Sāhitya* (Calcutta: Ratnāvalī, 1995).

15. M. M. Bose, *The Post-Caitanya Sahajiā Cult of Bengal* (Calcutta: University of Calcutta, 1930). Sahaja is "the natural tendency one poses from birth. . . . Love is a natural characteristic of the Supreme Being possessed by man by virtue of his origin from the Eternal Spirit" (vi).

16. Deben Bhattacharya, *Love Songs of Chandidas* (London: Allen & Unwin, 1967), 82.

17. H. P. Śāstrī, *Bauddhagān o Dohā* (Calcutta: Baṅgīya Sāhitya Pariṣat, 1917); Sukumār Sen, *Caryāgīti-padāvalī* (Burdwan: Sāhitya Sabhā, 1956); Atindra Mojumdar, *The Caryapadas* (Calcutta: Naya Prokash, 1973). On the use of *sandābhāṣā,* see chapter 3 (this volume).

18. Among the more important Vaiṣṇava Sahajiyā texts are the following: Ākiñcana Dāsa, *Vivarta Vilāsa* (Calcutta: Tārācāṅd Dās, 1948); the collection, *Sahajiyā Sāhitya* (SS), ed. M. M. Bose (Calcutta: University of Calcutta, 1932), which contains the *Ānandabhairava* and *Āmṛtarasāvalī*; the anthology *Baṅga-sāhitya paricaya,* ed. D. C. Sen (Calcutta: University of

Calcutta, 1914), which contains the *Prema-vilāsa, Sahajatattva* and other Sahajiyā texts; and the *Vaiṣṇava-granthāvalī,* ed. S. Basu (Calcutta: Basumatī Sāhitya Mandir, 1342 B.S. [1935]), which contains the *Durlabhasāra* and *Ātma-tattva.*

Secondary literature on the Vaiṣṇava Sahajiyās includes—in addition to the classic works of Dimock, Bose, and Dasgupta—Paritosh Das, *Vaiṣṇava Sahajiyā Cult of Bengal and Pañca Śākhā Cult of Orissa* (Calcutta: Firma KLM, 1988); Glen A. Hayes, *Shapes for the Soul: A Study of Body Symbolism in the Vaiṣṇava Sahajiyā Tradition of Medieval Bengal* (Ph.D. diss., University of Chicago, 1985). For a good overview of the literature see Stewart, "Sex, Secrecy and the Politics."

19. *Vivarta Vilāsa,* 10. Cf. Bose, *Post Caitanya Sahajiā Cult,* 278.

20. Dimock, *The Place of the Hidden Moon,* 15.

21. Bhattacharya, *Love Songs of Chandidas,* 156. "In the abandonment of the Vedas and the giving up of family is the birth of *prema*" (SS, pada 38, attributed to Caitanyadās).

22. Dimock, *The Place of the Hidden Moon,* 109.

23. Almost from the first penetration of Sufism into India, we find Sufis circulating classic yogic texts such as the *Āmṛta-Kuṇḍa,* which was translated into Arabic as early as the thirteenth century. By the sixteenth century, authors such as Saiyīd Sultān, Ali Rāzā, or Saiyīd Martūza had forged a rich synthesis of Sufi mysticism with Tantric and yogic techniques. See the works of Saiyīd Sultān, such as the *Jñān Pradīp, Nabī-baṃśa* and others in Āhmad Śarīph, ed., *Nabī-baṃśa* (Dhaka: Bangla Academy, 1978). See also M. R. Tarafdar, *Husain Shahi Bengal, 1494–1538, A Socio-Political Study* (Dhaka: Bangla Academy, 1965); Muhammad Enamul Haq, *A History of Sufi-ism in Bengal* (Dhaka: Asiatic Society, 1975); Asim Roy, *The Islamic Syncretistic Tradition in Bengal* (Dhaka: Academic Pub., 1983); Richard Eaton, *The Rise of Islam and the Bengal Frontier, 1204–1760* (Delhi: Oxford University Press, 1994).

24. Salomon, "Bāul Songs," in *Religions of India in Practice,* ed. D. Lopez (Princeton: Princeton University Press, 1995), 191.

25. There is much debate over the etymological origins of the term "Bāul." The most common view is that it derives from the Sanskrit term *vātula* or *vyākula,* meaning mad or upset; there is also a Hindi variant, *Baura.* Others, however, think it is from the Persian word *Āul.* The first use of the term appears in the *Kṛṣṇavijaya* of Śrī Mālādhāra Basu, to mean a "carefree and disheveled nature"; it also appears in the *Caitanya Caritāmṛta,* in which Caitanya is called "*Bāul*" or mad with divine love. Cf. Upendranāth Bhaṭṭācārya, *Bāṅglār Bāul o Bāul Gān* (Calcutta: Orient Book Co., 1981), 1–5.

26. Dimock, *The Place,* 251; cf. Deben Bhattacharya, *Songs of the Bards of Bengal* (New York: Grove Press, 1969), 30. The primary collections of Bāul songs include Motilāl Dās and Pīyūṣkānti Mahāpātra, *Lālan-Gītikā: Lālan Śāh Phakirer Gān* (Calcutta: University of Calcutta, 1958); Muhammad Mansur Uddin, *Hārāmaṇi: Lok Saṅgīt Saṃgraha* (Calcutta: University of Calcutta, 1942); Kṣitimohan Sen, *Bāṅglār Bāul* (Calcutta: University of Calcutta, 1954)

There is a large body of secondary literature on the Bāuls; see, for starters, Edward C. Dimock, "The Bāuls and the Islamic Tradition," in *The Sants: Studies in a Devotional Tradition of India,* ed. K. Schomer and W. H. McLeod (Delhi: Oxford, 1987); Charles Capwell, *Music of the Bāuls of Bengal* (Kent: Ohio State University Press, 1986); Carol Salomon, "Bāul Songs" and "The Comogonic Riddles of Lalan Fakir," in *Gender, Genre and Power in South Asian Expressive Traditions,* ed. A. Appadurai et al. (Philadelphia: University of Pennsylvania Press, 1991); Bhaṭṭācārya, *Bāṅglār Bāul o Bāul Gān*; Jhā, *Phakir Lālan Sāiṅ.*

27. *Bāul Saṅgīt,* in *Vividha-dharma-saṅgīt,* song 461, translated by Dasgupta, *Obscure Reli-*

gious Cults, 163. On the image of the "topsy-turvy land," see Capwell, *Music of the Bāuls*, 188–89.

28. On this point, see Hugh Urban, "The Politics of Madness: The Construction and Manipulation of the 'Bāul' Image in Modern Bengal," *South Asia* 12 (1999): 13–46; cf. Salomon, "Bāul Songs," 189.

29. The most severe attacks on the Bāuls occurred during the latter half of the previous century and the first half of this one. The Bengali Muslim community was swept with a series of radical reformist movements such as the *Tariqa-i Muhammadiyah* and the *Faraizi*. See Rafiuddin Ahmed, *The Bengali Muslims, 1871–1906: A Quest for Identity* (Delhi: Oxford, 1981), 184. Likewise, as Hindu reformers such as J. N. Bhattacharya charges, "The Bāuls are low class men and make it a point to appear as dirty as possible . . . they are a godless sect, sexual indulgence is the approved religious exercise . . . The moral condition of these sects . . . is deplorable indeed." *Hindu Castes and Sects*, 381.

30. See Capwell, *Music of the Bāuls of Bengal*, ch. II.

31. See De, *Kartābhajā Dharmer Itivṛtta*, 10–12. Throughout West Bengal, many calling themselves Kartābhajās are basically indistinguishable from Bāuls, as are their songs. This is probably due to the fact that since the beginning of this century, the "Bāul" has been valorized as a kind of "folk icon," while the Bāul songs have attained national and even international popularity. Cf. Capwell, *Music of the Bāuls*, ch. 1.

32. Chakrabarty has compiled a list of fifty-six "heterodox" sects. *Vaiṣṇavism in Bengal*, 349. See also Dasgupta, *Obscure Religous Cults*; Caṭṭopādhyāy, "Śrī Caitanya o Lokāyat Uttarādhikār."

33. "As organized Vaishnavism deepened its image of a neo-Brahman order, promoting social cohesion . . . the more radical Sahajiyā tradition . . . began to grow in popularity. . . . There developed a number of deviant sects . . . who disavowed all norms of caste distinction. . . . The various deviant sects, e.g., the Kartābhajās . . . repudiated idolatry and caste." Sekhar Bandyopadhyay, "Popular Religion and Social Mobility in Colonial Bengal: The Matua Sect and the Namasudras," in *Mind, Body and Society: Life and Mentality in Colonial Bengal*, ed. R. K. Ray (Calcutta: Oxford, 1995), 160.

34. Ajit Dās, *Jātvaiṣṇava Kathā* (Calcutta, 1993).

35. Chakrabarty, *Vaiṣṇavism in Bengal*, 346; "The assertion of Brahminical dominance in a religious movement . . . which was anti-caste and anti-intellectual, inevitably led to the growth of deviant orders" (ibid., 324; cf. Partha Chatterjee, *The Nation and Its Fragments*, ch. IX).

36. There is of course a vast and conflicted literature on the subject; see for starters Sugata Bose, ed., *South Asia and World Capitalism* (Delhi: Oxford, 1990); Hamza Alavi, ed., *Capitalism and Colonial Production* (London: Croom Helm, 1982); Irfan Habib, "Colonialism in the Indian Economy, 1857–1900," *Social Scientist* 3 (1975); Frank Perlin, "Precolonial South Asia and Western Penetration in the 17th–19th Centuries: A Problem of Epistemological Status," *Review* 4 (1980): 267–306; Ashok Rudra and B. D. Talid Majid, *Studies in the Development of Capitalism in India* (London: Rutledge, 1978); Kumkum Chatterjee, *Merchants, Politics and Society in Early Modern India: Bihar: 1733–1820* (Leiden: Brill, 1996); N. K. Sinha, *The Economic History of Bengal* (Calcutta: Firma KLM, 1962); David Ludden, "World Economy and Village India, 1600–1900: Exploring the Agrarian History of Capitalism," in *South Asia and World Capitalism*.

37. Washbrook, "Law, State and Agrarian Society." "Rather than a set of governing principles imported from a more advanced culture, the early East India Company state [was] a logical extension of processes with disitinctively indigenous origins." Washbrook, "Progress

and Problems: South Asian Economic and Social History, 1720–1860," *Modern Asian Studies* 22, no. 1 (1988): 57–96.

38. Bayly, *Rulers, Townsmen and Bazaars*, 229.

39. Washbrook, "Law, State and Agrarian Society." As Bose suggests, "in the complex negotiations between pre-capitalist and capitalist structures much remained unaltered. Colonial capitalists engaged in both contest and compromise with intermediate social." *Peasant Labour and Colonial Capital: Rural Bengal since 1770* (Cambridge: Cambridge University Press, 1993), 41.

40. Chatterjee, *The Nation and its Fragments,* 32. "There is something magical about a theory that can . . . spirit away the violent intrusion of colonialism and make all of its features the innate property of an indigenous history. . . . Like all feats of magic, however, this . . . is an illusion" (ibid.).

41. Bose, *Peasant Labour*, 41; cf. Asok Sen, "Subaltern Studies: Capital, Class and Community," in *Subaltern Studies V* (Delhi: Oxford 1987). As Guha argues, one of the great paradoxes of the Raj was that it did not in fact encourage the development of capitalism in India, but in many ways impeded it, while intensifying the "feudal exploitation" of the peasantry. The result was "to assign to the most advanced capitalist power in the world the task of fusing landlordism and usury in India so we well as to impede the development of capitalism both in agriculture and in industry." *Elementary Aspects,* 8.

42. For a summary of these different types of market, see David Curley, *Rulers and Merchants in Late 18th Century Bengal* (Ph.D. diss., University of Chicago, 1980); Chatterjee, *Merchants, Politics and Society,* 48–49. For contemporary British descriptions, see James Wise, *Notes on the Races, Castes and Tribes of Eastern Bengal* (London, 1883), 212–19.

43. Bhattacharya, "Traders and Trades in Old Calcutta," 209. For a good description of the life of the bazaar in a Bengali town, see Akos Oster, *Culture and Power: Legend, Ritual and Rebellion in a Bengali Society* (London: Sage, 1984), 94–100.

44. Sen, "Passages of Authority," 19–20. See also Sen, *Conquest of Marketplaces.*

45. Sen, "Passages of Authority," 26–27. "The conjunction of religious endowment, market exchange and support of ritual elders . . . suggests a form of redistribution of resources very different from . . . charity in the Victorian sense" (ibid., 28–29)

46. Sen, "Passages of Authority," 30–31. On the role of the marketplace in the *Caṇḍīmaṅgal*, see Curley, *Rulers and Merchants,* 1–39. In Narottom Dās's *Hāṭ Pattan*, the founding of the marketplace is used as a metaphor for Caitanya's founding of the Gauḍīya Vaiṣṇava tradition, as he appoints each of his disciples to act as officials or merchants in the bazaar (Sen, "Passages of Authority").

47. Sen, "Conquest of Marketplaces," 210–11.

48. "Zamindaris' control over rural markets remained unbroken and *hats* and *gunges* continued to function within the penumbra of zamindari authority. . . . The zamindars weathered the challenge to their control over markets." Chatterjee, *Merchants, Politics and Society*, 138.

49. See Rama Deb Roy, *Glimpses on the History of Calcutta, 1600–1800* (Calcutta, 1985), 24–25; P. J. Marshall, "The Company and the Coolies: Labour in Early Calcutta," in *The Urban Experience: Calcutta,* ed. Pradip Sinha (Calcutta: Riddhi, 1987), 25.

50. Pradip Sinha, "Calcutta and the Currents of History, 1690–1912," in *Calcutta, the Living City*, Vol. I, 33. "The Black Town, itself a division of a split metropolis (the other division being the whites) was in turn split into two societies—economically, politically, socially. . . . The stratification was ideologically buttressed by the bhadralok concept of *itarjan* and *chotolok*—pejorative terms to describe the lower orders." Banerjee, *The Parlour,*

71. For general descriptions of Calcutta, see Benoy Ghose, ed., *Selections from English Periodicals of 19th Century Bengal* (Calcutta: Papyrus, 1978); P. T. Nair, ed., *Calcutta in the 18th Century: Impressions of Travelers* (Calcutta: Firma KLM 1984). On the influx of migrant labor into Calcutta, see Marshall, "The Company and the Coolies": "Demands for labor are one of the most obvious ways in which a society subjected to colonial rule begins to experience its pressures, . . . The port cities of the Company had undergone rapid growth, creating demands for labour on an entirely new scale" (23).

51. Quoted in Bagchi, "Wealth and Work in Calcutta," 212–13.

52. Banerjee, *The Parlour and the Streets,* 1.

53. See David Kopf, *The Brahmo Samaj and the Shaping of the Modern Indian Mind* (Princeton: Princeton University Press, 1979); Wilhelm Halbfass, *India and Europe: An Essay on Understanding (*Albany: SUNY Press, 1988); R. C. Majumdar, *On Rammohun Roy* (Calcutta, 1972). As Kopf, *The Brahmo Samaj,* describes this *bhadralok* class:

> [They were the] Bengali equivalent of the comprador class that served Western colonialism as native intermediaries and agents. Compradors were brokers in the commercial sense or in the intellectual sense of interpreting the West to their countrymen. . . . This class . . . which was the closest thing to a "middle class" under colonialism, was best represented by the Brahmo Samaj. Side by side with the image of Brahmo liberal theism and reformism . . . is the image of Brahmo elitism characterized by hard work, financial success and social esteem vis à vis the Western world (87).

54. Banerjee, *The Parlour and the Streets*, 1.

55. Ibid., 29; cf. Sinha, *Calcutta in Urban History,* 30.

56. Banerjee, *The Parlour and the Streets,* 38.

57. Sinha, "Economic Background of the Century," 3. "Traditionally skilled craftsmen who had been lured away form the villages . . . gradually sank into poverty . . . unable to compete with the European tradesmen pouring into the growing metropolis." Banerjee, "The World of Ramjan Ostagar," 81.

58. Bagchi, "Wealth and Work in Calcutta," 212. "Bengal [was] the most exploited region in colonial India with Calcutta as the nodal point of this exploitation." Sinha, "Calcutta and the Currents of History," 32.

59. Banerjee, *The Parlour and the Streets*, 68, 70.

60. See especially Bose, *Peasant Labour,* "Introduction"; Ranajit Guha, *A Rule of Property for Bengal: An Essay on the Idea of Permanent Settlement* (Delhi: Oxford, 1963).

61. Sirajul Islam, *The Permanent Settlement in Bengal: A Study of Its Operation, 1790–1819* (Dacca: Rangla Academy, 1979), xi. Philip Lawson, *The East India Company: A History* (London: Longman, 1993), 110.

62. Guha, *A Rule of Property for Bengal.*

63. Bayly, *Indian Society*, 108–109; cf. Gyan Prakash, *Bonded Histories: Genealogies of Labor Servitude in Colonial India* (Cambridge: Cambridge University Press, 1990), 100; Islam, *The Permanent Settlement.*

64. Cf. Romesh Chunder Dutt, *The Peasantry of Bengal: A View of Their Condition under the Hindu, the Mahomedan and the English Rule* (Calcutta: Thacher, Spink, 1874), 153; Sinha, *Economic History of Bengal.*

65. Guha, *Elementary Aspects of Peasant Insurgency in Colonial Bengal* (Delhi: Oxford, 1983), 7; cf. Bose, *Peasant Labour,* 111–15; Islam, *Permanent Settlement,* 170–72.

66. Sen, "Subaltern Studies," 228. On the Indigo rebellion, see Blair Kling, *The Blue Mutiny: the Indigo Disturbances in Bengal, 1859–1862* (Philadelphia: University of Pennsylva-

nia Press, 1966). On the Faraizi and Wahabi movements, see Qeyamuddin Ahmad, *The Wahabi Movement in India* (Calcutta: Firma KLM, 1966).

67. *Friend of India* 14, vol. 2 (January 1836), 11.

68. The term *bhāva* is extremely difficult to translate and bears a wide range of meanings, designating everything from "mood, emotion or condition" to religious rapture and transcendental bliss. Following McDaniel, I would suggest that *bhāva* in this case is best translated as "ecstasy," in the sense of extreme religious emotion or divine madness (*The Madness of the Saints: Ecstatic Religion in Bengal* [Chicago: University of Chicago Press, 1989], 21–23).

69. The oldest known manuscript—which, rather significantly, every other scholar of the Kartābhajās has strangely ignored—is the "Kartābhajā Gīta" (1228–1233 B.S. [1821–26], Baṅgīya Sāhitya Pariṣat, MS. no. 964. The following the are the known printed editions of the Kartābhajā songs:

1. *Kartābhajār Gītāvalī*, ed. Nabīncandra Cakravartī (Calcutta: Caitanya Candrodaya, 1277 B.S. [1870]). Most authors believe this to be the first printed edition of the songs; however, apart from Sukumār Sen, no other scholar has actually seen this text. (Sen, *Bāṅgālī Sāhityer Itihāsa*, vol. II).
2. *Bhāver Gīta*, ed. Rameścandra Ghoṣe (Calcutta: Aurora Press, 1389 B.S.[1882]). Ghoṣe published the first full edition, containing 616 songs.
3. *Śrī Śrī Juter Pada / Bhāver Gīta*, ed. Bhuvanamohan Gaṅgopādhyāy (Calcutta: Author 1300 B.S. [1893]). The second half of the 1870 *Kartābhajār Gitāvalī* appeared in 1300/1893 with the title *Śrī Juter Pada*, containing 585 songs, and was reprinted in 1319 B.S. (1812) as *Bhāver Gīta* with 662 songs.
4. *Bhāver Gīta*, ed. Manulāl Miśra (Calcutta: Author, 1313, 1329 [1906, 1922]). Miśra, the most influential Kartābhajā theologian after Dulālcāṅd, published the most widely read editions of the *Bhāver Gīta*. The first contains only 573 songs, while the second has 590. Miśra's edition has since been reprinted numerous times, with varying numbers of songs—in 1356 (1949), with 573 songs, and in 1384 (1977), with 590. The most recent edition (1992), which I use in this book, is a reprint of the latter, published by Miśra's great grandson, Śāntirañjan Cakravartī (Calcutta: Indralekha Press, 1399 B.S.).

70. Miśra, *Kartābhajā Dharmer Ādi Vṛttānta Vā Sahajatattva Prakāśa* (Calcutta: Author, 1925); *Bhāver Gīta Vyākhyā Saha Sahaja Tattvaprakāśa* (Calcutta: Author, 1911).

71. Upendranāth Mukhopādhyāy, ed., *Saṇgītakośa* (Calcutta: Basumati Press, 1895); Pāl, *Ghospāṛār Satimā*; Dās, *Saṅgīta o Darśana* and *Śrī Satīmā Candrikā*. Datta also includes some songs and mantras in his *Bhāratavarṣīya Upāsaka Sampradāya*, 227–29, as does Dinesh Chandra Sen, *Chaitanya and His Age* (Calcutta: University of Calcutta, 1922), 342–43.

72. William Ward, *A Brief Memoir of Krishna Pal, the First Hindoo in Bengal who Broke the Chain of Caste by Embracing the Gospel* (London: J. Offor, 1823).

73. Garrett, *Bengal District Gazetteers*, 49–50.

74. Oddie, "Old Wine in New Bottles?" 329–31; cf. Rev. F. A. Cox, *History of the Baptist Missionary Society from 1792–1842,* 2 vols. (London: T. Ward and Co., 1842), 11.

75. Ward, *A View of the History, Literature and Religion of the Hindoos*, vol. I, 223.

76. Wilson, *Sketch of the Religious Sects of the Hindus*, 171–74.

77. James Long, *Handbook of Bengal Missions* (London: J. F. Shaw, 1848); Eugene Stock, *The History of the Church Missionary Society: Its Environment, Its Men and Its Work* (London: Church Missionary Society, 1899), vol. I, 314–15. The German missionary W. J. Deer baptized thrity Kartābhajās. In 1838, ten villages with 500 persons were converted at once.

Archdeacon Dealtry reported that the whole population of fifty-five villages wished to become Christian (see Oddie, "Old Wine in New Bottles").

78. Caitra, 1254 [March 30, 1848], reproduced in Subhāṣ Bandyopādhyāy, "Sekāler Saṃvādapatre Ghoṣpāṛār melā," in *Kartābhajā Dharmamata o Itihāsa*, vol. 1, 40–42. A similar account appeared in the journal *Somaprakāśa*, 23 Caitra, 1270 B.S. [April 4, 1864].

79. Akṣaykumār joined Debendranāth's Tattvabodhinī Sabhā in 1843 and became editor of the *Tattvabodhinī patrikā*—a high position in the Brāhmo Samāj. In 1850, Akṣaykumār published a detailed description of the Kartābhajās in *Tattvabodhinī* (4th part, no. 81, 12 Baiśākh), which relied on the information given by one Bhairavacandra Datta. This was later published in his later published in 1870 in his classic *Bhāratavarṣīya Upāsaka Smapradāya* (cf. Kopf, *The Brahmo Samaj*, 49).

80. D. C. Sen, *History of Bengali Language and Literature* (Calcutta: University of Calcutta, 1954). On his relation to Dulālcāṅd, see Chakrabarty, *Vaiṣṇavism in Bengal*, 379–81.

81. Ghoṣāl, *Karuṇānidhānavilāsa* (Calcutta, 1813); see Sen, "Kartābhajā Kathā o Gān," 37–38.

82. Sen, "Āmār Jīvana" in *Nabīncandra-Racanāvalī*, vol. 3, 174–76; cf. Kopf, *The Brahmo Samaj*, 120.

83. "Calcutta's *bhadralok* society was quick to condemn the *Kartābhajā* sect as a religion of *itar* people and prostitutes, who were promiscuous in their habits and violated the norms of Hindu religion." Banerjee, *The Parlour*, 69.

84. Rāy, *Dāśarathī Rāyer Pāñcālī*, 665. For a more scholarly, though equally cynical, view, see Jogendranath Bhattacharya, *Hindu Castes and Sects* (Calcutta: Firma KLM, 1896), 383–86.

85. Kripal, *Kālī's Child*, 123–25, 223–30. See *Śrīśrīrāmakṛṣṇakathāmṛta*, 5.180. 2.89, 3.21; and *Śrīśrīrāmakṛṣṇalīlāprasaṅga*, 4.1.28.

86. *Shri Ramakrishna the Great Master*, 507; cf. Kripal, *Kālī's Child* 124–26.

87. On the various legends of Āulcāṅd, see KDA 17–35; STP 1–10; Garrett, *Bengal District Gazetteers*, 47–49. De, *Kartābhajā Dharmer Itivṛtta*, 17–20; Chakrabarty, *Vaiṣṇavism in Bengal*, 353–55.

88. There are a wide number of opinions regarding the meaning of "āul." Although most scholars believe it derives from the Persian *waliya*, others suggest it dererives from an Arabic word āul, meaning "origin" (ādi in Sanskrit) (Pāl, *Ghoṣpāṛār Satī Mā*, 46). Others have tried to give the term a Sanskritic origin, tracing it to *ākula*, meaning "distressed, uneasy, fervent" and thus, like Bāul, mad or insane. As Sen comments, "From his childhood he was thought mad. That may be why he was called *'Āule'* (*ākul*, mad)." "Kartābhajār Kathā o Gān." For other derivations see Śarīph, *Bāṅgālī o Bāṅglār Sāhitya*, 103.

89. Tony K. Stewart, "Satya Pīr: Muslim Holy Man and Hindu God," in *Religions of India in Practice*, ed. D. Lopez (Princeton: Princeton University Press, 1995), 579, 580. As the eighteenth-century poet Bhāratacandra described Satya Pīr: "In this Kali age, the societal office of the twice born, the warriors, the common folk and the lowly servers have gradually disintegrated, succombing to the might of foreign Muslims. At this time Lord Hari came down, taking on the body of a fakir . . . he wore a beard and mustache, his body covered by a patchwork wrap, a cap on his head, in his hand a staff. From his mouth poured the speech of Muslim *pīrs* and the Prophet." *Satyanārāyaṇera Vrātakathā* in *Bhāratacandra Granthāvalī*, ed. V. Bandyopādhyāy (Calcutta: Baṅgīya Sāhitya Pariṣat, 1357 B.S. [1950]), 440, (trans. by Stewart).

90. Chakrabarty, *Vaiṣṇavism in Bengal*, 355; cf. Miśra, *Bhāver Gīta Vyākhyā*, 15–18; Garrett, *Bengal District Gazetteers*, 47; De, *Kartābhajā Dharma*, 21–22.

91. Gaṅgopādhyāy, "Preface," in *Śrī Śrī Juter Pada,* 3; This legend is also recounted in STP 5–6: "At the beginning of the war between Sirājudalah and Clive in 1757 . . . when the soldiers had returned to Murshidabad after plundering the factories, the Lord Fakir became manifest at the meeting place of the three rivers. A foot soldier came with a great trunk. He saw the Fakir, and, thinking him to be mad, put the trunk on his back and struck him with his rifle. The Lord . . . carried it. But a little distance away he put the trunk down. He said, *kocemāli uṭhegā phirāṅgi baiṭhegā* three times and disappeared."

92. Chakrabarty, *Vaiṣṇavism in Bengal,* 358; see KDA 17–20; Hunter, *Statistical Account,* 53.

93. As Bloom puts it, "Interpretation is revisionism and the strongest readers so revise as to make every text belated, and themselves into children of the dawn, earlier and fresher than any completed text could hope to be." *Kabbalah and Criticism,* 126.

94. Cf. KDA 1–71; Chakrabarty, *Vaiṣṇavism in Bengal,* 354. Let us pause here and consider this legend more carefully: Is this simply a popular folk story, or does it hold some deeper esoteric meaning? We should remember that the Triveṇi is one of the most common metaphors used in Sahajiyā and Bāul discourse to refer to the secret site in the body where the three interior veins—the *Iḍā, Suṣumṇā* and *Piṅgalā*—come together. In the female, this is the yoni, and the flowing of the Ganges is among the most common metaphors for the monthly flow of the menstrual blood. Let us also remember that the Moon—*cāṇd* or *candra*—and also the "Madman"—Āul, Bāul, Pāgal Mānuṣa—are common metaphors for the appearance of the Supreme Self, the Maner Mānuṣa, at the time of menstruation in the female body. For three days, He descends from His seat in the top of the head and dallies in the waters of the yoni, before returning to his divine abode. These three days are said to be the best time for Bāul practice and sexual rituals. See Bhattacharya, *Bāṅglār Bāul,* 413–4; Salomon, "Bāul Songs".

Hence, to say that "*Āulcāṅd*"—the divine Moon and supreme Madman—appeared at the *Triveṇi* could easily be taken as a reference to esoteric bodily practices, such as the technique of "catching the uncatchable Man", or realizing the Man of the Heart when he appears in the menstrual flow. Some later Kartābhajā songs appear to make this connection rather explicit—for example, the following song included in Advaita Dās's "Saṅgītamālā": "He floats within the Triveṇī. . . . The river of poison lies on two sides; The stream flows endlessly. Between them is the river of nectar . . . you must plunge within it; otherwise, you will drink poison and lose your life." *Śrī Satīmā Candrikā,* 86.

95. Pāl, *Ghoṣpāṛār Satī Mā,* 82.

96. KDA, cited in Bhaṭṭācārya, *Bāṅglār Bāul,* 62–63.

97. *Somaprakāśa* 23 Caitra, 1270 B.S. [1864].

98. KDA 9, 57–69; cf. Chakrabarty, *Vaiṣṇavism in Bengal,* 358.

99. KDA 17–20, cf. Chakrabarty, *Vaiṣṇavism in Bengal,* 358.

100. On the Sayta Guru sect which emerged in East Bengal near Bakarganj, see Henry Beveridge, *The Distrinct of Bakarganj: Its History and Statistics* (London: Trubner, 1876), cited in Pāl, *Ghoṣpāṛār Satīmā,* 100–101.

101. Riāzul Hāq, *Maramī Kabi Pañju Śāh: Jīban o Kābya* (Dhaka: Bangla Academy, 1990), 23–24; see Śarīph, *Bāul Tattva* (Dhaka: Bangla Academy, 1973), 41, and *Bāṅgālī o Bāṅglā Sāhitya,* 88, 99.

102. The twenty-two fakirs appear are listed variously in five different sources: *Bhāver Gīta* (1882 ed.), 231; Datta, *Bhāratavarṣīya Upāsaka Sampradāya,* 220–21; Miśra, *Bhāver Gīter Vyākhyā,* 22; Miśra, *Kartābhajā Dharmer Ādi Vṛttānta,* 27–28; anonymous Kartābhajā song, recorded in Bhaṭṭācārya, *Bāṅglār Bāul,* 64. For good comparison of the first four lists, see Chakrabarty, *Vaiṣṇavism in Bengal,* 356–57.

According to the 1882 BG, they are as follows: Āndirām, Becu Ghoṣe; Bhīma Rāy Rājput, Dedo Kṛṣṇa, Goda Kṛṣṇa, Haṭu Ghoṣe, Kānāi Ghoṣe, Kinu Govinda, Lakṣmīkānta, Manohar Dās, Nitāi, Nityānanda, Nayāna, Nidhirām, Pāñcakaṛi, Rāmśaraṇ Pāl, Rāmanāth Dās, Śaṅkara, Śiśurām, Śyāma, Viśu Dās The lists of Datta and Miśra contain a number of different names.

Rather signficantly, the list in the anonymous song reprinted in contained in Bhaṭṭācārya does not contain the name of Rāmśaraṇ Pāl, the first Kartā. The reason for this is not clear, but it may suggest an alternative tradition within the community which did not accept Rāmśaraṇ's authority; hence it could be related to the Satyasrot or "secret Kartābhajā" tradition begun by Kānāi Ghoṣe.

103. Pāl, *Ghoṣpāṛār Satī Mā,* 173.

104. On Kānāi Ghoṣe, see Pāl, *Ghoṣpāṛār Satī Mā,* 173–74.

105. Chakrabarty, Vaiṣṇavism in Bengal, 356. Miśra identifies the twenty-two, respectively, with Rāmānanda Basu, Jīva Gosvāmin, Dāmodara Paṇḍit, Vakreśvara, Govindānanda, Mādhvācārya, Raghunāth Bhaṭṭa, Kamalākar Piplāi, Gopāla Bhaṭṭa, Vāsu Ghoṣe, Gadādhara Paṇḍit, Sundarānanda, Gaurīdāsa, Banamālī Paṇḍit, Jāhṇavā Devī, Śivānanda Sen, Śikhi Māhiti, Rāmānanda Rāy, Kāśī Miśra, Jagannātha Dās, Kālā Kṛṣṇadās, and Vāsudeva Sārvabhauma (KDA 27–28).

106. Sarkār, "Ghoṣpāṛār Melā o tār Prāṇbhomrā," 5–6.

107. See D. C. Sen, "Ghoṣpāṛār Melā," *Baṅgabani* (Jaistha 1329 B.S. [1922]), 430–31.

108. Miśra, *Bhajanatattva Prakāśa, arthāt Mahājanadiger Bhāvānurūpa Pada* (Calcutta: Indralekha Press, 1389 B.S. [1982]), 10.

109. Miśra, *Satīmār Mahātmyā* (Calcutta: Indralekha Press, 1325 B.S. [1918]); see Kripal, *Kālī's Child*, ch. 4.

110. *Jelepāṛer Saṅg niye Haraberakam Raṅg* (Calcutta, 1322 B.S. [1915]), quoted in Cakravartī, *Sāhebdhanī Sampradāya*, 41–42.

111. Dās, *Ghoṣpāṛār Kartābhajā Dharma*, 26; cf. Hunter, *Statistical Account*, 53.

112. Letter of John Henry Barrows, Chairman, General Committee on Religious Congresses, to Sri Ramdulal Pal, April 17, 1893; an invitation to the World's Congress Auxiliary of the World's Columbian Exposition of 1893.

113. Cited in Sarkār, "Ghoṣpāṛār Melā o tār Prāṇbhomrā," 10.

114. *Calcutta Review* 6 (1849), 407.

115. Sen, "Kartābhajār Kathā o Gān," 39.

116. Chakrabarty, *Vaiṣṇavism in Bengal*, 360-61; cf. Banerjee, "From Aulchand to Satī Mā."

117. Cakravartī, *Gabhīr Nirjan Pathe,* 68; cf. Banerjee, "From Aulchand to Satī Mā."

118. Banerjee, "From Aulchand to Satī Mā," 44.

119. Although by far the majority of the Kartābhajā following was originally among the poor lower classes, there were also various attempts throughout the nineteenth century to attract the patronage of some wealthy upper-class Bengalis. This was above all the case under the leadership of Dulālcāṅd, who had become widely known even among the wealthy elites of Calcutta. We have already met the famous Zamindār and poet, Rājā Jayanārāyaṇ Ghoṣāl, who was praised as one of the "most progressive men of Calcutta," and is widely believed to have undergone initiation at the hands of his Dulālcāṅd himself. See Sen, "Kartābhajār Kathā o Gān," 37–38.

Later in the nineteenth century, a number of educated *bhadraloks* became increasingly curious about this new sect, with its rejection of caste and its seemingly unversal, nonsectarian ideals; as the *Saṃvāda Prabhākara* reported in 1847: "The numbers of the Kartā's devotees include not only lower classes; among them are men of pure castes, scholars and philosophers." As we have seen, several leading social reformers, such as Śaśīpad Bābu, and a number of prominent literary figures such as Nabīncandra Sen, were deeply impressed by the Kartābhajās' seemingly "modern" ideals of the brotherhood of man and the harmony of scriptures. See Kopf, *The Brahmo Samaj*: "no other Bengali was so beautifully in the image of the Brahmo social reformer" (120).

In fact, a few members of the Brāhmo Samāj, such as the Vaiṣṇava pundit, Vijaykṛṣṇa Goswāmi (d.1899), even underwent initiation and began to practice *prāṇāyāma* under a Kartābhajā guru in Calcutta. Born a Vaiṣṇava Brahmin, Vijaykṛṣṇa hoped to infuse elements of Vaiṣṇava devotion into Brāhmoism, and thereby "convey Brāhmo ideals to a larger mass of Bengalis." It would seem that his interest in the Kartābhajās was part of this broader Brāhmo agenda. Indeed, it was in large part becaue of his contact with the highly suspect Kartābhajās that Vijaykṛṣṇa was severely attacked by his fellow Brāhmos, and finally forced to resign from the Samāj in 1886. See Kopf, *The Brahmo Samaj*, 223; Āmṛtalāl Sengupta, *Śrī Śrī Vijayakṛṣṇa Gosvāmi: Sādhanā o Upadeśa* (Calcutta, 1992), 102.

Despite this brief appeal to the upper classes, however, the Kartābhajās appear to have progressively fallen into disfavor among Calcutta's *bhadralok* society; indeed, by the end of the nineteenth century, they would be widely ridiculed as a degenerate band of charlatans, thieves, and prostitutes.

120. Datta, *Bhāratavarṣīya Upāsaka Sampradāya*, 226.

121. *Somaprakāśa*, 20 Caitra 1270 B.S. [1864].

122. Oddie, "Old Wine in New Bottles?" 329.

123. Cakravartī, "Gabhīr Nirjan Pathe," 6. As Banerjee comments, "One popular sect that raised a lot of controversy was the *Kartābhajā* group. Although its headquarters was . . . Ghoshpara, a few miles from Calcutta, it drew a lot of people from the poorer classes of the city . . . the stress on equality of all peoples irrespective of caste . . . drew the lower orders in large numbers." *The Parlour and the Streets*, 69.

124. Cf. Cakravartī, *Sāhebdhanī Sampradāya*, 36–38; Chakrabarty, *Vaiṣṇavism in Bengal*, 360–63.

125. Jhā, *Phakir Lālan Sāin*, 218. As Jhā points out, a similar theme of the decline of the small merchants in the face of the new European and wealthy indigenous businessmen appears in many Bāul songs: "The hāṭ and bājār are mentioned again and again in the songs. . . . The metaphor of the wealth . . . of the small merchants becoming exhausted appears many times in the songs. . . . Because of the thievery of enemies or natural disasters, the small merchant fell into poverty" (ibid.).

126. BG 265. There are many satirical songs poking fun at the brokers; for example "Don't we honor these men as Brokers? For so many Princes and Nobles are always paying them respect! Without any power or capital of their own, they acquire wealth! Brother, that's why the Brokers have now attained such great status! The wise Broker can attain anything, finite or infinite. . . . And that's why, without any power of their own, they come and sit a if they were Princes!" (BG 268). For good discussion of the role of the Broker or Middleman in colonial Calcutta, see P. J. Marshall, *East Indian Fortunes: The British in Bengal in the Eighteenth Century* (Oxford: Clarendon Press, 1976), 38–39.

127. I interviewed these and many other Kartābhajās in Calcutta between 1994 and 1997. In the interest of privacy, I have chosen not to use their real names or addresses in this book.

128. Cf. Māṇik Sarkār, "Ghoṣpāṛār Melā," in *Kartābhajā Dharmamata o Itihāsa*, vol. 2, 57.

Chapter 2

1. As Comaroff puts it: "The rituals of Zion are a bricolage whose signs appropriate the power both of colonialism and Tshidi tradition, welding them into a transcendent synthesis that seeks . . . to reconstitute the divided self." *Body of Power,* 12. See also Taussig, *The Devil,* where he argues that the South American Indians "absorbed but also transformed Christian mythology" so that Christian elements were mixed with traditional pagan myths, and thus "gave poetic expression to the needs of the oppressed" (227).

2. de Certeau, *The Practice of Everyday Life,* xiv. Sekhar Bandyopadhyay makes a similar argument with regard to the Matua sect of Bengal: "We cannot take it for granted that popular religion was always conformist. . . . People were not always passive receivers of values of their superiors: they also adapted these in their own ways. Through this process of creative appropriation, popular religion developed its subversive edge. It began to question the hegemonic order and preached inversion of the social hierarchy." "Popular Religion and Social Mobility in Colonial Bengal: The Matua Sect and the Namasudras," in *Mind, Body and Society: Life and Mentality in Colonial Bengal,* ed. R. Ray (Calcutta: Oxford, 1995), 153; cf. Roger Chartier, "Culture as Appropriation: Popular Cultural Uses in Early Modern France," in *Understanding Popular Culture: Europe from the Middle Ages to the Nineteenth Century,* ed. S. Kaplan (Berlin: Mouton, 1984).

3. The Bengali term *Mānuṣa* is more literally translated by the nongendered English word "humanity"; however, I have chosen to translate it here somewhat ironically as "Man" because, as will become evident in this chapter, the Kartābhajā path is ultimately not as "egalitarian" as it might at first appear, and there are clear asymmetries between males and females within the tradition.

4. Caṭṭopādhyāy, "Śrī Caitanya o Lokāyat Uttaradhikār." On the Bengal Renaissance and Rammohun Roy, see Kopf, *British Orientalism,* 199–200; and Rammohun's *Abridgement of the Vedant,* in *Sources of Indian Tradition,* ed. T. De Bary (New York: Columbia University Press, 1958), 573–75.

5. Cf. Dick Hebdige, *Subculture: The Meaning of Style* (London: Routledge, 1979): "Subcultures . . . are cultures of conspicuous consumption. . . . It is through rituals of consumption, through style, that the subculture reveals its secret identity and communicates its forbidden meanings. It is the way in which commodities are used which mark the subculture off from more orthodox cultural formations" (103).

6. See especially Banerjee, "From Aulchand to Satī Mā," 29–60.

7. There is a vast literature on the concept of "syncretism"; for useful attempts to redefine and reformulate the category, see C. Stewart and R. Shaw, *Syncretism/Anti-Syncretism: The Politics of Religious Synthesis* (London: Routledge, 1994); Thomas Bryson, "The Hermeneutic of Religious Syncretism: Swami Vivekananda's Practical Vedānta," Ph.D. diss., University of Chicago (1992). For a good criticism of the concept, see Tony K. Stewart and Carl Ernst, "Syncretism," in *South Asian Folklore: An Encyclopedia,* ed. M. Mills and P. Claus (Garland Publishing, forthcoming); Eaton, *The Rise of Islam,* 302–303.

8. Fiske, "Cultural Studies," 157, 158; de Certeau, *The Practice of Everyday Life,* xiii.

9. Today, many devotees place themselves primarily within the Gauḍīya Vaiṣṇava tradition; many scholars also identify the Kartābhajās as essentially Vaiṣṇava, though as a heterodox or "deviant" variant of the mainstream tradition. Chakrabarty, *Vaiṣṇavism in Bengal,* for example, calls them "half Vaiṣṇava and half Sahajiyā," and thus a "major dissent from orthodox Vaiṣṇavism" (379). According to others such as Upendranāth Bhaṭṭācārya and Deben-

dranāth De, they are best understood as a later branch of the more general Bāul tradition. (De, *Kartābhajā Dharmer Itivṛtta,* ch. I; Bhaṭṭācārya, *Bāṅglār Bāul,* 69–71).

10. Mukhopādhyāy, "Pravartakakendrik Sahajiyā." As Caṭṭopādhyāy suggests, "the founder Āulcāṅd is said to be the avatar of Caitanya. But surely there is no close relationship between the Kartābhajā sect and the Vaiṣṇava tradition; rather, it was established on the basis of the Sahajiyā tradition." "Śrī Caitanya o Lokāyat Uttaradhikār," 280-81. See also Nandī, *Kartābhajā Dharma,* 64.

11. Dimock, *The Place,* 105

12. Miśra, *Satyadharma Upāsana vā Śukrabārer Yājana Praṇālī* (Calcutta: Indralekha Press, 1398 B.S. [1991), 66, 67. "At present," Aulcāṅd thought, "there is no easy method of worship for the lowly, powerless people; that's why I have revealed the easy (*sahaja*) path, so they can worship the truth within them, the worship of Man." KDA, in Bhaṭṭācārya, *Bāṅglār Bāul,* 62.

13. De, *Kartāhajā Dharmer Itivṛtta,* 104.

14. Dimock, *The Place of the Hidden Moon,* 109.

15. De, *Kartābhajā Dharmer Itivṛtta,* app. II.

16. Bhaṭṭācārya, *Bāṅglār Bāul,* 69.

17. Bhattacharya, *Religious Sects of the Hindus,* 383–86.

18. *Bhāver Gīta,* cited in Pāl, *Ghoṣpāṛār Satī Mā,* 97.

19. On the Muslim concept of *Haq,* see De, *Kartābhajā Dharmer Itivṛtta,* 2–3; Sen, "Kartābhajār Kathā o Gān." On Satya Pīr, see Stewart, "Satya Pīr" and "Competing Structures of Authority."

20. Mint Sayings (STP 61; III.46, 50). According to a Hadith, "You will die before you die." Cf. Haq, *History of Sufi-ism in Bengal,* 67, 101.

21. De, *Kartābhajā Dharmer Itivṛtta,* 17. "They don't deny outward religious laws. . . . Their practices are hidden from others, and no one knows they are devotees." Dās, *Śrī Satīmā Candrikā,* 62.

22. Garrett, *Bengal District Gazetteer, Nadia,* 48.

23. De, *Kartābhajā Dharmer Itivṛtta,* 12.

24. See Salomon, "Bāul Songs," 199; Capwell, *Music of the Bāuls,* ch. 1.

25. For example, "Everyone says, 'a Man is a Man;' but how is one a Man? Man is a Jewel, Man is life, Man is the heart's treasure. . . . Those Men who are dead while alive are the essence of Man" (*Sahajiyā Sāhitya* [SS], pada 21).

26. Caṭṭopādhyāy, "Ghoṣpāṛār Melā," 144–46, and "Śrī Caitanya o Lokāyat Uttaradhikār," 281.

27. Caṭṭopādhyāy, "Ghoṣpāṛār Melā," 144. Acording to another song attributed to Lālan, "What bliss there is in Ghoṣpāṛā! It is the rescue of both sinners and renunciants. With Dulālcāṅd, Mā has sat at the base of the Dālim tree . . . Lālan offers homage to you with the earth of the Dālim tree" (ibid.).

28. *Kartābhajār Gitāvalī,* cited in Sen, "Kartābhajār Kathā o Gān," 41–45. Interestingly, the Maner Mānuṣa songs do not appear in the earlier manuscript, "Kartābhajā Gīta" (1228–33 B.S. [1821–6]).

29. Compare the famous Bāul song: "When will I find him, that man of my heart? He is lost. In my search I have wandered near and far." Dimock, *The Place,* 261.

30. "Brother, I cannot know the Man of the Heart! . . . One day, having searched for this Man at home and abroad, I got to see a humorous spectacle upon the ocean of life! All the ships were loaded with jems and jewels—But where had their Master (Kartā) gone? Apart from all this merchandise, there was nothing else; These men had come upon

the ships to engage in business; and whatever sort of thing you desire, they'll give you!" (BG 241; II.78).

31. This was first pointed out to me by the respected scholar of economic history, Sirajul Islam (personal conversation, Dhaka, August 1996); however, it was noted 100 years ago by Bhattacharya in *Hindu Castes and Sects,* 383–84. On the *gadi,* see also Banerjee, "From Aulchand to Satī Mā."

32. Sen, "Kartābhajār Kathā o Gān," 37.

33. See Oddie, "Old Wine in New Bottles?"; Pāl, *Ghoṣpāṛār Satī Mā,* 156.

34. Pāl, *Ghoṣpāṛār Satī Mā,* 153.

35. De, *Kartābhajā Dharma,* 70f.

36. Dās, *Ghoṣpāṛār Kartābhajā Sampradāya,* 48.

37. Mukhopādhyāy, "Pravartakakendrik Sahajiyā," 8.

38. Beveridge, *The District of Bakarganj,* cited in Pāl, *Ghoṣpāṛār Satīmā,* 156–57.

39. Pāl, *Ghoṣpāṛār Satīmā,* 156–7; De, *Kartābhajā Dharmer Itivṛtta,* 1–10.

40. Sen, "Kartābhajār Kathā o Gān," 37.

41. Ghoṣāl, *Karuṇānidhānavilās,* quoted in Sen, "Kartābhajār Kathā o Gān," 37.

42. Kopf, *The Brahmo Samaj,* 11. Cf. Roy, *The Precepts of Jesus, the Guide to Peace and Happiness* (Calcutta, 1820).

43. BG (1882) 269, trans. (freely) by Chakrabarty, *Vaiṣṇavism in Bengal,* 375.

44. Kripal, *Kālī's Child,* 227 (emphasis in the original). Cf. *Kathāmṛta,* 2.98.

45. In his as yet unpublished sequel to *Kālī's Child* and in various personal communications (1996–98), Kripal has pointed to the role of Rāmakṛṣṇa as a kind of "Hindu answer to Christ" for many of his later devotees.

46. Cakravartī, "Kartābhajā Sampradāya," 26.

47. BG (1882) 158, q. 3, translated by Chakrabarty, *Vaiṣṇavism in Bengal,* 375.

48. Barthes, *Mythologies* (New York: Himan and Walsh, 1972), 131. On the role of bricolage as a source of "resistance, opposition and subversion," see Graeme Turner, *British Cultural Studies: An Introduction* (Boston: Unwin Hyman, 1990), 217.

49. Sen, *Caitanya and His Age,* 346. "The secret practitioners of this religion are averse to revealing it to ordinary people. In common society, they follow ordinary laws and injunctions. . . . But among their own company, the follow this rule: *lok madhye, lokācār, sadguru madhye ekācār.*" De, *Kartābhajā Dharmer Itivṛtta,* 33. Metaphorically, the conventional and ultimate Truths are said to be like the "Central City" (*Sadar*) and the "hinterland" or rural district: they must both be accepted as "true," as part of the same State, though in different spheres of operation: "If one doesn't understand that the Central City and the rural hinterland are both of one kind, then the Conventional and the Ultimate truths are not one. [One who doesn't understand this] cannot be called a 'Master' " (STP 63; SE III.83).

50. Dimock, *The Place of the Hidden Moon,* 109.

51. Chakrabarty, *Vaiṣṇavism in Bengal,* 362, 363–64.

52. Sen, *Chaitanya and His Age,* 402.

53. Caṭṭopādhyāy, "Ghoṣpāṛār Melā," 135.

54. Dās, *Śrī Satīmā Candrikā,* 61–62.

55. Chatterjee, *The Nation and Its Fragments,* 187.

56. Interviewed at his home in Calcutta, July–September, 1996.

57. Saradānanda, *Śrīśrīrāmakṛṣṇalīlāprasaṅga,* vol. 2, 22–23. Vaiṣṇavacaraṇ was the son and disciple of Utsavānanda Vidyāvagīśa; his mother was Padma, and his wife was Viṣṇusukhī. He met Rāmakṛṣṇa at the celebration of Daṇḍa Mahotsava (Kālījīvana Devasarma, *Śrīśrīrāmakṛṣṇalīlā abhidhāna* [Calcutta: Karuṇā Prakāśana, 1983], 215).

58. Akṣaykumār Sen, *Śrīśrīrāmakṛṣṇa-puṅthi* (Calcutta: Udbhodana Kāryālaya, 1976), 116. According to Rāmakṛṣṇa's account, Vaiṣṇavacaraṇ and his cohorts not only engaged in Tantric sexual rites, but they also made use of the most defiling substances—even the consumption of sexual fluids and excreta: "Vaishnavacharan followed the views of the Kartābhajās. . . . Many of them follow the view of the *Rādhā Tantra*. The essences of earth, fire, water, wind and space [become] shit, piss, menstrual blood and semen." *Kathāmṛta,* 5.180–81, trans. by Kripal, *Kālī's Child,* 290.

59. Kripal, *Kālī's Child,* 223; cf. *Śrīśrīrāmakṛṣṇa-Līlāprasaṅga,* 4.1.29–30.

60. Chatterjee, *The Nation and Its Fragments,* 187.

61. Pal, quoted in Garrett, *Bengal District Gazetteer, Nadia,* 49-50.

62. *Saṃvāda Prabhākara,* 18 Caitra, 1254 B.S. [1848]; Bandyopādhyāy, "Sekāler Saṃvādapatre Ghoṣpāṛer Melā," 42.

63. Cakravartī, *Sāhebdhanī Sampradāya,* 42.

64. Sen, "Āmār Jīvana," 184.

65. Trust deed of the Brāhmo Samāj, in Sophia Collet, *The Life and Letters of Rammohun Roy* (Calcutta: B.K. Biswas, 1962), 471. See Ahmed, *Social Ideals and Social Change in Bengal,* 33–36; Rāmmohun Roy, *Brief Remarks Regarding Modern Encroachment on the Ancient Rights of Females* (Calcutta: Sadharan Brahma Samaj, 1822).

66. Caṭṭopadhyāy, "Śrī Caitanya o Lokāyat Uttaradhikār," 280; Pāl, *Ghoṣpāṛār Satī Mā,* 300–302.

67. Nandī, Kartābhajā Dharma o Sāhitya, 131–33; cf. Pāl, *Ghoṣpāṛār Satī Mā,* 302.

68. Marshall, *Bengal: The British Bridgehead,* 178.

69. Mitra, "Kartābhajā: Saṃśaya o Samasyā," 89.

70. Hyram Haydn, *The Counter Renaissance* (New York: Grove Press, 1960); R. Kinsman, ed. *The Darker Vision of the Renaissance* (Berkeley: University of California Press, 1974).

71. Banerjee, *The Parlour and the Streets,* 68, 69.

72. Śrī J. (pseudonym), "Kartābhajāder Sambandhe Kroṛapatre," *Bāndhava* 6, no. 9 (1288 B.S. [1881]), 395; cf. Chakrabarty, *Vaiṣṇavism in Bengal,* 368.

73. Cakravartī, *Paścimbaṅger Melā o Mahotsava,* 176–77.

74. Cakravartī, *Paścimbaṅger Melā o Mahotsava,* 176.

75. Mitra, *Āmi Kān Pete Rai,* 46.

76. Interviewed in Ghosphara, July 19, 1996, and in Calcutta, July 24, 1996.

77. Cakravartī, "Kartābhajāner Rūpa o Svarūpa, xv. "At one time, it was said 'Man is truth,' but . . . it was transformed into 'the Guru is truth.' . . . The Kartābhajās brought the Guru between the worshipped and the worshipper. In the feudal system there was also a middle position between the Rājā and his subjects, in the hierarchy of Zamindār, Taluqdār and small land-holder." Cakravartī, *Sāhebdhanī Sampradāya,* 43.

78. *Saṃvāda Prabhākara,* 18 Caitra, 1254 B.S. [1848]; Bandyopādhyāy, "Sekāler Saṃvādapatre Ghoṣpāṛer Melā;" cf. Datta, *Bhāratavarṣīya Upāsaka Sampradāya,* 226–28.

79. Sarkār, "Ghoṣpāṛā Melā: Samājavijñ ānabhittik Samīkṣa," 56–60.

80. Datta, *Bhāratavarṣīya Upāsaka Sampradāya,* 226.

81. *Somaprakāśa,* 20 Caitra 1270 B.S. [1864]; Bandyopādhyāy, "Sekāler Saṃvādapatre Ghoṣpāṛer Melā," 46.

82. Kripal, *Kālī's Child,* 225.

83. Mālik, *Nadīya Kāhinī,* 240; cf. Datta, *Bhāratavarṣīya Upāsaka Sampradāya,* 225–27.

84 . "The new social conscience . . . of Unitarianism was in Rammohun almost entirely directed to the miserable state of women. He found them uneducated and illiterate, married before puberty imprisoned in purdah and murdered at widowhood. . . . [O]nly

by freeing women . . . could Indian society free itself from social stagnation." Kopf, *The Brahmo Samaj,* 15. See Rammohun's *Brief Remarks.*

For other studies of women in the Bengal Renaissance, see Judith Walsh, "The Virtuous Wife and the Well-Ordered Home: The Re-conceptualization of Bengali Women and their Worlds," in *Mind, Body and Society: Life and Mentality in Colonial Bengal,* ed. R. Ray (Calcutta: Oxford, 1955); Tanika Sarkar, "Politics and Women in Bengal—The Conditions and Meaning of Participation," in *Women in Colonial India: Essays on Survival, Work and the State* (Delhi: Oxford, 1989).

85. Chatterjee, *The Nation and its Fragments,* 116.

86. Ghulam Murshid, *Reluctant Debutante: Response of Bengali Women to Modernization* (Rajshahi: Sahitya Samsad, 1983), 123.

87. Chatterjee, *The Nation and its Fragments,* 127.

88. Apart from that of guru-ship, the Kartābhajā tradition also offered women important roles as religious singers or Kīrtanwalīs. Particularly in the nineteenth century, the role of the Kīrtanwalī was a lucrative one—though also an ambivalent role which aroused both respect and suspicion in mainstream society. Mitra's novel, *Āmi Kān Pete Rai,* offers a remarkable insight into the status of a Kartābhajā Kīrtanwalī in nineteenth-century Calcutta: On one hand, because of her unusual independence, she was regularly identified as a kind of prostitute, whose musical performances were followed by the sale of sexual favors. In fact, the more successful Kīrtanwalīs often became retainees of wealthy businessmen, who supported them, often extravagantly, in exchange for both musical and sexual favors: "All these women—. . . those women who pursued the life of a professional singer, as well as those who openly practiced prostitution—were affluent. And even if the Kīrtanwalīs . . . were not common prostitutes, they were often retained by reputed Zamindārs or Merchants. Some of them lived together with the same man as husband and wife for a long period of time." *Āmi Kān Pete Rai,* 62–63.

But as the character Sarabhāi explains, even if it is true that the Kīrtanwalīs sometimes invite a man to spend the night, they are by no means mere prostitutes: for they act freely and are well compensated by their affluent guests: "They're not the same as 'prostitutes.' . . . It's true that, once in a while, one of the Bābus may spend the night. But . . . those bābus are no small fries—they're very affluent men. . . . And there is no lack of money—indeed, there's heaps of money" (ibid., 71).

89. Tṛpti Brahma, "Satīmā," *Satyadhāraṇ,* Dol number (1390–91 B.S. [1983–84]).

90. Cakravartī, *Sāhebdhanī Sampradāya,* 39.

91. Interviewed July 12, 1996 at her home (Calcutta). To protect her privacy, I have chosen not to use her name in this book.

92. *Saṃvāda Prabhākara,* 18 Caitra, 1254 B.S. [1848]; Bandyopādhyāy, "Sekāler Saṃvādapatre Ghoṣpāṛār Melā," 40.

93. Sen, *Bṛhat Baṅga,* vol. II, 893.

94. *Saṃvāda Prabhākara,* 18 Caitra, 1254 B.S. [1848]; Bandyopādhyāy, "Sekāler Saṃvādapatre Ghoṣpāṛer Melā," 41.

95. *Somaprakāśa,* 23 Caitra 1270 B.S. [1864]; Bandyopādhyāy, "Sekāler Saṃvādapatre Ghoṣpāṛer Melā," 47.

96. Among the few studies on the role of women in Tantra are Shaw, *Passionate Enlightenment;* Sanjukta Gupta, "Women in Śaiva/Śākta Ethos," in *Roles and Rituals for Women,* ed. J. Leslie (London: Pinter, 1991); Rita Gross, "I Will Never Forget to Visualize that Vajrayogini Is My Body and Mind," *Journal of Feminist Studies in Religion* 3, no. 1 (Spring, 1987): 77–89.

Lee Siegel, "Bengal Blackie and the Sacred Slut: A Sahajiyā Buddhist Song," *Buddhist Christian Studies* 1 (1981): 51–58.

97. See, for example, Sir Monier Monier-Williams's account of Tantrism, in *Hinduism* (New York: Society for Promoting Christian Knowledge, 1985), 129–30.

98. Miranda Shaw, *Passionate Enlightenment: Women in Tantric Buddhism* (Princeton: Princeton University Press, 1994), 11. For similar romantic views, cf. Eliade, Yoga, 259–61.

99. The most important of these are Bholanath Bhattacharya's interviews with female Śākta and Sahajiyā sādhikās in Bengal. "Some Aspects of the Esoteric Cults of Consort Worhsip in Bengal: A Field Survey Report," *Folklore* 18, nos. 1–2 (1976). There are also some firsthand accounts among Bāul women. Cf. R. M. Sarkar, *Bāuls of Bengal: In Quest of the Man of the Heart* (New Delhi: Gain Publishing, 1990); Līnā Cākī, "Bāul Saṅginī—Mahilā Bāul," in *Bāul, Lālan, Rabīndranāth,* ed. S. Mitra (Calcutta: Pustak Bipaṇi, 1995).

100. *Jīvanvṛttānta,* 37, trans. Kripal, *Kālī's Child,* 123.

101. *Kathāmṛta,* 2.89, trans. by Kripal, *Kālī's Child,* 124. On another occasion, Vaiṣṇavacaraṇ took Rāmakṛṣṇa to meet a group of women belonging to a sect called the Navarasikas, which appears to be another name for the Kartābhajās. One of the women, it seems, began to make the rather odd gesture of sucking her own big toe; meanwhile, another woman—apparently commenting on the first act—"acted out a very obscene gesture" (*Jīvanvṛttānta,* 37; Kripal, *Kālī's Child,* 123).

102. Dās, *Saṅgīta o Darśana,* 122.

103. Ibid., 119.

104. Ibid., 115.

105. O'Flaherty, *Women, Androgynes and Other Mythical Beasts* (Chicago: University of Chicago Press, 1980), 38; see also Hayes, "Shapes for the Soul," 234–38.

106. Miśra, *Bhāva Lahari Gīta,* 57–58.

107. Dās, *Śrī Satī Mā Candrikā,* 70

108. David Snellgrove, *Indo-Tibetan Buddhism: Indian Buddhists and their Tibetan Successors* (Boston: Shambhala, 1987), 287. Many other scholars have made similar observations: "Women . . . are made subordinate to and dependent upon males and their ritual role is . . . limited to being a partner for male adepts." Brooks, *Auspicious Wisdom,* 25–26.

109. Gupta et al., *Hindu Tantrism,* 34.

110. *Ratnasāra,* quoted in Bose, *Post-Caitanya Sahajiā Cult,* 77.

111. Bose, *Post-Caitanya Sahajiā Cult,* 76.

112. Foucault, *The History of Sexuality, Volume 1,* 103; cf. *Power/Knowledge: Selected Interviews and Other Writings, 1972–1977* (New York: Pantheon 1980), 219–20. "Power is a pressure toward ever-greater optimization. Sex . . . becomes a thing not to be simply condemned . . . but managed, inserted into a system of utility, regulated, made to function to an optimum." Hubert Dreyfus, "On the Ordering of Things," in *Michel Foucault: Philosopher,* ed. T. Armstrong (New York: Routledge, 1992), 88.

113. Cakravartī, *Sāhebdhanī Sampradāya,* 39; cf. *Vrātya Lokāyata Lālan,* 104–105.

Chapter 3

1. See Dimock, *The Place of the Hidden Moon,* 103–105; Hayes, "Vaiṣṇava Sahajiyā Traditions."

2. Stewart, "Sex, Secrecy and the Politics of Sahajiyā Scholarship," 39, cited op. cit.

3. Cakravartī, *Gabhīr Nirjan Pathe,* 13; For good discussions of the Kartābhajās's unique form of *sandhābhāṣā,* see Cakravartī, "Kartābhajāner Rūpa o Svarūpa," xv–xvi. "There is no

doubt that this religion was influenced by Tantra. That is why it must be kept hidden from common people. . . . If one is not an intimate, it cannot be revealed." Dās, *Saṅgīta o Darśana,* 122.

4. Chakrabarty, *Vaiṣṇavism in Bengal,* 368.

5. See section "Coinage for the Poor." H. P. Śāstri and others had thought that the term was "twilight language" (*Sandhyā-bhāṣā*). *Bauddha Gān O Dohā,* 8. However, Vidhusekhar Shastri showed definitively that it is in fact "intentional language," *sandhābhāṣā,* which is a shortened form of *sandhāya,* a gerund formed from the root *dhā* with the prefix *sam,* meaning "aiming at, having in view, intending." "Sandhābhāṣā," *Indian Historical Quarterly* 4 (1928): 295. See Agehandanda Bharati, "Intentional Language in the Tantras," *Journal of the American Oriential Society* 81 (1961): 261–70; Eliade, *Yoga,* 250.

6. Śāstrī, *Bauddha Gān O Dohā,* 8. See Shastri, "Sandhābhāṣā," 295; Dasgupta, *Obscure Religious Cults,* 413–14; Bharati, "Intentional Language," 261–70.

7. See Dasgupta, *Obscure Religious Cults,* 413–14; Dimock, *The Place,* 124–25.

8. Hayes, "The Vaiṣṇava Sahajiyā Traditions," 334.

9. Eliade, *Yoga,* 253f. For a similar "cryptological" model, see Bharati, *Tantric Tradition,* 164–67.

10. Jha, "Cari-Candra-Bhed: Use of the Four Moons," in *Mind, Body and Society: Life and Mentality in Colonial Bengal,* ed. R.Ray (Calcutta: Oxford University Press, 1995), 69–71. Jha identifies at least eleven divergent interpretations of the four moons, ranging from whether the four substances are literal or merely symbolic, how they are to be ingested, order of ingestion, how often, and so on.

Rahul Peter Das has shown a similar conflict of interpretations among various Bāuls regarding sexual practices. "Problematic Aspects of the Sexual Rituals of the Bāuls of Bengal," *Journal of the American Oriental Society* 112, no. 3 (1992): 399–432.

11. "Among the songs there is some philosophy, but its value is not as great as their unusual simplicity and the originality in their composition. . . . There is no influence from the high-class *sādhubhāṣā.* The unrestricted emotion of Sahaja is expressed with the simple language of the spoken word. . . . Within these songs flows the life blood of Bengali literature which one cannot see anywhere prior to Rabindranath." Sen, "Kartābhajār Kathā o Gān," 39.

12. As Cakravartī comments, "Lālśaśī's *Bhāver Gīta* is half urban and half rural in its language. That's why it has found an audience among both contemporary and later generations." *Vrātya Lokāyat Lālan,* 131–32. Hence, it is difficult to classify the songs of the *Bhāver Gīta* among the genres of Bengali literature. They do not really fit into the better known forms of the nineteenth century, such as the popular *kheuḍ* songs (songs about the love of Rādhā and Kṛṣṇa), the *kathakatā* (mythological stories), or the *pāñcālī* (popular songs interspersed with short rhymes about Hindu divinities); nor do they appear to reflect Muslim forms such as the *dobhasi* literature. See Banerjee, *The Parlour,* 95–107. With their use of a "Question and Answer" (*Saoyāl-Jabāb*) format, and their extensive use of secular imagery drawn from life in Calcutta, the songs of the *Bhāver Gīta* bear some resemblance to the *Kabi* songs—or poetic duals between groups of performers, usually in a question-and-answer format—so popular in nineteenth-century Calcutta. Nagendranāth Basu, ed., *Viśvakoṣa* (Calcutta, 1299 B.S. [1892], 3:223).

In short, the *Bhāver Gīta* represents a complex and original mixture of both traditional Vaiṣṇava devotional songs with the more "secular" forms of nineteenth-century Calcutta, combining classic religious themes with vivid descriptions of contemporary social life. As Banerjee has shown in his study of nineteenth-century folk culture, this kind of fusion of rural and urban styles was part of a much broader cultural fusion taking place in colonial Calcutta, as poor peasants and workers migrated from the villages and resettled their homes and folk culture in the new urban environment. The result was the birth of a variety of new styles—dubbed "abominable entertainments" by the upper classes—"consisting of rural folk forms imported from village homes and innovations born of the new urban environment." "The World of Ramjan Ostagar," 81.

13. D. C. Sen, "Kartābhajā Dal," *Baṅgabani,* no. 4 (1 Barṣa, 1358 B.S. [1951]): 33.

14. Cakravartī, *Gabhīr Nirjan Pathe*, 13.

15. J. P. Losty, *Calcutta: City of Palaces: A Survey of the City in the Days of the East India Company, 1690–1858* (London: Arnold Publishers, 1990), 102.

16. This phrase is actually not included in Miśra's list of 204 Mint Sayings, but it is widely accepted as the most famous of the Kartābhajās' secret phrases; Miśra discusses it elsewhere (e.g., KDA 31). The term *Hijṛā* typically refers to a male who has had his penis and testicles removed in a ritual operation; he then becomes part of a semireligious community of similar men who dress as women and often engage in homosexual prostitution. For an excellent study of this community, see Serena Nanda, *Neither Man nor Woman: The Hijṛās of India* (Belmont: Wadsworth, 1990).

17. Sen, "Āmār Jīvana," 187.

18. See Nanda, *Neither Man nor Woman*, 12–13.

19. Pāl, *Ghoṣpāṛār Satīmā,* 219–21. As Dineścandra Sen comments, "everyone knows the verse of Baba Aul: the woman is a hijṛā, the man a eunuch, then you will be a Kartābhajā. If one cannot fully control the senses, one has no authority to enter this religion." "Kartābhajā Dal," 33.

20. See Bhaṭṭācārya, *Bāṅglār Bāul o Bāul Gān*, 69–71; Sen, *Śrīśrīrāmakṛṣṇa-puṅthi*: "Taking a woman is the true method of practice; but how many men in a million are capable of such a practice? The Lord said that this path is not easy—The woman must become a *hijṛā*, the man must become a eunuch. Then they will be Kartābhajās, otherwise, they will not. At every step the practitioners fear falling" (116).

21· Dās, *Saṅgīta o Darśana,* 69–72.

22. See Miśra, *Bhāva Lahari Gīta*, 57–58.

23. This is the explanation given by a Kartābhajā guru named Trailokya Mahānta, interviewed in Sudhīr Cakravartī, *Paścim Baṅger Melā o Mahotsava* (Calcutta: Pustak Bipaṇi, 1996): "One must remain in the formless state. It is as if the woman becomes a *hijṛā* and the man becomes a *khojā*" (177).

24. Kripal, *Kālī's Child*, 224–25.

25. See Dās, *Śrī Satīmā Candrikā*, 70–72; and Śrī J. (pseud.), "Kartābhajāder Saṃbandhe Kroṛapatre," *Bandhava* 6, no. 9 (1288 B.S. [1881]): 395.

26. Ricoeur, *Hermeneutics and the Human Sciences* (Toronto: University of Toronto Press, 1986), 161–62. As Mario Valdes, Introduction, in *A Ricoeur Reader: Reflection and Imagination* (Toronto: University of Toronto Press, 1991), comments, "Rather than a transposition of meaning from author to reader, literary criticism becomes a process, a movement, back and forth between text and critic. . . . There can be no claim to definitive meaning of the text, for this claim would kill the text" (11).

27. Clifford, *The Predicament of Culture*, 52, paraphrasing Barthes, *Image Music Text* (New York: Hill and Wang, 1977), 146, 148.

28 On the McGuffin metaphor, see Introduction, section titled "The Torment of Secrecy." See also Burkert, "Der Geheime Reiz des Verbogenen: Antike Mysterienkulte," and Apter, *Black Critics and Kings,* 107–108.

29. Roland Barthes, *Writing Degree Zero* (New York: Hill and Wang, 1977); cf. *The Barthes Reader*, ed. Susan Sontag (New York: Hill and Wang, 1995), xxiii.

30. Bellman, *The Language of Secrecy*, 144.

31. Miśra, *Satyadharma Upāsana vā Śukrabārer Yājana Praṇālī* (Calcutta: Indralekha Press, 1398 B.S. [1991]), 66–67.

32. Interviewed in Mazdia village, Nadiya district, September 10, 1996. It later turns out, interestingly enough, that this individual was not in fact an actual Kartābhajā , but simply a local musician who had heard that a Western scholar was coming, and so presented himself to me as a Kartābhajā master and the possessor of many esoteric teachings.

33. Barth, *Ritual and Knowledge*, 217.

34. This hierarchy is summarized in Miśra's STP*;* see also Nandī, *Kartābhajā Dharma*, 69–71.

35. Śrī J. (pseud.), "Kartābhajāder Saṃbandhe Kroṛapatre," 395.

36. Chakrabarty, *Vaiṣṇavism in Bengal*, 368.

37. Interviewed in Calcutta, July 14, 1996.

38· Bourdieu, *The Logic of Practice,* 141.

39. Thurman, "Vajra Hermeneutics," in *Buddhist Hermeneutics,* ed. D. Lopez (Honolulu: University of Hawaii Press, 1988). For a good analysis of its role in Aboriginal society, see Keen, *Knowledge and Secrecy in Aboriginal Religion*: "The constitution of guarded religious knowledge was founded in ambiguity. I posit a general structure in the control of knowledge . . . resting in the ambiguity of meaning. . . . Mystery was in the hands of the few, who deliberately used devices of obscurity in the control of religious ideology" (21).

40. Lindstrom, *Knowledge and Power*, 121–22.

41. Richard Kearney, *Poetics of Imagining: From Husserl to Lyotard* (London: Harper Collins, 1991), 152; Ricoeur, "The Metaphorical Process as Cognition, Imagination and Feeling," in *On Metaphor*, ed. S. Sacks (Chicago: University of Chicago Press, 1978): "The sense of a novel metaphor . . . is the emergence of a new semantic congruence . . . from the ruins of the literal sense shattered by semantic incompatibility or absurdity . . . the suspension of the reference proper to ordinary language is the condition for the emergence of a more radical way of looking at things" (151–52).

42. Ricoeur, *Reflection and Imagination,* 32.

43. Eliade, *Yoga,* 250.

44. Miśra, *Satyadharma Upāsana,* 66–67.

45. Ibid.*,* 59–60.

46. Thompson, Introduction to Bourdieu, *Language and Symbolic Power,* 22.

47. Chakrabarty, *Vaiṣṇavism in Bengal*, 365. "The Sahaja remains like one blind in the daylight, his eyes are opened in the night and his true life begins at night. In the daytime he has to do conventional things, to observe the rules of caste and pay respect to the Malik the Missionary and the Brahman. . . . But he becomes the true man at night in secret societies. . . . There they pay no heed to the rules of caste and other social relations." Sen, *Chaitanya and His Age,* 402.

48. Davis, *Dojo: Magic and Exorcism in Modern Japan* (Stanford: Stanford University Press, 1980), 239–41

49. Pāl, *Ghoṣpāṛār Satī Mā*, 255.

50. Cited in Garrett, *Bengal District Gazetteer, Nadia,* 49–50 (emphasis added).

51. The title of this section, "Meetings with Remarkable Madmen," is a play on the classic work of George Gurdjieff, *Meetings with Remarkable Men* (New York: Dutton, 1963). The term madman (*pāgal, kṣepā, bāul*) is commonly used to describe holy men of the

Kartābhajā and other sects, who are believed to be utterly beyond the boundaries and laws of mainstream society—hence seemingly insane or intoxicated with God.

52. Brooks, *The Secret of the Three Cities*, 6–7.

53. In the interest of privacy, I have chosen not to use the real names of these gurus and devotees.

54. Interviewed in Mazdia village, West Bengal, September 10, 1996. I had strong suspicions about this individual's credibility when I found that he knew none of the songs contained in the *Bhāver Gīta* and seemed to have only a rudimentary idea of what the Kartābhajā tradition was. Later, respected folklorist Dr. Vasudev Mandal of Krishnanagar informed me that this singer had no connection with the Kartābhajās and was widely known as something of a charlatan.

55. Interviewed July 19, 1996. As explained previously (Introduction, note 56), I have decided to respect the privacy of my informants by using pseudonyms in this book. Although it is not an ideal solution to the ethical-epistemological double bind, it is necessary, in the absence of informed consent, to protect the rights and reputations of these individuals.

56. He seemed in fact to be paraphrasing one particular song, which goes as follows: "From (God's) Forehead, the seed fell into the bottomless waters; and thus it fell into a prison and was bound within the net of Māyā. Within that lie both birth and death. Upon that ocean lies a Great Jewel of a Man. That jewel is an invaluable treasure, like the seed within a seed! But no one can grasp it without good spiritual compansions. Gaze upon this ray of light within the city of the Heart!" (BG 414)

57. This is also a paraphrase of a series of songs from the *Bhāver Gīta,* which describe the spiritual path with the allegory of "sailing to the Hidden City" (BG 159–60). For a more extended discussion of these metaphors, see chapter 5.

58. Pāl, *Ghoṣpāṛār Satīmā,* 246–54.

59. Interviewed numerous times at his home in North Calcutta, and in Ghoshpara, between July and October 1996.

60. See Pāl, *Ghoṣpāṛār Satīmā,* 246–54.

61. Although he claimed these to be highly secret and dangerous techniques, reserved solely for the most advanced disciples, most of them are basically adapted from very old and pan-Indian traditions of yoga and are easily accessible in any book store, both in India and in the United States.

62. Interview at his home, August 10, 1996.

63. Interview, August 10, 1996.

64. As Bourdieu points out, dominated groups often reproduce their own domination even in the very act of resisting it. The use of slang, for example, is a deliberate violation of the normal laws of language, which offers a kind of symbolic capital to lower-class groups. But at the same time, it reinforces the image of the lower class speaker as ignorant, uncivilized or "vulgar." As such, it cannot be grasped within a simple binarism of domination and resistance, but is a more ambivalent mixture of subordination and contestation: "[S]lang is the product of a quest for distinction that is none the less dominated and condemned to produce paradoxical effects which cannot be understood . . . within the alternatives of resistance or submission. . . . When the dominated quest for distinction leads the dominated to affirm . . . that in the name of which they are dominated and constituted as vulgar, do we talk of resistance? . . . Resistance may be alienating and submission may be liberating." *In Other Words*, 155. So, too, the paradox of the Kartābhajās is that the very practices which endowed them with power and freedom—the use of Tantric language and practices

which transgress social boundaries—would also become a new source of alienation: it made them all the more "vulgar" and despicable in the eyes of the exoteric world.

CHAPTER 4

1. At least some of this complex economic terminology was explained to me by Advaita Candra Dās (interviewed in Calcutta, June–August 1996).

2. De, *Kartābhajā Dharmer Itivṛtta*, 9–10. See also Banerjee, "From Aulchand to Satī Mā," 29–60.

3. Sen, "Passages of Authority," 31–35; see chapter 1. On Rāmakṛṣṇa's use of market images, see Sarkar, *An Exploration of the Ramakrishna Vivekananda Tradition*, 25–30. "It is the world of the chakri, of clerical jobs in mercantile and government offices, that dominates Ramakrishna's milieu" (ibid., 25).

4. Chakrabarty, *Vaiṣṇavism in Bengal*, 360.

5. See Guha, *Elementary Aspects*, chap. 2; Chatterjee, *The Nation and Its Fragments,* chap. 9. As Gayatri Spivak, "A Literary Representation of the Subaltern: Mahasweta Devi's *Stanadayini*," in *Subaltern Studies,* vol. 5, ed. R. Guha (Delhi: Oxford, 1987), comments: "One argument of Subaltern Studies has been that the subaltern persistently translates the discourse of religion into the discourse of militancy" (131).

6. See George Lakoff and Mark Johnson, *Metaphors We Live By* (Chicago: University of Chicago Press, 1980), 3–10; Mark Johnson, *Body in the Mind: The Bodily Basis of Meaning, Imagination and Reason* (Chicago: University of Chicago Press, 1987).

7. Fernandez, *Persuasions and Performances: The Play of Tropes in Culture* (Bloomington: Indiana University Press, 1986): "Culture . . . rests upon metonymic and metaphoric predications of sign images upon inchoate subjects. . . . These predications take place within an x-dimensional cultural quality space and give affective definition to pronouns which seek to be more aptly located within that space" (60–61).

8. de Certeau, *The Practice of Everyday Life*, xi–xii. This tactic of consumption is part of "a logic whose models go as far back as the age old ruses of fishes and insects that disguise themselves in order to survive. . . . Everyday life invents itself by poaching . . . on the property of others" (ibid.).

9. BG (1882), paraphrased by Chakrabarty, *Vaiṣṇavism in Bengal,* 377.

10. Sen, "The Conquest of Marketplaces," 229–31; see chapter 1 in this volume.

11. Bakhtin, *Rabelais and His World* (Bloomington: Indiana University Press, 1984), 153–54.

12. Guha, *Elementary Aspects*, 258.

13. *Hāṭ Pattan*, 195, trans. Sen, "Passages of Authority," 31.

14. Sen, "Passages of Authority," 32, quoting D. C. Sen, *Baṅgīya Sāhitya Paricaya,* 1838.

15. Jhā, *Phakir Lālan Sāiṅ*, 218. As Lālan sings, "O Madman, you've brought the Moneylender's wealth, and now you've lost it with the remaining debt, you'll go the world of the dead; your fate is sealed with indebtedness. . . . Come to the bazaar of bliss and engage in business" (ibid., 63).

16. Sarkar, *An Exploration of the Ramakrishna Vivekananda Tradition*, 31.

17. Banerjee, *The Parlour and the Streets,* 84. "Their cultural expressions [were] a radical manifestation of protest coming from the bottom, directed against both the new colonial influence and old feudal customs, in a language that was more earthy than that cultivated by the educated gentry" (ibid., 9).

18. On the role of the *Dālāls* and *Pāikārs* in the Bengali marketplace, see Marshall, *East*

Indian Fortunes, 38–9: "Production of commodities appears to have been arranged by men whose commonest title was *dālāl* or *pāikār.* . . . Merchants placed orders with *dālāls* and advanced money to them. The *dālāls* in turn commissioned *pāikārs* to set the weavers to work. Finished cloth was finally adjusted by the merchants with the *dālāls.*"

19. Chakrabarty, *Vaiṣṇavism in Bengal*, 374, paraphrasing BG (1882), 138, 148

20. BG (1882) 117, 126.

21. Ibid., 127, 138.

22. Ibid., 19. On the conversion of Kartābhajās by Christian missionaries, see Oddie, "Old Wine in New Bottles," 15–20

23. Chakrabarty, *Vaiṣṇavism in Bengal*, 378, paraphrasing BG (1882), 125–26, 138.

24. This refers to the conflict between the French and British in India, corresponding to their wars at home: It probably refers to the military campaigns waged by the Company against the French in 1795, dictated by the Revolutionary War in Europe. See Marshall, *East Indian Fortunes*, chap. III.

25. Arjun Appadurai, "Introduction: Commodities and the Politics of Value," in *The Social Life of Things: Commodities in Cultural Perspective,* ed. A. Appadurai (Cambridge: Cambridge University Press, 1986), 52. There is a vast literature on the cargo cults; see especially Peter Worsely, *And the Trumpets Shall Sound* (New York: Schocken, 1957); Glynn Cochrane, *Big Men and Cargo Cults* (Oxford: Clarendon Press, 1970).

26. See Banerjee, *The Parlour,* 38.

27. Chatterjee, *The Nation and Its Fragments,* 85. See *Rājāvalī* (Serampore: Baptist Mission Press, 1808); on Rāmprasād Mitra, see Das Gupta, "Old Calcutta as Presented in Literature," 118.

28. The image of the "Three Madmen" is common in many Bāul songs and refers to Caitanya and his foremost disciples, Nityānanda and Advaita Ācārya; according to the following song recorded by Capwell, "That rosik madman came and created an uproar in Nodia. . . . Nitai is mad, Gowr is mad, Caitanya is the root of madness. Advaita became mad and sank into *ras.*" *Music of the Bāuls*, 190.

29. Chakrabarty, *Vaiṣṇavism in Bengal,* 378, paraphrasing BG (1882), 147, app. 1.

30. Ibid., 124; cf. Mukhopādhyāy, "Pravartakendrik Sahajiyā," 4.

31. BG (1882) 122, trans. by Chakrabarty, *Vaiṣṇavism in Bengal,* 378. On the meaning of the Perso-Arabic term *ādab* and the image of the "Good-Mannered Company," see chapter 6. Essentially, *ādab* is used to refer to the characteristics of refinement, manners and good taste which distinguish the aristocracy: "Adherence to *ādab* (norms of refined behavior and taste) . . . was essential for aristocratic status and comprised the content of what aristocracy was supposed to mean. . . . *Ādab* consisted of certain . . . generally acknowledged modes of dress, interpersonal behavior and deportment." Chatterjee, *Merchants, Politics and Society,* 208–209. See Barbara Metcalf, ed. *Moral Conduct and Authority: The Place of Adab in Asian Islam* (Berkeley: University of California Press, 1984).

32. "A 100-petalled lotus floats upon the immeasurable waters, and upon it is a poor wretched Madman (*becārā pāgal*) . . . That heavy-bearded one completed the cycle. He wandered through heaven, earth and hell, and all that remained to complete the cycle was the land of the poor Wretched One. . . . The Distinguished Company goes to bring that Medicine, and when one gets it, he is filled with joy. At the gesture of the Bearded One, [the Company's] wandering is ended. The four [Madmen, i.e., Caitanya, Nityānanda, Advaita and Āulcāṅd] have joined together as one and have crossed over" (BG 190). Also "A Poor Wretched Man came; In due succession, he completed the cycle. This is the story of the Three [Caitanya, Nityānanda and Advaita]. . . . The Original Company was comprised of

the three worlds. Even if they went to travel to different lands, and found the three Men [Caitanya, Nityānanda and Advaita], why would they return and cease to wander? For only when the four Madmen [i.e., the three plus Āulcāṅd] join together and cross over is [their search] completed" (BG 189; II.8).

33. Chakrabarty, *Vaiṣṇavism in Bengal*, 375, paraphrasing BG (1882), 221. On the *ādab Kompānī,* see Mukhopādhyāy, "Pravartakendrik Sahajiyā," 4–5.

34 . "What shall I tell you about our state? The one who founded this Platoon of the Poor (*kāṅgāler palṭan*) is the Great Poor God (*gorib bidhātā*)! See the ragged clothing of our Creator—If anyone desires anything, He will import it! . . . Whether we want it or not, brother, we always get it—even if the room and the foundations are not to our liking. For, apart from a poor shanty, the Creator can build nothing else! And Śaśī Lāl laughs and says, 'His bed is a date-palm leaf!'" (BG 112; II.10).

35. "The Merchant of this city has prepared his ship; and with him, how many foodstuffs go! They look again at the list of rates—for something of one value, he gives the people a hundred times that. In this way, he gives the price, you know! He distributes it to the Poor people in this land. Such a thing has occurred in this gathering of the Poor!" (BG 123).

36. On the importance of the Company's seal on goods imported and exported in Bengal, see Marshall, *East Indian Fortunes*, 110–12.

37. Compare this line with the song of Lālan, "*tin pāgale melā holo. . . .*" Sanatkumār Mitra, *Lālan Phakir: Kabī o Kābya* (Calcutta: Pustak Bipaṇi, 1386 B.S. [1979), 113–14. Here is further evidence of the connections between Lālan and the Kartābhajās and the possible influence of the latter on the former.

38. Appadurai, "Commodities and the Politics of Value," 52.

39. Sahlins, *Culture and Practical Reason* (Chicago: University of Chicago Press, 1976), 169; on this subject, see also Igor Kopytoff, " The Cultural Biography of Things: Commoditization as Process," in *The Social Life of Things: Commodities in Cultural Perspective,* ed. A. Appadurai (Cambridge: Cambridge University Press, 1986): "For the economist, commodities simply are. . . . Certain things are produced and . . . circulate through the economic system. . . . From a cultural perspective, the production of commodities is also a cultural and cognitive process: commodities must be not only produced materially as things, but also culturally marked as being a certain kind of thing" (64).

40. Hebdige, *Subculture: The Meaning of Style*, 18 (emphasis added).

41. Taussig, *The Devil and Commodity Fetishism,* 181.

42. Comaroff, *Modernity and Its Malcontents*, xi–xii. As Sahlins, "Cosmologies of Capitalism," comments, "Western capitalism has loosed on the world enormous forces of production, coercion and destruction. Yet precisely because they cannot be resisted, the goods of the larger system take on meaningful places in the local scheme of things" (4).

43. Lakoff and Johnson, *Metaphors We Live By*, 236.

44. On this point, see Banerjee, "From Aulchand to Satī Mā," and Cakravartī, *Paścim Baṅger Melā*: "In the songs of the Kartābhajās there is a great deal of language of business, trade, scales, weighing, shopkeepers . . . the Company. In the purses of the Kartās today, too, many coins jingle" (173).

Chapter 5

1. De, *Kartābhajā Dharmer Itivṛtta,* 12.

2. Pāl, *Ghoṣpāṛār Satīmā,* 254, quoting *Kathāmṛta,* 5.10.2.

3. See Marcel Mauss, "Techniques of the Body," *Economy and Society* 2 (1978): 70–88; Mary Douglas, "The Two Bodies," *Natural Symbols: Explorations in Cosmology* (New York: Pantheon, 1970); Bryan S. Turner, *The Body and Society: Explorations in Social Theory* (Oxford: Basil Blackwell, 1988). As Bourdieu, *The Logic of Practice*, puts it, "All the symbolic manipulations of bodily experience, starting with . . . a symbolically structured space, tend to impose the integration of body space with cosmic space and social space, by applying the same categories . . . to the relationship between man and the natural world" (77).

On the "inscription" of the social law or Logos on the human body, see de Certeau, *The Practice of Everyday Life*, 139–42; Comaroff, *Body of Power*, 9–10.

4. Comaroff, *Body of Power*, 9–11; cf. Bynum, *Fragmentation and Redemption: Essays on Gender and the Human Body in Medieval Religion* (New York: Zone Books, 1992).

5. Douglas, *Natural Symbols*, 98–9. On the role of the body as an alloform of the social hierarchy, see Bruce Lincoln, *Myth, Cosmos and Society: Indo-European Themes of Creation and Destruction* (Cambridge: Harvard University Press 1986), 170–72.

6. Michel Foucault, *Discipline and Punish: The Birth of the Prison* (New York: Vintage, 1980), 25.

7. Bourdieu, *The Logic of Practice*, 69–70. "Spatial organization, built form and everyday practice were the silent bearers of a symbolic scheme . . . which impressed itself upon consciousness as the process of socialization inserted the person into the world. . . . [T]his process was centered upon the body, the medium through which the values of any social system become internalized as categories of individual experience and identity. . . . The signs and functions of the organism act as a 'memory,' a condensed model for the collective order." Comaroff, *Body of Power*, 124.

8. Bourdieu, *In Other Words*, 167.

9. Bill Ashcroft, Gareth Griffiths, and Helen Tiffin, eds., *The Post-colonial Studies Reader* (New York: Routledge, 1995), 321–22. As Homi Bhabha, "Postcolonial Authority and Post-Modern Guilt," in *The Post-Colonial Studies Reader,* puts it, "the native wears his psychic wounds on the surface of his skin like an open sore—an eyesore to the colonizer" (65). On "the importance of the body as a site of power and contestation between the colonized and the colonizers," see David Arnold, *Colonizing the Body: State Medicine and Epidemic Disease in Nineteenth Century India* (Berkeley: University of California Press, 1993).

10. Ashcroft, et al., *The Post-Colonial Studies Reader*, 321–22.

11. As Ong, *Spirits of Resistance,* argues in the case of women factory workers in Malaysia, the body itself often becomes the locus of a "struggle of resistance against a new capitalist and industrial system which dehumanizes and degrades individuals, which turns bodies into raw materials to be disciplined and molded for the purposes of production" (10).

12. Guha, *Elementary Aspects of Peasant Insurgency*, 164. As Chatterjee, *The Nation and Its Fragments,* observes, "Caste attaches itself to the body, not the soul. It is the biological reproduction of the human species through procreation with endogamous caste groups which ensures the permanence of marks of caste purity . . . It is the physical contact of the body with defiling substances that mark it with the conditions of pollution which can be removed by observing prescribed procedures of physical cleanings" (194).

13. Ronald Inden, *Marriage and Rank in Bengal Culture: A History of Caste and Clan in Middle Period Bengal* (Berkeley: University of California Press, 1976), 10.

14. Ronald Inden and Ralph Nicholas, *Kinship in Bengali Culture* (Chicago: University of Chicago Press, 1987), 37.

15. Ibid., 23

16. Ibid., 52.

17. Ibid., 55, 52–54. On these ideas in other Indian traditions, see White, *The Alchemical Body,* 184–202; E. Valentine Daniel, *Fluid Signs: Being a Person the Tamil Way* (Berkeley: University of California Press, 1987).

18. Hayes, "Shapes for the Soul," 337.

19. Bynum, *Fragmentation and Redemption,* 16–7. See also Lincoln, *Discourse,* 101–105.

20. Comaroff, *Body of Power,* 79.

21. As Datta described the initiation ritual in his account of 1870: "At the time of initiation, there is the following conversation between the Guru and disciple. *Mahāśay:* 'will you be able to perform this religious practice?' *Barātī:* 'I will.' *Mahāśay:* 'You will not speak false words, you will not steal, you will not sleep with another man's wife, and you will not sleep too often with your own wife.' *Barātī:* 'I will do none of these things.' *Mahāśay:* 'Say, "You are truth and your words are true."' *Barātī:* 'You are truth and your words are truth.' The Guru then gives him the mantra and says, 'without my permission, do not speak this name to anyone.'" (*Bhāratavarṣīya Upāsaka Sampradāya,* 223). Subsequently, once he has demonstrated his worthiness and true devotion to the Guru guru, the initiate will then be entrusted with the next degree of esoteric knowledge, the *ṣolo ānā* (or "complete") mantra: "*Kartā Āule Mahāprabhu: Āmi tomār sukhe cali phiri, tilārddha tomār hārā nāhi, āmi tomār saṅge āchi, dohāi mahāprabhu*" (ibid.). For a description and discussion of initiation by a contemporary devotee, see Dās, *Śrī Satīmā Candrikā,* 67–68.

22. Pāl, *Ghoṣpāṛār Satīmā,* 255.

23. Oddie, "Old Wine in New Bottles?" 335.

24. Datta, *Bhāratavarṣīya Upāsaka Sampradāya,* 224.

25. White, *The Alchemical Body,* 27.

26. Dās, *Saṅgīta o Darśana,* 119–20. For a good discussion of the Bāul's similar system of bodily cosmography, see Salomon, "Bāul Songs," 195–97. "The retrieval of the Sahaj Mānuṣ is the main focus of *sādhanā.* . . . On the third day of a woman's menstrual period the *Sahaj Mānuṣ,* who feels an irresistible attraction to the Śakti in menstrual blood, descends from the woman's *sahasrār* to her Triveṇī. . . . Through coitus the *Sahaj Mānuṣ* is separated out of the menstrual blood, attracted into the male practitioner's penis and brought back to the *sahasrār.* The resulting bliss . . . is called 'catching the Uncatchable, catching the thief, being dead while alive.'" (Ibid., 195–96).

27. Caṭṭopādhyāy, *Bhāver Gīta Vyākhyā,* 18–19.

28. Dās, *Śrī Satīmā Candrikā,* 70.

29. "As a result of this practice with a female companion, the Female Nature arises within one's own body. Once one has attained the female nature, an actual female partner is no longer needed. The *sādhaka* himself experiences the female nature." Dās, *Śrī Satīmā Candrikā,* 70.

30. "Saṅgītamālā," in Dās, *Śrī Satīmā Candrikā,* 87; trans. SE IV.9.

31. See Dās, *Śrī Satīmā Candrikā,* 70–72; on the penetration of the six *cakras* and the divinization or immortalization of the body, see Miśra, STP, 120–25.

32. On the river and boating metaphor, see Hayes, "Shapes for the Soul," 337–40, and Hugh Urban, "Secret Bodies: Re-Imagining the Body in the Vaiṣṇava-Sahajiyā Tradition of Bengal," *The Journal of South Asian Literature* 28, nos. 1 & 2 (1995): 45–62.

33. Much of this imagery of merchant trade and its references to Tantric bodily practices has been explained by later commentators, such as Rājanārāyaṇ Caṭṭopādhāyāy, *Bhāver Gīta Vyākhyā,* 13–14.

34. Datta, *Bhāratavarṣīya Upāsaka Sampradāya,* 228. This use of number symbolism (the

five sense organs, five physical organs, the six enemies, etc.) is common throughout Bāul and Sahajiyā songs. See Capwell, *Music of the Bāuls*, 185–86.

35. "Saṅgīta-Mālā," in Dās, *Śrī Satīmā Candrikā*, 90–91; trans. SE IV.8.

36. As Coudhurī comments, "within these words lies a slightly tricky problem. Hearing *ḍhākā,* one normally thinks of the city of Dhaka in Bangladesh. But it has another meaning besides this. In fact, it means that city which is concealed. The marketplace is where the buying and selling of love occurs. That is is the Hidden City." Cited in "Prasaṅga: Bāṅglā Bāul Gān," *Dhruvapada*, Bārṣik Saṅkalan (1997), 141.

37. Dr. Carol Salomon pointed out this image of the "Hidden City" (personal correspondence, 1997).

38. *Bhāver Gīta*, quoted in Dās, *Śrī Satīmā Candrikā*, 60. The image of *jyānte marā* appears in many earlier Sahajiyā and later Bāul songs: for example, "The inward longing is for the beloved—without whom there is the burning sensation in the heart that makes a man dead while living. This death in love is the most covetable death." Caṇḍīdāsa, trans. Dasgupta, *Obscure Religious Cults*, 137. So, too, according to a popular Bāul song, "Those who are dead and yet fully alive, and know the flavour and feeling in love will cross the river. . . . They kill lust with lust and enter the city of love unattached." Song of Haridās, in Bhattacharya, *Songs of the Bards*, 68.

39. Pāl, *Ghoṣpāṛār Satīmā*, 255.

40. Chakrabarty, *Vaiṣṇavism in Bengal,* 364.

41. Dick Hebdige, *Hiding in the Light: On Images and Things* (London: Routledge, 1988), 32.

42. Chatterjee, *The Nation and Its Fragments*, 195.

43. Chakrabarty, *Vaiṣṇavism in Bengal,* 362, 363–64. "The Sahaja remains like one blind in the daylight, his eyes are opened in the night and his true life begins at night. In the daytime he has to do conventional things, to observe the rules of caste and pay respect to the Mallik, the Missionary and the Brahman . . . and abide by their orders. But he becomes the true man at night in the secret societies . . . There they pay no heed to the rules of caste and social relations." Sen, *Chaitanya and His Age,* 402.

44. Chatterjee, *The Nation and Its Fragments*, 87.

45. Mary Douglas, *Purity and Danger: An Ananlysis of Concepts of Pollution and Taboo* (London: Routledge, 1966), 190–91. Not unlike the Tantric Aghori, who deliberately consumes the most defiling substances such as human flesh and excrement, the Kartābhajā engages in an "occult manipulation of impurity" in order to deconstruct the boundaries of conventional society itself: "Far from being orgiastic revels," Lincoln, *Discourse and the Construction of Society,* comments, "these are sacred rituals in which the Aghorins seek to enact their absolute liberation from the human condition, together with its arbitrary restraints" (114).

46. As Lincoln, *Discourse and the Construction of Society,* points out, "Egalitarianism . . . is never a simple matter, there being a multitude of ways in which hierarchy may be reasserted, the most egalitarian of claims notwithstanding" (85).

47. Pāl, *Ghoṣpāṛār Satīmā,* 218; cf. Datta, *Bhāratavarṣīya Upāsaka Sampradāya*, 226.

48. Dās, *Śrī Satīmā Candrikā,* 11–15. For a good discussion of the image of the body of the Deity as an alloform for the cosmic and social hierarchies, see Lincoln, *Myth, Cosmos and Society*, 143–46.

49. Datta, *Bhāratavarṣīya Upāsaka Sampradāya,* 226.

50. Dās, *Ghoṣpāṛār Kartābhajā Sampradāya,* 56.

51. See Sarkār, "Ghoṣpāṛār Melā," 59.

1. See, e.g., Monier Williams, *Hinduism*, 129.

2. As Heinrich Zimmer, *Philosophies of India* (New York: Meridian Books, 1956), for example, praises the Tantras, in his characteristically romantic style, "In the Tantra, the manner of approach is not that of Nay, but of Yea . . . the world attitude is affirmative . . . [M]an must rise through and by means of nature, not by rejection of nature" (576). See also Philip Rawson, *The Art of Tantra* (London: Thames and Hudson, 1973), 10. The most recent argument for the liberating and empowering nature of Tantra is Shaw's feminist reading in *Passionate Enlightenment.*

3. See Padoux, "Tantrism, an Overview," 271–72. For a more developed discussion of the imagining of "Tantrism" in colonial Bengal, see Urban, "The Extreme Orient," 123–46.

4. Monier Williams, *Hinduism,* 122–23, 116. On the "generally pejorative assessment of the Tantras" by European authors, see Halbfass, *India and Europe*, 205. As David Kopf comments, "An Historiographical Essay on the Idea of Kālī," in *Shaping Bengali Worlds, Public and Private,* ed. Tony K. Stewart (East Lansing: Asian Studies Center, 1989), "The enduring legacy of Orientalism is a contrasting set of images: the golden age, which is Indo-Aryan, Brahminical and elitist, versus a subsequent dark age, which is medieval, popular, orgiastic and corrupt. . . . An age of Kālī . . . descended upon the subcontinent as Indian culture became tribalized, its heroic classicism swamped by orgiastic religion and witchcraft" (114).

5. Sarkar, *An Exploration of the Ramakrishna-Vivekananda Tradition,* 45.

6. Stewart, "Sex, Secrecy and the Politics of Sahajiyā Scholarship," 39.

7. On this point, see Mukhopādhyāy, "Pravartakakendrik Sahajiyā," 1–5.

8. Kripal, *Kālī's Child,* 287–90. As Kripal points out, this image has profound bodily overtones: The back door is also the unclean aperture of the body, the anus. In a series of associations, Rāmakṛṣṇa links this "secret door" both with the practices of Tantrism and with the most unclean aspects of the body: "Tantra (the back door), the act of defecation (the hidden door in the thief's chamber), the anus (the secret door) . . . and the energy center that controls the process of evacuation and initiates early mystical experience" (ibid., 290; cf. *Kathāmṛta,* 5.180–81).

9. On the problem of secrecy and censorship, see introduction, section titled "The Torment of Secrecy"; cf. Jansen, *Censorship;* Scott, *Domination and the Arts of Resistance,* 138–40

10. Sushil Kumar De, *Early History of the Vaiṣṇava Faith and Movement* (Calcutta: Firma K.LM., 1961), 349; See Rūpa Gosvāmin's *Lalita Mādhava*, act 10. According to Jīva Gosvāmin, "Kṛṣṇa . . . is in fact the husband of the Gopīs, as he is with all women . . . the Gopas were never their real husbands but only appeared as such. They were the immaculate wives of Kṛṣṇa and their apparent relationship with the Gopas was an illusion created by divine Yogamāyā" (ibid., 409–10). For other discussions of the *parakīyā-svakīyā* debate, see Dimock, *The Place of the Hidden Moon,* 202–15; Bose, *The Post-Caitanya Sahajiā Cult of Bengal*, chap. 2.

11. De, *Vaiṣṇava Faith and Movement*, 349.

12. "He who understands only the external meaning . . . calls it *svakīyā* teaching; but the real inner meaning is *parakīyā*. Superficial people who do know what is in the depths of the heart of Jīva Gosvāmin count him among those of the *svakīyā* persuasion. But he who understands the real meaning knows that it is parakīyā." *Karṇānanda* of Yadunandana Dās, ed. R. Vidyāratna (Berhampur: Rādhā-ramaṇ Press, 1929), 88, trans. Dimock, *The Place of the Hidden Moon*, 206.

13. De, *Vaiṣṇava Faith and Movement*, 349–50n.

14. Dimock, *The Place of the Hidden Moon*, 210; cf. Bose, *The Post-Caitanya Sahajiā Cult*, chap. 2.

15. *Durlabhasāra*, 131, trans. Dimock, *The Place of the Hidden Moon*, 211.

16. *Rasaratnasāra*, 65, quoted in Bose, *Post-Caitanya Sahajiā Cult*, 46, n. 2.

17. Robert Sailley, "The Sahajiyā Tradition," in *Vaiṣṇavism: Contemporary Scholars Discuss the Gauḍīya Tradition,* ed. S. Rosen (New York: Folk Books, 1992), 144.

18. *Vairāgya Nirṇaya Grantha,* quoted in Sudarśan Rāy, *Vaiṣṇava Dharmer Kalaṇkita Adhyāy* (Calcutta: Śrī Gouraṇga Research Center, n.d.), 29. The text is probably falsely attributed to Narottama.

19. Inden, *Imagining India* (Oxford: Blackwell, 1990), 1–5.

20. Wilson, *Essays and Lectures, chiefly on the Religion of the Hindus,* 257–58.

21. Ward, *A View of the History, Literature and Religion of the Hindoos,* 2: 247.

22. Wheeler, *The History of India from the Earliest Age* (Edinburgh: Blackwood, 1893), 364.

23. Moreland, *A Short History of India* (New York: MacKay, 1936), 291.

24. Farquhar, *An Outline of the Religious Literature of India* (Oxford: Oxford University Press, 1920), 200.

25. On the *Mahānirvāṇa* and its engimatic role in colonial Bengal, see Urban, "The Strategic Uses of an Esoteric Text," 55–81, and J. Duncan M. Derrett, "A Juridical Fabrication of Early British India: The *Mahānirvāṇa Tantra,*" *Essays in Classical and Modern Indian Law* (Leiden: Brill, 1977), 2: 224–46.

26. Kopf, *The Brahmo Samaj*, 265. See Rāmmohun's, "A Defense of Hindoo Theism," in *The English Works of Rāja Rāmmohun Roy,* ed. I. C. Ghose. (New Delhi: Cosmo, 1982), 1: 9. Indian scholars of the early twentieth century are often even more virulent in their criticism of the Tantras. According to Benyotosh Bhattacharya, *An Introduction to Buddhist Esoterism* (Delhi: Motilal Banarsidas, 1980 [1931]), the Tantras represent a kind of infectious disease which must be eradicated: "If at any time the mind of the nation as a whole has been diseased, it was in the Tantric age. . . . The story related in the Tantric works is . . . so repugnant that . . . all respectable scholars have condemned them wholesale. . . . The Hindu population as a whole is even today in the grip of this Tantra . . . and is suffering from the very disease which originated 1300 years ago . . . Someone should take up . . . the diagnosis, aetiology, pathology and prognosis of the disease, so that more capable men may take up its eradication in the future" (vii).

27. Kripal, *Kālī's Child*, 32–33.

28. Charles R. Brooks, *The Hare Krishnas in India* (Princeton: Princeton University Press, 1989), 84–85; see Tridandi Bhakti Prajnan Yati, *Renaissance of Gaudiya Vaishnava Movement* (Madras: Sree Gaudiya Math, 1978), 39.

29. Thakur, *Shri Chaitanya Shikshamritam* (Madras: Sree Gaudiya Math, 1983), 248–50. See also *Jaiva Dharma* (Madras: Sree Gaudiya Math, 1975), 250, and Bhaktisiddhānta's discussion of *parakīyā* in *Shri Chaitanya's Teachings, part II* (Mayapur: Sree Chaitanya Math, 1974), 129–31.

30. *Shri Chaitanya's Teachings, part II,* 129, 270. Similar attacks on the Sahajiyās also appear in more scholarly works such as that of J. N. Bhattacharya, *Hindu Castes and Sects,* who describes them as "the lowest of the Chaitanite sects of Bengal" (482): "The Sahajias . . . inculcate that every man is Krishna and that every woman is Radha. . . . The result of these doctrines is the utter absence of any bar to promiscuous intercouse" (360).

31. Stewart, "Sex, Secrecy and the Politics of Sahajiyā Scholarship," 39.

32. On the term *ādab*, see Barbara Metcalf, ed., *Moral Conduct and Authority: The Place of Adab in Asian Islam* (Berkeley: University of California, 1984); and Chatterjee, *Merchants, Politics and Society*. As Chatterjee comments, "What allowed the aristocracy to claim a high status was not merely their display of wealth. Adherence to *ādab* (norms of refined behavior and taste) . . . was essential for aristocratic status. . . . *Ādab* consisted of certain . . . generally acknowledged modes of dress, interpersonal behavior and deportment. . . . *Ādab* was expected to bestow on the nobility the quality of discrimination—of being able to recognize socially approved virtues (spirituality, piety, charity, talents like poetry and music)" (208–209).

33. For example, according to a song from the collection, "Saṅgītamālā": "Make the frog dance in the mouth of the serpent, then you will be the king of Rasikas . . . You will still be a chaste wife; you won't be an adulteress, under the control of no one; even though you become unchaste and abandon your family . . . seeing another's husband, with passion radiant like gold . . . Swim in the ocean of impurity; let down your hair, but don't get wet and don't touch the water" (Dās, *Śrī Satīmā Candrikā*, 92).

34. "As a wondrous Royal Goose, He has plunged into the waters and floats upon them; Swinging and swaying, He dallies in union with his beloved Lady Goose. And I see the dawn of both the wondrous full Moon and Sun together! From time to time He appears upon Her Lotus, in order to adorn her in splendor. With joyful hearts, the bees make their buzzing sound. . . . Within the Lotus of the Heart, the bees all drink the nectar!" (BG 415).

The image of the male and female goose or swan appears in many Bāul songs as a key metaphor of sexual union and the technique of catching the Man of the Heart amidst the female menstrual flow; "The blood is white, and on the lake of blood float a pair of swans, copulating continuously in a jungle of lust and love" (song of Gopal, in Bhattacharya, *Songs of the Bards*, 62).

35. In one song, for example, we are told that "*Parakīyā* is gratifying for both persons; though one thinks it is good, it is the opposite (*hita bhāvite biparīta*)" (BG 52; II.82). However, in the very next song—the answer to the foregoing—we are told that "Both *rasas* [both *svakīyā and parakīyā*] are necessary; When [male and female] become one, there is love; then they worship in Sahaja" (BG 52; II.83).

36. The image of the "Company Fort," which is almost surely Calcutta's Fort William, appears numerous times in the *Bhāver Gīta*, usually referring to the secret dwelling place of the Man of the Heart: for example, "Show me, brother, where they've built the Company's Fort. Surely, there's a flag planted upon it. All around it is a deep moat. O how many guns and how many soldiers!" (BG 160).

37. Here I am relying on the interpretations offered by Manulāl Miśra, *Sahaja Tattva Prakāśa* (STP 127–30); Dās, *Saṅgīta o Darśana*, 113–15; Pāl, *Ghoṣpāṛār Satī Mā*, 246–50.

38. Pāl, *Ghoṣpāṛār Satī Mā*, 246–47

39. Jansen, *Censorship*, 14.

40. Scott, *Domination*, 138–39.

41. Jansen, *Censorship*, 81–82; cf. Strauss, *Persecution and the Art of Writing*.

42. Brill, ed., *The Basic Writings of Sigmund Freud*, 223.

43. Garrett, *Bengal District Gazetteers, Nadia*, 49–50.

44. Pāl, *Ghoṣpāṛār Satī Mā*, 246–48. A similar interpretation is suggested by Mukhopādhyāy, "Pravartakakendrik Sahajiyā": "There was a break with the earlier practices (of the Sahajiyās). The Lord of the fourteen worlds is the *ādab Kompānī*. . . . The garden was established by the Parakīyā practice. But within it, the 'foul smell,' arose. . . . In the first part of the eighteenth century in Bengal, Parakīyā love had become established over Svakīyā love. . . . When the Company got wind of this, it cut the root of the practice of Parakīyā

love (thus, the Kartābhajās speak of Svakīyā love)" (5–6).

45. See chapter 3; Pāl, *Ghoṣpāṛār Satī Mā*, 324–26. "Of what sort is the practice in this new fruit garden? . . . Neither the chaste wife nor the illicit lover . . . is a companion in practice. . . . There is no need for a female companion. . . . There is no question of union of men and women; it demands complete control of the senses" (324).

46. Miśra, *Bhāva Lahari Gīta* (Calcutta: Uma Press, 1914), 57–58.

47. Dās, *Saṅgīta o Darśana,* 115.

48. Dās, *Saṅgīta o Darśana,* 113.

49. "If one loses control due to lust, if one falls into the waves on the ocean of the erotic mood, it is a terrible failure. Thus the Kartābhajās' root mantra is *'Meye hijṛā, puruṣ khojā.'* " Dās, *Ghoṣpāṛār Kartābhajā Dharma*, 49–50.

50. "Saṅgītamāla," in Dās, *Śrī Satīmā Candrikā*, 92.

51. Dās, *Saṅgīta o Darśana*, 119.

52. Dās, *Śrī Satī Mā Candrikā,* 71–72.

53. Thurman, "Vajra Hermeneutics," cited in chapter 3.

54. Chatterjee, "Some Observations on Guru Cult," 207–10

55. Datta, *Bhāratavarṣīya Upāsaka Sampradāya,* 224.

56. "The Kartābhajā repudiated the Parakīyā theory. . . . The Kartābhajā emphasis [was] on Svakīyā relation and the combined sādhanā of the spiritual couple." Chakrabarty, *Vaiṣṇavism in Bengal*, 379.

57. Cakravartī, *Sāhebdhanī Sampradāya,* 50.

58. Scott, *Domination and the Arts of Resistance,* 158.

59. de Certeau, *The Practice of Everyday Life,* xi–xii.

60. On the Kartābhajās as a degenerate Tantric sect, see Datta, *Tattvasāra*, 99; on the Kartābhajās as the "foremost of the Aghora-panthīs" see Dāśarathī Ray's satirical poem, "Kartābhajā," *Dāśarathī Rāyer Pāñcālī,* 664–70 For a general discussion of the heated controversy surrounding the sect, see Cakravartī, *Paścim Baṅger Melā o Mahotsava,* 169–71. As Banerjee, *The Parlour and the Streets,* puts it, "Calcutta's bhadralok society was quick to condemn the Kartābhajā sect as a religion of *itar* people and prostitutes who were promiscuous in their habits and violated the norms of Hindu relgion" (69).

61. Bhattacharya, *Religious Movements of Bengal,* 47; cf. Kripal, *Kālī's Child,* 223–25.

62. Kedarnāth Datta, *Sacitra Guljār Nagar* (Calcutta, 1871), cited in De, *Kartābhajā Dharmer Itivṛtta*, 50.

63. Rāy, *Dāśarathī Rāyer Pāñcālī,* 664; see translation by Urban in SEV.

64. Majumdār, ed. *Bāṅglādeśer Itihāsa,* 264–65.

65. Smith, *Imagining Religion*, 18. See Brooks, *The Secret of the Three Cities*, 55–71; Padoux, "Tantrism, an Overview," 271–72; and Urban, "The Extreme Orient," 123–46.

66. The only one of Brooks's ten characteristics that the Kartābhajās do not share is the use of ritual diagrams such as as *yantras* or *maṇḍalas.*

67. Kripal, *Kālī's Child*, 28.

68. Ibid., 29.

Chapter 7

1. Simmel, "The Sociology of Secrecy," 332–33. On the strategy of "mystification" and the naturalization of the asymmetries of power, see Bourdieu, *Outline of a Theory of Practice,* 171–74.

2. Cakravartī, *Sāhebdhanī Sampradāya,* 35; cf. Bhattacharya, *Religious Movements of Bengal,* 53.

3. See Bourdieu, *Language and Symbolic Power,* 22–25.

4. See Cakravartī, *Paścim Baṅger Melā,* 158–60.

5. Bayly, *Indian Society and the Shaping of the British Empire,* 5; cf. Washbrook, "South Asia, the World System and World Capitalism," 479–508.

6. Bose, *Peasant Labour and Colonial Capital,* 1–2.

7. For good criticisms of post-colonial theory, see McClintock, *Imperial Leather,* 230–33. O'Hanlon, "Recovering the Subject," 197–224; Asad, *Genealogies of Religion,* 14–15.

8. Kelly, *A Politics of Virtue,* xiv.

9. Lincoln, *Discourse and the Construction of Society,* 85.

10. On the Vallabhācāris and their taxations, see Chakrabarty, *Vaiṣṇavism in Bengal,* 336–37.

11. Elizabeth Brandt, "On Secrecy and the Control of Knowledge: Taos Pueblo" in *Secrecy: Cross-Cultural Perspectives,* ed. S. Tefft (New York: Humanities Press, 1980), 126–27, 130. As Simmel, *The Sociology of Georg Simmel,* suggests, secret societies are an especially clear example of the "principle of hierarchy or graduated differentiation of the elements in a society. Secret societies above all others, carry through the division of labor and the gradation of their members with great thoroughness" (356–57).

12. Jean Chesneaux, *Secret Societies in China in the Nineteenth and Twentieth Centuries* (Ann Arbor: University of Michigan Press, 1971), 8.

13. See Cakravartī, *Paścim Baṅger Melā,* 11–12, 167–70; Dās, *Ghoṣpāṛār Kartābhajā Dharma,* 55–56.

14. Banerjee, "From Aulchand to Satī Mā," 38.

15. *Somaprakāśa,* 20 Chaitra, 1254 B.S. [1848]. "The policy of structuring the sect on the basis of organized collection of levy through the sub-gurus in a well-developed hierarchical network . . . led to the accumulation of capital in . . . Ghoshpara." Banerjee, "From Aulchand to Satī Mā," 39.

16. See Sarkār, "Ghoṣpārā Melā," 6–7. My own efforts to inquire into the Kartābhajās' finances were repeatedly denied by the living Kartās.

17. Mālik, *Nadīya Kāhinī,* 185–86.

18. Bhattacharya, *Hindu Castes and Sects,* 382; cf. Banerjee, "From Aulchand to Satī Mā," 36.

19. Dās, *Ghoṣpāṛār Kartābhajā Dharma,* 55–56.

20. Chatterjee, *The Nation and Its Fragments,* 83

21. Chakrabarty, *Vaiṣṇavism in Bengal,* 361. The *ṣolo ānā mantra* goes as follows: "O Sinless Lord—O great Lord, at your pleasure I go and return, not a moment am I without you, I am always with you, O great lord."

22. See chapter 2, section titled "The Subversive Bricolage of the Kartābhajā Path." According to the weekly "Friday Song," "Pardon my sins, Lord. My erring mind goes from birth to death. . . . How many millions are my sins. . . . Surely I have committed many offenses, abundantly, repeatedly, in my actions; they are innumerable. . . . I am the bailiff (*belik*) you are the Proprietor (*Mālik*) of everything . . . take and control all my wealth, my self-will, my strength. Save me, in your Office (*serestā* [typically a mercantile office]), from the guns of the slanderers . . ." (BG 3; II.95).

As Mukhopādhyāy, "Pravartakakendrik Sahajiyā," summarizes this practice, "Many devotees meet together and sing Satīmā's or Dulālcāṅd's name. . . . At the end of the worship everyone looks in the direction of the confessor. The confessor has to pay a fine for his sins of 5 1/2 annas. . . . After promising to pay his Dāyika he will touch his head to the earth. Then his heart is made clean" (8).

23. See chapter 1; cf. Sen, "Passages of Authority," Marshall, *East Indian Fortunes*, 26. As Curley, "Rulers," explains, there were basically three classes of taxes on marketplaces in Bengal: "those collected on goods in transit past a cauki or toll-post, those collected on goods traded at a particular market, and finally licensing fees . . . collected in the name of an official monopoly. . . . There were also tolls on shops, on weighing merchandise or on verifying scales and on ferries" (42).

24. Banerjee, "From Aulchand to Satī Mā," 37; cf. Satyavrata De, addendum to Debendranāth De, *Kartābhajā Dharmer Itivṛtta*, 87.

25. Dās, *Ghoṣpāṛār Kartābhajā Dharma*, 55–56.

26. Sarkār, "Ghoṣpāṛār Melā o tār Prāṇbhomrā," 6–7. This observation has been made by many others; cf. Cakravartī, *Sāhebdhani Sampradāya*, 48; Majumdār, "Kartābhajā Sampradāya," 36.

27. Banerjee, "From Aulchand to Satī Mā," 39.

28. On the Wahabi and The Farazi uprisings, see chapter 1; see Kaviraj, *Wahabi and Farazi Rebels*, 33, 60; Guha, *Elementary Aspects of Peasant Insurgency*, 26, 74, 171–73.

29. Sarkār, "Ghoṣpāṛā Melā o tār Prāṇbhomrā," 6.

30. Prakash, "Reproducing Inequality: Spirit Cults and Labor Relations in Colonial Eastern India," in *The World of the Rural Laborer in Colonial India*, ed. Gayan Prakash (Delhi: Oxford, 1992), 303.

31. The other primary holy days include, among others, the Śrīnirmalā Mātāṭhākurāṇīr Tirōbhāva Utsava in Boiśākh month; the Boiśākh-Pūrṇimā Rathjātrā; Rāmśaraṇ Pāl's Mahotsava in Āṣāṛ month; Satī Mā's Mahotsava (the day after the new moon preceeding Durgā Pūjā); and Dulālcāṅd's Tirobhāva Utsava in Caitra month. For a complete list of holy days, see Pāl, *Ghoṣpāṛār Satī Mā*, 193–94.

32. For a wonderful contemporary description of the Melā, see Nabīncandra Sen, "Ghoṣpāṛā Melā," part IV of *Āmār Jīvana*, 183–86 For more general accounts see Cakravartī, *Paścim Baṅger Melā*, 161; "Ghoṣpāṛār Satīmār Utsava o Melā," in *Paścimbaṅger Pūjā Parvan o Melā,* ed. Asok Mitra (Delhi: Govt. of India, 1375 B.S. [1968]), 351–56; Sarkār, "Ghoṣpāṛā Melā" ; Tarūṇ Mitra, "Ghoṣpāṛār Satīmār Melā," *Āmṛta* 2, no. 44 (1963): 438–39.

33. Banerjee, "From Aulchand to Satī Mā," 48.

34. My primary research on the Melā was conducted in March 1997. As Cakravartī, *Paścim Baṅger Melā*, describes the Melā: "Several kinds of people come to the festival: (1) the Mahāśays and Barātīs come to fulfill their annual duties and make new disciples; (2) the sick and those in need perform the three acts of smearing themselves with the earth from the Dālim tree, bathing in the Hīmsāgar pond and the *daṇḍikāṭhā;* (3) common devotees, who respect the sacred place with worship of Satī Mā; (4) beggars and ascetics in the hope of getting some money; (5) Bāuls and renunciants, who gather together to sing and engage in religious practice; (6) a large group of merchants, who come with the certainty of making a lot of money; (7) common sightseers who come to see the festival and buy a few things" (167).

35. *Somaprakāśa*, 23 Caitra, 1270 B.S. [1864]. As Banerjee, "From Aulchand to Satī Mā," comments: "Devotees from all parts of Bengal put up make shift shelters . . . for which they have to pay tax to the gadi of the Pal family. Shopkeepers have also to pay a fixed amount to the Pals. . . . Many devotees offer gold ornaments and other precious jewellery at the temple of Satī Mā. . . . All these taxes and rents and offerings are an important source of revenue for the gadi in Ghoshpara" (42).

36. On the role of the Melā as a marketplace, see Sen, "Passages of Authority," 1–40; Robert Mongommery Martin, ed., *The History, Antiquities, Topography and Statistics of Easten India*, 3 vols. (London: Allan and Co., 1883) 2: 1007–1008.

37. In his historical novel based on the life of a female Kīrtan singer of the 19th nineteenth century, Mitra vividly describes the oppressive financial burden of the Melā, which was especially difficult for the poor of rural Bengal. As the character Nistāriṇī enumerates the various expenses of a trip to the Melā, "First, absence from work; second heavy expense, no income and more expenditure; travel back and forth this long distance by boat. . . . It's considerably high for poor people like them. Besides, there would be expenses for food, offerings and depositing money in the gadi of the Kartā. Where would they get all this? Each year Bhavatāraṇ ran up a huge debt—it took three or four months to pay off" (*Āmi Kān Pete Rai*, 48).

38. See Bourdieu, *Language and Symbolic Power*, 22–24.

39. Scott, *Domination*, 121.

40. *Saṃvāda Prabhākara*, 18 Caitra, 1254 B.S. [1848].

41. Banerjee, "From Aulchand to Satī Mā," 44.

42. See Claude Lévi-Strauss, *The Raw and the Cooked* (New York: Harper and Row, 1969); Douglas, *Purity and Danger;* Marshal Sahlins, *Culture and Practical Reason* (Chicago; University of Chicago Press, 1978).

43. R. S. Khare, "Food with Saints: An Aspect of Hindu Gastrosemantics," in *The Eternal Food*, ed. R. S. Khare (Albany: SUNY, 1986); cf. Mckim Marriott, "Caste Ranking and Food Transactions: A Matrix Analysis," in *Structure and Change in Indian Society,* ed. M. Singer (Chicago: University of Chicago, 1968).

44. Lincoln, *Discourse and the Construction of Society*, 75.

45. Ibid., 88.

46. Rāy, "Kartābhajā," 668–69.

47. *Saṃvāda Prabhākara,* 18 Caitra, 1254 B.S. [1848].

48. Ibid.

49. Banerjee, "From Aulchand to Satī Mā," 41.

50. Ibid., 40.

51. Mitra, *Āmi Kān Pete Rai,* 49–50.

52. Letter of September 25, 1894, in *Vivekenanda: A Comprehensive Study,* ed. Swami Jyotirmayananda (Madras: Swami Jyotirmayananda, 1993), 508.

53. Bhattacharya, *Hindu Castes and Sects,* 384.

54. Rāy, "Kartābhajā;" 670; see SE V.

55. Cakravartī, *Gabhīr Nirjan Pathe*, 75.

56. Ibid., 77.

57. Sarkār, "Ghoṣpāṛā Melā," 60–63.

58. Bakhtin, *Rabelais and his World,* 123.

59. Scott, *Domination and the Arts of Resistance*, 181.

60. Banerjee, *The Parlour and the Streets,* 143, 144–45; cf. Bakhtin, *Rabelais and His World,* 90.

61. Marriot, "The Feast of Love," in *Krishna: Myth, Rites and Attitudes,* ed. M. Singer (Chicago: University of Chicago Press, 1966), 210–212.

62. Lincoln, *Discourse and the Construction of Society,* 90; cf. Gluckman, *Custom and Conflict in Africa* (Oxford: Oxford University Press, 1966): "This particular ritual, by allowing people to behave in normally prohibited ways, gave expression in a reversed form, to the normal rightness of a particular social order" (116).

63. Guha, *Elementary Aspects of Peasant Insurgency*, 35, quoting Victor Turner, *The Ritual Process*, 188. "Nothing happens at this festival to upset society in spite of the seemingly radical bouleversement. . . . The saturnalia, the systematic violation of structural distances between castes and the defiance of rules governing relationships between members of the community, the blatant underminig of . . . morality—add up not to a disruption of the social order . . . but to its reinforcement" (ibid., 33–34).

64. Scott, *Domination and the Arts of Resistance*, 191, 178.

65. See Foucault, "Space, Knowledge and Power," in *The Foucault Reader*, ed. P. Rabinow (New York: Pantheon, 1984), 239–56.

66. Chakrabarty, *Vaiṣṇavism in Bengal*, 362.

67. Extracts from Marshman's Journal, 266, cited in Oddie, "New Wine in Old Bottles?"' 15.

68. Kumudnāth Mālik, *Nadīya Kāhinī* (Calcutta, 1986 [first printed in 1317 B.S.]), 186.

69. Banerjee, "From Aulchand to Satī Mā," 38.

70. *Somaprakāśa*, 23 Caitra 1270 B.S. [1864].

71. Rāy, "Kartābhajā," 668; see SEV for a full translation of this very funny poem.

72. Oddie, "Old Wine in new Bottles?" 330–1. For records of these events, see *Christian Missionary Register* (June 1839): 305; Long, *Handbook of Bengal Missions*, 183–84; *Friend of India* (April 11, 1839).

73. Oddie, "Old Wine in New Bottles?" 340; cf. *Church Missionary Register* (October 1839): 461.

74. Rāy, "Kartābhajā," 669.

75. On this point, see *The Sociology of Georg Simmel*, 356–57.

76. McClintock, *Imperial Leather*, 15. As Kaplan, *Neither Cargo nor Cult*, argues, we must acknowledge not only "the power of colonized peoples to make their own history," and the power of the colonial state to shape and constrain that history; ultimately, we must also be aware of the subtle ways in which the boundaries between colonizer and colonizer begin to blur or overlap: "the distinction between that which is indigenous and that which is colonial is breached. Rather than indigenes and colonizer retaining separate systems of meaning, and rather than . . . the colonized either becoming hegemonized or resisting . . . new articulations are made" (16).

Chapter 8

1. Nandī, *Kartābhajā Dharma*, 69.

2. Banerjee, "From Aulchand to Satī Mā," 30, 42.

3. See Cakravartī *Sāhebdhanī Sampradāya*, 43–46; Pāl, *Ghoṣpāṛār Satīmā*, 162–65.

4. Cakravartī, *Sāhebdhanī Sampradāya*, 50.

5. On Kānāi and the "Secret Kartābhajās," see Nandī, *Kartābhajā Dharma*, 41–47; Pāl, *Ghoṣpāṛār Satīmā*, 173–74; and Haradhan Mukhopādhyāy, *Satyasrota* (Calcutta, 1385 B.S. [1978]). The legend is that Kānāi had initially renounced the world and become a Sannyāsī, but Āulcāṅd ordered him to give up the Sannyāsī life and become a wedded householder. Kānāi's foremost disciple, Jagat Sen, is reputed to have been the guru of the famous Vaiṣṇava pundit and Brahmo reformer, Vijaykṛṣṇa Gosvāmin.

6. In the following songs, for example, Kubir uses the images of the "human-body-Calcutta" and the "railway car of the body" to describe the state of man in this mortal world: "Oh, how wondrous are the habits of the human body-Calcutta! . . . You dwell in Calcutta's Bowbazaar; Brother, you're entangled in so many desires!!" (Cakravartī, *Sāhebd-*

hanī Sampradāya, 197, song 57). "Oh my mind, you ask about the railway-car of the human body—within it lies a precious Jewel! But not everyone can see the One who sat in Haora station and fashioned this human rail-car. . . . The initiatory Guru is the wishfulfilling Tree, in the guise of the Ticket Master [*ṭikiṭ māsṭār*]. . . . The Mind-Engineer has the task of controlling the ten senses and the six enemies, who wear the guise of Soldiers. . . . The Human Rail-Car is wondrous, for it has no need of rails! . . . It has an enclosure of skin, but inside, it's filled with diamonds, pearls and red gold! And this very car lies in the neighborhood of Calcutta" (ibid., song 56, 194–95).

Elsewhere Kubir describes contemporary economic events, such as the sorrows of Indigo cultivation and the seizure of poor farmers' lands by the Company: "Now Indigo [*nīl*] has come in the guise of Nīlakaṇṭha [the blue-throated, i.e., Śiva] and conquered the world! Driven by the madness of Indigo, where will I go? Because of Indigo, those wily, wicked men have taken away all our homesteads! Those who deal in Indigo are like the embassadors of Death! And whatever you get from them, they'll use to ruin and kill you, with their hands around your neck!" (ibid., 207).

7. See Cakravartī, "Kartābhajā Sampradāya," 28–30, and *Sāhebdhanī Sampradāya*: "The similarity of the Sāhebdhanīs and Kartābhajās is striking. Both are opposed to the Vedas and follow bodily practices. At the origin of both religions, the founder was an ascetic Muslim: Āulcāṅd and Sāhebdhanī. The primary organizer of the Kartābhajās was Rāmśaraṇ Pāl and his son Dulālcāṅd. The primary organizer of the Sāhebedhanīs was Dukhīrām (Mulīrām) Pāl and his son Caraṇ Pāl. Rāmśaraṇ was a Sadgop, and Dukhīrām was of the Gopa class. In both sects, the worship of the hereditary guru is practiced . . . the primary form of worship of both sects is song" (28–59).

8. Jhā, "Murśīdābād Jelār Vaiṣṇava Dharmer Itivṛtta," in *Murśīdābād Carcā*, ed. P. Maitra (Murśīdābād, 1395 B.S. [1988]), 93–122. "Ramakanta Chakrabarty and others have considered the Kartābhajā . . . as a subsect of Vaiṣṇavas. However if one examines their philosophy and worship . . . they can by no means be classified as Vaiṣṇavas . . . None of them would introduce themselves as Vaiṣṇavas."

9. See chapter 3, section titled "Meeting with Remarkable Madmen"; I interviewed both men between July and October 1996.

Conclusions and Comparative Comments

1. Bose, *Peasant Labour and Colonial Capital,* 41; cf. Bayly, *Indian Society*, 5–8.

2. de Certeau, *The Practice of Everyday Life*, 56–60; Comaroff, "Introduction, *Body of Power,*

3. On the subaltern use of religious imagery in the interests of political and economic goals, see Spivak, "A Literary Representation of the Subaltern," 131–35; Guha, *Elementary Aspects*, chap. 2; Chatterjee, *The Nation*, chap. IX.

4. See Asad, "Introduction," in *Genealogies of Religion*, and O'Hanlon, "Recovering the Subject."

5. Kelly, *A Politics of Virtue,* xiv.

6. Bourdieu, *In Other Words*, 155.

7. Smith, "Introduction," *Imagining Religion*.

8. Eco, *Interpretation and Overinterpretation,* 38–40. This preoccupation with secrecy in American culture had already been noted as early as the 1950s with the craze of conspiracy theory and the dawn of the Cold War; see Shils, *The Torment of Secrecy,* 41–45.

9. As Luther Martin, "Secrecy in Hellenistic Religious Communities," in *Secrecy and*

Concealment, argues, "a theoretical prominence attributed to secrecy in religion . . . is a consequence of 18th century intellectual formations which, shared by a 19th century Romantic mentality, still governs the modern academic study of religions" (121).

10. Goffman, *The Presentation of Self in Everyday Life*, 46. A similar argument is made by Jan Bremmer, "Religious Secrets and Secrecy in Classical Greece," with regard to the Greek Mystery cults: "Unlike many gullible moderns seem to think, there was no esoteric wisdom in ancient Mysteries" (72).

11. Clifford, *The Predicament of Culture*, 90. As the Comaroffs, *Ethnography*, suggest, "Ethnography . . . is not a vain attempt at literal translation, in which we take over the mantle of an-other's being . . . It is a historically situated mode of understanding historically situated contexts" (9–10).

12. See Lincoln, *Discourse and the Construction of Society*, 5–8.

13. See Bellman, *The Language of Secrecy*, 1–10. As Martin, "Secrecy in Hellenistic Religious Communities," argues, "As discursive formations, secrets are structured in such a way that they can be disclosed. . . . The rhetoric of secrecy . . . offers a seductive temptation to break [existing social] barriers" (113).

14. See Antonio Gramsci, *Selections from the Prison Notebooks* (New York: International Publishers, 1971), 144–45; Guha, *Elementary Aspects*, 1–17; Lincoln, *Discourse*, 5–6. "In the hands of elites . . . discourse of all forms—not only verbal but also the symbolic discourse of spectacle, costume, icon, musical performance and the like—may be strategically employed to mystify the inevitable inequities of any social order and to win the consent of those over whom power is exercised, thereby . . . transforming simple power into 'legitimate' authority. Yet discourse can also serve members of subordinate classes . . . in their attempts to demystify, delegitimate and deconstruct the established norms" (Ibid., 5).

15. Lincoln, *Authority*, 7.

16. On the use of secrecy by poor lower classes in the Vodou tradition, see Brown, *Mama Lola;* Davis, *Passages of Darkness*. As Michel Laguerre, has shown in the case of the Bizango society, the Vodou cults of the French colonial era served as refuge for Maroons or fugitive slave rebels; they thus represented a "constant threat to the local French establishment," and an ongoing source of resistance against slavery (Michel Laguerre, "Bizango: A Voodoo Secret Society in Haiti," in *Secrecy: A Cross-Cultural Perspective*, ed. Stanton Tefft (New York: Human Sciences Press, 1980), 148–49). On the Mau Mau, see Carl Rosberg and John Nottingham, *The Myth of the Mau Mau: Nationalism in Kenya* (Stanford: Stanford University Press, 1966); on the Triad and White Lotus groups, see Chesneaux, *Secret Societies in China*, and Susan Naquin, *Millenarian Rebellion in China* (New Haven: Yale University Press, 1976).

17. On the Chishti Sufi order, which was closely involved with the political hierarchy of the Mughal empire in India, see Eaton, *The Rise of Islam*, 89–91; on the political role of Shingon in Japan, see Taiko Yamasaki, *Shingon: Japanese Esoteric Buddhism* (Boston: Shambhala, 1988); on esotericism in Tantric Buddhism, see Thurman, "Vajra Hermeneutics"; Lopez, "The Heart Sūtra as Tantra."

18. I have undertaken such a comparison between Tantric and Masonic secrecy in my article, "Elitism and Esotericism." On the elitist and aristocratic nature of the European and American Masonic lodges, see Jacob, *Living the Enlightenment;* Dumenil, *Freemasonry and American Culture;* William Weisberger, *Speculative Freemasonry and the Enlightenment: A Study of the Craft in London, Paris, Prague and Vienna* (New York: Columbia University Press, 1993).

19. On the hegemonic use of secrecy in Australian Aboriginal society, see Keen, *Secret Knowledge*. Chesneaux, *Secret Societies in China,* 8–10. "Secret societies took the diametrically

opposed view to the established order while at the same time, by a curiously mimetic process, drawing from it their inspiration to define their own parallel order" (ibid., 187–88).

20. Apter, *Black Critics and Kings*, 17–18. "In the context of . . . colonial rule, the totalizing transpositions of Orisa worship appropriated church and state . . . within the metaphysical horizons of the cults. White missionaries, district officers and their African employees . . . entered Yoruba power relations, but they . . . did not displace it . . . The work of the cults became more important, not less. If the missionaries and colonial administrators were dangerous forces to reckon with, all the more reason to regulate their powers by traditional . . . ritual means" (ibid., 177).

On the general role of secret societies in colonial contexts, see Tefft, *Secrecy*, 55–58. For a good discussion of the changing role of specific secret traditions under colonial rule, see Lindstom, *Knowledge and Power*, 196–200, and Kempf, "Ritual, Power and Colonial Domination," 110–112.

21. Tefft, *The Dialectics of Secret Societies*, 109–111.

Select Bibliography

Bengali and Sanshrit Sources

Editions of Bhāver Gīta (in chronological order)

Kartābhajā Gīta. Bengali manuscript no.964. Bāṅgīya Sāhitya Pariṣat Library, Calcutta, 1228–33 B.S. (1821–26).

Kartābhajār Gītāvalī. ed. Navīncandra Cakravartī. Calcutta: Caitanya Candrodaya, 1277 B.S. (1870).

Bhāver Gīta. ed. Romeścandra Ghoṣe. Calcutta: Aurora Press, 1389 B.S. (1882).

Śrī Śrī Juter Pada. ed. Bhuvanamohan Gaṅgopādhyāy. Calcutta: Author, 1894, 1900, and 1905.

Bhāver Gīta. ed. Manulāl Miśra. Calcutta: Author, 1313, 1325, 1329 B.S. (1906, 1918, 1922).

Bhāver Gīta. ed. Govardhan Cakravartī. Calcutta: Indralekha Press, 1950.

Bhāver Gīta. ed. Indrabhūṣan Cakravartī. Calcutta: Indralekha Press, 1977

Bhāver Gīta. ed. Śāntirañjan Cakravartī. Calcutta: Indralekha Press, 1399 B.S. (1992).

Other Primary Kartābhajā Sources (Bengali)

Cakravartī, Govardhan, ed. *Bhajanatattva Gīta, arthāt Mahājanadiger Bhāvānurūpa pada.* Calcutta: Indralekha Press, 1398 B.S. (1991).

Kartābhajā Saṅgīta." In *Saṅgītakośa*, ed. Upendranāth Mukhopādhyāy. Calcutta: Basumati Press, 1895.

Miśra, Manulāl. *Sahaja Tattva Prakāśa.* Calcutta: Author 1309 B.S. (1902).

———. *Bhāver Gīta Vyākhyā Saha Sahaja Tattvaprakāśa Vā Sanātana Sahaja Satya Dharmer Ādi Itihāsa.* Calcutta: Author, 1911.

———. *Bhāva-Lahari-Gīta.* Calcutta: Umā Press, 1914.

———. *Kartābhajā Dharmer Ādi Vṛttānta Vā Sahajatattva Prakāśa.* Calcutta: Author, 1925.

———. *Satyadharma Upāsana vā Śukrabārer Yājana Prāṇālī.* Calcutta: Indralekha Press, 1398 B.S. (1981).

———. *Bhajanatattva Prakāśa, arthāt Mahājanadiger Bhāvānurūpa Pada.* Calcutta: Indralekha Press, 1389 B.S. (1982).

Other Contemporaneous Sources on the Kartābhajās (Bengali)

Āhmed, Muhammad Riāzzudin, ed., *Islām Pracārak* (January 1903).

Biśvas, Jyotiścandra. *Jelepāṛār saṅg niye Haraberakam raṅg.* Calcutta, 1322 B.S. (1915).

Ghoṣāl, Jayanārāyaṇ. *Karuṇānidhānavilāsa.* Calcutta, 1811.

Rāy, Dāśarathī. "Kartābhajā." In *Dāśarathi Rāyer Pāñcālī,* ed. Haripad Cakravartī. Calcutta: University of Calcutta Press, 1962.

Saṃvāda Prabhākara (18 Caitra 1254 B.S. [1848]).

Sen, Nabīncandra. "Ghoṣpāṛār Melā," part IV of *Āmār Jīvana.* In *Kavibara Nabīncandra Sen, Granthāvalī.* Calcutta: Basumatī, 1974.

Somaprakāśa (20 Caitra 1270 B.S. [1864]).

Śrī J. (pseud.). "Kartābhajāder Sambandhe Kroṛapatre," *Bandhava* 6, no. 9 (1288 B.S. [1881]).

Modern Secondary Sources on the Kartābhajās (Bengali)

Cakravartī, Jāhnavīkumār, "Kartābhajāner Rūp o Svarūp." In *Kartābhajā Dharmamata o Itihāsa,* vol. 2, ed. S. Mitra. Calcutta: De Book Stores, 1976–77.

Cakravartī, Sudhīr. "Kartābhajā Sampradāya: Dharmata o Sādhanatattva." In *Kartābhajā Dharmamata o Itihāsa,* vol. 2, ed. S. Mitra. Calcutta: De Book Stores, 1976–77.

———. "Gabhīr Nirjan Pathe," *Ekṣan,* Autumn (1392 B.S. [1985]).

Caṭṭopādhyāy, Tuṣār. "Ghoṣpāṛār Melā, Kartābhajā o Lālan." In *Lālan Sāhitya o Darśana,* ed. K. R. Hāq. Dhaka: Bangla Academy, 1976.

———. "Śri Caitanya o Lokāyata Uttarādhikāra." In *Gouṛaṅgasaṃskṛti o Śrīcaitanyadeva,* ed. S. Gosvāmī. Calcutta: Calcutta Publishers, 1988.

Dās, Śrī Advaita Candra. *Ghoṣpāṛār Kartābhajā Sampradāya.* Calcutta: Kālī Press, 1983.

———. *Śrī Satīmā Candrikā.* Calcutta: Firma KLM, 1986.

———. *Saṅgīta o Darśana.* Calcutta: Cayanikā, 1992.

De, Debendranāth. *Kartābhajā Dharmer Itivṛtta.* Calcutta: Jiggasa Agencies, 1968.

Kālakūṭa, *Kothāy Se Jan Āche.* Calcutta: De's Publishing, 1983.

Mitra, Sanatkumār, ed. *Kartābhajā Dharmamata o Itihāsa.* Calcutta: De Book Stores, 1976–77, 2 vols.

Mukhopādhyāy, Bimalkumār. "Pravartakakendrik Sahajiyā: Kartābhajā." In *Kartābhajā Dharmamata o Itihāsa,* vol. 2, ed. S. Mitra. Calcutta: De Book Stores, 1976–77.

Nandī, Ratan Kumār. *Kartābhajā Dharma or Sāhitya.* Naihati: Asani Press, 1984.

Pāl, Satyaśiva. *Ghoṣpāṛār Satī Mā o Kartābhajā Dharma.* Calcutta: Pustak Bipaṇi, 1990.

Sarkār, Māṇik. "Kartābhajā Melā o tār Prāṇbhomrā." In *Kartābhajā Dharmamata o Itihāsa,* vol. 1, ed. S. Mitra. Calcutta: De Book Stores, 1976–77.

———. "Ghoṣpāṛā Melā." In *Kartābhajā Dharmamata o Itihāsa,* vol. 2, ed. S. Mitra. Calcutta: De Book Stores, 1976–77.

Sen, Sukumār. "Kartābhajār Kathā o Gān." In *Kartābhajā Dharmamata o Itihāsa,* vol. 2, ed. S. Mitra, Calcutta: De Book Stores, 1976–77.

Other Bengali and Sanskrit Sources

Basu, Manindra Mohan, ed. *Sahajiyā Sāhitya.* Calcutta: University of Calcutta Press, 1932.

Basu, S., ed. *Vaiṣṇava-Granthāvalī.* Calcutta: Basumati Sahitya Mandir, 1342 B.S. (1935).

Bhaṭṭācārya, Upendranāth. *Bāṅglār Bāul o Bāul Gān.* Calcutta: Oriental Book Co., 1981.

Cakravartī, Sudhīr. *Sāhebdhanī Sampradāya, tāder Gān.* Calcutta: Pustak Bipaṇi, 1985.

———. *Balahāṛī Sampradāya ār tāder Gān.* Calcutta: Pustak Bipaṇi, 1986.

———. *Gabhīr Nirjan Pathe.* Calcutta: Ānanda, 1989.

———. *Paścim Baṅger Melā o Mahotsava.* Calcutta: Pustak Bipaṇi, 1995.

———. *Bāṅglār Dehatattva Gān.* Calcutta: Prajñā Prakāśana, 1990.

Dās, Ākiñcana. *Vivarta Vilāsa.* Calcutta: Tārācānd Dās, 1948.

Dās, Upendrakumār, ed. *Kulārṇava Tantra*. Calcutta, Navabhārata, 1383 B.S. (1976).

Datta, Akṣayakumār. *Bhāratavarṣīya Upāsaka Sampradāya*. Calcutta: Karuṇā Prakāśanī, 1987. First published 1870.

Datta, Rāmacandra. *Tattvasāra*. Calcutta: Śaśadhar Prakāśana, 1983. First published 1885.

Devaśarmā, Kālījīvana. *Śrīśrīrāmakṛṣṇa abhidhāna*. Calcutta: Karuṇā Prakāśanī, 1981.

Gupta, Mahendranāth. *Śrīśrīrāmakṛṣṇa-kathāmṛta*. Calcutta: Udbodhan Kāryālay, 1987.

Jhā, Śaktināth. *Phakir Lālan Sāin: Deś, Kāl Ebang Silpa*. Calcutta: Saṃvād, 1995.

Kavirāja, Kṛṣṇadāsa. *Śrī Śrī Caitanyacaritāmṛta,* ed. Rādhāgovinda Nāth. Calcutta: Bhakti-pracāra-bhāṇḍar, 1355 B.S. (1948), 6 vols.

Mahānirvāṇa Tantra. Calcutta: Ādi Brāhma Samāj, 1876.

Majumdār, Rameścandra, ed. *Bāṅglādeśer Itihāsa*. Calcutta: General Printers and Publishers, 1957.

Mallik, Kumud Nāṭh. *Nadīya Kāhinī*. Rāṇāghāṭ: Author, 1910.

Mitra, Gajendrakumār. *Āmi Kān Pete Rai*. Calcutta: Mitra and Ghose, 1992.

Naskār, Sanatkumār. *Mughal Juger Bāṅglā Sāhitya*. Calcutta: Ratnāvalī, 1995.

Saradānanda, Swāmi. *Śrīśrīrāmakṛṣṇa-Līlāprasaṅga*. Calcutta: Udbodhan Kāryālay, 1986.

Śāstrī, H. P. *Bāuddha Gān o Doha*. Calcutta: Baṅgīya Sāhitya Pariṣat, 1917.

Sen, Akṣaykumār. *Śrīśrīrāmakṛṣṇa-puṅthi*. Calcutta: Udbhodana Kāryālay, 1976.

Sen, Dineścandra, ed. *Baṅga Sāhitya Paricaya*. Calcutta: University of Calcutta, 1914.

———. *Bṛhat Baṅga: Suprācīna Kāla haite Plāsir Juddha Parjanta*. Calcutta: De's, 1993.

Sen, Sukumār, ed. *Caryāgīti-padāvalī*. Burdwan: Sāhitya Sabhā, 1956.

English Sources

Nineteenth Century English Sources on the Kartābhajās

Beveridge, Henry. *The District of Bakarganj*. London: Trübner, 1876.

Bhattacharya, J. N. *Hindu Castes and Sects*. Calcutta: University of Calcutta, 1896.

Calcutta Christian Observer 25 (1856).

Church Missionary Register (June–October 1839).

Friend of India (April 11, 1839).

Garrett, J. H. E. *Bengal District Gazetteers, Nadia*. Calcutta: Bengal Secretariat Book Stall, 1910.

Hunter, William Wilson. *Annals of Rural Bengal*. London: Smith, Elder & Co., 1897.

Long, James. *Handbook of Bengal Missions*. London: J. F. Shaw, 1848.

Stock, Eugene. *The History of the Church Missionary Society, Its Environment, Its Men and Its Work*. London: Church Missionary Society, 1899.

Ward, William. *Account of the Writings, Religion and Manners of the Hindus*, 4 vols. Serampore, Mission Press, 1811.

———. *A Brief Memoir of Krishna Pal, the First Hindoo in Bengal Who Broke the Chain of Caste by Embracing the Gospel*. London: J. Offor, 1823.

Wilson, H. H. *Sketch of the Religious Sects of the Hindus*. London: Trübner, 1861–62 (first published 1846).

Secondary Comparative and Methodological Sources

Ahmad, Aijaz. In *Theory*. New York: Verso, 1992.

Appadurai, Arjun, ed. *The Social Life of Things: Commodities in Cultural Perspective* Cambridge: Cambridge University Press, 1986.

Apter, Andrew. *Black Critics and Kings: The Hermeneutics of Power in Yoruba Society.* Chicago: University of Chicago Press, 1992.

Arnold, David. *Colonizing the Body: State Medicine and Epidemic Disease in Nineteenth Century India.* Berkeley: University of California Press, 1993.

Asad, Talal. *Geneologies of Religion: Discipline and Reasons of Power in Christianity and Islam.* Baltimore: Johns Hopkins University Press, 1993.

Ashcroft, Bill, Griffiths, Gareth, and Tiffin, Helen, eds. *The Post-Colonial Studies Reader.* London: Routledge, 1995.

Bagchi, Amiya Kumar. "Wealth and Work in Calcutta, 1860–1921." In *Calcutta: The Living City,* ed. S. Chaudhuri. Calcutta: Oxford University Press, 1990.

Bandyopadhyay, Sekhar. "Popular Religion and Social Mobility in Colonial Bengal: The Matua Sect and the Namasudras." In *Mind, Body and Society: Life and Mentality in Colonial Bengal,* ed. R. Ray. Calcutta: Oxford University Press, 1995.

Banerjee, Sumanta. *The Parlour and the Streets: Elite and Popular Culture in Nineteenth Century Calcutta.* Calcutta: Seagull, 1989.

———. "The World of Ramnaj Ostagar, the Common Man of Old Calcutta." In *Calcutta, the Living City,* vol. 1, *The Past,* ed. S. Chaudhuri. Calcutta: Oxford, 1990.

———. "From Aulchand to Satī Mā: The Institutionalization of the Syncretist Kartabhaja Sect in Nineteenth Century Bengal." *Calcutta Historical Journal* 16, no. 2 (1994): 29–60.

Barth, Fredrick. *Ritual and Knowledge among the Baktaman of New Guinea.* New Haven: Yale University Press, 1975.

Barthes, Roland. *Mythologies.* New York: Himan and Walsh, 1972.

———. *The Barthes Reader,* ed. S. Sontag. New York: Hill and Wang, 1982.

Bayly, C. A. *Indian Society and the Making of the British Empire.* Cambridge: Cambridge University Press, 1988.

———. *Rulers, Townsmen and Bazaars: North Indian Society in the Age of British Expansion.* Cambridge: Cambridge University Press, 1983.

Bellman, Beryl. *The Language of Secrecy: Symbols and Metaphors in Poro Ritual.* New Brunswick: Rutgers University Press, 1984.

Bhabha, Homi. *The Location of Culture.* London: Routledge, 1994.

Bhattacharya, Aparna. *Religious Movements of Bengal, 1800–1850.* Calcutta: Vidyasagar Pustak Mandir, 1981.

Bhattacharya, Deben, ed. *Love Songs of Candidas.* London: George Allen & Unwin, 1967.

———. *Songs of the Bards of Bengal.* New York: Grove Press, 1976.

Bhattacharyya, Swapan Kumar and Ray, Gayatri. "The Car Festival of Dulalcand at Ghoshpara in the District of Nadia, West Bengal." *Folklore* 18, no. 1 (January 1977).

Bloom, Harold. *Kabbalah and Criticism.* New York: Seabury Press, 1975.

———. *A Map of Misreading.* New York: Oxford University Press, 1975.

Bok, Sisella. *Secrets: On the Ethics of Concealment and Revelation.* New York: Pantheon, 1982.

Bolle, Kees, ed. *Secrecy in Religions.* New York: E. J. Brill, 1987.

Bonacich Phillip. "Secrecy and Solidarity." *Sociometry* 39 (1976): 200–208.

Bose, Manindra Mohan. *The Post-Caitanya Sahajiā Cult of Bengal.* Calcutta: University of Calcutta, 1930.

Bose, Sugata. *Peasant Labour and Colonial Capital.* Cambridge: Cambridge University Press, 1993.

———. *South Asia and World Capitalism.* Delhi: Oxford University Press, 1990.

Bourdieu, Pierre. "The Economics of Linguistic Exchange." *Social Science Information* 16 (1977): 645–68.

———. *Outline of a Theory of Practice*. Cambridge: Cambridge University Press, 1977.

———. *The Logic of Practice*. Stanford: Stanford University Press, 1981.

———. "The Forms of Capital." In *Handbook of Theory and Research for the Sociology of Education*, ed. J. Richardson. New York: Greenwood, 1983.

———. *Language and Symbolic Power*. Cambridge: Harvard University Press, 1984.

———. *In Other Words: Essays toward a Reflexive Sociology*. Stanford: Stanford University Press, 1990.

Brooks, Charles R. *The Hare Krishnas in India*. Princeton: Princeton University Press, 1989.

Brooks, Douglas R. *The Secret of the Three Cities: An Introduction to Hindu Śākta Tantra*. Chicago: University of Chicago Press, 1990.

———. *Auspicious Wisdom: The Texts and Traditions of Śrīvidyā Śākta Tantrism in South India*. Albany: SUNY, 1992.

———. "Encountering the Hindu "Other": Tantrism and the Brahmans of South India." *Journal of the American Academy of Religion* 60 (1992): 405–36.

Brown, Karen McCarthy, *Mama Lola: A Vodou Priestess in Brooklyn*. Berkeley: University of California Press, 1991.

Bryson, Thomas. "The Hermeneutics of Religious Syncretism: Swami Vivekananda's Practical Vedānta." Ph.D. diss., University of Chicago, 1992.

Burkert, Walter. "Der geheime Reiz des Verbogenen: Antike Mysterienkulte." In *Secrecy and Concealment: Studies in the History of Mediterranean and Near Eastern Religions*, ed. H. Kippenberg and G. Stroumsa. Leiden: Brill, 1995.

Bury, J. B. *A History of Freedom of Thought*. London: Oxford, 1913.

Bynum, Caroline. *Fragmentation and Redemption: Essays on Gender and the Human Body in Medieval Religion*. New York: Zone, 1992.

Calhoun, Craig, Lipuma, Edward, and Postone, Moishe, eds. *Bourdieu: Critical Perspectives*. Chicago: University of Chicago Press, 1993.

Capwell, Charles. *Music of the Bauls of Bengal*. Kent: Kent State University Press, 1986.

Chakrabarty, Ramakantha. *Vaiṣṇavism in Bengal, 1486–1900*. Calcutta: Sanskrit Pustak Bhandar, 1985.

Chartier, Roger. "Culture as Appropriation: Popular Cultural uses in Early Modern France." In *Understanding Popular Culture: Europe from the Middle Ages to the Nineteenth Century*, ed. S. Kaplan. Berlin: Mouton, 1984.

Chatterjee, Kumkum. *Merchants, Politics and Society in Early Modern India*. Leiden: Brill, 1996.

Chatterjee, Partha. *The Nation and Its Fragments: Colonial and Postcolonial Histories*. Princeton: Princeton University Press, 1993.

Chesneaux, Jean. *Popular Movements and Secret Societies in China, 1840–1950*. Stanford: Stanford University Press, 1972.

Chirol, Valentine. *Indian Unrest*. London: Macmillan, 1910.

Clarke, J., Hall, S., Jefferson, T., and Roberts, B., eds. *Resistance through Rituals*. London: Routledge, 1993.

Clifford, James. *The Predicament of Culture: Twentieth Century Ethnography, Literature and Art*. Cambridge: Harvard University Press, 1988.

Cohen, Abner. *The Politics of Elite Culture: Explorations in the Dramaturgy of Power in Modern African Society*. Berkeley: University of California Press, 1981.

Collet, Sophia. *The Life and Letters of Rammohun Roy*. Calcutta: D. K. Biswas, 1962.

Comaroff, Jean. *Body of Power, Spirit of Resistance: The History and Culture of a South African People.* Chicago: University of Chicago Press, 1985.

Comaroff, Jean, and Comaroff, John, eds. *Modernity and Its Malcontents: Ritual and Power in Postcolonial Africa.* Chicago: University of Chicago Press, 1993.

Curley, David. "Rulers and Merchants in Late Eighteenth Century Bengal." Ph.D. diss., University of Chicago, 1980.

Das, Paritosh. *Sahajiyā Cult of Bengal and Pañca Śākhā Cult of Orissa.* Calcutta: Firma KLM, 1988.

Dasgupta, Shashibhushan. *Obscure Religious Cults, as a Background to Bengali Literature.* Calcutta: Firma KLM, 1968.

De, S. K. *Early History of the Vaiṣṇava Faith and Movement in Bengal.* Calcutta: University of Calcutta Press, 1942.

De Bary, T., ed. *Sources of Indian Tradition.* New York: Columbia University Press, 1958.

de Certeau, Michel. *The Practice of Everyday Life.* Berkeley: University of California Press, 1984.

Dimock, Edward C., Jr., trans. *The Caitanya Caritāmṛta of Kṛṣṇadāsa Kavirāja.* Cambridge: Harvard University Press, 2000.

———. *The Place of the Hidden Moon: Erotic Mysticism in the Vaiṣṇava Sahajiyā Cult of Bengal.* Chicago: University of Chicago Press, 1966.

Dirks, Nicholas. *Colonialism's Culture: Anthropology, Travel and Government.* Princeton: Princeton University Press, 1994.

Douglas, Mary. *Purity and Danger: An Analysis of the Concepts of Pollution and Taboo.* Harmondsworth: Penguin, 1970.

Dumenil, Lynn. *Freemasonry and American Culture, 1880–1930.* Princeton: Princeton University Press, 1984.

Eaton, Richard. *The Rise of Islam and the Bengal Frontier.* Oxford: Oxford University Press, 1993.

Ebersole, Gary. *Ritual Poetry and the Politics of Death in Early Japan.* Princeton: Princeton University Press, 1989.

Edwardes, Michael. *Plassey: The Founding of an Empire.* New York: Taplinger, 1970.

Eliade, Mircea. *The Quest: History and Meaning in Religion.* Chicago: University of Chicago Press, 1969.

———. *Yoga: Immortality and Freedom.* Princeton: Princeton University Press, 1971.

———. *Occultism, Witchcraft and Cultural Fashions.* Chicago: University of Chicago Press, 1976.

Faivre, Antoine. "Esotericism." In *Encyclopedia of Religion*, vol. 5, ed. M. Eliade. New York: Macmillan, 1986.

Faivre, Antoine, and Needleman, Jacob, eds. *Modern Esoteric Spirituality.* New York: Crossroad, 1992.

Faivre, Antoine, and Voss, Karen-Claire. "Western Esotericism and the Science of Religions." *Numen* 42 (1995): 48–77.

Farquhar, J. N. *An Outline of the Religious Literature of India.* Oxford: Oxford University Press, 1920.

Fiske, John. "Cultural Studies and Everyday Life." In *Cultural Studies,* ed. L. Grossberg et al. London: Routledge, 1992.

Fong, Mak Lou. *The Sociology of Secret Societies: A Study of Chinese Secret Societies in Singapore and Peninsular Malaysia.* New York: Oxford University Press, 1981.

Foucault, Michel. *Power/Knowledge: Selected Interviews and Other Writings*, ed. C. Gordon. New York: Random House, 1977.

———. *The History of Sexuality*. Vol. 1: *An Introduction*. New York: Vintage, 1978.

———. *Discipline and Punish: The Birth of the Prison*. New York: Vintage, 1980.

———. *The History of Sexuality*. Vol. 2: *The Use of Pleasure*. New York: Vintage, 1986.

Freud, Sigmund. *The Basic Writings of Sigmund Freud*, ed. A. A.Brill. New York: Modern Library, 1938.

Ghose, I. C., ed. *The English Works of Rāja Rāmmohun Roy*. New Delhi: Cosmo, 1982.

Gordon, Leonar *Bengal: The Nationalist Movement, 1876–1940*. New York: Columbia University Press, 1974.

Gramsci, Antonio. *Selections from the Prison Notebooks*. New York: International Publishers, 1971.

Guénon, René. *Aperçus sur l'initiation*. Paris: Gallimard, 1946.

Guha, Ranajit. *A Rule of Property for Bengal: An Essay on the Idea of Permanent Settlement*. Delhi: Oxford, 1963.

———. "Neel Darpan: the Image of a Peasant revolt in a Liberal Mirror." *Journal of Peasant Studies* 2, no. 1 (October 1974): 1–46.

———. *Elementary Aspects of Peasant Insurgency in Colonial India*. Delhi: Oxford, 1983.

———. ed. *Subaltern Studies: Writings on South Asian History and Society*. 6 vols. Delhi: Oxford University Press, 1982–90.

Gupta, Sanjukta, Goudriaan, Teun, and Hoens, Dirk Jan. *Hindu Tantrism*. Leiden: E. J. Brill, 1979.

Gurdjieff, George. *Meetings with Remarkable Men*. New York: Dutton, 1963.

Haberman, David. *Acting as a Way of Salvation: A Study of Rāgānugā Bhakti Sādhanā*. New York: Oxford University Press, 1988.

Halbfass, Willhelm. *India and Europe: An Essay on Understanding*. Albany: SUNY, 1988.

Hall, Stuart, and Jefferson, Tony. *Resistance through Rituals: Youth Subcultures in Post-War Britain*. London: Routledge, 1993.

Haq, E. M. *History of Sufi-ism in Bengal*. Dhaka: Asiatic Society of Bangladesh, 1975.

Haydn, Hyram. *The Counter-Renaissance*. New York: Grove Press, 1960.

Hayes, Glen A. "Shapes for the Soul: A Study of Body Symbolism in the Vaiṣṇava Sahajiyā Tradition of Medieval Bengal." Ph.D. diss., University of Chicago, 1985.

———. "The Vaiṣṇava Sahajiyā Traditions of Medieval Bengal." In *Religions of India in Practice*, ed. D. Lopez. Princeton: Princeton University Press, 1995.

Haynes, Douglas, and Prakash, Gyan, eds. *Contesting Power: Resistance and Everyday Social Relations in South Asia*. Berkeley University of California Press, 1991.

Hebidge, Dick. *Subculture: The Meaning of Style*. London: Methuen, 1979.

———. *Hiding in the Light: On Images and Things*. London: Methuen, 1988.

Heckerthorn, C.W. *The Secret Societies of all Ages and Countries*. New York, 1965.

Hobsbawm, E. J. *Primitive Rebels: Studies in Archaic Forms of Social Movement in the 19th and 20th Centuries*. Manchester: Manchester University Press, 1959.

Inden, Ronal *Marriage and Rank in Bengali Culture*. Berkeley: University of California Press, 1976.

———. *Imagining India*. London: Blackwell, 1990.

Inden, Ronald and Nicholas, Ralph. *Kinship in Bengali Culture*. Chicago: University of Chicago Press, 1986.

Jacoby, Russel. "Marginal Returns: The Problem with Post-Colonial Theory." *Lingua Franca* 5, no. 6 (1995): 30–38.

Jansen, Sue Curry. *Censorship: The Knot that Binds Power and Knowledge.* New York: Oxford University Press, 1988.

Jenkins, Peter. *Pierre Bourdieu.* London: Routledge, 1990.

Kaplan, Martha. *Neither Cargo nor Cult: Ritual Politics and the Colonial Imagination in Fiji.* Durham, N.C.: Duke University Press, 1995.

Keen, Ian. *Knowledge and Secrecy in an Aboriginal Religion.* Oxford: Clarendon Press, 1994.

Kelly, John. *A Politics of Virtue: Hinduism, Sexuality and Countercolonial Discourse in Fiji.* Chicago: University of Chicago Press, 1991.

Kermode, Frank. *The Genesis of Secrecy.* Cambridge: Harvard University Press, 1979.

Khare, R. S. "Food with Saints: An Aspect of Hindu Gastrosemantics." In *The Eternal Food,* ed. R. S. Khare. Albany: SUNY, 1986.

Kinsely, David. *The Divine Player: A Study of Kṛṣṇa Līlā.* Delhi: Motilal Banarsidas, 1979.

Kinsman, Robert S., ed. *The Darker Vision of the Renaissance.* Berkeley: University of California Press, 1974.

Kippenberg, Hans, and Stroumsa, Guy, eds. *Secrecy and Concealment: Studies in the History of Mediterranean and Near Eastern Religions.* Leiden: Brill, 1995.

Kopf, David. *British Orientalism and the Bengal Renaissance.* Berkeley: University of California Press, 1969.

———. "An Historiographical Essay on the Goddess Kālī." In *Shaping Bengali Worlds, Public and Private,* ed. Tony K. Stewart. East Lansing: Asian Studies Center, 1975.

———. *The Brahmo Samaj and the Shaping of the Modern Indian Mind.* Princeton: Princeton University Press, 1979.

Kripal, Jeffrey J. *Kālī's Child: The Mystical and the Erotic in the Life and Teachings of Ramakrishna.* Chicago: University of Chicago Press, 1998.

Lawson, Philip. *The East India Company: A History.* London: Longman, 1993.

Lévi-Strauss, Claude. *The Raw and the Cooked.* New York: Harper and Row, 1969.

Lincoln, Bruce. *Discourse and the Construction of Society: Comparative Studies of Myth, Ritual and Classification.* New York: Oxford University Press, 1989.

———. *Authority: Construction and Corrosion.* Chicago University of Chicago Press, 1994.

———. "Theses on Method." *Method and Theory in the Study of Religion* 8, no. 3 (1996).

Lincoln, Bruce and Grotanelli, Cristiano. "A Brief Note on (Future) Research in the History of Religions." *Method and Theory in the Study of Religion* 10 (1998): 311–25.

Lindstrom, Lamont. *Knowledge and Power in a South Pacific Society.* Washington, DC: Smithsonian Institute, 1990.

Luhrmann, T. M. "The Magic of Secrecy." *Ethos* 17, no. 2 (1989).

MacKenzie, Norman, ed. *Secret Societies.* New York: Holt. Rinehart and Winston, 1967.

MacMunn, Sir George. *The Underworld of India.* Delhi: Discovery, 1933.

Majumdar, Ranesh Chandra. *History of Bengal.* Calcutta: D. Bharadwaj, 1978.

Mandal, P. K. "The Fair of Satima: A Sociological Inquiry." *Folklore* 18, no. 12 (1977): 375–84.

Marshall, P. J. *Bengal: The British Bridgehead: Eastern India, 1740–1828.* Cambridge: Cambridge University Press, 1987.

Matter, Jacques, *Histoire critique du gnosticisme et de son influence.* Paris: Levrault, 1828.

Mauss, Marcel. "Techniques of the Body." *Economy and Society* 2, no. 1 (1973): 70–88.

McClintock, Anne. *Imperial Leather: Race, Gender and Sexuality in the Colonial Context.* New York: Routledge, 1995.

McDaniel, June. *The Madness of the Saints: Ecstatic Religion in Bengal.* Chicago: University of Chicago Press, 1989.

Monier-Williams, Sir Monier. *Hinduism.* New York: Society for Promoting Christian Knowledge, 1885.

Moreland, W. H. *A Short History of India.* New York: MacKay, 1936.

Muller-Ortega, Paul Eduardo. *The Triadic Heart of Śiva: Kaula Tantricism of Abhinavagupta in the Non-dual Śaivism of Kashmir.* Albany: SUNY, 1989.

Nair, T. P., ed. *Calcutta in the Nineteenth Century.* Calcutta: Firma KLM, 1989.

Nanda, Serena. *Neither Man nor Woman: The Hijras of India.* Belmont: Wadsworth, 1990.

O'Connell, Joseph. "Social Implications of the Gauḍīya Vaiṣṇava Bhakti Movement." Ph.D. diss., Harvard University, 1970.

Oddie, Geoffrey. "Old wine in New Bottles? Kartabhaja (Vaishnava) Converts to Christianity in Bengal, 1835–1845." *Indian Economic and Social History Review* 32, no. 3 (1995): 327–43.

O'Flaherty, Wendy Doniger. *Women, Androgynes and Other Mythical Beasts.* Chicago: University of Chicago Press, 1980.

O'Hanlon, Rosalind. "Recovering the Subject: *Subaltern Studies* and Histories of Resistance in Colonial South Asia." *Modern Asian Studies* 22, no. 1 (1988): 189–224.

O'Keefe, Daniel. *Stolen Lightning: The Social Theory of Magic.* New York, 1982.

Ong, Aihwa. *Spirits of Resistance and Capitalist Discipline: Factory Women in Malaysia.* Albany: SUNY, 1987.

Ownby, David and Heidhues, Mary Somers, eds. *Secret Societies Reconsidered: Perspectives on the Social History of Modern South China and Southeast Asia.* London: M. E. Sharpe, 1993.

Padoux, André. "A Survey of Tantrism for the Historian of Religions." Review article of *Hindu Tantrism* by S. Gupta, D. J. Hoens and T. Goudriaan. *History of Religions* 20, no.4 (1981).

———. "Tantrism: An Overview." In *Encyclopedia of Religion,* vol. 14, ed. M. Eliade. New York: Macmillan, 1986.

———. *Vāc: The Concept of the Word in Selected Hindu Tantras.* Albany: SUNY, 1990.

Peleg, Ilan, ed. *Patterns of Censorship around the World.* Boulder: Westview Press, 1993.

Perlin, Frank. "Proto-Industrialization and Pre-Colonial South Asia." *Past and Present* 98 (1983): 30–95

Ponse, Barbara. "Secrecy in the Lesbian World." *Urban Life* 5 (1976): 313-38.

Prakash, Gyan, ed. *The World of the Rural Laborer in Colonial India.* Delhi: Oxford, 1992.

———. *After Colonialism: Imperial Histories and Postcolonial Displacements.* Princeton: Princeton University Press, 1995.

Rosberg, Carl, and Nottingham, John. *The Myth of the "Mau Mau:" Nationalism in Kenya.* Stanford: Hoover Institution Press, 1966.

Roszak, Theodore. *The Making of a Counter-Culture.* Garden City: Doubleday, 1969.

Roy, Rammohun. *The Precepts of Jesus, the Guide to Peace and Happiness.* Calcutta: Baptist Mission Press, 1820.

———. *Brief Remarks Regarding Modern Encroachment on the Ancient Rights of Females.* Calcutta: Sadharan Brahmo Samaj, 1922.

Sahlins, Marshall. *Culture and Practical Reason.* Chicago: University of Chicago Press, 1976.

———. *Historical Metaphors and Mythical Realities: Structure in the Early History of the Sandwich Islands Kingdom.* Ann Arbor: University of Michigan Press, 1981.

———. *Islands of History.* Chicago: University of Chicago Press, 1985.

———. "Cosmologies of Capitalism: The Trans-Pacific Sector of the World System." *Proceedings of the British Academy* 74 (1988).

Said, Edward. *Culture and Imperialism*. New York: Knopf, 1994.

Sailley, Robert. "The Sahajiyā Tradition." In *Vaiṣṇavism: Contemporary Scholars Discuss the Gauḍīya Tradition,* ed. S. Rosen. New York: Folk Books, 1992.

Salomon, Carol. "Cosmogonic Riddles of Lālan." In *Gender, Genre and Power in South Asian Expressive Traditions*. ed. A. Appadurai. Philadelphia: University of Pennsylvania Press, 1991.

———. "Bāul Songs." In *Religions of India in Practice,* ed. D. Lopez. Princeton: Princeton University Press, 1995.

Sanderson, Alexis. "Purity and Power among the Brahmins of Kashmir." In *The Category of the Person,* ed. M. Carrithers et al. Cambridge: Cambridge University Press, 1985.

Saraswati, Bhaktisiddhanta. *Shri Chaitanya's Teachings, part II*. Mayapur: Sree Chaitanya Math, 1974.

Sarkar, Sumit. *An Exploration of the Ramakrishna-Vivekananda Tradition*. Simla: Institute of Indian Studies, 1993.

Schaefer, Richard. "The Ku Klux Klan's Successful Management of Secrecy." In *Secrecy: A Cross-Cultural Perspective*, ed. S. Tefft. New York: Human Sciences Press, 1980.

Schuon, Frithjof. *Esoterism as Principle and as Way*. Bloomington: World Wisdom, 1986.

Scott, James C. *Domination and the Arts of Resistance: Hidden Transcripts*. New Haven: Yale University Press, 1990.

Sen, Dinesh Chandra. *Chaitanya and His Age*. Calcutta: University of Calcutta Press, 1922.

———. *History of Bengali Language and Literature*. Calcutta: University of Calcutta Press, 1954.

Sen, Sudipta. "Conquest of Marketplaces: Exchange, Authority and Conflict in Early Colonial North India." Ph.D. diss., University of Chicago, 1994.

———. "Passages of Authority: Rulers, Traders and Marketplaces in Bengal and Benaras, 1700–1750." *Calcutta Historical Journal* 17 no. 1 (1996): 1–40.

Sen, Sukumar. *History of Bengali Literature*. New Delhi: Sahitya Academy, 1960.

Sen Gupta, P. K. *The Protestant Missions in Bengal, 1793–1833*. Calcutta: Firma KLM, 1971.

Shaw, Miranda. *Passionate Enlightenment: Women in Tantric Buddhism*. Princeton: Princeton University Press, 1994.

Shils, Edward. *The Torment of Secrecy: The Background and Consequences of American Security Policies.* Carbondale: Southern Illinois University Press, 1956.

Simmel, George. "The Sociology of Secrecy and Secret Societies." *American Journal of Sociology* 11 (1905), reprinted in *The Sociology of Georg Simmel,* ed. K. Wolff. New York: Free Press, 1950.

———. *The Philosophy of Money.* London: Routledge, 1978.

Smith, Jonathan Z. *Map Is not Territory: Studies in the History of Religions.* Chicago: University of Chicago Press, 1978.

———. *Imagining Religion: From Babylon to Jonestown*. Chicago: University of Chicago Press, 1982.

———. *Drudgery Divine: On the Comparison of Early Christianities and the Religions of Late Antiquity.* Chicago: University of Chicago Press, 1990.

Spivak, Gayatri. "A Literary Representation of the Subaltern: Mahasweta Devi's *Stanadayini*." In *Subaltern Studies,* vol. 5, ed. R. Guha. Delhi: Oxford, 1987.

———. "Subaltern Studies: Deconstructing Historiography." In *In Other Worlds: Essays in Cultural Politics.* London: Routledge, 1987.

Stewart, C., and Shaw, R., eds. *Syncretism/ Anti-Syncretism: The Politics of Religious Synthesis.* London: Routledge, 1994.

Stewart, Tony K. "Sex, Secrecy and the Politics of Sahajiyā Scholarship, Or: Caveats from a Faint-hearted Student of Tantra." Unpublished manuscript, 1990.

———. "Satya Pīr: Muslim Holy Man and Hindu God." In *Religions of India in Practice,* ed. D. Lopez. Princeton: Princeton University Press, 1995.

———. "Competing Structures of Authority: Satya Pīr on the Frontiers of Bengal." Unpublished manuscript, 1997.

Stewart, Tony K., and Ernst, Carl. "Syncretism." In *South Asian Folklore: An Encyclopedia,* ed. M. Mills and P. Claus. Garland, forthcoming.

Strauss, Leo. *Persecution and the Art of Writing.* Glencoe: Free Press, 1952.

Suleri, Sara. *The Rhetoric of British India.* Chicago: University of Chicago Press, 1992.

Sumanta, Suchitra. "The Self-Animal and Divine Digestion: Goat Sacrifice to the Goddess Kālī in Bengal." *Journal of Asian Studies* 53, no. 3 (1994): 779–803.

Tagore, Rabindranath. *The Religion of Man.* Boston: Beacon Press, 1961.

Taussig, Michael. *The Devil and Commodity Fetishism in South America.* Chapel Hill: University of North Carolina Press, 1980.

———. *Shamanism, Colonialism and the Wild Man: A Study in Terror and Healing.* Chicago: University of Chicago Press, 1987.

———. *Mimesis and Alterity: A Particular History of the Senses.* London: Routledge, 1993.

Tefft, Stanton K., ed. *Secrecy: A Cross-Cultural Perspective.* New York: Human Sciences Press, 1980.

———. *The Dialectics of Secret Society Power in States.* New Jersey: Humanities Press, 1992.

Thakur, Bhaktivinod. *Jaiva Dharma.* Madras: Sree Gaudiya Math, 1975.

———. *Shri Chaitanya Shikshamritam.* Madras: Sree Gaudiya Math, 1983.

Thurman, Robert. "Vajra Hermeneutics." In *Buddhist Hermeneutics,* ed. D. Lopez. Honolulu: University of Hawaii Press, 1986.

Tiryakian, Edward. "Toward the Sociology of Esoteric Culture." *American Journal of Sociology* 78 (1952): 491–512.

Torgovnick, Marianna. *Gone Primitive: Savage Intellects, Modern Lives.* Chicago: University of Chicago Press, 1990.

Turner, Graehme. *British Cultural Studies: An Introduction.* Boston: Unwin Hyman, 1990.

Urban, Hugh B. "Secret Bodies: Re-Imagining the Body in the Vaiṣṇava-Sahajiyā Tradition of Bengal." *Journal of South Asian Literature* 28, nos. 1 & 2 (1995): 45–62.

———. "The Strategic Uses of an Esoteric Text: The *Mahānirvāṇa Tantra.*" *South Asia* 18, no. 1 (1995): 55–82.

———. "The Poor Company: Economics and Ecstasy in the Kartābhajā Sect of Colonial Bengal." *South Asia* 19, no. 2 (1996): 1–33.

———. "Elitism and Esotericism: Strategies of Secrecy and Power in South Indian Tantra and French Freemasonry." *Numen* 44 (1997): 1–38.

———. "The Torment of Secrecy: Ethical and Epistemological Problems in the Study of Esoteric Traditions." *History of Religions* 37, no. 3 (1998): 209–48.

———. "The Extreme Orient: The Construction of 'Tantrism' as a Category in the Orientalist Imagination." *Religion* 29 (1999): 123–46.

———. "The Politics of Madness: The Construction and Manipulation of the 'Bāul' Image in Modern Bengal." *South Asia* 22, no. 1 (1999): 13–46.

———. "India's Darkest Heart: Kālī in the Colonial Imagination." In *Encountering Kālī:*

In the Margins, at the Center, In the West, ed. Jeffrey J. Kripal and Rachel Fell McDermott. Berkeley: University of California Press, forthcoming (2001).

———. *Songs of Ecstasy: Tantric and Devotional Songs from Bengal.* New York: Oxford University Press, 2001.

Wali, Maulavi Abdul. "On Some Curious Tenets and Practices of a Certain Class of Fakirs of Bengal." *Journal of the Anthropological Society of Bombay* (November 30 1898).

Walsh, Judith. "The Virtuous Wife and the Well-Ordered Home: The Re-conceptualization of Bengali Women and their Worlds." In *Mind, Body and Society: Life and Mentality in Colonial Bengal,* ed. R. Ray. Calcutta: Oxford, 1995.

Warren, Karen, and Laslett, Barbara. "Privacy and Secrecy: A Conceptual Comparison." In *Secrecy: A Cross-Cultural Perspective,* ed. S. Tefft. New York: Human Sciences Press, 1980.

Washbrook, D. A. "Law, State and Agrarian Society in Colonial India." *Modern Asian Studies* 15 (1981).

———. "Progress and Problems South Asian Economic and Social History, 1720–1860." *Modern Asian Studies* 22, no. 1 (1988): 57–96.

Wheeler, Talboys. *The History of India from the Earliest Age.* Edinburgh: Blackwood, 1893.

White, David Gordon. *The Alchemical Body: Siddha Traditions in Medieval India.* Chicago: University of Chicago Press, 1996.

———, ed. *Tantra in Practice.* Princeton: Princeton University Press, 2000.

Woodroffe, Sir John [Artur Avalon]. *Principles of Tantra: The Tantratattva of Śrīyukta Śiva Candra Vidyārṇava Bhaṭṭācārya Mahodaya.* Madras: Ganesh & Co., 1960.

———. *Shakti and Shākta.* New York: Dover, 1978.

Yati, Tridandi Bhakti Prajnan. *Renaissance of Gaudiya Vaishnava Movement.* Madras: Sree Gaudiya Math, 1978.

Index

Kṛṣṇa, 34–35, 54, 65, 87, 89, 123, 146, 148, 173, 200
Kartā as, 70, 85, 200
Kṛṣṇadāsa Kavirāja, 164
kṣepa, khepā, 130, 169–70, 249n.51
Kubir, 44, 205, 265n.6
Kulārṇava Tantra, 105
kuṇḍalinī (serpent power), 7, 76, 113, 142, 145, 147–48
Vāsuki as, 145

Lālan Shāh (Lālan Fakir), 36, 44, 68, 118, 205
and Ghoshpara festival, 44, 68, 242n.27, 251n.15
and Kartābhajās, 68
and Man of the Heart, 68–69
Lālśaśī (Śaṣī Lāl). *See* Dulālcāṅd
latrine door, 48, 161
līlā (play), 65, 165, 200
Lincoln, Bruce, xi, 11, 183, 192, 213, 214, 223n.42, 226n.78, 256n.45, 263n.44, 263n.62. 266n.14
lotus, 144, 153, 175
lotus of the heart, 152–53
see also sahasrāra
love. *See prema*
lower classes, 8–9, 25, 41, 56, 68, 119, 190–92, 215, 234n.50, 239n.119
see also itar lok
lust. *See kāma*

Mā Gosāiṅ, 84–85, 89, 142
madmen, 108, 133, 252n.32
Āulcāṅd, Caitanya, Nityānanda and Advaita as, 252n.32
madness, 35, 108–9, 117, 133, 237n.88,
see also bāul, kṣepa, pāgal
māgī, 10, 178
mahājan, 39, 57–58, 124
Mahānirvāṇa Tantra, 28, 166
mahāśay, 80–82, 84, 89, 102, 142, 156, 181, 184–85, 187, 190, 198, 255n.21
maithuna, 111, 113
see also parakīyā, sex, *svakīyā,* Tantra
mālik, 71, 148, 156, 157, 185–86, 188, 249n.47, 261n.22
Man of Ecstasy. *See bhāver mānuṣa*
Man of the Heart. *See maner mānuṣa*
maner mānuṣa, 68–70, 110, 113, 148, 152, 238n.94,
and Bāuls, 68–70
mantra, 7, 45, 131, 178
mānuṣer dharma, 8, 46, 47, 60–62, 67, 78, 90, 173, 241n.3
marketplace, 22, 31–33, 38, 39–40, 42, 94, 97, 106, 114, 116–136, 190, 234n.46–48, 256n.36
black market, 22, 94, 105–6, 114, 213–14
and British East India Company, 33, 40
marketplace of love, 32, 119, 123–24, 130, 157
marketplace of the world, 22, 32, 37–38, 40, 117
metaphor in Bengali literature, 22, 32–33, 38, 40, 116–17
metaphor for religious life, 13, 33, 60, 119, 123, 234n.46
secret marketplace. *See gupta hāṭ,* Vṛndāvana
social and cultural significance of, 32, 39, 119
see also bājār, hāṭ
Marx, Karl, 20, 22, 125, 134
māyā, 120, 143, 250n.56
melā. See Ghoshpara Melā
menstrual blood, 138, 140, 143–45, 146, 148, 169, 171, 238n.94, 255n.26
see also raja
merchants, 33, 37, 54, 120, 124, 253n.35
merchant of love, 149
see also mahājan, shopkeepers
metaphors, 14, 104, 110, 114, 116–18, 135–36, 168–69, 249n.41, 251n.7
economic, 14, 106, 116–36
sexual, 89, 104, 105, 110, 168–69, 259n.34
mint. *See ṭyāṅkśālī*
miracles, 53, 56, 85, 88, 192–95
Miśra, Manulāl, xi, 46, 64, 82, 96, 101, 174, 236n.69
money, v, 94, 96–97, 106
see also ṭyāṅkśālī
moneylenders, 33, 39, 57–58, 97, 116, 120–25, 231n.10
mūlādhāra, 145, 148

nāḍīs, 143, 145, 147–48
Nietzsche, Friedrich, vii
Nirañjana, 144
Nityānanda, 65, 120, 128, 130, 252n.32
nivṛtti, 102–103, 154

pāgal, 15, 108–9, 117, 133, 252n.32
pāgal kompānī, 8, 117, 133
see also bāul, kṣepa, madmen, madness
Pāl, Rāmśaraṇ, 47, 50–53, 73, 79, 186, 204–5
Pāl, Satyaśiva, 98, 107, 137, 153, 173
parakīyā, 51–52, 76, 146, 162–80, 204, 257n.12, 259–60n.44, 260n.56, 257n.12, 259n.35
paramārthik (ultimate truth), 6, 62, 67, 75–76, 107, 138, 154–55